Speaking and Instructed Foreign Language Acquisition

SECOND LANGUAGE ACQUISITION
Series Editor: **Professor David Singleton**, *Trinity College, Dublin, Ireland*

This series brings together titles dealing with a variety of aspects of language acquisition and processing in situations where a language or languages other than the native language is involved. Second language is thus interpreted in its broadest possible sense. The volumes included in the series all offer in their different ways, on the one hand, exposition and discussion of empirical findings and, on the other, some degree of theoretical reflection. In this latter connection, no particular theoretical stance is privileged in the series; nor is any relevant perspective – sociolinguistic, psycholinguistic, neurolinguistic, etc. – deemed out of place. The intended readership of the series includes final-year undergraduates working on second language acquisition projects, postgraduate students involved in second language acquisition research, and researchers and teachers in general whose interests include a second language acquisition component.

Full details of all the books in this series and of all our other publications can be found on http://www.multilingual-matters.com, or by writing to Multilingual Matters, St Nicholas House, 31–34 High Street, Bristol BS1 2AW, UK.

SECOND LANGUAGE ACQUISITION
Series Editor: David Singleton, *Trinity College, Dublin, Ireland*

Speaking and Instructed Foreign Language Acquisition

Edited by
Mirosław Pawlak, Ewa Waniek-Klimczak
and Jan Majer

MULTILINGUAL MATTERS
Bristol • Buffalo • Toronto

Library of Congress Cataloging in Publication Data
A catalog record for this book is available from the Library of Congress.
Speaking and Instructed Foreign Language Acquisition/Edited by Miroslaw Pawlak, Ewa Waniek-Klimczak and Jan Majer.
Second Language Acquisition: 57.
Includes bibliographical references.
1. Language and languages–Study and teaching. 2. Second language acquisition.
I. Pawlak, Miroslaw. II. Waniek-Klimczak, Ewa. III. Majer, Jan.
P51.S587 2011
418.0071–dc22 2011015610

British Library Cataloguing in Publication Data
A catalogue entry for this book is available from the British Library.

ISBN-13: 978-1-84769-411-9 (hbk)

Multilingual Matters
UK: St Nicholas House, 31-34 High Street, Bristol BS1 2AW, UK.
USA: UTP, 2250 Military Road, Tonawanda, NY 14150, USA.
Canada: UTP, 5201 Dufferin Street, North York, Ontario M3H 5T8, Canada.

The policy of Multilingual Matters/Channel View Publications is to use papers that are natural, renewable and recyclable products, made from wood grown in sustainable forests. In the manufacturing process of our books, and to further support our policy, preference is given to printers that have FSC and PEFC Chain of Custody certification. The FSC and/or PEFC logos will appear on those books where full certification has been granted to the printer concerned.

Typeset by Datapage International Ltd.
Printed and bound in Great Britain by the MPG Books Group.

Contents

Contributors vii
Preface xiii

**Part 1: Theoretical Perspectives on Instructed
Acquisition of Speaking**

1 Instructed Acquisition of Speaking: Reconciling
  Theory and Practice
  Mirosław Pawlak 3

2 Authenticity in Oral Communication of Instructed
  L2 Learners
  Agnieszka Nowicka and Weronika Wilczyńska 24

3 Formulaic Sequences in the Output of Instructed
  L2 Learners
  Piotr Białas 42

4 Formulaicity vs. Fluency and Accuracy in Using English
  as a Foreign Language
  Agnieszka Wróbel 55

5 Talking the Same Language: Sociocultural
  Aspects of Code-Switching in L2 Classroom Discourse
  Jan Majer 66

6 Speaking in English for Academic Purposes in the
  Light of Lingua Franca English and Sociocultural Theory
  Anna Niżegorodcew 84

Part 2: Speaking and Individual Variables

7 Near-Nativeness as a Function of Cognitive and Personality
  Factors: Three Case Studies of Highly Able Foreign
  Language Learners
  Adriana Biedroń 99

8 "I Am Good at Speaking, But I Failed My Phonetics Class" –
  Pronunciation and Speaking in Advanced
  Learners of English
  Ewa Waniek Klimczak 117

9   Oral Skills Awareness of Advanced EFL Learners
     Krystyna Droździał-Szelest 131
10   Pronunciation Learning Strategies – Identification and
     Classification
     Aneta Całka 149
11   Metaphonetic Awareness in the Production of Speech
     Magdalena Wrembel. 169
12   Foreign Language Speaking Anxiety from the Perspective
     of Polish Students of German Studies
     Krzysztof Nerlicki 183
13   The Relationship between Language Anxiety and the
     Development of the Speaking Skill: Results of a
     Longitudinal Study
     Ewa Piechurska-Kuciel 200

Part 3: Research into Instructed Acquisition of Speaking
14   On the Authenticity of Communication in the Foreign
     Language Classroom
     Sebastian Piotrowski 215
15   Ways to Proficiency in Spoken English as a Foreign
     Language – Tracing Individual Development
     Irena Czwenar. 230
16   Task Repetition as a Way of Enhancing Oral Communication
     in a Foreign Language
     Anna Mystkowska-Wiertelak. 245
17   The Use of the Internet and Instant Messengers in Assisting
     the Acquisition of Speaking Skills in English Lessons
     Mariusz Kruk 258
18   Investigating the Perception of Speaking Skills with
     Metaphor-Based Methods
     Dorota Werbińska 268
19   Phonetically Difficult Words in Intermediate
     Learners' English
     Jolanta Szpyra-Kozłowska. 286
20   Transcultural Interference, Communities of Practice and
     Collaborative Assessment of Oral Performance
     Przemysław Krakowian 300

Contributors

Piotr Białas is a foreign language teacher of English at the State Higher Vocational School in Tarnów and a PhD student at the University of Warsaw. His academic interests are basically pedagogical grammar and language acquisition with particular emphasis on the role of memory and psychology in the context of formulaic language research.

Adriana Biedroń received her doctoral degree in applied linguistics from Adam Mickiewicz University in Poznań in 2003. She is an assistant professor at the Pomeranian Academy in Słupsk. She teaches second language acquisition, psycholinguistics and descriptive grammar. Her fields of interest include applied psycholinguistics and second language acquisition theory. Her research focuses on individual differences in second language acquisition, in particular, foreign language aptitude, attributional processes and cognitive factors. Recent publications include *Attribution Related Affects in Second Language Acquisition* (Słupsk: Wydawnictwo Naukowe Akademii Pomorskiej, 2008) and (coauthored with Anna Szczepaniak) 'The cognitive profile of a talented foreign language learner' (*Psychology of Language and Communication*, vol.13, no.1, 2009).

Aneta Całka is a teacher at the English Department of the Teacher Training College in Szczytno. Her research interests include learner autonomy, learner strategies, pronunciation learning and teaching. Currently, she is working on her doctoral dissertation on instruction in pronunciation learning strategies and its effects.

Irena Czwenar has experience in teaching English and foreign language teaching methodology at the tertiary level. She has been involved in both pre- and in-service teacher training programs in Poland. Her main research interest is the teaching and assessment of oral proficiency of upper-intermediate and advanced learners of English. She received her PhD in 2008 from the University of Łódź.

Krystyna Droździał-Szelest is Professor of Applied Linguistics, currently at Teacher Training College, Adam Mickiewicz University. She teaches BA, MA and PhD seminars in English Language Teaching methodology and applied linguistics. Her PhD and post-PhD degrees, obtained from Adam Mickiewicz University in Poznań, are both in applied linguistics. Her present research interests cover English Language Teaching methodology, teacher training and teacher development, foreign language education and language teaching materials. She has published a number of research papers and one book and supervised 18 PhD theses.

Przemysław Krakowian, PhD, is a graduate of the Lodz University, where he is now an assistant professor in the Department of English Language. His research interests include new orientations in English Language Teaching, applications of computers, virtual learning environments, the internet and corpora in English Language Teaching. He has been involved in a number of projects connected with online and asynchronous web-based assessment of oral skills in intercultural settings.

Mariusz Kruk, PhD, studied Russian philology (Pedagogical University in Zielona Góra) and English philology (Adam Mickiewicz University). He has been working for a number of years as a senior high-school teacher as well as a teacher of English at the College of Education and Therapy in Poznań. His main interests include computer-assisted language instruction and learner autonomy.

Jan Majer received his doctoral degree from Adam Mickiewicz University and his postdoctoral degree from the University of Lodz. He is Professor of English and Head of the Department of Psycholinguistics and English Language Teaching, Institute of English Studies, Faculty of Philology, University of Lodz, Poland. His main areas of interest are bilingualism, second language acquisition theory and research, analysis of classroom communication and English as an International Language. His most significant publication of the last few years, among several articles on bilingual communication in educational discourse, is the book titled *Interactive Discourse in the Foreign Language Classroom* (University of Łódź Press, 2003).

Krzysztof Nerlicki, PhD, is a lecturer at the Institute of Germanic Studies at the University of Szczecin. His main research interest is in the area of foreign language acquisition with a particular consideration of the influence of cognitive emotional social factors on learning and communicative processes and the role of subjective learner beliefs.

Anna Niżegorodcew took her PhD at the Philosophical Faculty of the Jagiellonian University of Krakow, Poland. She is Professor in Applied Linguistics and Chair of the Applied Linguistics Section of the English Department at the same university. She has published a number of books and articles in the areas of teaching English, second language acquisition and second/foreign language teacher education. Her recent interests have focused on the application of Relevance Theory in the L2 classroom (*Input for Instructed L2 Learners: The Relevance of Relevance*, Multilingual Matters, 2007) and using English as a lingua franca in intercultural communication.

Agnieszka Nowicka is involved in research focusing on conversation analysis of lingua franca interactions, ethnomethodology, membership categorization analysis, and foreign language learning and teaching. She is currently researching ethnic descriptions in interactions in English as a lingua franca.

Mirosław Pawlak is Professor of English in the English Department at the Faculty of Pedagogy and Fine Arts of Adam Mickiewicz University in Kalisz, Poland. His main areas of interest are second language acquisition theory and research, form-focused instruction, classroom discourse, learner autonomy, communication and learning strategies, individual learner differences and pronunciation teaching. His recent publications include *The Place of Form-Focused Instruction in the Foreign Language Classroom* (Adam Mickiewicz University Press, 2006) and several edited collections on learner autonomy, language policies of the Council of Europe, form-focused instruction and individual learner differences.

Ewa Piechurska-Kuciel is a professor of English at Opole University where she teaches EFL methodology and second language acquisition courses. She specializes in the role of affect in the foreign language acquisition process.

Sebastian Piotrowski works in the Institute of Romance Languages at John Paul II Catholic University of Lublin. His research combines the fields of second language acquisition and foreign language pedagogy, with special attention to discourse strategies and the specificity of exolingual communication in formal settings.

Jolanta Szpyra-Kozłowska is Associate Professor of English Linguistics and Chair of Phonetics and Phonology in the Department of English at Maria Curie-Skłodowska University, Lublin, Poland. She has published extensively (six books and more than 100 papers) on English and Polish phonology, theory of phonology, the phonology–morphology interaction, modern pronunciation pedagogy and gender linguistics. Her books include *The Phonology-Morphology Interface. Cycles, Levels and Words* (1989), *Three Tiers in Polish and English Phonology* (1995), *Wprowadzenie do współczesnej fonologii* [Introduction to Contemporary Phonology], 2002, *Lingwistyka płci. Ona i on w języku polskim* [Gender Linguistics. Her and Him in Polish], coauthored by M. Karwatowska, 2005. Currently, she is working on a book titled *English Pronunciation Pedagogy. A Polish Perspective*.

Ewa Waniek-Klimczak is professor of English linguistics and the Director of Studies in the Institute of English at the University of Łódź.

She teaches courses in phonetics, phonology, accents of English and spoken discourse. Her main research interests are the acquisition and usage of the second language sound system, cross-linguistic phonetics and phonology and pronunciation teaching. Her recent publications include *Socio-psychological Conditioning in ESL Pronunciation: Consonant Voicing in English Spoken by Polish Immigrants to Britain* (PWSZ Press, 2009), *Temporal Parameters in Second Language Speech: An Applied Linguistic Phonetics Approach* (University of Łódź Press, 2005) and edited collections of papers *Issues in Accents of English I and II* (Cambridge Scholars Publishing, 2008 and 2010).

Dorota Werbińska, PhD, works at Pomeranian Academy in Słupsk. She has been involved with the changing scene of Polish education with regard to teaching and learning foreign languages since the beginning of the 1990s (the INSETT program, the New Matura project, teachers' professional promotion project and recently the implementation of the new curriculum core). Her main interests include language teachers' cognition, teacher professional development, teacher dilemmas, teacher burnout, teacher identity and hidden curriculum. She is the author of two books: *Skuteczny nauczyciel języka obcego* [The Effective Teacher of a Foreign Language], Warsaw: Wydawnictwo Fraszka Edukacyjna, 2004, and *Dylematy etyczne nauczycieli języków obcych* [Ethical Dilemmas of Foreign Language Teachers], Wydawnictwo Fraszka Edukacyjna, 2009.

Anna Mystkowska Wiertelak, PhD, is a teacher and teacher trainer at the English Department of the Faculty of Pedagogy and Fine Arts of Adam Mickiewicz University in Poznań. Her main interests include teacher education and language instruction.

Weronika Wilczyńska is the author of numerous books and articles devoted to foreign language learning and teaching, communication competence theory, intercultural communication, motivation in L2 learning, foreign language teacher training and learner autonomy. Currently, her interests concentrate on foreign language learning research. She cooperated with the coauthor in a multiphilological group project on learner autonomy.

Magdalena Wrembel is Assistant Professor at the School of English, Adam Mickiewicz University, Poznań, Poland. She specializes in English practical phonetics and teacher training. She has conducted several workshops on the teaching of L2 pronunciation as part of in-service training. Her main areas of research involve second and third language phonological acquisition, language awareness, phonological metacompetence as well as innovative trends in pronunciation pedagogy. She has published several articles in international journals and edited collections, including, for example, 'An overview of English pronunciation teaching materials. Patterns of change: Model accents, goals and priorities' (2005), 'Metacompetence-oriented model of phonological acquisition' (2005), 'In search of cross-modal reinforcements in the acquisition of L2 practical phonetics'(2007), 'On hearing colours – cross-modal associations in vowel perception in a non-synaesthetic population' (2009) and 'L2-accented speech in L3 production' (2010).

Agnieszka Wróbel is an English teacher and teacher trainer. She is interested in phraseology and lexical approaches to foreign language teaching. Currently, she is involved in research into explicit teaching of formulaic language to Polish learners of English in formal classroom setting. The research is part of her PhD thesis at the University of Warsaw.

Preface

Few of those involved in instructed language acquisition would disagree
that, whatever be learners' aptitude or motivation, developing the ability
to speak in a foreign language is an extremely difficult and arduous task.
This is because the acquisition of speaking involves the mastery of the
different language subsystems to the point that they can be employed
automatically in spontaneous communication, simultaneous focus on
comprehension and production, which is difficult to achieve because of
limited attentional resources, as well as the impact of a wide range of
social factors that often determine successful attainment of communicative goals. The challenge is further compounded in a situation in which
learners have rather limited access to the target language both inside and
outside the classroom, which is the norm in the majority of foreign
language contexts. For this reason, there is a need to explore issues
connected with teaching, learning and testing speaking with a view to
translating the guidelines stemming from theoretical positions and
research findings into feasible and context-sensitive pedagogical recommendations. Such is the rationale behind the present volume, which
considers speaking in terms of influential theoretical perspectives,
representative of both the psycholinguistic and sociolinguistic approaches, investigates various individual variables that can affect the
development of speaking skills and reports the findings of research
projects focusing on different aspects of instructed acquisition of speaking in a foreign language. The book brings together 20 contributions by
Polish scholars, experts in the field of applied linguistics and second
language acquisition specialists, which are divided into three parts
according to their dominant theme, with similarity of topic rather than
alphabetic order being the main principle of organization in each of
them.

The first part, titled *Theoretical perspectives on instructed acquisition of
speaking*, comprises six papers that strive to show how leading theories
and hypotheses can be applied to explaining the processes of acquiring,
producing and teaching different aspects of a foreign language. It opens
with a chapter by Mirosław Pawlak who demonstrates how influential
psycholinguistic perspectives on second language acquisition can
provide insights into instructed acquisition of speaking and proposes
on that basis a tentative model of developing oral communication skills

in the foreign language classroom. Agnieszka Nowicka and Weronika Wilczyńska, in turn, tackle the issue of authenticity of oral communication, postulating integration of the individual and sociocultural dimensions of communicative actions as well as arguing that successful speaking instruction requires the existence of a pragmatic context and anchoring teaching practices in social-function models such as genres. The contributions by Piotr Białas and Agnieszka Wróbel focus on the role of formulaic sequences in learning how to speak in a foreign language. Both of them recognize the contributions that these multiword units can make to the acquisition of speaking skills, with the former emphasizing the need for their proceduralization and the latter cautioning that their application may lead to fluent but inaccurate target language use and offering a handful of pedagogical implications. In the next chapter, Jan Majer seeks to account for the occurrence of code switching in negotiated repair in the foreign language classroom from the perspective of sociocultural theory and recommends relaxation of the language policy in educational discourse so that it resembles nonclassroom bilingual interaction. Sociocultural theory is also invoked by Anna Niżegorodcew who combines this perspective with that afforded by Lingua Franca English and makes the point that English for Academic Purposes can be viewed not only from a pedagogical but also from a sociocultural angle as a distinctive type of interaction coconstructed by speakers in nonnative discourse and as a regulatory process of identifying with an academic community of practice.

The seven chapters included in Part 2, *Speaking and individual variables*, focus on the way in which individual variation can affect instructed acquisition of speaking. First, Adriana Biedroń discusses the cognitive and affective characteristics that enable learners to reach a near-native level of proficiency when it comes to their speaking skills and reports the findings of a qualitative study that investigated the profiles of three such exceptional learners. Then, Ewa Waniek-Klimczak describes the findings of a research project that was aimed at correlating advanced learners' grades in pronunciation, speaking, grammar and writing courses, and then relating these to such personality traits as self-image, inhibition, risk-taking, ego-permeability and ambiguity tolerance. The chapter by Krystyna Droździał-Szelest, in turn, stresses the role of learners' awareness of oral skills as a key factor in developing their ability to communicate in a foreign language and discusses the results of a small-scale study that examined this kind of awareness among advanced learners of English. Aneta Całka brings our attention to pronunciation learning strategies, an area that has been thus far surprisingly neglected, and reports the findings of a preliminary study the aim of which was to identify strategies of this type used by advanced learners of English and put to the test a classification that she devised.

Pronunciation is also the focus of the contribution by Magdalena Wrembel who explores the role of awareness in learning this language subsystem and discusses the results of a research project in which think-aloud protocols were employed with an eye to identifying the strategies used by English philology students to consciously monitor pronunciation while speaking. The last two chapters included in this part deal with the impact of language anxiety on the ability to speak in a foreign language. In the first of these, Krzysztof Nerlicki concludes on the basis of a diary study conducted among Polish students of German studies that anxiety appears before the act of speaking, often as a result of negative experiences, and has a detrimental effect on language production. In the second, Ewa Piechurska-Kuciel conceives of anxiety as a factor producing communication barriers in a foreign language and reports the findings of a longitudinal research project that investigated the relationship between language anxiety and senior high-school students' assessment of their speaking skills.

The last part of the volume, *Research into instructed acquisition of speaking*, includes texts primarily devoted to empirical investigations of different facets of speaking in a foreign language. In the first contribution, Sebastian Piotrowski revisits the problem of authenticity, analyzing it empirically from the perspective of a focus on meaning, focus on form and focus on the process of task performance, and concludes that its presence depends on the extent to which classroom discourse fosters authentic interaction in the target language. Subsequently, Irena Czwenar reports the findings of a longitudinal investigation in which she traced the oral development of nine upper-intermediate and advanced students of English in terms of fluency, accuracy and lexical and grammatical complexity over a three-year period, finding that although the participants improved on these measures, they advanced their oral proficiency in different ways by prioritizing some of the dimensions over the others. Improvement in oral production in terms of fluency, accuracy and complexity is also investigated by Anna Mystkowska-Wiertelak who reports the results of a study that examined the effects of task repetition. Emphasis is then shifted to the role of modern technology as Mariusz Kruk looks into the use of the internet and instant messengers in instructed acquisition of speaking and reports the results of a quasi-experimental study that demonstrate that such tools can indeed promote the acquisition of speaking skills by senior high-school learners. In another empirical contribution, Dorota Werbińska applies metaphor-based approaches of processing metaphor and metaphor processing to the investigation of learners' beliefs regarding the acquisition of speaking skills in English, German and Russian. Jolanta Szpyra-Kozłowska focuses on errors in the pronunciation of entire words as being more detrimental than segmental or prosodic inaccuracies, and reports the results of a study that sought to pinpoint the sources of such problems on the basis of subjective perceptions of intermediate learners of English. In the last chapter in this part, Przemysław Krakowian touches upon problems with interrater variability that arose as a consequence of transcultural interference in the course of assessment of oral production of the members of a community of practice made up of the participants of a web-based project.

This publication is primarily intended for second language acquisition theorists and researchers who are interested in various issues related to instructed acquisition of speaking, but it will also be a valuable resource for undergraduate, graduate and doctoral students dealing with this important area. The book can also provide useful guidelines for methodologists and materials writers who can use the insights offered by individual chapters to improve the actual practice of developing speaking skills in the language classroom. We are hopeful that, thanks to the breadth and diversity of topics covered as well as an evidently pedagogic orientation of the contributions, this anthology will contribute to more effective instructional practices with respect to the development of speaking skills in the foreign language classroom as it is in this context that this area is often neglected and is therefore in urgent need of improvement.

Mirosław Pawlak
Ewa Waniek-Klimczak
Jan Majer

Part 1

Theoretical Perspectives on Instructed Acquisition of Speaking

Chapter 1
Instructed Acquisition of Speaking: Reconciling Theory and Practice

MIROSŁAW PAWLAK

Introduction

It is perhaps fitting to start this chapter with a quote from Bygate (2002: 27) who so aptly comments that 'The study of speaking – like the study of other uses of language – is properly an interdisciplinary field. It involves understanding the psycholinguistic and interpersonal factors of speech production, the forms, meanings and processes involved, and how these can be developed'. Indeed, when reading recent overviews of critical issues involved in learning, using, teaching and testing this crucial skill (e.g. Burns & Seidlhofer, 2010; Bygate, 2002, 2008, 2009; Hughes, 2002; Luoma, 2004; Tarone, 2005; Thornbury, 2005), it becomes clear that describing, understanding and explaining these complex processes requires insights from such disciplines as theoretical and applied linguistics, psychology, sociology, neurology or educational studies. More specific contributions, in turn, accrue from particular branches or combinations of these disciplines including, among others, phonetics, phonology, syntax, morphology, pragmatics, conversation analysis, corpus linguistics, second language acquisition, psycholinguistics, sociolinguistics or neurolinguistics. Such a huge diversity of influences and the inherent intricacy of their manifold relationships testify to the tremendous complexity of the speaking skill, the inevitable outcome of which is the difficulty involved in its successful development when acquiring a second or foreign language, be it naturalistically, in the classroom or with the benefit of both of these conditions. This difficulty is particularly acute, however, in the case of instructed language acquisition in the foreign language context where out-of-class exposure is often restricted, language instruction is confined to just several hours a week and the quality of classroom discourse is far from conducive to the development of effective communicative skills (Majer, 2003; Ortega, 2007a; Pawlak, 2000, 2004, 2009).

An important source of ideas on how these problems can be tackled are theories, models and hypotheses that specialists have put forward over the last few decades to explain different aspects of the process of second and foreign language acquisition, including the reception and production of speech as well as the appropriation of the requisite knowledge, abilities and skills. This chapter aims to demonstrate how such theoretical perspectives can provide a basis for formulating a set of useful guidelines for learning and teaching speaking in a foreign language setting, such as the one typical of language education in Poland. Following a brief overview of the main challenges in instructed acquisition of speaking, firstly, the key tenets of influential psycholinguistic theories and hypotheses which are more or less directly relevant to the development of speaking skills will be presented, that is the model of speech production (cf. Kormos, 2006; Levelt, 1989, 1999), interactionist approaches (cf. Gass, 1997; Long, 1981, 1996; Swain, 1985, 1995), skill-learning theory (cf. DeKeyser, 1998, 2001) and the model of language proficiency (Skehan, 1998). Secondly, the pedagogical implications stemming from these theoretical positions will be discussed and the feasibility of implementing them in the foreign language classroom will be addressed. The chapter will conclude with a proposal for a tentative model of teaching speaking which is based on the recommendations of theorists but at the same time recognizes the constraints that teachers have to face daily in their classrooms.

Challenges of Instructed Acquisition of Speaking

Before embarking on the task of reconciling theory and practice for the benefit of more effective instructed acquisition of speaking in a foreign language, it appears warranted to take a closer look at what is involved in the mastery of this skill as well as the resultant challenges that have to be faced when learning and teaching it. What must be emphasized from the very outset is that there is a broad consensus among specialists that the ability to engage in oral language production, although it tends to be taken for granted, is '(. . .) the most complex and difficult to master' (Tarone, 2005: 485). This complexity, which is clearly reflected in the contributions to the present volume, is related to a number of issues, such as the fact that the act of speaking is rarely a monologue and typically also involves simultaneous listening and comprehending; it happens in real time, thus being transient and dynamic; it involves mobilizing various aspects of communicative competence, including non-linguistic resources; it is heavily reliant on the situational context and it must take account of the broader cultural and social milieu. It also impinges upon the process of the acquisition of this skill because, as Burns and Seidlhofer (2010: 197) point out, '(. . .) learning speaking, whether in a first or other language, involves developing subtle and detailed knowledge about why, how, when to communicate, and complex skills for producing and managing interaction, such as asking a question or obtaining a turn'. Such difficulties, in turn, inevitably generate a number of problems for teachers, particularly those in foreign language settings, as they have to create in their classrooms optimal conditions for the acquisition of all the components of the skill of speaking as well as ample opportunities for contextualized, meaningful and integrated practice in using it.

A description of the characteristics of speaking in a foreign language can be approached from different angles, but typically it is conceptualized in terms of two interrelated facets, that is the various types of knowledge that learners possess and their expertise in adeptly using this knowledge in real communication, which have been, respectively, labelled in latest state-of-the-art articles as *language as a system* and *language in contexts of use* (Bygate, 2002), *form* and *function* (Tarone, 2005), *what learners know* and *what learners do* (Thornbury, 2005) and *oral repertoires* and *oral processes* (Bygate, 2008). The current discussion, however, draws upon a more detailed characterization of the construct of spoken language offered by Bygate (2009), who breaks it down into (1) *the spoken repertoire*, (2) *the conditions of speech* and (3) *the processes of oral language production*. With respect to the first of these categories, it includes a range of linguistic elements, which can be subdivided into *phonological* (i.e. both segmental and suprasegmental), *lexicogrammatical* (morphological and syntactic resources, lexis, as well as formulaic and pragmalinguistic units) and *discourse features* (i.e. socio-pragmatic features and pragmatic discourse structures), and different constellations of which are used with a view to attaining social or informational purposes in specific situations (cf. Roever, 2009). Broadly speaking, these purposes are related to three overarching functions of oral discourse, namely *interactional* (i.e. maintaining social relationships), *transactional* (i.e. conveying information) and *ludic* (i.e. using language for entertainment) (cf. Brown & Yule, 1983; Tarone, 2005). As demonstrated by the findings of research in corpus linguistics (e.g. Chafe, 1985; Cullen & Kuo, 2007; O'Keefe *et al.*, 2007), the occurrence and distribution of various linguistic features is characterized by *fragmentation*, or relative lack of modification and subordination, high incidence of sub-clause-level units or fragments and frequent evidence of editing, and *involvement*, which manifests itself in the use of elements signalling personal identity or group membership, or expressing feelings and attitudes towards the interlocutor or discourse content. As a result, spoken language is typically associated with short turns and frequent turn-taking, pausing, false starts, hesitations, fillers, backchannels, negotiation, repairs, communication strategies, the use of deictic pronouns, ellipsis, questions, negatives or disjuncts, although some of these are by no means confined to speech (cf. Biber *et al.*, 2002). As regards the conditions in which spoken language is produced, Bygate (2009) points to *the presence of an interlocutor*, as well as conditions closely related to it. *reciprocity*, entailing making adjustments to allow smooth communication, and *time pressure*, deriving from lack of planning time and the need to listen to what is being said, both of which operate simultaneously and are responsible for the occurrence of fragmentation and involvement. Finally, the processes of language production are accounted for in terms of the stages of *conceptualization, formulation, articulation* and *monitoring*, posited by most models of speech production (de Bot, 1992; Kormos, 2006; Levelt, 1989), as well as *controlled* and *automatic processing*, viewed as gradable rather than categorical (cf. Segalowitz, 2003).

A question that arises at this juncture is whether it is at all feasible to acquire such a complex and multifaceted inventory of features, abilities and subskills, automatize them to such an extent that they can be used in real-time processing and apply them successfully to achieve specific communicative goals in an appropriate way in various culturally bound contexts. In the light of the fact that even prolonged, massive exposure to the target language (TL) together with its pragmatic and sociocultural norms, such as that available in second language contexts or, to some extent, in immersion education, by no means guarantees the attainment of high levels of proficiency, including accurate, appropriate and distinct speaking skills (e.g. Harley, 1989; Klatter-Folmer & Van Avermaet, 1997, cited in Van den Branden, 2007; Schmidt, 1983), such problems are bound to be exacerbated in foreign language settings. It is difficult to see, for example, how an average learner who attends four or five lessons a week, hardly ever uses the foreign language in a meaningful way in these lessons because of the nature of classroom interaction, has scant access to that language outside school and does not interact with native speakers can ever be expected to gain control over even a fraction of the repertoire described above, not to mention its skilful use in face-to-face communication. In fact, even advanced learners, such as those studying foreign languages for professional reasons (i.e. teachers, translators, linguists), who have apparently mastered their formal aspects, experience great difficulty with deploying these resources in spontaneous communication, let alone the fact that emulating the distinctive characteristics of speech and adjusting it to various contextual, social and cultural variables is typically beyond their reach.

It is obvious that there is a ceiling effect for interlanguage development, even for learners endowed with exceptional language aptitude, and thus their speaking skills are unlikely to ever mirror those of native speakers, and perhaps there is little reason why they should. Nonetheless, oral communication is such an important goal for most learners, irrespective of their level of proficiency, that effective instruction in this area should be at the top of the agenda for all foreign language teachers. Sadly, there are still situations where learners have virtually no opportunities for developing this skill due to frequent reliance on the

L1, teacher-fronted classes with rigid control over all classroom discourse or excessive preoccupation with other skills and subsystems. Even when efforts are made to teach spoken language, they are either aimed at preparing students for specific examination formats or simply misguided since the activities, such as role-plays that students recite from memory or exchanges that require minimal output, have little to do with authentic communication. When it comes to specialized foreign language instruction in institutions of higher education, although students have the benefit of separate speaking classes in which opportunities for oral communication abound, a major woe of such classes is that they seldom, if ever, focus upon such issues as colloquial, situation-specific phrases, appropriateness of expression, levels of formality, turn-taking mechanisms, negotiation of meaning, communication strategies and so on. As a consequence, students who consider themselves to be effective communicators are in for an unpleasant surprise on their first trip to the TL country when eyebrows are raised over the language that they produce and phrases that they would never have thought of uttering are used in specific situations. All of these problems testify to the challenges involved in instructed acquisition of speaking but at the same time point to the urgent need to provide a framework for effectively developing this key skill in response to learner expectations, such that would specify curricular decisions, materials, resources and practicable instructional options. A good point of reference for designing such a model are insights derived from influential theoretical perspectives on the processes of second language acquisition and use to which we now turn.

Tenets of Selected Psycholinguistic Perspectives on Foreign Language Acquisition

Before discussing the claims of the second language acquisition theories, models and hypotheses that may be germane to instructed acquisition of speaking, a few important qualifications are in order. For one thing, the author is fully aware that the theoretical perspectives dealt with below represent only what Sfard (1998) refers to as the *acquisition metaphor* and focus mainly on cognitive processes. In doing so, they ignore sociocultural perspectives which adopt the *participation metaphor* and place emphasis on contextual factors and interpret language learning as a dynamic, ongoing activity embedded in experience (see e.g. Batstone, 2007; Lantolf & Thorne, 2007; Ortega, 2007b; Zuengler & Miller, 2006). Still, although the latter have grown in prominence in recent years and provided an impetus for many empirical investigations (e.g. Brooks & Swain, 2009; Suzuki & Itagaki, 2009; Swain & Lapkin, 2002), this decision was intentional and was dictated by the desire to provide a coherent account of instructed acquisition of speaking, space limitations and the fact that such issues are touched upon elsewhere in this publication (see Majer, this volume; Niżegorodcew, this volume). It should be added that the following discussion is confined to those psycholinguistic theories and hypotheses which the author considers as best suited to providing insights into the teaching and learning of speaking skills and that only key tenets of each position are highlighted.

Model of speech production

The discussion in the present section draws upon a model of speech production which was initially proposed by Levelt (1989) to account for this process in the first language and was later adapted to bilingual speech production in the publications of, among others, de Bot (1992), Pienemann (1998), Bygate (2002), Izumi (2003) and Kormos (2006), with the last of these attempts being the main point of reference in our further considerations. Kormos (2006) argues that the modular approach adopted by Levelt (1989) is superior to *spreading activation theories* (Dell, 1986; Stemberger, 1985) and writes that 'Despite a few shortcomings (...) the modular theory of speech processing provides the most detailed and systematic account of the generation of verbal messages to date and has therefore been the most influential in the study of L2 speech' (2006: 11). In keeping with the original formulation, she claims that bilingual speech production consists of three separate modules, that is the *conceptualizer*, the *formulator* and the *articulator*, and makes the following additional assumptions: (1) although learners at higher proficiency levels can engage in parallel processing, encoding can only be serial when it requires conscious attentional control; (2) cascading of activation is allowed because lexical items which are activated but not selected can in turn activate relevant phonological nodes; (3) backward flow of activation between levels is impossible, with monitoring involving the use of the system of speech comprehension and (4) the nature of speech processing in the L1 and the L2 is similar. When it comes to the types of knowledge that a foreign language learner has at his or her disposal, Kormos (2006) postulates the existence of one long-term memory store which comprises (1) *episodic memory* (i.e. memory of autobiographical events); (2) *semantic memory*, which is hierarchically organized and includes the mental lexicon consisting of *concepts* (linguistic or non-linguistic notions as well as associated meaning-related memory traces), *lemmas* (containing syntactic information) and *lexemes* (storing morpho-phonological information); (3) *the syllabary* (holding automatized articulatory scores used to produce syllables) and (4) *declarative memory of syntactic and phonological rules*. What should be emphasized is that the first three of these are shared between first and additional languages and only the last one is particular to bilingual speakers, such as instructed foreign language learners. It is also assumed that attentional resources are limited, which inevitably affects speech production in L2, and thus automatization of encoding procedures is necessary, which can be explained in terms of both rule-based approaches, such as adaptive control of thought theory (Anderson, 1983, 1995), and item-based approaches, such as instance theory (Logan, 1988) or strength theory (MacKay, 1982).

The model posits that the process of speech starts with *message conceptualization* where relevant semantic concepts are activated and the language in which these concepts are to be encoded is set, with the effect that the output of this stage is a preverbal plan accompanied by a language cue. In order to account for the use of formulaic non-creative formulaic sequences, Kormos (2006) points out that semantic memory also holds chunks of concepts necessary to express various communicative functions such as apologizing, requesting or criticizing which are activated as one unit in a specific situation. It also has to be emphasized that this process does not happen in a vacuum and has a very strong social dimension since in conceptualizing a particular pragmatic purpose, the speaker has to take into account a number of factors such as the overall topic of the interaction, the relationship with the interlocutor, interpretation of preceding and upcoming discourse, prototypical patterns of interaction, content knowledge or ongoing negotiation, to name but a few (cf. Bygate, 2002). In the second phase, referred to as *formulation*, the preverbal message has to be converted into a speech plan, which involves the processes of *lexical, syntactic* and *phonological encoding*. To be more precise, the learner has to (1) match these concepts or chunks of concepts together with accompanying language cues with appropriate lexical entries, or lemmas in the form of single words or multiword units that get activated for both L1 and L2; (2) retrieve relevant syntactic information (gender, number, etc.) and put together phrases and clauses using the information held by lemmas and lexemes, falling back upon declarative (i.e. explicit) and procedural (i.e. implicit) knowledge and then (3) prepare a phonological plan of an utterance by activating phonological word forms with possible cascading of activation to other lexemes, access phonemes stored as whole units and retrieve articulatory gestures for syllables from the syllabary, with such automatized programs being L1-based for beginners and separate for L2 in more advanced learners. Also at this phase, according to Bygate (2002), pragmatic factors may come into the picture as well and they are reflective, for instance, of prototypical memories of distinctive features of lexical items or reliance on rapidly fading traces in working memory. Finally, in the last stage, labelled *articulation*, the phonetic plan is executed, which entails retrieving chunks of internal speech from the articulatory buffer, thus transforming internal knowledge into audible sounds.

The current discussion of the model of speech production in a foreign language would be incomplete without commenting on the processes of monitoring, transfer, code-switching and the application of communication strategies. As regards the former, it is similar to the L1 and involves three loops where the output of the conceptualization stage is compared with the initial intention of the speaker, the phonetic plan is scrutinized internally and the articulated message is externally monitored in terms of it accuracy, appropriacy and effectiveness, with the caveat that modifications can be made only in the conceptualizer. The main difference lies in the fact that because of their incomplete TL knowledge, L2 learners have to direct their restricted attentional resources to the processes of lexical, grammatical and phonological encoding as they are likely to be controlled rather than automatic, which results in ineffective monitoring and prioritization of meaning over form, vocabulary over grammar, accuracy over fluency or the other way around (Kormos, 1999; Muranoi, 2007). With respect to transfer and code-switching, these processes can be explained by the fact that L1 and L2 knowledge stores are shared, and items and procedures in both languages are activated, the ramification of which is that learners unintentionally (e.g. erroneous syntactic information is used) or intentionally (i.e. to compensate for their lacking resources or in the hope that L1 and L2 are similar) resort to their mother tongue. When it comes to communication strategies, these can be defined from a psycholinguistic position as 'the expression of an alternative speech plan when the original proved to be unencodable' (Poulisse, 1997: 5). As Dörnyei and Scott (1997) explain, they can be employed to deal with resource deficits in vocabulary, grammar or phonology, processing time pressures and deficiencies that learners perceive in their output or comprehension problems, and they involve, for example, modification of concepts or features of lemmas and lexemes.

Interactionist approaches

Following Gass and Mackey (2007), the label *interactionist approaches* as it is used in the present chapter is an umbrella term which is meant to refer to various theoretical positions seeking to establish a link between interaction and language learning, with the qualification that, for reasons spelled out above, it does not include social perspectives which are viewed by some specialists as part and parcel of interactionist research (see Philp, 2009). Although this line of inquiry has its roots in the 1970s (e.g. Hatch, 1978), research of this kind started to gain momentum with the appearance of Long's (1983) interaction hypothesis, which built on Krashen's (1981) input hypothesis and posited that discourse modifications played a more important role than *a priori* linguistic modifications in making input comprehensible. More precisely, it gave weight to *negotiation of meaning*, or interactive work done by interlocutors to forestall or resolve communication impasses, and *interactional modifications*, understood as adjustments to conversation structure intended to tackle such problems. This resulted in a spate of laboratory and classroom-based studies which were descriptive in nature and mainly aimed at exploring the various patterns of interaction as well as the factors impacting them (see e.g. Spada & Lightbown, 2009), but failed to directly address the link between negotiation and language learning.

This evident shortcoming led Long (1996) to propose a revised version of the interaction hypothesis, which draws upon Schmidt's (1990, 2001) noticing hypothesis in recognizing the crucial role of attention and noticing in the process of language learning, and, in this way, ties in with research on instructed language acquisition. This new formulation is based on the assumption that '(...) environmental contributions to acquisition are mediated by selective attention and the learner's developing L2 processing capacity, and that these resources are brought together most usefully, although not exclusively, during *negotiation for meaning*' (Long, 1996: 414) [emphasis original]. As a consequence, it is hypothesized that the benefits of negotiated interaction go beyond the provision of better quality *positive evidence* and they also include a more direct contribution to interlanguage development thanks to the availability of *negative evidence* in the form of different forms of corrective feedback as well as opportunities for producing *modified output* as a result of *noticing the gap* (cf. Schmidt & Frota, 1986) in TL knowledge. Long (1996) emphasizes in particular the value of *recasts*, defined as utterances which rephrase erroneous utterances without changing their intended message, which are relatively implicit and unobtrusive, thus ensuring a constant flow of interaction and continued focus on meaning. Notwithstanding its main emphasis on input-based error correction, such a view fits in closely with the output hypothesis advocated by Swain (1985, 1995, 2005) in order to accommodate research findings demonstrating partial failure of Canadian French immersion programme to develop productive skills, accuracy and appropriacy. The hypothesis stresses the role of production in triggering syntactic processing and the need to generate *pushed* or *comprehensible output*, or such that not only succeeds in conveying messages but does so in an accurate, appropriate, coherent and precise manner. This is accomplished through reacting to learner errors in the course of communicative tasks in such a way that learners become aware of their inaccurate utterances and attempt to fix them without compromising their communicative intent. Swain (1995, 2005) also elaborates on the functions of output in L2 learning, pointing out that, apart from enhancing fluency, it promotes noticing by helping learners realize their linguistic deficiencies, fosters hypothesis formation and testing, and allows conscious refection on TL use.

Both the revised interaction hypothesis and the output hypothesis have given an impetus to numerous studies, many of which have become an integral part of empirical investigations into form-focused instruction and have considerably extended our understanding of this field. In particular, such research projects have addressed the issue of the effectiveness of different types of corrective feedback provided during message conveyance (e.g. implicit vs. explicit, input-based vs. output-based, intensive vs. extensive), both in terms of immediate output modifications in the form of uptake and repair, and long-term effects of the intervention, thus fulfilling DeKeyser's (1998) requirement of meaningful practice (see e.g. Lyster & Saito, 2010). Another fruitful line of inquiry has been the investigation of the occurrence and effects of *language-related episodes* in which learners consciously reflect on their TL use, either questioning the accuracy of their output or engaging in self- or peer-correction (see e.g. Leeser, 2004). What should also be noted is the recognition of the impact of linguistic (e.g. complexity of the target form), individual (e.g. language aptitude) and contextual (e.g. type of activity) factors on the impact of corrective feedback, and the need to take into account learners' response to such feedback, or their engagement (cf. Ellis, 2010).

Skill-learning theory

Skill-learning theory derives from rule-based theories of automatization, in particular Anderson's (1983, 1995) adaptive control of thought theory, and has been applied to the field of language learning mainly through the work of Johnson (1996) and DeKeyser (1998, 2001). As DeKeyser (2007a: 97) explains,

> The basic claim of skill acquisition theory is that learning of a wide variety of skills shows a remarkable similarity in development from initial representation of knowledge through initial changes in behavior to eventual fluent, spontaneous, largely spontaneous, and highly skilled behavior, and that this set of phenomena can be accounted for by a set of basic principles common to the acquisition of all skills.

To be more precise, such a process entails a move from *explicit, declarative knowledge*, which is conscious knowledge of rules and fragments, to *implicit, procedural* knowledge, which is subconscious and enables fast and effective use of these rules and fragments in spontaneous communication. Since the development of fully implicit representation may be an unattainable goal for foreign language learners due to grossly inadequate opportunities for TL exposure and interaction,

DeKeyser (2007b) prefers to talk about *automatized knowledge*, which may still be conscious but is available for actual communication, with the qualification that automaticity is a matter of degree rather than an all-or-nothing affair. Leaving aside such technicalities, the conversion of declarative knowledge into procedural knowledge is indispensable for the ability to use the TL in spontaneous oral communication as it accelerates the processes of lexical, grammatical and phonological encoding (see above) and frees up learners' limited attentional resources, which can be allocated to discourse planning, deciding on message content as well as monitoring rather than selection of accurate linguistic forms (cf. Segalowitz, 2003).

Such a transformation requires both a quantitative and a qualitative change in the initial declarative representation and involves the processes of *automatization* (i.e. speeding up the performance of a skill, reducing the error rate and interference from other tasks) and *restructuring* (i.e. changing the subcomponents of knowledge and the way in which they interact). For these processes to take place, it is necessary to provide learners with practice opportunities, but the type of practice has to be carefully adjusted to the specific stage of skill acquisition, that is the development of declarative knowledge, its proceduralization and automatization. As regards the first two of these, teachers must provide learners with appropriate rules and examples, and opportunities to apply this knowledge in understanding and producing correct sentences, although, in the light of his experience of teaching English to senior high-school learners, the present author finds it difficult to concur with DeKeyser (1997, 2007b) that the move from declarative to procedural knowledge does not take much time and may be complete by means of a dozen or so relevant sentences. Automatization, in turn, is a much more ambitious goal in a classroom context, as it takes a considerable amount of time and effort, and it requires *meaningful practice*, that is such that goes beyond mechanical drills or exercises which do not aid learners in establishing form-meaning connections, and consists in the use of the structures taught to achieve genuine communicative goals (cf. DeKeyser, 1998). As DeKeyser (2007b: 292) notes, 'Good practice needs to involve real operating conditions as soon as possible, which means comprehending and expressing real thoughts, and this necessarily involves a variety of structures, some of which be much further along the declarative-procedural-automatic path than others'. Practice of this kind can naturally be accompanied by timely corrective feedback in the form of recasts or prompts (e.g. clarification requests) and thus can also be considered from the perspective of interactional approaches (see 'Interactionist approaches' section).

By DeKeyser's (2007a, 2007b) own admission, skill-learning theory is not without its share of problems and it is not intended to explain all aspects of instructed foreign language acquisition. For one thing, there is considerable controversy over the contributions of *output-oriented practice* as recommended by Johnson (1996) and DeKeyser (1998) and *input-based practice*, which lies at the heart of VanPatten's (2002) input processing theory, with research findings being inconclusive in this respect. Secondly, there is the issue of transferability of automatized procedural knowledge, which, in contrast to declarative knowledge, is highly skill-specific and subject to transfer-appropriate processing, with the result that effective practice in one mode or context is unlikely to affect performance in another, a good case in point being the interface between comprehension and production or a picture-description task and a whole-class discussion. Thirdly, the theory is mainly applicable to adults endowed with high aptitude, relatively simple structures and early stages of instructed learning, although all of these conditions do not have to be present (cf. DeKeyser, 2007a). Finally, similarly to negotiated interaction, the outcomes of practice in learning a foreign language are a function of a learner's developmental readiness and a wide array of individual variables, not only age and aptitude but also learning styles, learning strategies, personality or motivation.

Model of language proficiency

The model of language proficiency to be discussed in the present section draws upon the idea of a *dual-mode system* proposed by Skehan (1998) which bears some resemblance to Pinker's (1999) *dual-mechanism model*. In this view, both native speakers and learners have at their disposal an analytic *rule-based system* and a formulaic *exemplar-based system*, or, to employ Reber's (1989) terminology, an *abstract memory system* and an *instantiated memory system*, neither of which is by itself sufficient for effective oral language production and which thus have to be used in tandem. As regards the former, it is highly structured, well organized and parsimonious; it allows creativity and flexibility and it is open to restructuring as new rules replace or subsume older ones, but, at the same time, it is difficult to utilize in comprehension and production because of limited attentional resources and working memory which cannot effectively accommodate the recombination of numerous small elements needed for utterance-construction on the basis of rules. By contrast, the latter system is redundant as it is made up of multiple representations of the same formulaic chunks in different configurations, the utilization of which is relatively easy under real operating conditions and does not deplete attentional resources, which can be allocated to message planning and formulation (see 'Model of speech production' section). The drawback of these memory-based multiword units, though, is that they have a limited potential for creating novel utterances, with the effect that such a system does not guarantee the expression of precise meanings suited to a specific situation (see Skehan, 1998).

While native speakers use the two systems with ease depending on circumstances, this issue is far more intricate in the case of foreign language learners as their dependence on rules and formulaic chunks is bound to be a function of a multitude of factors such as opportunities for naturalistic exposure offered by the educational context, type of instruction or a range of individual differences (cf. Pawlak, 2006), and there is scant empirical evidence to support the model in the case of L2 learning (cf. Ellis, 2008). Another difference between first and second language acquisition is that while natives inevitably move through the stages of *lexicalization* (i.e. reliance on exemplars), *syntacticalization* (i.e. emergence of a rule-based system) and *relexicalization* (i.e. appearance of functionally autonomous multiword units based on rules), given the tendency to prioritize meaning over form in tackling processing demands, '(. . .) there is a danger that the second language learner will not progress beyond the first of the three stages (. . .)' (Skehan, 1998: 91). A solution that Skehan (1998) proposes is to create conditions that would be conducive to going beyond the phase of lexicalization, to the stages of syntacticalization and relexicalization, and claims that this goal can best be accomplished by means of task-based instruction. Since different tasks are likely to aid this move in specific ways, channelling learners' attentional resources in particular ways, there have been a number of studies which have looked at how manipulating various task parameters can affect oral production. Researchers have investigated, among others, different types of planning (cf. Ellis, 2009), task repetition (e.g. Bygate, 2001; Mystkowska-Wiertelak, this volume) or cognitive complexity (cf. Robinson *et al.*, 2009), typically evaluating learners' speech in terms of fluency, accuracy and complexity (cf. Czwenar, this volume; Hausen & Kuiken, 2009).

Implications for Instructed Acquisition of Speaking

Taken together, the theoretical perspectives described above provide a solid basis for a number of useful pedagogical implications for instructed acquisition of speaking which will be outlined here mainly with respect to the foreign rather than second language context. In the first place, given the processing demands of spontaneous oral production and comprehension, it is necessary to equip learners with requisite systemic knowledge in terms of grammar, lexis, multiword units, pronunciation, pragmatic routines and paralinguistic means; sensitize them to the distinctive features of the spoken language and to make them cognizant of how such resources can be employed to convey intended meanings in a range of situations. In view of blatantly inadequate exposure, learners can hardly be expected to develop much of this knowledge incidentally, which is likely to happen to a greater or lesser extent in second language settings, and thus there is a need for formal instruction which would focus not only on specific linguistic features but also on important pragmatic and sociocultural aspects, such as contextual determinants of appropriacy or rules of turn-taking. Learners should also be provided with copious opportunities to activate these types of knowledge in order to employ the TL to perform interactional, transactional and ludic functions. This will clearly require a high degree of contextualization of activities aimed at developing speaking skills, a chance to decide about what and how to say rather to recite from memory, as this will activate the processes of conceptualization, formulation and articulation, and integration of different skills and subsystems in communicative tasks as is the case in real-life situations. Since, as argued by Kormos (2006), there is ample evidence that L1 and L2 concepts and lemmas and lexemes share the same memory space and receive some degree of activation in speech production, it would also make sense to view the first language as an ally that can aid learners in retrieving the required target items, rules and articulatory plans by, for example, instructing them in the use of relevant memory or cognitive learning strategies (e.g. making associations and analysing contrastively). Equally beneficial can be training in the use of communication strategies, which, as pointed out above, may help learners replace or modify preverbal plans to handle deficits in their systemic competence or gain extra time for planning and monitoring, as well as other learning strategies useful in practicing and monitoring speaking skills.

Apart from such general considerations, more specific recommendations can be made on the types of activities that should be used in the classroom with a view to fostering the ability to effectively take part in spontaneous oral communication. For one thing, even though drills and exercises can be useful up to a point, what learners need is meaningful practice in which they can employ specific structures of formulaic chunks under real operating conditions (cf. DeKeyser, 1998), as only in this way can they be expected to develop implicit knowledge in addition to explicit knowledge or, as DeKeyser (2007b) would have it, transform declarative knowledge into procedural knowledge and then automatize the latter. Particularly useful for this purpose are communicative tasks which require learners to employ the TL for message conveyance but are constructed in such a way that their attention is also directed at specific features, such as rules, lexical units, pragmalinguistic items or articulatory patterns. They can take the form of production-based focused communication tasks where the use of a feature is essential for their completion (cf. Ellis, 2003); activities with a built-in element that deflects part of the available attention from the targeted form, in line with the $ra - 1$ (required attention minus one) formula (cf. Johnson, 1996); tasks triggering automatization, such as the 4/3/2 technique (i.e. telling the same story to different interlocutors with less time on each occasion) (cf. Arevart & Nation, 1991) or repetition of the same or similar task (cf. Bygate, 2001). As mentioned above, it is also possible to shift learners' attention between accuracy, fluency and complexity by adjusting the design features of tasks, which may involve providing opportunities for planning, introducing a post-task activity or manipulating its cognitive complexity (e.g. the amount of context or information) (cf. Skehan, 1998).

Also useful in promoting instructed acquisition of speaking are different activities which encourage learners to engage in negotiated interactions of the kind suggested by Long (1996) or Swain (1995, 2005). For example, tasks could be designed, both in group-work and whole-class teaching modes, which induce learners to engage in exchanges fostering interactional modifications and pushed output, their awareness of these sequences could be raised and pertinent training could be undertaken in this area. Yet another possibility is enhancing the likelihood of occurrence of language-related episodes in learners' conversations by utilizing text-reconstruction activities such as those described by Muranoi (2000) or Swain (2000), or supplying instructions about the use of given structures prior to the performance of the task. There is also a place for the provision of corrective feedback in the course of communicative activities, which should not deprive them of their meaning-oriented character but still ensure that learners notice the corrective move and interpret it as such, require them to produce the correct form and be intensive in the sense of targeting a single form (cf. Ellis, 2007).

Towards a Model of Teaching Speaking Skills in the Foreign Language Classroom

As Bygate (2002) illustrates, various approaches to the development of speaking skills have been proposed by methodologists over the years, such as the *skill-getting and skill-using approach* (i.e. controlled practice of the system followed by communicative activities) (Rivers & Temperley, 1978), the *whole-skill: part-skill approach* (communicative tasks followed by controlled practice activities) (Littlewood, 1981), manipulating task parameters to emphasize accuracy, fluency and complexity (Skehan, 1998), the *focus on form approach* (i.e. integrating form and meaning in communicative tasks) (Long, 1996) and the *proportional approach* with a shift of focus from accuracy to fluency with learners' growing proficiency (Brumfit, 1984). Valuable as they are, such proposals fail to address the complexities of instructed acquisition of speaking in a comprehensive way as they focus only on some aspects of this process, often in keeping with the theoretical persuasions of their proponents, but tend to ignore other issues which may be crucial in a specific context. For this reason, in conclusion to the present chapter, an attempt is made to propose a model of teaching speaking in the foreign language classroom which, although admittedly imperfect and tentative, may provide a useful point of reference for materials designers, methodologists and teachers.

Effective instructed acquisition of speaking involves making a number of decisions at the level of the curriculum, lesson planning, the choice of specific techniques and promoting learner independence. In the first place, the development of speaking skills must be viewed as an integral part of the curriculum, it must be a priority from the very beginning of instruction and it should draw upon different approaches such as those enumerated above. It is the belief of the present author that it would be the most beneficial to adopt a proportional syllabus for that purpose, which could be partly modular and partly integrated depending on the situation and learners' needs (cf. Pawlak, 2006). In other words, as learners become more proficient, there should be a gradual shift from form-focused to meaning-oriented activities, but the latter should be present to some extent from the outset, either as an extension of controlled practice or entirely on their own. With respect to the organization of language lessons, speaking can obviously be practiced throughout them as long as teachers choose to use the TL as much as possible, which is sadly often not the case, but there is also a need to dedicate entire activities to this skill, particularly those that require real communication and not just performance based on memorization. These tasks can be implemented at any point in the lesson (i.e. beginning, middle or end) in accordance with its objectives and while they may be conducted with the whole class, especially advantageous will be setting up pair or group-work activities for this purpose. Of equal significance is systematic teaching of TL forms, including morphosyntactic features, words, multiword units, pronunciation patterns and sociopragmatic routines, creating opportunities for their automatization as well as promoting noticing and hypothesis formation, for example, through timely, narrowly focused error correction during communicative tasks. Learners can also benefit from awareness-raising focusing upon verbal and non-verbal aspects of discourse, distinctive features of spoken language, the occurrence of negotiated interaction, monitoring and skilful use of communication strategies. Given the skimpy access to the TL, learners should also be encouraged to adopt an autonomous approach to developing speaking skills, by being shown, for instance, how to search for extra sources of exposure and trained in the use of learning strategies that will help them to fully exploit the potential of such affordances. Finally, complicated as it might be in a classroom setting, it would be advisable to make performance of communicative tasks an integral part of assessment procedures.

Clearly, these specifications are very general and should be subject to modification in accordance with learners' age, educational level, goals or individual differences as well as the exigencies of particular local contexts. Nonetheless, such guidelines constitute a set of core principles which should be heeded by foreign language teachers if the development of their learners' speaking skills is of concern to them. And no matter what class they may teach, it definitely should be for the simple reason that for the vast majority of learners, it is the ability to engage in successful oral communication, whether this success is defined as achieving nativelike mastery or merely getting messages across, that drives their motivation to learn a particular foreign language.

References

Anderson, J.R. (1983) *The Architecture of Cognition.* Cambridge, MA: Harvard University Press.

Anderson, J.R. (1995) *Learning and Memory: An Integrated Approach.* New York: Wiley.

Arevart, S. and Nation, P. (1991) Fluency improvement in a second language. *RELC Journal* 22, 84–94.

Batstone, R. (2007) A role for discourse frames and learner interpretations in focus on form. *New Zealand Studies in Applied Linguistics* 31, 55–68.

Biber, D., Conrad, S. and Leech, G. (2002) *Longman Students Grammar of Spoken and Written English.* Harlow: Pearson Education.

Brooks, L. and Swain, M. (2009) Languaging in collaborative writing: Creation of and response to expertise. In A. Mackey and C. Polio (eds) *Multiple Perspectives on Interaction. Second Language Research in Honor of Susan M. Gass* (pp. 58–89). New York: Routledge.

Brown, G. and Yule, G. (1983) *Teaching the Spoken Language.* Cambridge: Cambridge University Press.

Brumfit, C.J. (1984) *Communicative Methodology in Language Teaching.* Cambridge: Cambridge University Press.

Burns, A. and Seidlhofer, B. (2010) Speaking and pronunciation. In N. Schmitt (ed.) *An Introduction to Applied Linguistics* (3rd edn, pp. 197–214). London: Hodder Education.

Bygate, M. (2001) Effects of task repetition on the structure and control of language. In M. Bygate, P. Skehan and M. Swain (eds) *Task-based Learning: Language Teaching, Learning and Assessment* (pp. 23–48). London: Longman.

Bygate, M. (2002) Speaking. In R.B. Kaplan (ed.) *The Oxford Handbook of Applied Linguistics* (pp. 27–38). Oxford: Oxford University Press.

Bygate, M. (2008) Oral second language abilities as expertise. In K. Johnson (ed.) *Expertise in Second Language Learning and Teaching* (pp. 104–127). New York: Palgrave Macmillan.

Bygate, M. (2009) Teaching and testing speaking. In M.H. Long and C.J. Doughty (eds) *The Handbook of Language Teaching* (pp. 412–440). Oxford: Wiley-Blackwell.

Chafe, W.L. (1985) Linguistic differences produced by differences between speaking and writing. In D.R. Olson, L. Torrance and A. Hildyard (eds) *Literacy, Language and Learning* (pp. 105–123). Cambridge: Cambridge University Press.

Cullen, R. and Kuo, I.-C. (2007) Spoken grammar and ELT course materials: A missing link? *TESOL Quarterly* 41, 361–386.

de Bot, K. (1992) A bilingual production model: Levelt's "speaking" model adapted. *Applied Linguistics* 13, 1–24.

DeKeyser, R.M. (1997) Beyond explicit rule learning. Automatizing second language morphosyntax. *Studies in Second Language Acquisition* 19, 195–221.

DeKeyser, R.M. (1998) Beyond focus on form: Cognitive perspectives on learning and practicing second language grammar. In C.J. Doughty and J. Williams (eds) *Focus on Form in Classroom Second Language Acquisition* (pp. 42–63). Cambridge: Cambridge University Press.

DeKeyser, R.M. (2001) Automaticity and automatization. In P. Robinson (ed.) *Cognition and Second Language Instruction* (pp. 125–151). Cambridge: Cambridge University Press.

DeKeyser, R.M. (2007a) Skill acquisition theory. In B. VanPatten and J. Williams (eds) *Theories in Second language Acquisition: An Introduction* (pp. 97–113). Mahwah, NJ: Erlbaum.

DeKeyser, R.M. (2007b) The future of practice. In R. DeKeyser (ed.) *Practice in a Second Language: Perspectives from Applied Linguistics and Cognitive Psychology* (pp. 287–304). Cambridge: Cambridge University Press.

Dell, G.S. (1986) A spreading activation theory of retrieval in sentence production. *Psychological Review* 93, 283–321.

Dörnyei, Z. and Scott, M.L. (1997) Communication strategies in a second language: Definitions and taxonomies. *Language Learning* 47, 173–210.

Ellis, R. (2003) *Task-based Language Learning and Teaching*. Oxford: Oxford University Press.

Ellis, R. (2007) The differential effects of corrective feedback on two grammatical structures. In A. Mackey (ed.) *Conversational Interaction in Second Language Acquisition* (pp. 339–360). Oxford: Oxford University Press.

Ellis, R. (2008) *The Study of Second Language Acquisition* (2nd edn). Oxford: Oxford University Press.

Ellis, R. (2009) The differential effects of three types of task planning on the fluency, complexity and accuracy in L2 oral production. *Applied Linguistics* 30, 474–509.

Ellis, R. (2010) Epilogue: A framework for investigating oral and written corrective feedback. *Studies in Second Language Acquisition* 32, 335–349.

Gass, S.M. (1997) *Input, Interaction, and the Second Language Learner.* Mahwah, NJ: Erlbaum.

Gass, S.M. and Mackey, A. (2007) Input, interaction and output in second language acquisition. In B. VanPatten and J. Williams (eds) *Theories in Second Language Acquisition: An Introduction* (pp. 175–199). Mahwah, NJ: Erlbaum.

Harley, B. (1989) Functional grammar in French immersion: A classroom experiment. *Applied Linguistics* 19, 331–359.

Hatch, E. (ed.) (1978) *Second Language Acquisition.* Rowley, MA: Newbury House.

Hausen, A. and Kuiken, F. (2009) Complexity, accuracy and fluency in second language acquisition. *Applied Linguistics* 30, 461–473.

Hughes, R. (2002) *Teaching and Researching Speaking.* Harlow: Pearson Education.

Izumi, S. (2003) Comprehension and production processes in second language learning: In search of the psycholinguistic rationale of the output hypothesis. *Applied Linguistics* 24, 168–196.

Johnson, K. (1996) *Language Teaching and Skill Learning.* London: Blackwell.

Klatter-Folmer, J. and Van Avermaet, P. (1997) Language shift among Italians in Flanders and Turks in the Netherlands. Paper presented at the 1st International Symposium on Bilingualism, Vigo.

Kormos, J. (1999) Monitoring and self-repair in L2. *Language Learning* 49, 303–342.

Kormos, J. (2006) *Speech Production and Second Language Acquisition.* Mahwah, NJ: Erlbaum.

Krashen, S. (1981) *Second Language Acquisition and Second Language Learning.* Oxford: Pergamon.

Leeser, M.J. (2004) Learner proficiency and focus on form during collaborative dialogue. *Language Teaching Research* 8, 55–81.

Lantolf, J.P. and Thorne, S.L. (2007) Sociocultural theory and second language learning. In B. VanPatten and J. Williams (eds) *Theories in Second language Acquisition: An Introduction* (pp. 201–224). Mahwah, NJ: Erlbaum.

Levelt, W.J.M. (1989) *Speaking: From Intention to Articulation.* Cambridge, MA: MIT Press.

Levelt, W.J.M. (1999) Language production: A blueprint for the speaker. In C. Brown and P. Hagoort (eds) *Neurocognition of Language* (pp. 83–122). Oxford: Oxford University Press.

Littlewood, W.T. (1981) *Communicative Language Teaching. An Introduction.* Cambridge: Cambridge University Press.

Logan, G.D. (1988) Towards and instance theory of automatization. *Psychological Review* 95, 492–527.

Long, M. H. (1981) Input, interaction and second language acquisition. In H. Winitz (ed.) *Native Language and Foreign Language Acquisition* (pp. 259–278). New York: Annals of the New York Academy of Sciences 379.

Long, M. H. (1983) Native speaker/non-native speaker conversation and the negotiation of comprehensible input. *Applied Linguistics* 4, 126–141.

Long, M.H. (1985) Input and second language acquisition theory. In S.M. Gass and C.G. Madden (eds) *Input in Second Language Acquisition* (pp. 377–393). Rowley, MA: Newbury House.

Long, M.H. (1996) The role of the linguistic environment in second language acquisition. In W. Ritchie and T. Bhatia (eds) *Handbook of Second Language Acquisition* (pp. 413–468). New York: Academic Press.

Luoma, S. (2004) *Assessing Speaking.* Cambridge: Cambridge University Press.

Lyster, R. and Saito, K. (2010) Oral feedback in classroom SLA: A meta-analysis. *Studies in Second Language Acquisition* 32, 265–302.

MacKay, D.G. (1982) The problems of flexibility, fluency and speed-accuracy trade-off in skilled behavior. *Psychological Review* 89, 483–506.

Majer, J. (2003) *Interactive Discourse in the Foreign Language Classroom.* Łódź: University of Łódz Press.

Muranoi, H. (2000). Focus on form through guided summarizing and EFL learners' interlanguage development. Paper presented at the 39th conference of Japan Association of College English Teachers (JACET), Okinawa, Japan.

Muranoi, H. (2007) Output practice in the L2 classroom. In R.M. DeKeyser (ed.) *Practice in a Second Language: Perspectives from Applied Linguistics and Cognitive Psychology* (pp. 51–84). Cambridge: Cambridge University Press.

O'Keefe, A., McCarthy, M. and Carter, R. (2007) *From Corpus to Classroom Language Use and Language Teaching.* Cambridge: Cambridge University Press.

Ortega, L. (2007a) Meaningful L2 practice in foreign language classrooms. A cognitive-interactionist SLA perspective. In R.M. DeKeyser (ed.) *Practice in a Second Language: Perspectives from Applied Linguistics and Cognitive Psychology* (pp. 180–207). Cambridge: Cambridge University Press.

Ortega, L. (2007b) Second language learning explained? SLA across nine contemporary theories. In B. VanPatten and J. Williams (eds) *Theories in Second Language Acquisition: An Introduction* (pp. 225–250). Mahwah, NJ: Erlbaum.

Pawlak, M. (2000) Optimizing interaction in the second language classroom. *Studies Anglica Posnaniensia* 35, 234–258.

Pawlak, M. (2004) *Describing and Researching Interactive Processes in the Foreign Language Classroom*. Konin: State School of Higher Education in Konin Press.

Pawlak, M. (2006) *The Place of Form-focused Instruction in the Foreign Language Classroom*. Poznań – Kalisz: Adam Mickiewicz University Press.

Pawlak, M. (2009). *Rola nauczyciela w kształtowaniu procesów interakcyjnych podczas lekcji języka obcego*. Poznań – Kalisz: Adam Mickiewicz University Press.

Philp, J. (2009) Epilogue: Exploring the intricacies of interaction and language development. In A. Mackey and C. Polio (eds) *Multiple Perspectives on Interaction. Second Language Research in Honor of Susan M. Gass* (pp. 254–273). New York: Routledge.

Pienemann, M. (1998) *Language Processing and Second Language Development: Processability Theory*. Amsterdam: John Benjamins.

Pinker, S. (1999) *Words and Rules*. New York: Basic Books.

Poulisse, N. (1997) Compensatory strategies and the principles of clarity and economy. In G. Kasper and E. Kellerman (eds) *Communication Strategies: Psycholinguistic and Sociolinguistic Perspectives* (pp. 49–64). London: Longman.

Reber, A. (1989) Implicit learning and tacit knowledge. *Journal of Experimental Psychology: General* 118, 219–235.

Rivers, W. and Temperley, M.S. (1978) *A Practical Guide to the Teaching of English as a Second Language*. Oxford: Oxford University Press.

Robinson, P., Cadierno, T. and Shirai, Y. (2009) Time and motion: Measuring the effects of the conceptual demands of tasks on second language speech production. *Applied Linguistics* 30, 533–554.

Roever, C. (2009) Teaching and testing pragmatics. In M.H. Long and C. J. Doughty (eds) *The Handbook of Language Teaching* (pp. 560–577). Oxford: Wiley-Blackwell.

Schmidt, R. (1983) Interaction, acculturation, and the acquisition of communicative competence. In N. Wolfson and E. Judd (eds) *Sociolinguistics and Language Acquisition* (pp. 137–174). Rowley, MA: Newbury House.

Schmidt, R. (1990) The role of consciousness in second language learning. *Applied Linguistics* 11, 129–158.

Schmidt, R. (2001) Attention. In P. Robinson (ed.) *Cognition and Second Language Instruction* (pp. 3–32). Cambridge: Cambridge University Press.

Schmidt, R. and Frota, S. (1986) Developing basic conversational ability in a second language: A case study of an adult learner of Portuguese. In R. Day (ed.) *Talking to Learn: Conversation in Second Language Acquisition* (pp. 237–326). Rowley, MA: Newbury House.

Segalowitz, N. (2003) Automaticity and second languages. In C.J. Doughty and M.H. Long (eds) *The Handbook of Second Language Acquisition* (pp. 382–408). Oxford: Blackwell.

Sfard, A. (1998) On two metaphors for learning and the dangers of choosing just one. *Educational Researcher* 27, 4–13.

Skehan, P. (1998) *A Cognitive Approach to Language Learning*. Oxford: Oxford University Press.

Spada, N. and Lightbown, P.M. (2009) Interaction research in second/foreign language classrooms. In A. Mackey and C. Polio (eds) *Multiple Perspectives on Interaction. Second Language Research in Honor of Susan M. Gass* (pp. 157–175). New York: Routledge.

Stemberger, J.P. (1985) An interactive activation model of language production. In A.W. Ellis (ed.) *Progress in the Psychology of Language* (pp. 143–186). Hillsdale, NJ: Erlbaum.

Suzuki, W. and Itagaki, N. (2009). Languaging in grammar exercises by Japanese EFL learners of differing proficiency. *System* 37, 217–225.

Swain, M. (1985) Communicative competence: Some roles of comprehensible input and comprehensible output in its development. In S.M. Gass and C.G. Madden (eds) *Input in Second Language Acquisition* (pp. 235–253). Rowley, MA: Newbury House.

Swain, M. (1995) Three functions of output in second language learning. In G. Cook and B. Seidlhofer (eds) *Principle and Practice in Applied Linguistics: Studies in Honor of H. G. Widdowson* (pp. 125–144). Oxford: Oxford University Press.

Swain, M. (2000) The output hypothesis and beyond: Mediating acquisition through collaborative dialogue. In J.P. Lantolf (ed.) *Sociocultural Theory and Second Language Learning* (pp. 97–114). Oxford: Oxford University Press.

Swain, M. (2005) The output hypothesis: Theory and research. In E. Hinkel (ed.) *Handbook of Research in Second Language Teaching and Learning* (pp. 471–483). Mahwah, NJ: Erlbaum.

Swain, M. and Lapkin, S. (2002) Talking it through: Two French immersion learners' response to reformulation. *International Journal of Educational Research* (Special issue on the role of interaction in instructed language learning) 37, 285–304.

Tarone, E. (2005) Speaking in a second language. In E. Hinkel (ed.) *Handbook of Research in Second Language Teaching and Learning* (pp. 485–502). Mahwah, NJ: Erlbaum.

Thornbury, S. (2005) *How to Teach Speaking.* Harlow: Pearson Education.

Van den Branden, K. (2007) Second language education: Practice in perfect learning conditions? In R.M. DeKeyser (ed.) *Practice in a Second Language: Perspectives from Applied Linguistics and Cognitive Psychology* (pp. 161–179). Cambridge: Cambridge University Press.

VanPatten, B. (2002) Processing instruction: An update. *Language Learning* 52, 755–803.

Zuengler, J. and Miller, E. (2006) Cognitive and sociocultural perspectives: Two parallel SLA worlds? *TESOL Quarterly* 40, 35–58.

Chapter 2
Authenticity in Oral Communication of Instructed L2 Learners

AGNIESZKA NOWICKA and WERONIKA WILCZYŃSKA

Introduction

Speaking is widely considered to be the principal *skill* that stands for an overall knowledge of a foreign language. However, because of its transitory and thus elusive nature, it is challenging to both analyze the process of speaking itself and to observe the skill development in L2, not to mention its learning and teaching. In addition, the multiplicity of current theoretical approaches exacerbates such problems. Even though a clear-cut and comprehensive demarcation of these issues seems extremely difficult and even risky in such a short chapter, yet, such an attempt to formulate an integrative and didactically motivated view of the problems need to be undertaken. The concept of individual communicative competence (ICC), discussed later in the chapter, proposes a person-oriented view of the competence that claims to unify the social and individual aspects of learning and teaching L2 discourses, thereby providing, as it is claimed, a more integrative approach to the didactics of L2 speaking

The notion of communicative competence aims at such an integrative approach to the development of the speaking skill, as in proposing a person-oriented dimension, it aims to combine the individual and social dimensions of communicative competence. The person-oriented perspective views an L2 speaker and learner in terms of an individualistic approach, treating an individual as an independent and self-regulating actor both in communication and in learning.

The Complexity of Speaking: Expanding the Conceptual Framework

The difficulties of creating a comprehensive view of the speaking process become evident already on the level of concepts, which can be divided into the following two groups:

- The terms belonging to the colloquial register, characterized by a wide and highly imprecise spectrum of usage:
  - *speaking*: an observable, physical and more specifically, acoustic phenomenon, describing one of human activities (*speaking*

appears here on a par with other actions such as *walking, standing, doing something*);

- *expressing oneself*: a wider term since it can also concern written discourse; it suggests the connection between speaking as an activity and a speaking actor that produces it as an expression of his or her intentions, thoughts and feelings;
- *communication*: the term emphasizes rather a communicative sense or an effect and an aim of speaking.
- Specialized terms from language and communication research:
  - *text, utterance, discourse* – they indicate, respectively, a material 'product' of the speaking activity and connect it to the speaking person or the context of an utterance;
  - *speech acts/speech (communicative) actions, (communicative) inter-actions* – this group of terms defines speaking in a wider context, emphasizing their action aspect or a pragmatic value as it is viewed by an individual; this selection of terms focuses as well on the structures and dynamics of communication.

Without doubt, the terms themselves reflect the ways of comprehending speaking. However, for the purposes of this chapter, a more developed arrangement of conceptual landscape is proposed, as represented in Figure 2.1.

The upper plane of the schemata represents the society, understood as a *language community*, consisting of smaller communities (professional, social, generational, religious ones, etc.), differing in their way or style of

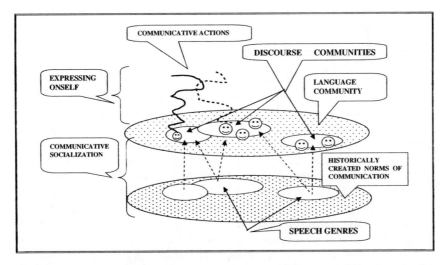

Figure 2.1 Schematic presentation of the main factors conditioning the L1 speaking skill.

'using' a given language, and more specifically, distinguished by their *discursive practices*. Practicing semiotic systems shared within a given community not only determines communication but also serves the purpose of marking one's identity and personal autonomy in relation to other communities. In the history of a given community, these practices are assigned to specific, important sociocommunicative functions, simultaneously shaping more or less ritualized forms of interaction and discourse types – genres. Social discourse practices fulfill certain social functions perceived by the members of a society as appropriate in a given context. Thus, they can be defined as having a social value in a given culture. On the level of communicative expectations, they are perceived as a part of norms and patterns that are present in education and that become criteria of evaluating social actions.

Theoretical references both to *discourse communities* defined in such a way and to the relations between them and within them broaden a general conceptual framework allowing us to grasp more comprehensively and accurately individual acts and communicative interactions. The speakers' performance appears not to be a merely spontaneous and completely arbitrary reflection of their internal states, but becomes a purposeful, intentional *action* or *coaction*. At the same time, an individual's specific communicative style, even though anchored within social norms, depends on his or her individually conditioned interpretation of and involvement in discourse. In relation to these norms, an individual's communicative style can be perceived as his or her selective and specific of each individual combination. It should be emphasized that *communicative practices* and *genres* (see 'Speech Structures and the Teaching of Speaking' section), as 'inherited' within given communities, despite undergoing a more or less visible evolution, on the whole, retain a relative stability of form, which makes them a significant reference in L1 and L2 studies.

Furthermore, another insufficiently appreciated but crucial fact is that our speech, in its individual and social dimension, is a part of our *self* or our personality. In natural or native culture conditions, an individual develops his or her language/discursive and sociocultural identity while gaining the membership in various social groups and discourse communities in the process of *socialization*, mainly, in the social interaction. This enculturation, however, in its semiotic-discursive dimension should be understood as a person's *individual* and *creative adaptation* to a given community (or communities). At the same time, the process is stimulated or even forced by educational activities, while outside the educational context, by social feedback or reactions to our communicative actions (e.g. incomprehension, critical reactions and disagreements, positive reinforcement and comprehension). Analogously, successful L2 learning on the whole also depends on the process of identity construction in that language, but in most cases, because of the different context of enculturation and language learning as well as a person's aims and the already developed L1 identity, the process proceeds in a different and usually more conscious way, and often results in a more complex, multilingual or multicultural identity. This identity is essentially different from an L1 cultural identity and very rarely emulates the cultural identity of a native L2 speaker.

Such interpretation of the processes of social interaction closely corresponds to the ethnomethodological approach, which also perceives social identity as construed by its members and situated in social interactions (Coulter, 2001; Jayyusi, 1984; Sacks, 1992). Both in endolingual or monocultural and exolingual and/or intercultural interactions, the identity is a social and dynamic phenomenon happening as a practice situated in various interaction types and discourses. Thereby, from the speakers' emic perspective, their identity, existing on the level of macro-social structure, is reconfirmed, invoked as relevant, interpreted and in fact construed in interactions on the micro-level of communicative acts such as descriptions referring to social categories and types. Social identity concerns the meaning of social categories or social types that a person can be interpreted as belonging to. One can simultaneously belong to basic conversational categories (speaker/listener), as well as ethnic, gender, age ones or intercultural or institutional categories (native/nonnative speaker, teacher, epistemic expert, learner, novice), or type collectives (Catholics, Hell's Angels, nice persons), all of which become visibly oriented to or co-selected by interlocutors as relevant for sense-making in different moments and contexts of communication. Thereby, identity, although anchored in the so-called macro-social structures, is strongly discursive and thus it represents a cultural phenomenon perceived as actually happening on the micro-level of interactions or discourses of speech communities.

In comparison with the contexts of L1 identity creation described above, the impoverished L2 learning conditions do not open up many possibilities of identity construction in L2 or even significantly limit them. The predominant and immediate discourse community in institutional learning is usually the community of learners and the virtual L2 community, often limited at best to model native speakers observed in learning materials or represented by native teachers. The prevailing relational pairs of categories and types (see Sacks, 1992) in this context have been observed to be institutional ones such as learner/teacher, epistemic expert/novice, native speaker/nonnative speaker. That is why, especially in earlier stages of L2 learning, the learner tends to experience a general sense of a lack of authenticity, which can be understood as both a socially shared and individually perceived and gradable sense of estrangement from native situations of language/discourse learning and processing (thinking, comprehending and production), and thus from his or her primary L1 identity.

Speaking: A Skill or Personal Competence?

The general perspective delineated above serves here as a background for the discussion of the following question: *how can contemporary studies of communicative actions in individual and interpersonal perspective influence the teaching of speaking?* This discussion takes into account the following domains of knowledge:

(a) the process of utterance construction, including complex and controversial problems of modeling speech production processes (see e.g. http://chat.carleton.ca/ ~ ceby/Serial.html);
(b) communicative cooperation – a process of interaction and co-construction of meanings and mutual interaction between communication participants;
(c) construing the competence – the process is understood as correlated with conscious and intentional actions undertaken by the learner with teacher's cooperation;
(d) the knowledge of an individual's control over (a) and (c), which is the result of the hereby proposed person-centered framework;
(e) the knowledge of how it can be supported didactically with a substantial cooperation on the part of the learner.

Because of the high complexity of the presented problems, it is almost an impossible task to discuss all these aspects here. For this reason, the following discussion focuses on the last problem (e), while the remaining ones are treated selectively as an indispensable and complementary background.

The notion of ICC, as proposed in earlier studies (Wilczyńska, 2002), becomes the main reference point for our considerations for the following reasons:

- such a perspective seems sufficiently extensive in that it takes into consideration the psychosocial determinants of *speaking/expressing oneself* and more generally, *communicating* and
- it is oriented at foreign language didactics in such a way that the process of learning and teaching integrates institutional aims with an individual's potential, focusing on personal effectiveness.

The premise of the following argument is that mastering and using communication skills is a person-tailored process, referring, on the one hand, to language-discourse patterns, and, on the other, to possibilities, needs and personal ambitions. Correspondingly, the term *competence* is understood as a set of personal skills. As an individual dynamically adjusts to his or her aims, contexts and types of undertaken actions, these skills also become changeable and shaped under the influence of value systems and individual experiences (Wilczyńska, 2002: 74). Such a definition foregrounds the dynamic 'action-perspective' and does not constrain itself to general psychosocial factors. Furthermore, what is more important, the perspective seems to illustrate well the *coherence* and *economy* of ICC, as features perceived by the speaker as his or her communicative operationality.

What is essential from the point of view of language instruction and learners themselves, this theoretical perspective complies with the demand of *(self)didactic effectiveness*. Thus understood ICC suggests a key role for the learner's personal activity in its construction in all essential and mutually complementary aspects, such as his or her awareness as to the nature of the competence and its conditions, the knowledge of training techniques (especially the semi-creative ones) and, finally, his or her authentic communicative experience. In this perspective, developing the 'speaking skill' means consciously construing or making one's own chosen social communicative practices. This process is to a large extent linguistic in nature and does not merely come down to producing an idiolect, but rather aims at creating a personal communicative style tailored to one's possibilities and ambitions. The style becomes part of an individual's general style of functioning and should be seen as a set of complex strategies of developing and using one's communicative skills. Consequently, *internalizing* learning units implies an integration of two traditionally contradictory dimensions – an individual and a social one – and determines an autonomy and authenticity of personal actions. Their authenticity, in turn, must be founded on the sociopsychic identity of a multilingual person.

Contemporary Speaking Instruction: Positive Tendencies and Challenges

Our subsequent discussion of fostering the competence in L2 speaking focuses upon the sociopsychological context of teaching and learning. The three groups of difficulties in developing ICC are discussed one by one, taking especially into account the specificity of L2 *taught as a school subject* in an institutional context of L2 learning and teaching. The specificity is determined by the fact that the preparation for communication in an L2 affects the learner *personally*, as it encompasses his or her personal style of acting and mental-cultural habits. All this requires significant work expenditure, high personal and creative engagement and at the same time, a fully mature and a realistic approach on the part of the learner. Therefore, it is a challenge for the teacher – in that it requires an equally substantial assistance in the sense of creating conditions for developing communicative awareness and accessibility of models as well as the organization of communication training.

Sociopsychological meaning of learning units

When meaning is considered from a foreign language speaker's perspective, in a natural context of language acquisition and learning, units of learning and their different formats (Wilczyńska, 1999) are claimed to be constituted in the reservoir of learner's communicative competence in a threefold relationship of meaning potential. An L1 or L2 learner acquires more easily those learning units in which all three meaning constituents are not perceived analytically as separate constituents but interpreted as unified and as producing one complex meaning. The most typical example of such learning units would be a (cluster) of context-sensitive formulaic expressions, their characteristic articulation and accompanying routine actions.

The less commonly associated meaning entities can vary from a single word to a whole genre such as poems, proverbs or routine comments. The meaning unfolds on the level of phonetic, pragmatic and semantic realizations, such as for instance in a congratulation formula that can be expressed with a characteristic intonation and with the use of appropriate lexical formulae whose precise semantic meaning in this communicative situation is a rather background matter. Such learning units in their different formats become the bases for developing competence out of pragmatically oriented nets of meaning that grow out of it. This is not to imply the determining nature of learning units, as they leave a space for individual modifications. The specifics of learning units can be described as follows (see Figure 2.2):

- The first one, *pragmatic value*, can be defined as an action value or a pragmatic effect of a communicative action, as existing in the system of social customs and routines (i.e. a series of potential realizations in different communicative contexts, discourses and styles, in different forms). In fact, the pragmatic meaning is situated in actual communication context in the sense that is construed there 'online' and interpreted by interaction participants in the immediate context of social interaction. Thus, it somehow fuses with the linguistic referent, realizing the meaning of an utterance.
- The second one, *semantic meaning*, is also understood as a propositional or grammatical-lexical meaning. In other words, it refers to a 'dictionary meaning' of linguistic forms. However, pure propositional meaning appears to be only an analytical abstraction of its possible contextualized forms or uses in a communicative action. From the speaker's perspective, the lexical-grammatical

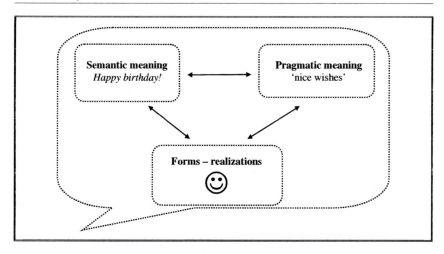

Figure 2.2 The threefold structure of the learning unit.

meaning extends paradigmatically to its uses in various contexts; namely, it allows the speaker to understand an utterance on a level of the linguistic code.

- Finally, *forms understood here as realizations in actual discourse*, where meaning is particularized in a phonetic form with its situation-specific intonation contours, a timbre of voice, characteristic mimics and so on that also display specific features of an individual's communicative style.

This threefold structure, which somehow reminds us of the Ogden-Richards' Triangle, corresponds to the analysis carried out from an etic or external perspective, resulting in a static and balanced model of meaning in its idealized form, while, actually, all these three dimensions overlap in a communicative act. The speaker initiates a communicative activity, being aware of a communicative value and the relations between learning units in a given language and finally, this activity assumes a concrete, physical form of discourse. Needless to say, for an L1 speaker, the processes of meaning interpretation, that is of connecting forms and their semantic or pragmatic meaning, run faster and more efficiently than in the case of L2 speakers (depending on their competence in L2). This fluency further develops on the basis of diversified and more intensive communicative experience in learning an L2. The impact of this interactional practice results in a learner combining three kinds of memory, that is motor, verbal and sociointeractional memory, the latter of which is considered here to be the most significant locus of fostering one's communicative competence.

Individual variability and conventions

For every individual who is competent in his or her native tongue, this threefold 'unit of meaning' is either strongly cohesive (internally integrated) and constitutes a continuum in the case of highly conventionalized sociocultural types of discourse or it can manifest relative openness, that is, some independence of these three dimensions. This openness, in turn, allows creativity of personal utterances in comparison to those more conventionalized or typical kinds. Consequently, the variability of utterances ranges from their relative typicality to creativeness. Contextualized observation of learning units as unified meaning entities makes it possible for the learner to develop an awareness concerning the degree of possible conventionality and openness to individualized realizations of those learning units.

A vitally important feature of mature communicative competence is an individual's sensitivity and awareness as to what extent a given format can be treated as a strongly conventionalized discourse type and to what degree it permits individual variation or a more creative interplay with conventions, that is, if it allows a less conventionalized interpretation and realization of norms. The choices that an individual tends to make in those respects reflect his or her cognitive and communicative style. An individual communicative style does not manifest itself only through lexical or grammatical choices that constitute only one of its aspects. It may also be seen in pragmalinguistic choices concerning, for example, the directness of expression visible in the usage of hedges or discourse markers or even on the level of preferred genres. There are speakers who tend to prefer less typical realizations even in highly conventionalized discourses; however, risking a misunderstanding or a communication breakdown, they cannot allow themselves for completely arbitrary performance. Thus, in this sense, the norm always remains a communicative reference point, a determinant of shared communicative competence, that is an open-ended, situated in practice and individually interpretable but nevertheless obliging communicative traffic sign, to use Goffman's analogy (cf. Goffman et al., 1997).

Developing L2 speaking skills in an institutional environment

For the most part, L2 learners study a foreign language in an institutional context, which, although variable depending on the specific aims of a given institution, and in consequence also on the teaching approach adopted, is characterized by relatively stable limitations. As far as the development of speaking skills is concerned, the source of those limitations resides, on the one hand, in learners' and instructors' attitudes concerning the development of speaking skills and, on the other, in the process of L2 speech learning and at the same time in interactional institutional practices. As far as the former are concerned, probably because of the relative impalpability of speech and the complexity of communication processes and, ironically, because of the assumption of the Communication Approach that the acquisition of both the L1 and L2 can take place subconsciously, there is a widespread belief visible in teaching and learning practices about the incidental nature of speech learning. According to this belief, L2 speaking skills can only be acquired in the same way as in the mother tongue, which ignores the fact that the learner is not provided with ample exposure to concrete speech learning units in the way allowing for their systematic observation, practice and also for their evaluation as a measurable aspect of his or her expertise in L2.

Those interactional limitations concern both students' opportunities for getting engaged in authentic L2 communication and learning various L2 discourses. One of the features of the L2 classroom discourse that distinguishes it from other school subjects is the foreign language being both a vehicle and a subject of instruction and communication (Seed-house, 2005). This, in turn, implies the existence of different types of interactions creating various types of contexts for learning a foreign language in training institutions. The well-known IRE (Initiation – Response – Evaluation) sequence characterizing teacher–student talk prevails in L2 discourse in many instructional settings (cf. Mehan, 1998). Even though it has justifiable instructional purposes, it has already justly earned an infamous reputation for itself as limiting students' possibilities of learning and practicing L2 communication, since the first initiating and the third evaluating turns in the sequence always belong to an instructor, thereby leaving the learner in a passive and reactive role. If teachers were to focus mainly on this form of interaction, it would undoubtedly result in serious constraints for learners when it comes to construing meaningful and intentional communication, thus further exacerbating the already existing rift between the forms and their meaning in the comprehension and production of L2 discourse. Taking into account the existence of a very limited context for authentic L2 practice in institutional conditions, the need to depart from the domina-tion of asymmetrical interactions and to train students in diversified types of discourses becomes an even more apparent necessity.

It would be highly unrealistic to expect a complete recreation in the classroom of natural conditions in which an individual would develop his or her personal communicative competence by acquiring discourse norms in the process of socialization/enculturation and at the same time shaping language and discourse identity, because of students' age and, in most cases, because of the discussed limitations of institutional learning. When learning an L2 or L3, the learner has already developed some discourse competence and identity in the L1 and mostly learns the language in institutional settings. While it is true that some types of discourse community of L2 language learners/speakers, sharing some forms of lingua franca discourse, can be observed to come into being, especially in foreign languages departments, when compared with natural acquisition, this context seems to lack both the intensity of submersion and the diversity of discourse types available to learners.

In order to remedy the deficiencies of an instructional setting, L2 instruction should focus on such tasks as project work and other semi-creative task types, opening up space for more personalized self-expression, such as, for example, discussions and mini-presentations that, even in institutional conditions, require a substantial degree of communicative authenticity. This includes as well the pragmatic authenticity of the lexis and grammatical forms used, whose control in communication, as Niżegorodcew observes (2007: 148–168), has been systematically disregarded in some classroom applications of the communicative approach. Hence, another major challenge for the teaching of L2 speaking is the problem formulated by some researchers as the inclusion of *focus on form* in communication (Pawlak, 2009). Authors working within the framework of conversation analysis (see e.g. Markee, 2000; Seedhouse, 2005) use the conversation analytic, constructivist, dynamic framework to explore the interactional conditions of usage and control of forms in interactional contexts, as they get construed, oriented to or interpreted by interaction participants themselves.

The contextual communicative scarcity of L2 institutional settings needs to be dealt with by exploring multiple and diversified L2 discourses and genres in institutional learning. Such exploration should aim at developing a learner's *awareness* of communication processes in the L2 in tasks focusing on communication or language in action, which in institutional conditions can be implemented by guided observation of audio and video recordings of media texts or everyday conversations. These tasks, however, require defining new objectives of learning, distinguished by the degree of generality in reference to the process of communication. For example, CA-based objectives of learning (Brouwer & Wagner, 2004: 30, 40; Kasper, 2006: 83–99) include such universal but culturally variable interactional actions as turn-taking, repair strategies, turn shapes and discourse-specific actions. In the L2 context, they become targets of learning or more complex skills that only partially and only sometimes can be transferred from native discourse and because of context scarcity in the L2 language, for the most part, they need to be observed and used consciously to be learned (Kasper & Rose, 2003: 260–261).

On the psycholinguistic level of speech production, the conscious nature of skill development in an L2 correlates with an L2 speaker's difficulty with sign processing. This concerns both the phonetic and the lexico-grammatical encoding. In addition, the encoding difficulty concerns not only the lexis and structures but also interactional learning targets such as discourse strategies. One can presume that meaning creation consisting in connecting the signifier and the signified, the form and its content in context, also in the case of discourse strategies takes more time and is a more conscious process in the L2 than in the L1, both in discourse comprehension and production. In addition, in the case of learners opting for mental translation from the L1, the process is accompanied by an intensified processing especially on the level of lexis and structures. If the L2 differs from learners' native language in the speech rate, it further impedes comprehension and speech production in the L2, as the learner has difficulty with auditory-articulatory adaptation to the L2. Hence, the importance of intensive listening as well as repetitions and extended memorization practice aimed at developing the basis for articulation, which consequently results in accelerating the conceptualization processes in the L2 and enhances the fluency in the use of target language forms. Furthermore, the targeted structures need to be simultaneously adapted by the learner to create his or her individual communicative style, which translates into communicative competence.

The relationship between spoken and written discourse

Genuine oral discourse should be seen as distinct from what is labeled as the 'spoken language.' Spoken language does not always equal actual physical speech production, as can be observed in written and stylized renditions of oral discourses frequently encountered in the literature. They aim more at highlighting certain personality and community traits of a represented character, rather than retaining the exact transcript of speech. Besides that, thanks to such stylized and *written* form, utterances become more comprehensible for readers than actual accurate transcripts. This peculiar paradox points to essential features of communication, since authorial translation interprets for the reader the possible interpretation of the listener, as he or she would comprehend the speech of a given character in actual social interaction. On the other hand, oralization or expressing the written text (i.e. reading it or reciting from memory) differs significantly from casual talk, both in terms of structure and the mode of creating it (e.g. a TV presenter in fact reading out a text visible to him or her on the screen would be commonly perceived as just talking). This does not mean that speaking manifests itself in the most complete manner or solely in the so-called free oral expression, but full spontaneity remains its key attribute.

In fact, the difference between speech and writing does not concern the form of expression alone, as is often emphasized in comparisons between written and spoken texts (the latter in the form of transcripts).

This indeed striking distinctness actually reflects the mode of construing and processing or comprehending verbal utterances in communicative interactions. Both of these aspects show their own specificity in the L2, which becomes evident in higher redundancy in production and in the so-called verbocentrism (with the lesser share of guessing in reception). Incidentally, the same features can be observed in communicative actions in L1. However, the most important factor is efficiency, as the procedural schemata cannot be formed if an utterance is not anchored in comprehensive action schemata.

Taking into consideration the above observations, the so-called spoken language as it appears, for example, in literary works frequently differs from instances of genuine oral discourse, which in literature are processed and stylized. Our beliefs about the spoken language and the teaching of speech remain under the influence of the teaching of writing. It exposes certain patterns but also the processes of their formation and understanding in reading. The analysis of utterance, such as those in video recordings, in the native language on the basis of appropriately detailed transcripts can help one realize these differences.

Speech Structures and the Teaching of Speaking

Recent research on speaking clearly shows an evolution of our beliefs as to the spontaneous nature of everyday interaction. Once research focused mainly on the written discourse, as it was driven by a pervasive conviction that, in contrast to writing, speaking is too spontaneous and disorganized to be observed systematically. Currently, empirical studies focus on the structures of speech, exploring their most ritualized and stabilized aspects manifest especially in genres. Consequently, L2 speaking instruction refers to them and to other speaking practices, at the same time observing how our individual utterances inscribe into them and possibly modify those patterns.

Observing and practicing oral utterances as threefold meaning units in their diverse forms appears to be an important preliminary condition of effective teaching of speaking. Frequently, classroom practice revolves around the so-called 'talking exercise,' which, in fact, proves to be a nonspecific school type of talk, unconnected to any type of discourse community practice other than the school one, and devoid of any communicative relevance other than a vaguely instructional one. This kind of exercise represents too broad a category to be useful for a learner who is often unaware of the diversity of interaction types. Hence, it would be useful to refer to some typology of talk such as, for instance, the one proposed in the theories of genres and text types. However, the development of communicative competence requires some degree of metalingual and metacommunicative awareness.

Unfortunately, in Polish education, especially at advanced levels of learning, these bases of communicative competence development are either insufficiently allowed for or even omitted. Anyway, from the perspective of the current discussion, it would be extremely valuable to integrate into L2 teaching the practice of at least general reflection concerning the conditions of communicative actions and their specificity.

Genres

Geneva center researchers (Bronckart & Plazaola Giger, 1998; Schneuwly, 1995) define genre as an autonomous entity integrating (a) certain content, (b) characteristic communicative and semiotic structures and (c) a specific arrangement of textual-discursive elements that exert a certain influence on the speaker. Genres are treated as a characteristic bridge between social communicative practices and a speaker's speech activities and imply a type of realization, its assessment and relevant expectations. This stability of the genre is a fundamental tool in the creation of coherent speech behavior and its interpretation. Mastering a genre by an individual can constitute an important element of his or her communicative competence; it also determines the effectiveness of communicative competence with respect to operative action schemata (situation/communicative value/utterance). The existence of genre patterns is also motivated by the existence of more or less deliberate deviations from the norm, ranging from casual via semiformal to formal styles.

So far the best explored and thus most clearly defined oral genres are *formal ones* such as speeches, oral presentations (fr. *exposé*), debate, discussion and a semi-formal interview. As was already mentioned, everyday conversation passes as the most casual type that can be treated as a general genre with certain subtypes (e.g. a neighborly or a party chat). In the conversation analysis framework, *face-to-face conversation* is considered to be a primary and basic form of social interaction. All other genres, especially institutional interactions, are treated as its transformation created by discourse communities for specific social aims; thus, genre-specific features are often analyzed against the background of conversations (Drew & Heritage, 1992; Schegloff, 1992). This typology comes in handy when analyzing actual discourses; however, the so-called pure genres are rarely encountered beyond formalized communicative situations. Representations concerning pertinent models determine not only concrete realizations but also our expectations and evaluations.

Text types

Text types fulfill certain discourse functions: one speaks in order to *describe, tell, compare, explain* and *justify something*. As opposed to genres, text types rarely exist separately in a pure form but they tend to intermingle in larger texts, as is the case, for instance, in discussions where descriptions interchange and fuse somehow with narrative and argumentative passages.

Routine interactional sequences

Routine interactional sequences are typical comments or reactions in common, everyday situations. They tend to be highly predictable with a rather limited range of possible modifications. Within the framework developed here, metalinguistic and metacommunicative awareness should be anchored in the learner's L2 identity, which finds its expression in his or her communicative style. As has already been pointed out, an individual should be allowed certain autonomy in adjusting himself or herself to 'norms.' This adaptation to norms in some less formalized genres can even become desirable though never completely arbitrary.

Speech structures–based didactics of speaking

According to Geneva researchers, genres epitomize a relatively stable form and a way of functioning; that is why, they may prove useful in the process of L2 speaking instruction. Their application can be observed in L2 teaching in the Canadian province of Québec; however, the genres taught there represent public rather than private communication types, so being relatively rare, they will not be all necessarily useful for learners. If one were to limit instruction to such patterns alone, this could, in fact, result in the distortion of the image of speech genres as always being subject to such highly formalized patterns whereas equally important is also developing lower-level scale skills, used in different genres and situations (e.g. finding out information in interviews, formulating questions in debates and conversations).

Another important aspect of genre-based teaching is allowing students to develop speaking skills in task situations constructed on the level of complexity adjusted to students' abilities (within Vygotsky's zone of proximal development) (Vygotsky, 1978). Tasks should open up the possibilities of developing such discourse features as dynamics, interactivity, totality, spontaneity and negotiability. One should not forget as well that the task should be perceived as a dynamic co-construction of participants rather than a determinant of what is happening in task interactions; in other words, the task features are, in fact, determined by interaction (task) participants as relevant in varying degrees in different interactional moments or tasks phases. While authentic school genres such as already-mentioned *casual school talk, lecture* and *presentation* are rehearsed somehow 'naturally' in institutional settings, training in communication genres, normally practiced in contexts other than L2 classroom, still seems to be a challenge. On the whole, there appears to exist a discrepancy between discourse genres as subjects taught in the instructional setting and their social functioning as communication tools, hence, a certain social fictitiousness of discourses practiced in the institutional context.

A tool that can prove very useful in making learners aware of differences between written and spoken genres is a guided observation of both audio–video recordings and their transcripts. They can be contrasted with written discourses or written stylizations of spoken utterances, such as, for example, literary ones. An important constraint is that these texts should not be the only tool of teaching but should rather serve the purpose of sensitizing students to essential elements of speech, such as concrete communicative actions observed and practiced by students in model genre contexts in different stylistic configurations. The tasks can focus, for instance, on such interactional objects as turn-taking and turn-holding in talk, culture-dependent repair strategies, turn shapes and sequences such as pre-/closure and opening formulas, audience-oriented strategies in presentations, interview information seeking turns, intercultural differences in argumentative turn shapes and specific speech acts such as apologies and requests, meta-textual signals and structures used to control the course of talk, indirectness and politeness formulas, hedges and discourse markers. Discourse observation practice appears to be more effective when accompanied by corresponding production tasks such as conversations, discussions and game-oriented role plays in L2. In addition, practicing shorter sequences or text types aimed at the controlled use of chosen interactional objects can prove to be an important phase in building students' fluency in chosen forms before letting them practice more complex genres. It needs to be emphasized that this latter apparently uncomplicated task also rests on identity construction in L2.

If one is to create genre-specific communicative actions in the L2, one needs to be aware of roles or social categories. More specifically, they are supposed to understand how members of a given speech community use a genre as a tool to realize its specific communicative and professional aims. This all translates into the awareness of communicative actions considered to be socioculturally normative for given person categories. Since, as was discussed above (see 'Introduction' section), these categories somehow comprise an individual's social identity and are culturally bound, the learner is faced with the challenge of negotiating, selecting and construing one's social identity in L2 also in this dimension, when the simple transposition of categories from L1 or a complete emulation of L2 roles is possible only in very rare cases. Thus, some learners' problems in producing genre- or even conversation-related actions, as well as developing a good, native-like pronunciation in L2, may have their roots in the sense of 'sociocategorical' estrangement or a strong identification with L1 categories.

A separate issue is the *evaluation* of students' competence in terms of oral discourse. Such assessment frequently concerns only the contents and linguistic accuracy of discourse without a special focus on discourse or genre forms. Clear criteria of evaluating oral discourse and communicative competence still remain to be developed, while research, mainly concentrating on examination assessment, has only recently begun to explore possible interactional and discourse criteria and in such situations (see Egbert & Seedhouse, 2006; Lazaraton, 2002). All in all, what remains open is the issue of learning progress, that is how L2 learning translates into a learner's out-of-classroom discourse and how such communication can be actually observed and evaluated.

Conclusion

The perspective of ICC discussed in this chapter proposes to evaluate the authenticity of learner's activity in the framework of integrated individual and sociocultural determinants of communicative actions. The major challenge of the L2 speaking instruction on all levels of learner's proficiency still appears to be its decontextualization, which in the long run negatively influences communicative authenticity and hinders the development of socially contextualized speech behaviors. Fostering communicative competence requires a pragmatic context for the learner to perceive the learning target as an integrated entity emerging in the connection between forms and their semantic and pragmatic meaning. Equally necessary appears to be anchoring of the teaching of speaking in social-functional models such as genres. Therefore, what emerges is the need to discuss the problems of approach to defining possible learning objectives in developing L2 speaking skills and determining their progression, that is the optimal sequence of learning. The learning units should be selected and prepared for use in the classroom to support their effective memorization and usage. Further studies of these units would benefit from a focus on individual perception of not solely semantic, pragmatic or phonetic meanings but on their combination in a meaningful unity as well.

References

Bronckart, J.P. and Plazaola Giger, I. (1998) La transposition didactique. Histoire et perspectives d'une problématique fondatrice. *Pratiques* 97–98, 35–58.

Brouwer, C.E. and Wagner, I. (2004) Developmental issues in second language conversation. *JAL* 1/2004, 29–47.

Coulter, J. (2001) Logic: Ethnomethodology and the logic of language. In G. Button (ed.) *Ethnomethodology and the Human Sciences* (pp. 20–50). Cambridge: Cambridge University Press.

Drew, P. and Heritage, J. (1992) Analyzing talk at work: An introduction. In P. Drew and J. Heritage (eds) *Talk at Work* (pp. 3–65). Cambridge: Cambridge University Press.

Egbert, M. and Seedhouse, P. (2006) The interactional organization of the IELTS speaking test. *IELTS Research Reports* 6, 161–206.

Goffman, E., Lemert, Ch.C. and Branaman, A. (1997) *The Goffman Reader*. United Kingdom: Blackwell.

Jayyusi, L. (1984) *Categorization and Moral Order*. Boston: Routledge & Kegan Paul.

Kasper, G. (2006) Conversation analysis as an approach to SLA. *AILA Review* 19, 83–99.

Kasper, G. and Rose, K. (2003) *Pragmatic Development in a Second Language*. London: Wiley-Blackwell.

Lazaraton, A. (2002) *A Qualitative Approach to the Validation of Oral Language Tests*. Cambridge: Cambridge University Press.

Markee, N. (2000) *Conversation Analysis*. Mahwah, NJ: Erlbaum.

Mehan H. (1998) The study of social interaction in educational settings: Accomplishments and unresolved issues. *Human Developments* 41, 245–269.

Niżegorodcew, A. (2007) *Input for Instructed L2 Learners. The Relevance of Relevance*. Clevedon: Multilingual Matters.

Pawlak, M. (2009) Nauczanie gramatyki języka obcego – kierunki i metody badań. *Neofilolog* 32, 33–48.

Sacks, H. (1992) Lecture 6. The MIR membership categorization device. In H. Sacks (ed.) *Lectures on Conversation* (Vol. 1, pp. 40–48). Oxford: Blackwell.

Schegloff, E.A. (1992) On talk and its institutional occasions. In P. Drew and J. Heritage (eds) *Talk at Work* (pp. 101–134). Cambridge: Cambridge University Press.

Schneuwly, B. (1995) De l'utilité de la transposition didactique. In J-L. Chiss, J. David and Y. Reuter (eds) *Didactique du français* (pp. 47–62). Paris: Nathan.

Seedhouse P. (2005) *The Interactional Architecture of the Language Classroom: A Conversation Analysis Perspective*. London: Blackwell.

Vygotsky L.S. (1978) *Mind in Society. The Development of Higher Psychological Processes*. Cambridge: Harvard University Press.

Wilczyńska W. (2002) Podmiotowość i autonomia jako wyznaczniki osobistej kompetencji komunikacyjnej. In W. Wilczyńska (ed.) *Autonomizacja w dydaktyce języków obcych. Doskonalenie się w komunikacji ustnej* (pp. 51–67). Poznań: Wydawnictwo Naukowe UAM.

Wilczyńska W. (1999) *Uczyć się, czy być nauczanym*. Warszawa: Państwowe Wydawnictwo Naukowe.

Chapter 3
Formulaic Sequences in the Output of Instructed L2 Learners

PIOTR BIAŁAS

Formulaicity Reconsidered

The range of the phenomenon of formulaicity is subject to abundant studies and lengthy discussions which lead to numerous contradictory conclusions. On the one hand, it is estimated that up to 80% of the words (at least in the *London-Lund Corpus of Spoken English*, in this instance) form part of prefabricated patterns (Altenberg, 1998). On the other, there are voices sustaining that these lexical bundles are a marginal phenomenon (Pinker, 1994). There also exist various labels in the literature to be attached to the phenomenon itself. The most influential and the most extensive discussions, at the same time, are proposed by the English literature. One of the contemporary, most recognizable researchers in the area of formulaicity is Alison Wray. Her research findings constitute an excellent overview of the present-day knowledge of the subject. She introduces into the literature the term *formulaic sequence*, adopted in this discussion, which is 'a sequence, continuous or discontinuous, of words or other meaning elements, which is, or appears to be, prefabricated: that is, stored and retrieved whole from memory at the time of use, rather than being subject to generation or analysis by the language grammar' (Wray, 2000: 465), which largely paraphrases Ellis (1996) claiming that the words within the sequence are 'glued together' and stored in memory as a 'big word', although the construction has the potential to be analysed into smaller segments.

In one of the first publications on formulaicity, Andrew Pawley and Frances Hodgetts Syder (1983) address this problem directly. In their discussion, the authors explicitly bring to light the problem of why the learner's production will sound non-native, no matter how highly developed his grammatical competence is. As noted by Pawley and Syder (1983: 195–196), a sentence such as *Your coming has brought me real gladness* illustrates a grammatically perfect sentence. A learner who would be able to produce such a sentence proves a number of skills that he has mastered. Firstly, he seems to know the rules concerning the use of the present perfect tense, is able to form the gerund, knows what the object pronouns are and how to use them in a sentence. Moreover, such a learner can construct a double-object sentence and knows the word *gladness,* which for most average learners seems to be beyond their reach. In a similar fashion, we can make the following sentences: *That you could come makes me so glad* or *That you could come gladdens me so* or even *Your having been able to come gladdens me so.* They are all grammatically perfect sentences; nonetheless, how can these sentences be compared with *I'm glad that you could come*? Although a much less elaborated one than the preceding examples, Pawley and Syder (1983) maintain that this last utterance, that is *I'm glad that you could come,* not the more complex ones, is much more likely to appear in the native speaker's production. Consequently, if it is more likely to appear in the native speaker's output, it means that this particular sequence ought to be employed in a given sociolinguistic context for the interaction to proceed smoothly and naturally. Clearly, the preceding paraphrases cannot be rejected as utterly wrong, but this kind of nativelike selection is one of the puzzles for linguistic theories and it is this puzzle that has been recently influencing a great deal of research work on a new approach to foreign language learning where lexis and grammar are not separate types of knowledge any longer.

The Functions of Formulaic Sequences

In the literature there exist two sound reasons which explain the sense of the phenomenon of formulaicity in language. Wray (2000, 2002, 2008) sustains that formulaic sequences perform several, neither reciprocally exclusive nor necessarily supplemental, functions. They depend to a large extent on 'the motivation *behind* the desire to speak fluently, express identity, organize text and help the hearer to understand what you say' (Wray, 2002: 93). She goes on to say that, consequently, formulaic sequences do not function as a solution to purely linguistic problems but they aid the speaker in meeting his or her extralinguistic needs. To extract a common core of a long list of the possible functions of formulaic sequences, Wray (2002: 95–96) claims that they all serve a single purpose: the promotion of the speaker's interests, which include the following:

- having easy access to information (via mnemonics, etc.);
- expressing information fluently;
- being listened to and taken seriously;
- having physical and emotional needs satisfactorily and promptly met;
- being provided with information when required;
- being perceived as important as an individual;
- being perceived as a full member of whichever groups are deemed desirable.

Saving effort in processing

Despite the variety of functions, according to Wray (2000, 2002), it is possible to subsume them into two primary aims that underlie motivations for the speaker's output. The *saving effort in processing function* is the first one. Becker (1975: 17) describes this function of formulaic sequences by saying that they '[...] give us ready-made frameworks on which to hang the expression of our ideas, so that we do not have to go through the labour of generating an utterance'. As pointed out by Wray (2000), this sort of savings in processing is undoubtedly beneficial when performing complicated concurrent tasks in particular, such as oral interaction, which, if to be successfully rendered, is actually a compilation of different sorts of tasks that, to a large extent, reminds a problem-solving enterprise. Indisputably, time pressure has every potential to multiply the problems and to impinge on the interaction process.

Not only continuous but also discontinuous, lengthy lexicalized stems can provide a structural skeleton on which to rely when constructing an utterance. Pawley and Syder (1983: 210) refer to the following pattern *NP be-TENSE sorry to keep-TENSE you waiting* as potentially generating a sentence such as *Mr Smith will be sorry to have kept you waiting*. In this single sentence stem, there are gaps, open to any semantically acceptable member of the required word class, which, when being filled in correctly, can generate a possibly infinite number of sentences. In a similar vein, Wray (2000: 474) argues that most of the sequences with no gaps for 'open class' items allow for a considerable amount of morphological variation, fitting tense, voice, person and number depending on a given context, for example *I've done really well* can be easily transformed into *You'll do really well* or *They did really well* not depriving it of its formulaicity at the same time. These adjustments, that is filling in open class slots or fitting morphological forms into a seemingly fossilized sequence, however, involve a degree of analytical processing on the part of the speaker. Still, according to Wray (2000: 474) 'there is [...] less effort involved in this than in creating the whole construction from scratch'.

In describing the saving effort in processing function, Wray and Perkins (2000) suggest further subcategorizing the processing functions of formulaic sequences into three subfunctions, that is (a) processing short cuts, (b) time buyers and (c) phrases to manipulate information. The first subcategory of formulaic sequences is illustrated by standard phrases with or without gaps, such as *Best foot forward* or *I have known __ for __ years in my capacity as __* or by standard referential labels being attached to certain sociological or economic phenomena, such as *personal computer* or *the current economic climate*. If stored in the mental lexicon, they are retrieved whole from memory and they increase production speed and fluency (Wray & Perkins, 2000). The second subcategory, time buyers, refers to those sequences which aid the speaker in the construction of discourse. By inserting time buyers, effortless and low time-consuming elements, into the novel material, the speaker provides for himself or herself a temporal space to better organize the output of analytical processing. Consequently, he or she is able to plan time without losing the turn and to maintain a smooth rhythm of the communication process. There are a number of types (Wray & Perkins, 2000) that fall into this subcategory, for example fillers such as *if you want my opinion* ..., turn-holders like *and let me just say* ..., discourse shape markers, for example *There are three points I want to make. Firstly,* ... *Secondly,* .... *Thirdly/ Lastly,* ..., or repetitions of preceding input, for instance (*A: What's the capital of Peru?*) *B: What's the capital of Peru?* ... (*Lima, isn't it?*). The last subcategory, namely manipulation of information, is built of mnemonics, lengthy texts required to learn and rehearse. This particular group is exemplified by sequences such as *Thirty days hath September* ..., *Shall I compare thee to a summer's day?* or the action of rehearsing a telephone number while looking for a pen. By storing this sort of information in the form of a formulaic sequence, one is able to gain and retain access to information which would be otherwise forgotten.

The socio-interactional function

Although the saving effort in the processing function of formulaic sequences must be accounted for when discussing the obstacles that the learner needs to overcome when engaging in an act of communication, what is of equal importance in the context of developing speaking skills is the second function proposed by Wray (2000), namely *the socio-interactional function* that most of the sequences illustrate. This category is frequently associated with lexical frames used in greeting, thanking, apologizing, inviting, instructing and so on. According to Wray and Perkins again (2000), there can be three primary socio-interactional functions of formulaic sequences. The first one, that is manipulation of others, is about satisfying our physical, emotional and cognitive needs to transform our surroundings by instructing others to do so. To fulfil this function, there is an extensive set of formulas to pick from. These are commands, for example *Keep off the grass,* requests, such as *Could you repeat that please?,* politeness markers, such as *I wonder if you'd mind* ... or bargains, such as *I'll give you __ for it,* etc. The other two functions relate to the way the speaker can demonstrate his or her individual or group identity in his or her environment to be taken seriously and how he or she can manipulate others to be perceived in a particular way. At his or her disposal the speaker has an apparently endless list of formulas that form different types of expressions, for example personal turns of phrase, such as *You know what I mean Harry* (Frank Bruno); 'in' phrases, such as *Praise the Lord!...*; group chants, for instance *We are the champions!*; institutionalized forms of words, rituals, proverbs, threats, quotations and so on, such as *Happy birthday* or *A stitch in time*, and *I wouldn't do that if I were you*, and so on.

Wray and Perkins (2000) propose to accommodate the two functions, that is the processing advantages and the socio-interactional benefits, within one model. The inseparability of the two functions seems to be self-evident, since 'the speaker selects a formulaic sequence in the interests of efficient production' (Wray, 2000: 477). Nonetheless, what is meant by 'efficient production' is not at all obvious. On the one hand, a given stretch can be chosen to reduce the strains of information processing to give the interaction a sense of fluency and smoothness. On the other, the speaker may pick a particular formulaic frame for a purely interactional goal just to evoke a verbal effect on the hearer. In this instance, the success of this exchange is not measured in terms of fluency and easiness but rather by whether the hearer reacted in the expected way. To put it differently, the function of a formulaic stretch in the socio-interactional setting is to bring about the maximally efficient comprehension. The model proposed by Wray and Perkins (2000) indicates that while the effort saving in processing function of formulaicity aids the speaker's production, the profits of formulaic stretches in the socio-interactional context aid the hearer's comprehension. According to Wray (2000), it is possible to represent the two functions in the same strategy since they seem to intersect and to form a common set of sequences which aid both the speaker's production and the hearer's comprehension. Wray believes that this common set is made up of discourse markers, such as *There are three points I want to make. Firstly, … . Secondly, … . Thirdly/Finally …* (Wray, 2000: 475). The centrality of this type of markers lies in the fact that 'they both anchor the structure of the speaker's output, so it is easier to sequence the ideas fluently, and, simultaneously, signal to the hearer where it will be most appropriate, and inappropriate, to begin a turn and what the overall character of the speaker's message is' (Wray, 2000: 478). Nonetheless, as admitted by Wray herself, this model does not account for the fact that the hearer has his or her own processing agenda and that the speaker is somehow forced to anticipate the condition of the hearer's mental lexicon and his or her knowledge of formulaic stretches. Therefore, she predicts that 'the most efficient and successful communication will occur where the speaker and hearer are very familiar with each other's speech patterns, or indeed share the same microvariety' (Wray, 2000: 479).

Formulaic Sequences and Classroom Interaction – Pedagogical Implications

Ellis (1994: 85) claims that in the early years of language acquisition 'formulaic language' appears in every learner's output, regardless of his or her age. Much research, however, shows that there are huge differences as to the extent learners use formulaic sequences. In Hanania and Gradman's (1977, quoted in Wray, 2002: 173) study, much cited in the literature as it is claimed that the naturalist adult learner operates at a high level of formulaicity, but on closer consideration, they seem to provide counter-evidence to this opinion, indicating that the role of formulas is facilitatory at most (for more detail, see Wray, 2002). Similarly, in Bohn's opinion (1986, quoted in Wode, 1981), on the basis of the Kiel Project data from four German children's naturalistic acquisition of English, formulaic language plays only a secondary role in L2 acquisition. He sustains that the chunks appearing in the learner's output are first selected and then built-in according to the economy-based strategies employed for effective production to serve an instant communicative purpose and that they do not interact with syntactic development.

Nonetheless, there is some evidence that resorting to formulaic sequences greatly maximizes the chances of achieving a communicative success because formulas allow L2 learners to engage in minimal communication effortlessly and, in some way, compensate for the lack of competence in terms of target language rules (Krashen & Scarcella, 1978). Similarly, Yorio (1989, quoted in Wray, 2002: 174) sustains that his subject, an 18-year-old Korean, was able to achieve a high level of formulaic accuracy in his L2 English written output since he skilfully used formulaic stretches in his production. However, their instant efficiency ensures the learner that he truly improves his L2 competence, causing the learner to stay at the 'intermediate plateau' (Lewis, 2000), which is exemplified by Schmidt's subject Wes who mastered a large number of formulas used with a great communicative success, while at the same time showing a fossilized grammatical system (Schmidt, 1983).

Wray (2002) admits that there are individual differences in the extent of using formulaic sequences which should be associated with the pressures, either processing or interactional or most probably both, experienced by the learner. The factors that should be considered in discussing this pressure, according to Wray (2002), are the pressure exerted on the learner to achieve particular goals and the level of the learner's need to interact with the L2 native speaker, that is 'there seems to be a link between the use of formulaic sequences and a need and a desire to interact, these two together contributing to the overall achievement of communicative competence' (Wray, 2002: 175). There are other studies which show that those learners who attained a much lower level of the overall language competence kept a socio-psychological distance from the L2 native speakers at the same time. Rehbein (1987) discovered that his subject Gastarbeiter applied a communication strategy consisting in avoiding situations in which he would have to use structures that he had not mastered yet. This strategy badly reduced the chances of meeting his actual communicative needs and thus the subject was depriving himself of the opportunity to raise the level of his L2 competence.

Formulas for pedagogic purposes

From a pedagogical perspective, a serious problem arises which formulaic sequences are the most optimal to be adopted into teaching materials to pursue the speaker's and the hearer's interests. An interesting account of how to approach formulaicity in the context of foreign language learning is proposed by Gozdawa-Gołębiowski (2008: 84) who presents the following categorization of the very term *formula*: (a) formulas as bundles of opaque features, (b) formulas as recurrent units, (c) formulas as social tokens and (d) formulas as morphosyntactic exemplars.

To bring the proposed categorization closer, Gozdawa-Gołębiowski (2008: 82) gives the following German sentence, highlighting the verb *abheben*: *Ich muss noch schnell zum Bankautomaten, um Geld abzuheben* (I must still quickly to-the cashpoint (for) money to-withdraw). As claimed by Gozdawa-Gołębiowski, this sentence may be (therefore, should be) approached as an example of a formulaic sequence. Although the most distinguishing feature of a formula is that it is retrieved whole from memory, as a fossilized lexical bundle rather than generated from scratch by a statistically large group of native speakers, Gozdawa-Gołębiowski sustains that the way native speakers process a particular stretch of words is of no use for a foreign language learner. For pedagogical purposes, he proposes to give up the formulaic/non-formulaic continuum and to consider the distinction between what is idiosyncratic and what is rule-based instead. Eventually, he goes on to say that

> any material that has been automatized is recognised by the language faculty as formulaic. (...) A string of words should be treated as a formulaic sequence for classroom purposes if there is no accessible rule that can explain the specific co-occurrence pattern or if there is no L1 analogue to draw upon. (Gozdawa-Gołębiowski, 2008: 83)

To expand on his argumentation, Gozdawa-Gołębiowski puts forward a proposal that 'a strong formula is one where a false L1 analogy suggests itself' and resembles the *'take under consideration'* para-formula[1] that regularly appears in the learner's rendition of the *take into consideration* formula (Gozdawa-Gołębiowski, 2008: 83). Consequently, the debate over what is and what is not formulaic does not bear any significant pedagogical implications for the learner. What is central to the problem, according to Gozdawa-Gołębiowski (Gozdawa-Gołębiowski, 2008: 83), is the question of what is and what is not predictable, which is largely determined by L1 transfer and grammatical generalization.

Interestingly, 'committing non-formulaic sequences into memory and thus turning them into formulas serves a useful pedagogical purpose and will frequently be encouraged by the teacher' (Gozdawa-Gołębiowski, 2008: 83). Rule-based processing is a psychologically real phenomenon, particularly with adult learning where constructing utterances out of individual lexemes implies relying heavily on a set of available structural rules, largely predictable guidelines, as put by Gozdawa-Gołębiowski: 'the learner naturally strives to build his interlanguage on stable foundations' (2008: 80). Although the memorization process in foreign language teaching until recently has fallen out of favour, Ellis and Sinclair (1996: 246–247) maintain that it is a central process in successful learning and claim that 'much of language learning is the acquisition of memorized sequences of language [...] ... Short-term representation and rehearsal allows the eventual establishment of long-term sequence information for language'.

Overall, a strong implication pointed out by Gozdawa-Gołębiowski is that the formulaic/non-formulaic continuum is irrelevant for the learner and the development of his interlanguage. Consequently, vigorous debates that are frequently sparked off in the field of foreign language pedagogy over what is formulaic and what is not cannot bring any conclusive outcomes. One of the reasons is perhaps the multitude of criteria, often mutually exclusive ones, for spotting formulas in the native speaker's output. For the apparent lack of consensus in this respect, the idiosyncratic/rule-based continuum, suggested by Gozdawa-Gołębiowski, offers a pedagogically oriented indication that any material that has been proceduralized is categorized as formulaic by the language faculty. Consequently, even the already cited German sentence *Ich muss noch schnell zum Bankautomaten, um Geld abzuheben* (I must still quickly to-the cashpoint (for) money to-withdraw), although it stands a good chance of being generated from scratch, seems to be framed on the following lexicalized stem: *Ich muss ... (zu) ... um... zu...*, which can be further explored in teaching a multitude of functions and concepts, thus to develop the learner's communicative competence.

Strictly speaking, the approach proposed by Gozdawa-Gołębiowski (2008) assumes that both opaque and rule-driven sentences can be (therefore, should be) memorized in the learning process to acquire the status of a pedagogical formula which can work wonders for the learner; it helps the learner to satisfy immediate communicative purposes and has the potential to trigger the development of his interlanguage system.

Formulas in interaction

To create a meaningful communicative situation in the classroom, which is the most typical environment for foreign language learning, is a truly demanding task. Besides, in the era of the increased role of mass culture and unlimited possibilities of acquiring information, it is more and more difficult to define the factors that truly influence the level of a given L2 and, consequently, it is hard to separate the impact of formal instruction offered in the classroom from the 'outside' influence, that is television, press, the internet, contacts with foreign language speaking friends and so on. Nonetheless, it is frequently assumed (cf. Ellis, 1994) that the primary impact comes from the classroom where formal instruction is the dominant foreign language teaching strategy.

Wray (2002) claims that the measure of learning formulaic sequences successfully depends on many factors. Most important, it is determined by the amount of formulas adapted to the teaching materials that the learner is exposed to. Nonetheless, it must be highlighted that not all sequences, considered as formulaic, can aid the learner's motivation to make his or her L2 output similar to the native speaker's production. The learner, in addition, may not be able to recognize properly the extralinguistic contexts that a particular formula can fit, which is why he or she truly needs instruction on how to manage formulas that he or she encounters in the data that he or she is exposed to in order to improve his or her L2 performance.

It is not surprising that one of the first strategies used by the learner is repeating a whole sequence of lexical items as a single entry without any internal inspections into the structure. The efficiency of this process frequently lies behind the construction of a great deal of foreign language teaching materials, such as course books, particularly at lower levels, which introduce typical conversational routines and useful classroom language, for example *What's your name? Where do you live? What job do you do? Please, would you repeat that? I don't know; I don't understand* (Jaworski, 1990: 397–398).

This approach to teaching a foreign language and to developing speaking skills is often referred to in the literature as the *phrasebook approach*. If it is to be applied at the beginner level, this approach proposes already pre-constructed sequences to be memorized and retrieved whole, as autonomous stretches of lexicalized stems, from memory when required as formulaic sequences. Resorting to such prefabricated items allows the beginner to 'exceed' his current level of grammatical and lexical competence and successfully engage in an interactional event to eventually satisfy his communicative goals. A learner who successfully uses the phrase *Can I have a* ... may have no idea of the phenomenon of inversion or the intricacies of the modal verb *can*, not to mention the use of articles. This indicates that the construction of formulaic sequences remains beyond the actual state of the learner's knowledge of the L2 he or she is aiming at. Many researchers believe that this property is the most distinctive feature of formulas. Hakuta (1974) maintains that when learners are obliged to wait with a particular sequence to be used in interaction until the moment they are introduced to a given grammatical rule necessary to construct this particular formula on their own, it leads to severe motivational problems.

An interesting example where particular attention is paid to the ways formulas can be used in interaction is Gatbonton's teaching method (Gatbonton & Segalowitz, 2005). The method assumes that formulaic sequences can be taught in the classroom with great success provided that certain criteria are considered in designing teaching material to be used. The guidelines look as follows:

- the activity must remain truly communicative, that is the outcome of the information exchange must be genuinely important to the learner;
- there must be psychological authenticity, that is the activity must 'allow learners to experience some of the normal psychological pressures felt by people engaged in real communication' (Gatbonton & Segalowitz, 1988: 486);
- the task must oscillate around every-day activities that learners can be part of, for example giving directions, apologizing and negotiating;
- the sequence must be formulaic, that is, it appears with a statistically significant frequency in characteristic contexts with hardly any modification of its form;
- the task-design must allow the learner to repeat the introduced formulas many times over.

Thus, Gatbonton (Gatbonton & Segalowitz, 2005) stresses the need for what is called *creative automatization* within the communicative language teaching framework, postulating that repetition through meaningful communicative drills of valuable utterances, in a context that originally forces the learner to exhaust substantial attentional resources to achieve the goal, feeds eventually into their automatization. What I claim here is that these communicatively valuable utterances (following Gozdawa-Gołębiowski, 2008; Wray, 2008) can be of two origins. They can be either word strings that are formulaic for the native speaker or 'word strings that are rich in such potential [to generate new patterns from them], such as ordinary sentences of regular construction that the learner *makes* formulaic by virtue of memorization' (Wray, 2008: 228). I insist here that the latter type of 'formula' is perhaps an equally or even more pedagogically useful item. A simple example of a drilling activity with such items (Gatbonton & Segalowitz, 2005) is the *Family Tree Activity* where students drill the phrase *How are you related to ...?* by asking each other questions about their families. An interesting example of the application of Gatbonton's teaching strategy and eventually the learner's formula concept (Gozdawa-Gołębiowski, 2008; Wray, 2008) is the *EJ programme* (a programme to teach Japanese at elementary level). The subjects of the study (Taguchi & Iwasaki, 2008), which was designed to verify the efficiency of this strategy, were 22 students (10 males and 12 females; 9 native English speakers, 7 Chinese speakers and 6 Korean speakers), all, basically, with no previous contact with the Japanese language. The findings reveal that the memorization of dialogues with embedded patterns via meaningful communicative drills promotes the acquisition of the system and the development of language processing mechanisms, thus developing oral production skills in terms of accuracy, complexity and fluency (for more details of the study, see Taguchi & Iwasaki, 2008).

Others, such as Myles *et al.* (1998), advise caution when applying formulaic sequences on a wider scale in foreign language pedagogy. They associate the early use of formulas with satisfying communicative needs, but they note that the period of intensive application of formulas is relatively short since the complexity of the learners'communicative purposes quickly overwhelms the potential of formulas. Then, those early formulas lose their original function and start to feed into productive use, promoting the process of grammar acquisition. Assuming, however, that the ultimate goal of language learning is to master a foreign language system, the above claim, quite conversely, is a good enough reason to introduce formulas into teaching.

Concluding Remarks

In this chapter I have looked at the well-acknowledged functions of formulaic sequences, mainly from the perspective of saving effort in processing and the socio-interactional function that some of the sequences possess. In the context of foreign language learning and developing speaking skills in particular, having at one's disposal a set of easily accessible prefabricated chunks in an act which itself exposes the learner to a number of extralinguistic pressures seems to be a perfect 'linguistic solution[s] to a nonlinguistic problem' (Wray, 2002: 94). Although it is perhaps not possible to eliminate these strains, teachers can equip learners with a collection of safe means, labelled collectively formulaic sequences, which, if proceduralized, give the learner a feeling of higher safety in a linguistic exchange. I stressed the importance of the proceduralization process by means of memorization in handling formulaic frames. By briefly presenting Gozdawa-Gołębiowski's account which redefines the commonly agreed status and the functions of formulas, I have brought to light the fact that developing speaking skills can be enhanced by operating in the holistic mode but that it might be the more beneficial if it combines with the non-holistic one, that is the analytic and the contentive modes (for more details on the contentive mode, see Gozdawa-Gołębiowski, 2003), provided that the new status of formulas, namely the learner's formula, is applied in foreign language pedagogy.

Note
1. The phenomenon and the term 'para-formula' is itself widely discussed in Masiejczyk (unpublished PhD dissertation, University of Warsaw, 2008).

References

Altenberg, B. (1998) On the phraseology of spoken English: The evidence of recurrent Word-combinations. In A. Cowie (ed.) *Phraseology: Theory, Analysis and Applications* (pp. 145–160). Oxford: Oxford University Press.

Becker, J. (1975) The phrasal lexicon. Bolt Beranek & Newman Report no. 3081, AI Report no. 28. Reprinted in R. Shank and B.L. Nash-Webber (eds) *Theoretical Issues in Natural Language Processing* (pp. 60–63). Cambridge, MA: Bolt Beranek & Newman.

Bohn, O.S. (1986) Formulas, frame structures, and stereotypes in early syntactic development: Some new evidence from L2 acquisition. *Linguistics* 24, 185–202.

Ellis, N.C. (1996) Sequencing in SLA: Phonological memory, chunking, and points of order. *Studies in Second Language Acquisition* 18, 9–126.

Ellis, N.C. and Sinclair, S. (1996) Working memory in the acquisition of vocabulary and syntax. *Quarterly Journal of Experimental Psychology* 49, 234–250.

Ellis, R. (1994) *The Study of Second Language Acquisition*. Oxford: Oxford University Press.

Gatbonton, E. and Segalowitz, N. (1988) Creative automatization: Principles for promoting fluency within a communicative framework. *TESOL Quarterly* 22, 473–492.

Gatbonton, E. and Segalowitz, N. (2005). Rethinking communicative language teaching: A focus on access to fluency. *Canadian Modern Language Review* 61, 325–353.

Gozdawa-Gołębiowski, R. (2003) *Interlanguage Formation: A Study of the Triggering Mechanisms*. Warszawa: Instytut Anglistyki UW.

Gozdawa-Gołębiowski, R. (2008) Grammar and formulaicity in foreign language teaching. *Glottodidactica* 34, 75–86.

Hakuta, K. (1974) Prefabricated patterns and the emergence of structure in second language acquisition. *Language Learning* 24, 287–297.

Hanania, E. and Grandman, H. (1977) Acquisition of English structures: A case study of an adult native speaker of Arabic in an English-speaking environment. *Language Learning* 27, 75–91.

Jaworski, A. (1990) The acquisition and perception of formulaic language and foreign language teaching. *Multilingua* 9, 397–411.

Krashen, S. and Scarcella, R. (1978) On routines and patterns in language acquisition and performance. *Language Learning* 28, 283–300.

Lewis, M. (ed.) (2000) *Teaching Collocation. Further Developments in the Lexical Approach.* Hove: LTP.

Myles, F., Hooper J. and Mitchell R. (1998) Rote or rule? Exploring the role of formulaic language in classroom foreign language learning. *Language Learning* 48, 323–364.

Pawley, A. and Syder, F.H. (1983) Two puzzles for linguistic theory: Nativelike selection and nativelike fluency. In J.C. Richards and R.W. Schmidt (eds) *Language and Communication* (pp. 191–226). New York: Longman.

Pinker, S. (1994) *The Language Instinct.* Harmondworth: Penguin.

Rehbein, J. (1987) Multiple formulae: Aspects of Turkish migrant workers' German in intercultural communication. In K. Knapp, W. Enninger and A. Knapp-Potthoff (eds) *Analysing Intercultural Communication* (pp. 215–248). Berlin: Mouton.

Schmidt, R.W. (1983) Interaction, acculturation and the acquisition of communicative competence: A case study of an adult. In N. Wolfson and E. Judd (eds) *Sociolinguistics and Language Acquisition.* Rowley, MA: Newbury House.

Taguchi, N. and Iwasaki, Y. (2008) Goals, beliefs and outcomes of an elementary Japanese program: Implementation of chunk learning in the development of interpersonal communicational ability. In H.J. Siskin (ed.) *AAUSC. From Thought to Action: Exploring Beliefs and Outcomes in the Foreign Language Program* (pp. 92–111). Boston: Heinle and Heinle.

Wode, H. (1981) *Learning a Second Language.* Tubingen: Narr.

Wray, A. (2000) Formulaic sequences in second language teaching: Principle and Practice. *Applied Linguistics* 21, 463–489.

Wray, A. (2002) *Formulaic Language and the Lexicon.* Cambridge: Cambridge University Press.

Wray, A. (2008) *Formulaic Language: Pushing the Boundaries.* Oxford: Oxford University Press.

Wray, A and Perkins, M.R. (2000) The functions of formulaic language: An integrated model. *Language and Communication* 20, 1–28.

Yorio, C.A. (1989) Idiomaticity as an indicator of second language proficiency. In K. Hyltenstam and L.K. Obler (eds) *Bilingualism Across Lifespan* (pp. 55–72). Cambridge: Cambridge University Press.

Chapter 4

Formulaicity vs. Fluency and Accuracy in Using English as a Foreign Language

AGNIESZKA WRÓBEL

Introduction

Anyone involved in language teaching is probably familiar with the fact that no matter how much practice students put into it, they do make mistakes. Their language is communicative but often far from the English that they would like to use. This may even be considered a disaster as the idealistic goal for many involved in foreign language teaching and learning is nativelike fluency and accuracy. A nativelike control over a foreign language is not restricted to the knowledge of and ability to manipulate morpho-syntactic rules or the possession of vast vocabulary consisting of separate lexical entries as well as idioms and idiomatic expressions. Of equal importance is the ability to choose those of them which would be used by a native speaker in a given situation. And native speakers' choice is usually predictable, as they depend on conventiona-lized forms and lexical units of varying complexity to express concepts, emotions or functions, rather than novel utterances. Of course, such preferences do not rule out linguistic creativity; yet, novelty seems to be a second choice, often with a certain purpose in mind. Advanced learners of English, or other languages, do need a command of a wide range of such prefabricated chunks of language – or formulaic language, as it is more and more often called – to be both accurate and fluent. However, it is easier said than done, and beneficial as it undoubtedly is for foreign language learning, its use may not always work in favour of non-native speakers.

Formulaicity in Native Language

Being a native speaker of a given language, we can convey any message in multiple ways. Our ability to produce numerous versions is credited to the generative potential of our grammar. Yet, we do not exercise this ability to the fullest. What is more, a great number of possible utterances seem not to be appropriate, even though there is nothing wrong with grammatical structures and vocabulary selection.

They just do not sound natural, they do not sound native. And more often than not, the only justification one can give is that 'this is not how we say this'. The reason is that native speakers do not really use the creative potential of grammar rules to the full extent. In 1983, Andrew Pawley and Frances Syder published an influential article in which they drew our attention to this nativelike selection – the ability of native speakers to convey their meaning by expressions that are both grammatical and at the same time nativelike. Generative grammar, usually understood as a set of rules that specify all and only the well-formed sentences of the language, is not enough for any learner to achieve a nativelike control. As Pawley and Syder put it, 'only a small proportion of the total set of grammatical sentences are nativelike in form – in the sense of being readily acceptable to native informants as ordinary, natural forms of expression, in contrast to expressions that are grammatical but are judged to be "unidiomatic", "odd" or "foreignisms"' (1983: 193).

Such preferences, concerning both lexical and grammatical choices, lie at the root of idiomaticity in native language. One may assume then that a fluent and accurate foreign language user should be as idiomatic as possible. A common belief has it that idiomaticity equals the ability to use those colourful idioms and idiomatic expressions such as the often-cited 'kick the bucket' or 'it's raining cats and dogs'. However, this conviction does not hold true. Idiomaticity is connected rather with the fact that native speakers rely on formulaicity, a large repository of formulas – ready-to-use expressions stored and retrieved holistically, of which idioms (like those above) are just a small part.

There is a multiplicity of terms used in studies and literature concerning formulaicity: *prefabs, ready-made expressions, routine formulae, idioms, multi-word chunks* and so on. The fact that the phenomenon is widespread across different fields has resulted in the presence of numerous definitions adopted by linguists working in these fields. What is more, formulaicity itself has a lot in common with phraseology, especially in corpus linguistics. Nonetheless, there have been attempts to provide a clear-cut definition which would encompass all aspects and dimensions of formulaicity/phraseology. Alison Wray (e.g. Wray, 2002), one of the leading researchers into formulaicity, points out that between what is for sure formulaic and what is not, there lies a huge amount of linguistic material that may, but does not have to, be formulaic. Sometimes, the research seems to be similar to looking for black cats in a dark room – you know they are there, but it is extremely difficult to spot them.

Recently, one of the most widely used definitions is that of *formulaic sequence*, a term introduced to replace all the other terms 'which have something useful to say, but none of which seems fully to capture the essence of the wider whole' (Wray, 2002: 8). In her 2002 book, Wray attempts to analyse and find common grounds for the findings of research into formulaicity from different fields and that, she claims, justifies the introduction of yet another term 'which does not carry previous baggage, and which can be clearly defined' (2002: 9). The introduced term – formulaic sequence – entails a habitual and holistic character of the phenomena as well as their apparent multi-unit structure. A *formulaic sequence*, according to Wray (2002), is 'sequence, continuous or discontinuous, of words or other elements, which is, or appears to be, prefabricated: that is, stored and retrieved whole from memory at the time of use, rather than being subject to generation or analysis by the language grammar' (2002: 9). This definition is dubbed *a working definition* as its aim is to encompass 'any material that *appears to be* prefabricated, not just that which *is*' (Wray, 2008: 95) [emphasis in original] and cover 'any kind of linguistic unit that has been considered formulaic in any research field' (2002: 9). The result is that the term *formulaic sequence* may serve as a coverall name for all and any instances suspected to have formulaic character as the definition of formulaic sequence is, purposely, extremely inclusive. An extensive and thorough analysis of data and evidence from different fields led Wray (2002) to the claim that mental lexicon is heteromorphic in nature and consists of *Morpheme Equivalent Units* (MEU) where an MEU is defined as 'a word or word string, whether incomplete or including gaps for inserted variable items, that is processed like a morpheme, that is without recourse to any form-meaning matching of any sub-parts it may have' (2008: 12).

The two definitions share the same principal views on formulaicity – its holistic nature of processing and, at the same time, consent for variability. Both are, however, very broad and, consequently, any instances of language which occupy the compositionality and/or flexibility continuum may be classified as formulaic. Formulaicity seems to be a significant component of almost all types of discourse. Various studies suggest that at least one-third to one-half of language is formulaic (e.g. Erman & Warren, 2000; Howarth, 1998) depending on register or mode (Biber *et al.*, 1999).

In an attempt to justify the very existence of the phenomenon, Wray (2000, 2002, 2008) focuses on the functions that formulaic language performs rather than on its degrees of variability or compositionality, which have been the criteria adopted by, for example, Moon (1997, 1998) or Nattinger and DeCarrico (1992). Although other criteria are acknowledged, it is the functions of formulaic sequences that are given priority in the Wray paper from 2000 on which what follows is based. There are two functions, generally speaking, that formulaic language performs: saving effort in processing (formulaic sequences function as compensatory devices for memory limitations) and helping, or even enabling, individuals to establish social relations of different kinds. These two broad categorical functions – processing effort reduction and social interaction

– may be divided further in terms of the benefits that they provide in the following way:

(1) *Reduction of processing effort* can be achieved by the use of

    (a) standard phrases including those with gaps ('(...) I have known for ___ years or best foot forward') and standard referential labels with agreed meanings ('the current economic climate' or 'bullet point'), which increase the speed and fluency of language production and so they act as *processing short-cuts*;

    (b) standard phrases with simple meanings ('one way or another' or 'make a decision'), fillers ('if you want to know my opinion' or 'if you like'), turn-holders ('and another thing' or 'and let me just say ...'), discourse shape markers ('There are three points I want to make. Firstly... Secondly ... Lastly') and repetitions of preceding input ('A: What's the capital of Peru? B: What's the capital of Peru? Lima, isn't it?'), which constitute vehicles for fluency, rhythm and emphasis. These also help planning time without losing the turn and that is why they are called *time-buyers*;

    (c) mnemonics ('Thirty days hath September...') or lengthy texts that are rote-learned ('Shall I compare thee to a summer's day?'), which enable the user to gain and retain access to information otherwise unlikely to be remembered and the speaker is capable of *manipulation of information*.

(2) *Social interaction* is supported by the use of

    (a) commands ('keep off the grass'), requests ('could you repeat that please?'), politeness markers ('I wonder if you'd mind ...'), bargains ('I'll give you ___ for it') and the like, which help the speakers satisfy their physical, emotional and cognitive needs through *manipulation of others*;

    (b) story-telling skills ('you're never going to believe this, but ...'), turn claimers ('Yes, but the thing is ...') and personal turns of phrase, which help the speaker be taken seriously or be separated from the crowd when *asserting separate identity* is what he or she wants or needs;

    (c) 'in' phrases, group chants, institutionalized forms of words ('happy birthday' or 'Dearly beloved, we are gathered here today...'), rituals ('Our Father, which art in Heaven...'), proverbs ('look before you leap'), threats, quotations, forms of address, hedges and the like, which help the speaker prove his or her overall membership and the place in hierarchy when *asserting group identity* is what he or she needs or wants.

Such a somehow reversed typology – with the shift of focus on a superordinate – is intentional. Wray (2000, 2002, 2008) claims that both functions are two sides of the same coin and 'all formulaic sequences can be characterized in terms of their function in bypassing processing, whether it be the speaker's or the hearer's, or both' (2000: 479). The overriding purpose is making communication as efficient as possible:

> when an individual chooses a prefabricated stretch of language in order to reduce the pressure on processing, the aim is to be fluent and to succeed in producing the entire message without interruption, or to ensure that information is reliably to hand when needed (...) when the speaker selects a formulaic sequence for socio-interactional purposes, what is paramount is the effect of the words on the hearer. (2000: 477)

Communication is most efficient when both the speaker and the hearer share speech patterns – the speaker chooses language which he or she presumes is known to the hearer. Although it might seem to be genuine altruism, it is not – 'it is in the speaker's interests to ensure that the hearer understands, since the intended effect of the utterance is to create a situation beneficial to the speaker' (Wray, 2002: 95). After all, what really matters is getting what we want and the use of formulaic language might be seen as one of the means of doing it.

It has been said so far that native speakers benefit tremendously from formulaicity, and, as Conklin and Schmitt point out, 'given their utility, it is not uprising that the use of formulaic sequences is widespread in language' (2008: 74). Being as beneficial and common as formulaic sequences undoubtedly are for native speakers, a question inevitably arises whether the formulaicity phenomenon can be of equal use to non-native users.

Formulaicity in Foreign Language Learning

The features discussed so far may lead to an assumption that formulaic language is something worth reaching for in foreign language teaching and learning. If it works so efficiently for native speakers, it may as well work in a language classroom. However, it might not be so obvious. As was said earlier, an ideal foreign language user has a good command of a range of formulaic language, meaning that he or she can use it both accurately and fluently. Beneficial as it might be, there seem to be certain problems concerning formulaicity in language learning and teaching.

Formulaicity and fluency

The feature of formulaic language that appears to be beneficial to both native and non-native users is the reduction in processing effort. Formulaic sequences, despite their length, are processed faster than the same sequences of words generated creatively. Prefabs compensate for a limited capacity of working memory, which seems to be overloaded when language is generated online from syntactic rules and individual lexical items. However, as Conklin and Schmitt point out, 'it must be said that this explanation, even though intuitive, is still more assertion than demonstrated fact' (2008: 76). More research is needed into the ways of formulaic and non-formulaic language processing although the research done so far seems to prove it (cf. de Bot, 1992; Conklin & Schmitt, 2008; Schmitt, 2004; Underwood *et al.*, 2004).

According to many researchers, formulaicity, being somehow synonymous with memory-based processing (Skehan, 1998) or the idiom principle (Sinclair, 1991), is the default setting for comprehension and production. Such ready-made formulaic sequences allow native speakers to use analytic resources to deal with any difficulties caused by a speaker's thick accent, non-native grammar, background noise, dysfluency, but also poetry or word plays. The moment they hear the beginning of the phrase, they recognize it and have time to evaluate what they hear and get ready for a reply. The same might apply to non-native speakers. Prefabricated chunks of language buy time required to prepare the rest of the utterance. This speeds up language production. The language flow seems less interrupted, there might be fewer hesitation pauses and the utterance, as a whole, appears to be more fluent. If a foreign language student possesses a number of such memorized sequences, he or she uses them without worrying about their internal structure, which, to some extent, often lessens their uncertainty whether the string is produced correctly. Otherwise, generating it from scratch overloads the memory capacity as one needs to manipulate rules, vocabulary, register and message, which, in case of lower levels of foreign language proficiency, is a rather consciously controlled process.

Formulaic sequences, especially those conventionalized language forms (Yorio, 1980), also help to ensure that a participant operates within an appropriate register and style in a verbal exchange. Well-chosen formulas make an utterance more polite and, which might be important, positively influence the interlocutor who, in turn, needs less effort to process the incoming message. Another benefit that learners can obtain from the use of formulaic sequences is that their language may sound more natural. In an attempt to help students achieve better fluency as well as help them sound more nativelike, modern course books contain sections on formulaic language, usually in the form of lists of functional expressions. These phrases, which are grouped according to their functions (asking the way, giving advice, ordering meals), serve as models of native use and are at hand saving learners the effort of generating them from scratch. It seems that all a learner has to do is to memorise them. When learners are able to retrieve memorized lexical items of various lengths, their oral (and written) production appears to be more organized and adequate in terms of the requirements of linguistic savoir vivre. Simple retrieval and, probably to a greater degree, the ability to manipulate such sequences with respect to any syntactic changes concerning tense, person and so on often help to cover up at least some of the grammatical and lexical deficiencies which, otherwise, would be exposed.

All the benefits that foreign language learners can enjoy from the knowledge of formulaic sequences and the ability to use them are possible when the sequences are used correctly. That is somehow unrealistic, as no matter how much formulaic language improves the fluency of non-native production, the problem lies in the accuracy of such production. A learner might seem fluent almost to the way native speakers can be in terms of conveying messages and/or the speed of the language production, but he or she hardly ever attains the idiomaticity of native speakers.

There is one aspect of formulaic language which, when it comes to English, may not be useful for non-native users around the world as it may not contribute to fluency. This feature concerns the fact that formulaicity gives language users a sense of belonging to the group that uses the language. For most non-native speakers of English, it might not be the case. Most non-native users communicate in English with other non-native speakers (Graddol, 2006). Yet, non-natives are still at a disadvantage in the globalized world. Graddol's comment might be revealing here: 'ELF approaches, like all foreign language teaching, positions the learner as an outsider, as a foreigner; one who struggles to attain acceptance by the target language community' (2006: 82). Globalization of the English language requires new approaches to the language itself. However, maybe it is Barbara Seidlhofer who is right in claiming that '(. . .) native-speaker language use is just one kind of reality, and one of very doubtful relevance for lingua franca contexts' (2001: 138). Any native language is highly culture-dependent in its phraseology, connotations or literature, history or politics references. Lack of such knowledge makes a non-native the 'outsider'. Yet, in most international contexts, it is rather redundant. For example, a situation where a person from China and a person from Zanzibar has a small talk about the weather is doubtful. What is more, formulaicity may hinder communication even between native speakers from different countries (Crystal, 2003). In English as Lingua Franca, the use of culture-flavoured formulaic strings seems unwelcome (Seidlhofer, 2001, 2002). The language is a means which enables learners to get a job, do business or research, or simply to deal with everyday situations when abroad. Non-native speakers' English is not a symbol of cultural identity any more.

Formulaicity and accuracy

Having to speak in a foreign language is undoubtedly a stressful situation in which our memory often fails us and what comes to our mind is what we remember best (due to stronger associations, more frequent encounters etc). In these moments, learners either rely on their abilities to generate utterances using all their language resources that they are convinced they possess, or try to retrieve a formula that they think they remember more or less correctly. The former might partially explain why so many learners painfully struggle to build their speech from individual units rather than use formulas that they are not sure of. In the latter case, the formulas are usually far from being nativelike (*Can I help you ice?/*can I help you a sandwich?/*I would you like to go). The inability to retrieve a required English formula also leads to a partial or complete transfer from learners' native language (*If I were on your place, I'd buy him . . . /*From the other side, it's not bad . . . /*You have to see it. It won't be the lost time!/*The movie, which lately paid my attention is cartoon X). When interlocutors do not share it, communication breaks down.

Probably the main problem concerning formulaicity in a foreign language lies at the very psycholinguistic core of the phenomenon. A formulaic sequence is acquired, stored and retrieved holistically, which is contradictory to the way adult and teenage learners encounter a foreign language (Gozdawa-Gołębiowski, 2003; Skehan, 1998; Wray, 2000, 2002, 2008). Processing in the native language is either holistic or analytic, whereas in a foreign language, there appears to be a third mode – contentive (Gozdawa-Gołębiowski, 2003) – which is usually the default one. Learners prioritize meaning over form the way they do in the native language. Being preoccupied with meaning, they usually do not pay much attention to grammatical words or morphological markers, which in case of native language do not have to be attended consciously. As a result, the content, open-class items of a phrase, is present, yet the phrase is far from being a native formula (*on other hand/*by a way/(*love at the first sight etc.).

Formulaic language, being highly culturally and socially marked, is a dynamic phenomenon and the rules that govern its use might be extremely difficult, if not impossible, to teach or learn. Does that mean that formulaicity is of little use to language learners? Definitely not. The common belief among students and learners that formulaicity consists mainly of idioms, clichés, proverbs, rhymes and fixed collocations needs to be changed. The problem with idioms is that they are very often not remembered exactly and lose their idiomatic meaning because of that. Another problem with idioms is that they are misused by students – either because they are falling out of use – the infamous 'raining cats and dogs' or because they are used in wrong contexts, which may result in a completely different meaning than the intended one ('Don Antonio kicked the bucket by accident'). Idiomatic expressions cannot be escaped as the language is full of them, but a distinction should be made between what is called passive and active knowledge. Students should know these colourful expressions, but they need to be cautious when using them. Learners need quite a lot of context, notes on register and attention to form. What is meant here is that learners must be aware that if they decide to use an idiom or formula, they cannot change or omit its parts as that may change its meaning.

Teaching hardly ever equals learning so one can never be sure what learners will remember, not to mention how they will use it. What can be done is, firstly, to provide them with enough input and, secondly, draw their attention to the language items that we would like them, hopefully, to remember. If students are to remember something as a whole, it must repeatedly appear not only in the input provided in the course book material but also in teacher's speech. One of the reasons why these students who learn a foreign language in classroom conditions are less formulaic than those learning in the given language speaking community is the little amount of formulaicity in the input that they get (Yorio, 1989). A lot of students use expressions, even long ones far above their assumed level, because they pick them up from films, the internet and so on. Formulaic input in classroom situations is, however, not enough. Left alone, students concentrate on extracting meaning and real-time processing limitations make them neglect form. Comprehension seems not to be followed by development of their interlanguage or production accuracy. What can be done here? Learners need help and guidance in searching for, noticing, sometimes even analysing expressions. Looking for and noticing idioms or collocations should not be difficult. The task gets more demanding when it comes to sentence stems; these are often neglected by both teachers and learners.

Productive sentence stems are complete sentences or, more often, expressions which are something less than a complete sentence, and their grammatical form and lexical content are wholly or largely fixed (Pawley & Syder, 1983). They are not true idioms but rather regular form-meaning pairings, and they have a specific conversational force which is, very often, not fully predictable from its literal meaning. The examples might be as follows: 'I hate to mention this, but ...'/'Would you mind (not) Verb+ ING (NP)'/'Think twice before you Verb Phrase'/'NP be-TENSE sorry to keep-TENSE you waiting' ('I'm sorry to keep you waiting', 'I'm so sorry to have kept you waiting', 'Mr X is sorry to keep you waiting all this time') Their fixedness may differ as many of them allow some grammatical transformations or lexical substitutions but, nonetheless, they still might be retrieved as wholes or automatic chains from the long-term memory. That lessens the amount of effort needed to process them. And this is how formulaicity can find its place in foreign language teaching.

Foreign language learners need help if their interlanguage is to benefit from formulaic sequences. Nevertheless, it remains an open question whether explicit teaching of formulaic sequences can result in interlanguage development. Wray (2000: 470) presents an extensive discussion of research findings stating that 'there is disagreement regarding the ability of taught learners to make generalizations about the grammar from formulaic input'. The problem seems to be the diversity of formulaic phenomena. Formulaic sequences occupy spectra from semantically opaque to transparent, from syntactically irregular to regular, with morphological modification possible or not. Without conscious assistance in noticing and analyzing, learners are left on their own, not knowing which sequences may be subjects for generalization.

Conclusions

In formal classroom learning and teaching, formulaic language might be a double-edged sword. On the one hand, it improves the fluency since it improves the flow of the language: the utterance seems not to be interrupted by hesitation pauses or self-corrections. On the other hand, very often, such an improvement is superficial, the formulas are broken and, to a native ear, they seem more foreign than a made-from-scratch utterance where a non-native speaker is struggling to put the words right according to the knowledge of rules that he or she is able to manipulate. Broken formulas often result from the way non-native users process language, and so it seems reasonable that in formal setting, assistance is needed to overcome the inadequate amount of input the native speakers acquiring language get otherwise. Moreover, both teachers' and learners' awareness should be developed that formulaicity is not only catchy idioms and proverbs or time-fillers and slangish expressions but, most of the time, it is hidden in grammatically regular and semantically transparent sequences which happen to be just the way native speakers say something.

References

Biber, D., Johansson, S., Leech, G. and Conrad, S. (1999) *Longman Grammar of Spoken and Written English*. London: Longman.

Conklin, K. and Schmitt, N. (2008) Formulaic sequences: Are they processed more quickly than nonformulaic language by native and nonnative speakers? *Applied Linguistics* 29, 72–89.

Crystal, D. (2003) *English as a Global Language* (2nd edn). Cambridge: Cambridge University Press.

de Bot, K. (1992) A bilingual production model: Levelt's 'speaking' model adapted. *Applied Linguistics* 13, 1–25.

Erman, B. and Warren, B. (2000) The idiom principle and the open choice principle. *Text* 20, 29–62.

Gozdawa-Gołębiowski, R. (2003) *Interlanguage Formation. A Study of the Triggering Mechanisms.* Warszawa: Instytut Anglistyki UW

Graddol, D. (2006) *English Next. Why Global English May Mean the End of 'English as a Foreign Language'.* London: British Council.

Howarth, P. (1998) Phraseology and second language proficiency. *Applied Linguistics* 19, 24–44.

Moon, R. (1997) Vocabulary connections: Multi-word items in English. In N. Schmitt and M. McCarthy (eds) *Vocabulary: Description, Acquisition and Pedagogy* (pp. 40–63). Cambridge: Cambridge University Press.

Moon, R. (1998) *Fixed Expressions and Idioms in English. A Corpus-Based Approach.* Oxford: Clarendon Press.

Nattinger R.J. and DeCarrico, J.S. (1992) *Lexical Phrases and Language Teaching.* Oxford: Oxford University Press.

Pawley, A and Syder, F.H. (1983) Two puzzles for linguistic theory: Nativelike selection and native like fluency. In J.C. Richards and R.W. Schmidt (eds) *Language and Communication* (pp. 191–225). New York: Longman.

Schmitt, N. (ed.) (2004) *Formulaic Sequences.* Amsterdam: John Benjamins.

Seidlhofer, B. (2001) Closing a conceptual gap: The case for a description of English as a lingua franca. *International Journal of Applied Linguistics* 11, 133–158.

Seidlhofer, B. (2002) The shape of things to come? Some basic questions about English as a lingua franca. In K. Knapp and C. Meierkord (eds) *Lingua Franca Communication* (pp. 269–302). Frankfurt/Main: Peter Lang. Online version: http://www.basic-english.org/member/articles/seidlhofer.html

Sinclair, J. McH. (1991) *Corpus, Concordance, Collocation.* Oxford: Oxford University Press.

Skehan, P. (1998) *A Cognitive Approach to Language Learning.* Oxford: Oxford University Press.

Underwood, G., Schmitt, N. and Galpin, A. (2004) The eyes have it: An eye-movement study into the processing of formulaic sequences. In N. Schmitt (ed.) *Formulaic Sequences*(pp. 155–172). Amsterdam: John Benjamins.

Wray, A. (2000) Formulaic sequences in second language teaching: Principle and practice. *Applied Linguistics* 21, 463–489.

Wray, A. (2002) *Formulaic Language and the Lexicon.* Cambridge: Cambridge University Press.

Wray, A (2008) *Formulaic Language: Pushing the Boundaries.* Oxford: Oxford University Press.

Yorio, C.A. (1980) Conventionalised language forms and the developments of communicative competence. *TESOL Quarterly* 14, 433–442.

Yorio, C.A. (1989) Idiomaticity as an indicator of second language proficiency. In K. Hyltenstam and L.K. Obler (eds) *Bilingualism Across the Life-Span* (pp. 55–72). Cambridge: Cambridge University Press.

Chapter 5

Talking the Same Language: Sociocultural Aspects of Code-Switching in L2 Classroom Discourse

JAN MAJER

Introduction

This chapter is concerned primarily with a specific characteristic of oral communication, namely code-switching – a language-contact phenomenon triggered by speakers sharing access to more than one linguistic system. In interactional terms, code-switching means alternate use of elements from two separate languages or dialects creating one utterance or an exchange (Winford, 2003: 14) 'tied together prosodically as well as by semantic and syntactic relations equivalent to those that join passages in a single speech act' (Romaine, 1995: 121). From a structural point of view, in any given instance of language alternation, one of the systems can be treated as 'the source of the morphosyntactic frame for the clause', while items from the other system are embedded in that base (Myers-Scotton, 2006: 241). Finally, a distinction is commonly observed between (Matras, 2009: 101)

- insertional code-switching – the placement of an L1 element in an utterance or sentence formed in L2 (i.e. the frame language) and
- alternational code-switching – changing the system between utterances or sentences.

The above principles underlie many sociolinguistic and psycholinguistic elaborations of the topic in question published to date. Treating these generalizations as a point of departure, the approach adopted in the present study takes language choice and language alternation beyond naturalistic talk in multilingual speech communities and focuses on pedagogic discourse in the institutionalized setting of the foreign-language classroom.

Rationale and Aims

As a sociolinguistic construct, 'speech community' has enjoyed a long tradition of exploration. However, besides relying on the seminal works of Labov (1972), Gumperz (1972) and Hymes (1974) which offer linguistic and social descriptions of variability, ethnicity and identity, more and more researchers (e.g. Davies, 2005; Eckert & Wenger, 2005) are shifting their inquiry towards communities of practice. This is because 'in today's increasingly mobile and multilingual world, conversations across linguistic and cultural boundaries are multiplying. As speakers with different repertoires come into contact with each other, the concept of the speech community is being transformed' (Lo, 1999: 461). And if we accept that communities of practice are characterized by constitutive features of mutual endeavour, a joint enterprise and a shared repertoire (Davies, 2005: 560), then these criteria are met by many educational environments.

In order to maximize output opportunities in L2, foreign language teaching relies on collaborative interaction. However, whether this is carried out via pair/group-work in learner-centred settings or through dyadic discourse in teacher-fronted formats, exchanges among participants sharing a common mother tongue inevitably lead to frequent switches between the available linguistic systems. As a result, what from a methodological point of view should be considered teacher talk and learner communicative practice often turns out to be bilingual discourse. Fortunately, however, the goal of modern language pedagogy is often defined as creating bilinguals (cf. Blyth, 1995; Cook, 2001). For example, when specifying ways of speaking to a language class, Seligson (1997: 21) adds this word of caution for English language teaching instructors: 'Remember, we're not training students to become fluent monolingual speakers of English but effective switchers between codes, i.e. bilingual users'. Furthermore, as pointed out by Halmari (2004), 'becoming bilingual does not only mean that an individual acquires discourse competence in more than one language; it also means that the speaker develops a competence to alternate between the two available languages to convey subtle pragmatic messages while in the company of other bilinguals' (p. 115). But exploiting bilingual resources can do more for the learner than facilitating interaction – it can also enhance learning. This is because among the many justifiable reasons for code-switching in educational contexts (cf. Eldridge, 1996; Majer, 2003, 2006, 2009; Niżegorodcew, 2007; Üstünel & Seedhouse, 2005), there is a heuristic function (cf. Holmes & Stubbe, 2004) which is realized in the form of scaffolding that assists not only collaboration in problem-solving activities but also language learning in a more general sense.

Over the years, research on child bilingualism and bilingual educational discourse – be it language pedagogy or content-based classrooms – has developed the following approaches to instruction mediated by

L1 (or L3), the contexts ranging from submersion in L2 to foreign languages taught to homogeneous classes:

- using the minority child's vernacular throughout the curriculum (e.g. Leggarreta, 1977);
- fostering minority languages to promote linguistic awareness, multilingualism and multiculturism (cf. Helot & Young, 2002);
- maintaining and developing the mother tongue in bilingual education (e.g. Cummins, 2003; Harding-Esch & Riley, 2003; Halmari, 2004);
- recognizing heritage language competence as a learning resource (e.g. Cummins, 2005, 2008);
- translanguaging (code-switching without the diglossic functional separation; cf. García, 2007);
- assuming a language ecology perspective and teaching bilingual children via bilingual instructional strategies based on the interdependence of skills and knowledge across systems (e.g. Creese & Blackledge, 2010);
- involving resourceful bilingual practitioners and bilingual support teachers (e.g. Hornberger, 2003; Martin-Jones & Saxena, 2003);
- using L3 as lingua franca in bilingual contexts (e.g. Björklund & Suni, 2000; Ife, 2007; Sanz, 2008);
- developing immersion programmes (e.g. Baker, 2001; Björk-Willén, 2008);
- promoting Content and Language Integrated Learning (CLIL; e.g. Butzkamm, 1998; Dalton-Puffer, 2007; Liebscher & Dailey-O'Cain, 2005);
- adhering to the 'L2-only' policy as much as possible (Harbord, 1992; Willis, 1981);
- advocating a judicious, sparing use of L1 in L2 instruction (e.g. Atkinson, 1993; Niżegorodcew, 1998; Schweers, 1999);
- treating L2 learners as multicompetent language users rather than as 'imperfect' native speakers (e.g. Cook, 2001) and
- organizing collaborative, consciousness-raising tasks in the L2 classroom by giving learners the opportunity to verbalize inner speech in L1 and to take advantage of natural cognitive processes that support L2 learning (e.g. Antón & DiCamilla, 1999; Macaro, 2001; Scott & de la Fuente, 2008).

By adopting the sociocultural perspective of some of the approaches listed above, in this chapter we consider bilingual discourse in the L2 classroom as an instance of language contact in which skilful involvement of the stronger linguistic system (i.e. L1) is believed to (1) sustain collaborative interaction, (2) promote semiotic mediation between learners, (3) reduce cognitive overload and (4) enhance the development of metalinguistic terminology (Antón & DiCamilla, 1999: 234; Scott & de la Fuente, 2008: 109–110). This position is hoped to move the discussion beyond the confines of a methodological issue. And that is how the problem of language alternation and language policy in the L2 classroom was treated for many years. Thus, advocates of the 'L2 only' approach spoke of the possibility of creating a rich linguistic environment for second language acquisition, as well as of the necessity to bridge the gap between educational and naturalistic discourse. At the same time, they warned that if too much native language was permitted, this automatically meant reduced quantity and quality of L2 input, with detrimental effects on the development of productive and receptive skills. What is more, the status of the target language seemed degraded if its use was confined to the realization of core pedagogical goals, with framework and social goals typically displaying a preponderance of L1. In contrast, opponents of the radical approach dismissed the 'L2 only' position as unrealistic when it came to, for example, dealing with discipline problems, maintaining rapport or explaining grammar and vocabulary. Besides, beginner-level students, especially young learners, were thought to feel insecure if the teacher did not switch to L1 when going through such classroom routines as issuing instructions or providing corrective feedback. Finally, having to negotiate meaning in L2 when in fact the teacher and the learners had a more straightforward means of communication at their disposal simply appeared artificial. These are some of the issues that have dominated the methodological approach to code-switching in the foreign language classroom.

While pedagogical implications remain an additional goal of the present study, the main objective is to focus on sociocultural aspects. The samples analysed for the purposes of the discussion to follow are displayed in the form of transcripts extracted from longer exchanges between teachers and students, collected by the author over many years of ethnographic research as well as reported in the literature, representing a cross-section of age groups, levels of proficiency and target languages – both positive and negative examples. Special attention in the analysis is devoted to negotiated repair in oral communication tasks. This is a specific issue in bilingual classroom interaction since, as pointed out by Buckwalter (2001), negotiation of repair differs from negotiation of meaning in that the latter merely aims to indicate that there is a communication problem, while the former is also concerned with the resolution. Apart from that, it seems that sociocultural theory (cf. Daniels, 2001; Lantolf, 2006) is particularly well suited to account for interactive patterns in negotiating corrective feedback, which involves adjustments going beyond the enhancement of comprehension.

Data Analysis

The qualitative analysis of L2 and L1 alternation in this chapter uses a typical design of exemplification. As is conventional in the literature (cf. Martin, 2003), L2 is given in regular text, whereas L1 (or L3) is signalled by bold print. Utterances in languages other than English are translated (in italics in pointed brackets). The account makes use of the author's own examples, unless specified otherwise.

We begin our discussion with a typical example of a teacher–student dyad where the instructor's switch from L2 to L1 is a reaction to the young learner's failure to respond in the target language. To be sure, it is not quite clear whether she does not know the answer or simply cannot comprehend the teacher's question. In any case, in order to sustain interaction and to give the pupil a chance of providing a meaningful answer, the teacher first acknowledges the student's insufficient preparation but then encourages a response in L1. Once that is given, the instructor offers a contextualization clue in the form of translation. This helps the learner to form the right answer, which is then met with positive cognitive feedback.

Extract 1 (lower primary school student; L2 = English, L1 = Polish)

> T: **What else is there in the room?**
> S: (SILENCE)
> T: **Co dalej? Chyba nazwy się nie nauczyłaś, co? No dobrze, powiedz, co jest w pokoiku**. *< any further [items]? you didn't quite learn the word, did you? well all right, tell me what's in the [little] room >*
> S: **Lawa**. *< coffee table >*
> T: **Lawa?** *< coffee table? >* (PAUSE) **No Karolinko, takie proste, no jak to było 'kawa i stół'?** *< come on, Karolinka, [it's] so simple, how did [we] say 'coffee and table'? >*
> S: (VERY SLOWLY) Coffee table.
> T: Coffee table, **dobrze**. *< good >*

Extract 1 represents a pedagogical approach in which in the beginner stages of learning code-switching may serve to provide young learners with a chance to practise L2 in a stress-free setting. One way to create this kind of atmosphere is to make certain that the students remain connected to their L1 (Halmari, 2004: 143).

Another example of the same approach, this time involving the whole class, is shown in Extract 2. More than merely arousing attention, the teacher switches the code as a reaction to S1's apparently inappropriate answer to a general solicit. Again, the encouragement aimed at eliciting the correct response is in the form of translation, but the difference is that the teacher also cues the class by prompting the respective constituents of the target phrase. This helps the learners to arrive at the right answer.

Extract 2 (lower primary school students; L2 = English, L1 = Polish)

> **T:** Why did the little girl cry? Why did she cry?
> **S1:** Because was not close to home.
> **T:** Not exactly. **Jak jest 'daleko od domu', misiaczki?** < *how do you say 'far from home', darlings?* > Far–
> **S2:** Far away.
> **T:** Fro–
> **S3:** From the house.
> **T:** From ho–
> **Ss:** From home.
> **T:** Yes, far from home.

The teacher's objective in the above-illustrated elicitation of repair is to minimize the young learners' contribution to the interaction. Accordingly, she leads them step by step through asking questions which require very short responses. In this way, she provides a scaffold by simplifying the students' role rather than their task (Daniels, 2001: 107). Eventually, the pupils' joint effort brings about a successful outcome.

The spontaneous material shown in the first two samples is too modest to make any generalizations, but research reported by Moore (2002: 280) indicates that teachers working with young learners are flexible towards code-switching, knowing that the growth of linguistic competence and the development of cognitive competence cannot be separated. In contrast, more ritualized switches are found in Extract 3, in which, admittedly, the teacher addresses the learners in the mother tongue as well as uses translation to elicit repair and encourage further attempts, but at the same time she fails to provide all the appropriate clues. More important, however, while resorting to L1 the teacher still ignores a serious error in S1's first question, namely the lack of concord between the verb and the subject, no doubt induced by negative transfer. In fact, what the translation does is emphasize the plural concept of 'hair' in Polish, whereas in the negotiation of repair the students' attention is drawn to the choice of pronoun and the word order – problems that were not present in S1's original utterance.

Extract 3 (upper primary school students; L2 = English, L1 = Polish)

> **T:** What else would you like to ask?
> **S1:** Are his hair dark?
> **T:** **E tam!** < *go on!* > **'Czy jego włosy są ciemne?'** No jak to będzie? < *'is his hair dark?' how do you say that?* >
> **Ss:** Is it– Is his–

S2: Is his–
T: **Jeszcze raz.** < *one more time* >
S1: Is her hair–
T: Is his hair.
S1: Is his hair is dark?
T: **Jeszcze raz.** < *one more time* >
S3: Is his hair dark?
T: **No ślicznie!** < now [that's] beautiful! >

When making a decision to switch the code the teacher needs to choose adequate contextual clues in order to determine cognitive focus. The transcript above demonstrates that in the course of the exchange, S1 makes two unsuccessful attempts at self-correction, which indicate that he misunderstood the teacher's feedback. It seems, then, that the choice of L1 affected both interaction and cognition to a greater extent than the teacher presumably intended.

In the fourth extract, derived from a transcribed lesson involving more mature students, code-switching occurs upon the teacher's provision of negative feedback and has a function of a personal appeal. But interaction is later sustained in L1 even when it enters the phase of unsuccessful elicitation of correction with a subsequent metalinguistic comment.

Extract 4 (senior secondary school students; L2 = English, L1 = Polish)

T: So why didn't you like 'Toy Story'?
S1: It's for the childrens.
T: Childrens? That's– That's very interesting. **Maciek, jak chcesz egzaminy zdawać?** < *Maciek, how do you expect to pass [your] exams?* >
Ss: **Dzieci.** < *children* >
T: **No właśnie,** < *that's it* >say **"dziecko".** < *child* >
S1: **"Dziecko"** – child, **"dzieci"** – childs.
T: Children. **Nie ma żadnego –s.** < *there isn't any –s* >**To jest nieregularna liczba mnoga.** < *it's irregular plural* >

The teacher elicits the singular form *child* by means of translation. On this basis, the learner (S1) is given a chance to reformulate his answer and perform self-correction. But the clue aimed to increase awareness of the exception to the rule appears to draw the learner's attention to the regular plural morpheme more than to the vocalic alternation. In any case, it is not certain whether S1 is thus able to revise prior knowledge.

A metalinguistic comment also happens to be the longest feedback turn provided by the native-speaker teacher in the learner's L1 in the dyadic exchange displayed as Extract 5. But the difference is that the instructor first negotiates repair in L2 and switches codes only when this attempt fails.

Extract 5 (adult student; L2 = Polish, L1 = English)

> T: Czy możesz powiedzieć, co to jest neurologia? < *can you tell*
> *[me] what neurology is?* >
> S: To jest– To takie są badania na głowę, jak ktoś straca
> przytomność. < *it's when– those are tests of the head when*
> *someone loses* [WRONG FORM] *consciousness* >
> T: Jak ktoś co? < *when someone what?* >
> S: Utraca przytomność? < *has lost* [WRONG FORM] *consciousness?* >
> T: **Look. You can only use the perfective with the past or the**
> **complex future tense, but not with the present. Drop the**
> **prefix.**
> S: Jak ktoś traca przytomność? < *when someone loses* [WRONG
> FORM] *consciousness?* >
> T: **Not bad, not bad, but try again**.
> S: Straci. < *has lost* >[CORRECT FORM]
> T: Chryste! Traci. < *Christ! loses* >

As shown above, when the teacher switches to English (the student's
L1), he chooses a metalinguistic clue instead of strategic mediation,
which would be in order given such a complex issue as aspect in Polish
(L2). What is more, this prescriptive attitude causes the teacher to
overlook efficient self-repair in the learner's final turn which he does not
accept on the grounds of the bid not conforming to his rule. Besides, the
feedback offered in the form of encouragement is misleading, since
the learner has actually approximated the target form by dropping the
perfective prefix of her previous attempt without still arriving at
the solution. It appears that the teacher's reaction at that stage is
affective rather than cognitive. The final observation is that negotiated
repair slows down the progression of this interaction.

Metacommunication, also called metatalk and defined in the
literature (e.g. Chaudron, 1988: 87) as discourse concerned with the
linguistic code and the content of teaching, is still the main issue in
the next few examples in which we look at bilingual exchanges
in student–student dyads. For example, in Extract 6, learners involved
in a collaborative task in L2 digress from it briefly in order to negotiate
repair in L1 in a lateral sequence. In the course of this interaction,
going through a series of approximations to the target form, S1 is
finally able to perform self-correction thanks to working with a more
capable peer (S2).

Extract 6 (adult students; L2 = English, L1 = Polish)

> S1:   So leader one party must to agree with the leader ah the other
> party.
> S2:   **Poczekaj, coś nie tak**. < *wait, something [is] wrong* >

S1:   Another party? The another?
S2:   **Nie o to chodzi.** < *that's not the point* >The leader–
S1:   **Z przyimkiem?** < *with a preposition?* > The leader of one party?
S2:   **Rezczownik musi być z apostrofem.** < *the noun has to have an apostrophe* >
S1:   **No to już.** < *here we go* >The leader of one's party. **Albo** < *or* >of one party's leader?
S2:   One party's–
S1:   One party's leader.

Faerch (1985: 190) wrote that metatalk is 'an important heuristic tool to be used for eliciting information about the FL'. While it would be unrealistic to expect students sharing a common L1 to engage in metacommunication in L2, their joint achievement in the excerpt quoted above is that they can make successful use of metalanguage and solve the problem without the teacher's intervention. It also has to be said that one learner turns out to act as tutor towards the other.

Tutor talk (cf. Flanigan, 1991) is even more forcibly illustrated in Extract 7 (after Majer, 2003: 144–146) – another example of bilingual interaction between two students involved in a collaborative task. Going over a pre-reading activity, they are supposed to find out from each other whether they believe in the supernatural, are superstitious and so on. For this reason, they are going over a checklist. The questions from the textbook and the elicited answers are naturally in L2, but most of the tutor talk and negotiation of repair coincides with the participants' switches to L1. In the course of this exchange, S2 appears to derive a lot in terms of learning by profiting from S1's corrective feedback and task management.

Extract 7 (senior secondary school students; L2 = English, L1 = Polish)

S1:   Do you believe in ghosts?
S2:   **Nie, to ja miałam cię spytać!** < *but it's my turn to ask you* >
S1:   **Wszystko jedno.**   [**No to**– < *never mind. so*– >
S2:   [Do you afraid of ghosts?
S1:   **Nie** afraid. **Nie chodzi o to, czy się boję, tylko czy wierzę.** < *not 'afraid'. it's not about whether I am afraid, but whether I believe* > Do I believe in ghosts? No, I don't. What about you?
S2:   I don't believe in ghosts too.
S1:   Are you at all superstitious?
S2:   **Co to jest**– supers-**co?** < *what's that 'supers-what'?* >
S1:   Superstitious **to jest przymiotnik od** superstition, **czyli 'zabobonny'.**
       < *'superstitious' is an adjective from* 'superstition', *that is* 'superstitious' >

S2: **Przesądny?** < *fearful?* >
S1: **Też.** < *[that] as well* > OK, so ask me a question if I am superstitious.
S2: Are you superstitious?
S1: Yes, I am afraid of the black cat. What about you?
S2: I am superstitious of thirteen – number thirteen.
S1: 'Superstitious' **to chyba będzie z** 'about'. < *I think you need* 'about' *with* 'superstitious' > OK, so have you ever had or know someone who has had a supernatural experience?
S2: 'Supernatural' **to jest właściwie co?** < *what's* 'supernatural', *anyway?* >
S1: **Nadprzyrodzony.** < *supernatural* >
S2: **Że niby jakieś doświadczenie nadprzyrodzone?** < *sort of like supernatural experience?* >
S1: **Nieważne, powiedzmy, że nie. Dalej:** < *never mind, let's say it's not. [let's] go on:* > Do you believe in telepathy and premonitions of the future?
S2: **Telepatia i co? Co to jest** 'premonitious' [*sic*: premonitions]? < *telepathy and what? what does it mean* 'premonitious'? >
S1: Premonitions. **Zobacz, tu jest napisane** < *look, it's written here* > (SHOWS WORD IN TEXTBOOK). **To nie jest przymiotnik tak jak** superstitious, **tylko rzeczownik w liczbie mnogiej.** < *it isn't an adjective like* 'superstitious', *but a plural noun* >
S2: **Ale co znaczy?** < *but what does it mean?* >
S1: **Jak się ma takie, no, złe przeczucie.** < *when you have, what's the word, a premonition* >
S2: No, I am not.

In the foreign language classroom, scaffolded negotiations over task completion going on in pairs or small groups are typically bilingual, particularly when no monitoring is involved. Yet, as evidenced above, even without the teacher's supervision, input and output opportunities for the learners can be substantial, with potential learning effects not only in terms of enhancing the development of metalinguistic terminology.

A similar exchange is represented by Extract 8. But although the participants' roles appear to be the same, code-switching is not directly related to the use of metalanguage, presumably due to the learners' lack of sophistication in this respect. On the other hand, there is negotiation of form which proceeds smoothly thanks to S2 tutoring S1.

Extract 8 (junior secondary school students; L2 = English, L1 = Polish)

S1: In the city centre it's difficult to find a parking.
S2: Parking **no to nie.** < *is out* >

S1: **A niby dlaczego nie** < *and why would that not [be]* >parking?
S2: **Bo nie. Właśnie że nie jest tak samo, tylko ten, no–**
< *because. it actually happens not to be the same, only what's the name–* >
S1: Par cark. **Tfu!** < *oops* > Park car.
S2: **Chyba coś odwrotnie.** < *I think it's the other way round* >
S1: Car park.

In contrast to 7 and 8, the next example (partly adapted from Scott & de la Fuente, 2008: 105) involves learners of equal competence and it shows how a form-focused oral task can be transformed into a consciousness-raising activity. Even though the interactants in this bilingual exchange (Extract 9 below) engage in metatalk, interlingual comparisons and translation, they still make the effort to practise speaking L2 for communication.

Extract 9 (adult students; L2 = Spanish, L1 = English)

S1:   Pues– yo pienso que 'que' < *well– I think that 'that'* > **is like 'that' in English, you know? Like** 'una ciudad que muchas turistas visitan' **is like–** es como **'a city that many tourists visit'. It's the same thing, right? I mean,** en español, es la misma cosa, ¿sí? < *in Spanish it's the same thing, right?* >
S2:   Sí, sí, y también 'los turistas que yo veo' es– < *yes, yes, and also 'the tourists that I see' is–* >
S1:   **'The tourists that I see'.**
S2:   'Cuyas' **is–** es– **'whose', like 'whose' in English,** porque < *because* > 'ciudad cuyas ruinas'– **'city whose ruins'–**
S1:   **Yes,** sí, y– un amigo < *yes, and– a friend* > **whose name is Roberto.**

What also makes this heuristic learning experience different from the samples discussed so far is that while reflecting about grammar the students are able to express their observations in L2, not just in L1. That is because, as Scott and de la Fuente (2008: 109) conclude, owing to the activation of the two linguistic systems and sources of knowledge, processes such as reading, thinking, and speaking appear to be simultaneous and integrated.

A certain modification of the bilingual system described in this study can be found in Extract 10 (partly adapted from Ife, 2007: 85). Here, upon encountering a communication problem, the learner switches to L3 for the simple reason that the L2 course is organized in a lingua franca English environment, it involves a heterogeneous multilingual class, while the teacher does not appear to understand the learner's L1.

Extract 10 (adult students; L2 = Spanish, L3 = English, L1 = no data)

> **T:** Doscientas fans. ¿Qué me podéis decir de los fans? Doscien-
> tas– ¿Por qué doscientas? < *two hundred* [FEMININE] *fans.*
> *what can you tell me of the fans? two hundred*—[FEMININE] *why*
> *two hundred* [FEMININE]*?* >
>
> **S:** **It's a number, no?**
>
> **T:** Sí es la cantidad, pero no dice 'doscientos', dice 'doscientas'
> fans. " < *yes, it's the quantity, but he doesn't say 'two hundred'*
> [MASCULINE], *he says 'two hundred'* [FEMININE] >
>
> **S:** **They are all female.**
>
> **T:** Sí, son todas chicas. < *yes, they are all girls* >

Adhering to Spanish and accepting the learner's contributions in a system other than the target language, the native-speaker teacher manages what might be called parallel talk (Majer, 2003: 408). It is a rather liberal approach to code-switching in classroom discourse, since while the instructor pursues the strategic goal of communicative language teaching by using L2 only, the learner is free to expresses herself in either L2 or L3. Still, even though communication is form-focused, neither of the student's turns seems conceptually or linguisti-cally complicated to justify the switch. Ife (2007: 85) concludes that the learner might have believed that to say for example *They are all female* sounded more sophisticated in lingua franca English than in L2.

As shown in Extract 10, parallel talk does not really involve language alternation within the same utterance, or indeed any translation. Complete utterances are expressed uniformly since L2 and L1 (L3) are clearly separated. That is why communication appears to be very efficient, which makes parallel talk seem much more natural than some other categories of bilingual classroom discourse described in this section of the chapter. However, not all instructors are prepared to respect the ecological rights of the learners' L1, and so in more mixed interactions there can be teacher feedback in L2 functioning as a gloss for the student's answer. A typical example is given below (after Majer, 2003: 409–410).

Extract 11 (senior secondary school students; L2 = English, L1 = Polish)

> **S:** **To chyba będzie drut kolczasty.** < *I think it's barbed wire* >
>
> **T:** Is that right? OK, so why don't you say it in English?
>
> **S:** **Ale nie wiem jak jest 'drut kolczasty'.** < *but I don't know how*
> *to say 'barbed wire'* >
>
> **T:** Oh, but you can try to say it in your own words.
>
> **S:** Some kind of wire. With uh– Like in concentration camps.
>
> **T:** OK, listen class. Janek here thinks DeKalb, Illinois is famous
> for the invention of barbed wire.

S: **Ale nie na sto procent.** < *but [I'm not] one hundred percent [certain]* >

T: What's that you said?

S: I'm not sure.

In Extract 11, the teacher acknowledges the student's turns expressed wholly in L1, yet she also issues reminders that it is his task to try and engage in negotiated interaction in L2. This actually results in the learner's reformulations which, even if somewhat reduced proposition-ally as communication strategies, nonetheless render the intended meaning. The student's effort, in turn, is rewarded with teacher feedback which provides the target phrase *barbed wire*. In this way, bilingual interaction achieves its pedagogical goal without interrupting the flow of talk (cf. Söderberg Arnfast & Jørgensen, 2003: 44). There is less negotiation in an exchange, hence greater facilitation of discourse progression.

However, language policies in the L2 classroom are not always as neat as shown above. Non-native teachers can sometimes send confusing and conflicting signals that negatively influence not just language pedagogy, but also sociolinguistic patterns of classroom interaction, as well as the learners' confidence. For example, the teacher in Extract 12 moves between L1 and L2, using both alternational and insertional switches, while – ironically – dealing with the very problem of language policy in classroom interaction.

Extract 12 (junior secondary school students; L2 = English, L1 = Polish)

T: **Cicho!** < *quiet!* >OK, one condition, **jeden warunek.** < *one condition* >

S: We don't speak Polish.

T: We don't speak Polish, that's one thing. Number two, **to już mogę wam powiedzieć po polsku, bo by było za trudno po angielsku.** < *that one I might as well tell you in Polish, because it would be too difficult in English* >

Another complication is that the pupils' linguistic rights do not extend as far as the teacher's. In other words, tolerance of unrestricted language choice on their part would almost certainly not be reciprocated. Furthermore, the cognitive message communicated by the teacher's bilingual instructions is that it may not be worth trying to restructure or reformulate discourse in L2 if what one intends to express appears to be rather complex. Finally, this kind of disorderly approach is generally discouraged by language teaching methodologists.

On the other hand, the code-switching system displayed above would not be considered artificial in naturalistic bilingual discourse or even in less typical educational settings such as native speaker–non-native speaker encounters arranged for communicative and cross-cultural purposes. Our next example in the present discussion (Extract 13; partly adapted from Holtzer, 2003: 48) illustrates precisely that situation.

Extract 13 (adult student; L2 = French, L1 = English)

> **NS:** J'ai un petit frère de 24 ans. Tu comprends? < *I've a younger brother who is 24. do you understand?* >
> **NSS:** Oui. < *yes* >
> **NS:** Qui vit á Singapour. < *who lives in Singapore* >
> **NNS:** (SILENCE)
> **NS:** Singapour. **Singapore**.
> **NNS:** Oh oui. < *oh yes* >

The cooperative strategy employed by the native speaker to overcome a communication breakdown is another instance of code-switching, namely replacing a L2 lexical item with its counterpart in L1. In terms of the alternational mechanism underlying the sub-category in question, the native speaker's bilingual utterance would not be different from a few instances already dealt with in the present study. However, it seems that in this case the only problem blocking comprehension is an unfamiliar pronunciation of the otherwise familiar place name.

Commenting on the simple incidence of lexical substitution, Holtzer (2003) writes: 'Such examples of code-switching as a communication strategy are relatively common in exolingual-bilingual interactions. We suspect that they are much less frequent in the language classroom where such strategies are rarely accepted' (p. 48). However, contrary to this claim, language classrooms are very typical environments for bilingual sequences (cf. Py, 1992), particularly in teacher talk. Such is the structure and content of the interaction in the final excerpt (partly adapted from Moore, 2002: 282) in our analysis of sociocultural aspects of language alternation. The only difference with respect to Extract 13 is the opposite directionality – from the learners' L1 to L2.

Extract 14 (primary school students; L2 = French, L1 = Spanish)

> **T:** Comment s'appellent? < *what do you call them?* >
> **S:** **Las frambuesas**. < *raspberries* >
> **T:** ¿**Las frambuesas**? Les framboises. < *raspberries? raspberries* >

In Extract 14, the bilingual sequence is made up of formal and semantic counterparts within a pair of closely related languages. Owing to this, the teacher's reaction to the student's response can be considered as a simple reminder that many lexical items in L2 and L1 are not too far apart – a consciousness-raising move. Moore (2002) argues that 'the echoing in Spanish on the part of the teacher and her rising tone in French both accentuate and emphasize the new data offered to the learner' (p. 282).

Implications

In order to sum up the foregoing considerations and ponder pedagogical implications going beyond the scope of the present chapter, we can formulate the following concluding remarks:

- Code-switching in pedagogic discourse deserves to be investigated because besides being an intriguing language contact phenomenon (cf. de Bot, 2002) it is simply widespread across foreign language classrooms. For example, it follows from the observations made by Polio and Duff (1994) and van der Meij and Zhao (2010) that the actual use of L1 by non-native teachers may be many times more frequent and longer than those teachers' declared bilingual practices.
- Apart from research on the structural patterns of bilingual interaction, the study of code-switching in classroom communication offers insights into cognitive processes underlying language learning and problem-solving strategies. One way of discovering how learners deal with such challenges could be analyzing meta-comments about linguistic tasks made in the form of private speech.
- The goal of present-day language pedagogy, both mainstream and integrated with content-based instruction, is to educate bilingual speakers. If so, then learners should be given the opportunity to experiment with using L2 and L1 in the same speech situation (Liebscher & Dailey-O'Cain, 2005: 245) and exploit their communicative resources in ways that resemble naturalistic bilingual and multilingual discourse.
- The sociocultural approach to language learning is generally opposed to methodologies which advocate the monolingual constraint, that is the 'L2-only' classroom policy, since L1 deprivation of for example younger learners is believed to negatively affect the process of cognitive development by posing unnecessary obstacles to concepts and knowledge already stored in L1 (Macaro, 2001: 531).
- Among the factors most frequently triggering code-switching in both teacher–student and student–student exchanges is negotiated repair (Majer, 2008: 87). Such interactions often involve metacommunication which, in turn, requires language awareness and knowledge of terminology.
- When engaging in repair and metatalk, language instructors often exploit bilingual resources by setting translation tasks. However, such sequences tend to interrupt the progression of interaction.
- In collaborative tasks, better students act as tutors to less able students building metaphorical scaffolds and providing corrective feedback.

References

Antón, M. and DiCamilla, F.J. (1999) Socio-cognitive functions of L1 collaborative interaction in the L2 classroom. *Modern Language Journal* 83, 233–247.

Atkinson, D. (1993) *Teaching Monolingual Classes*. London: Longman.

Baker, C. (2001) *Foundations of Bilingual Education and Bilingualism* (3rd edn). Clevedon: Multilingual Matters.

Björk-Willén, P. (2008) Routine trouble: How preschool children participate in multilingual instruction. *Applied Linguistics* 29, 555–577.

Björklund, S. and Suni, I. (2000) The role of English as L3 in a Swedish immersion programme in Finland: Impacts on language teaching and language relations. In J. Cenoz and U. Jessner (eds) *English in Europe. The Acquisition of a Third Language* (pp. 198–221). Clevedon: Multilingual Matters.

Blyth, C. (1995) Redefining the boundaries of language use: The foreign language classroom as a multilingual speech community. In C. Kramsch (ed.) *Redefining the Boundaries of Language Study* (pp. 145–183). Boston: Heinle.

Buckwalter, P. (2001) Repair sequences in Spanish L2 dyadic discourse: A descriptive study. *Modern Language Journal* 85, 380–397.

Butzkamm, W. (1998) Code-switching in a bilingual history lesson: The mother tongue as a conversational lubricant. *International Journal of Bilingual Education and Bilingualism* 1, 81–99.

Chaudron, C. (1988) *Second Language Classrooms: Research on Teaching and Learning*. Cambridge: Cambridge University Press.

Cook, V.J. (2001) Using the first language in the classroom. *Canadian Modern Language Review* 57, 402–423.

Creese, A. and Blackledge, A. (2010) Translanguaging in the bilingual classroom: A pedagogy for learning and teaching? *Modern Language Journal* 94, 103–115.

Cummins, J. (2003) Bilingual education: Basic principles. In J.M. Dewaele, A. Housen and Li Wei (eds) *Bilingualism. Beyond Basic Principles. Festschrift in Honour of Hugo Baetens Beardsmore* (pp. 56–66). Clevedon: Multilingual Matters.

Cummins, J. (2005) A proposal for action: Strategies for recognizing heritage language competence as a learning resource within the mainstream classroom. *Modern Language Journal* 89, 585–592.

Cummins, J. (2008) Teaching for transfer: Challenging the two solitudes assumption in bilingual education. In J. Cummins and N.H. Hornberger (eds) *Encyclopedia of Language and Education: Vol. 5. Bilingual Education* (2nd edn, pp. 65–75). Boston: Springer.

Dalton-Puffer, C. (2007) *Discourse in Content and Language Integrated Learning (CLIL) Classrooms*. Amsterdam: John Benjamins.

Daniels, H. (2001) *Vygotsky and Pedagogy*. London: Routledge.

Davies, B. (2005) Communities of practice: Legitimacy and choice. *Journal of Sociolinguistics* 9, 557–581.

de Bot, K. (2002) Cognitive processes in bilinguals: Language choice and code-switching. In R. Kaplan (ed.) *The Oxford Handbook of Applied Linguistics* (pp. 287–300). Oxford: Oxford University Press.

Eckert, P. and Wenger, É. (2005) Communities of practice in sociolinguistics. What is the role of power in sociolinguistic variation? *Journal of Sociolinguistics* 9, 582–589.

Eldridge, J. (1996) Code-switching in a Turkish secondary school. *ELT Journal* 50, 303–311.

Faerch, C. (1985) Meta-talk in FL classroom discourse. *Studies in Second Language Acquisition* 7, 184–199.

Flanigan, B. (1991) Peer tutoring and second language acquisition in the elementary school. *Applied Linguistics* 12, 141–158.

García, O. (2007) Foreword. In S. Makoni and A. Pennycook (eds) *Disinventing and Reconstituting Languages* (pp. xi–xv). Clevedon: Multilingual Matters.

Gumperz, J.J. (1972) Introduction. In J.J. Gumperz and D. Hymes (eds) *Directions in Sociolinguistics* (pp. 1–25). New York: Holt, Rinehart and Winston.

Halmari, H. (2004) Codeswitching patterns and developing discourse competence in L2. In D. Boxer and A.D. Cohen (eds) *Studying Speaking to Inform Second Language Learning* (pp. 115–148). Clevedon: Multilingual Matters.

Harbord, J. (1992) The use of the mother tongue in the classroom. *ELT Journal* 46, 350–355.

Harding-Esch, E. and Riley, P. (2003) *The Bilingual Family. A Handbook for Parents* (2nd edn). Cambridge: Cambridge University Press.

Helot, C. and Young, A. (2002) Bilingualism and language education in French primary school: Why and how should migrant languages be valued? *International Journal of Bilingual Education and Bilingualism* 5, 96–112.

Holmes, J. and Stubbe, M. (2004) Strategic code-switching in New Zealand workplaces. Scaffolding, solidarity and identity construction. In J. House and J. Rehbein (eds) *Multilingual Communication* (pp. 133–154). Amsterdam: John Benjamins.

Holtzer, G. (2003) Learning culture by communicating: Native-non-native speaker telephone interactions. In M. Byram and P. Grundy (eds) *Context and Culture in Language Teaching and Learning* (pp. 43–50). Clevedon: Multilingual Matters.

Hornberger, N.H. (2003) Afterword: Ecology and ideology in multilingual classrooms. In A. Creese and P. Martin (eds) *Multilingual Classroom Ecologies. Inter-relationships, Interactions and Ideologies* (pp. 136–142). Clevedon: Multilingual Matters.

Hymes, D. (1974) *Foundations of Sociolinguistics: An Ethnographic Approach.* Philadelphia: University of Pennsylvania Press.

Ife, A. (2007) A role for English as lingua franca in the foreign language classroom? In E. Alcón Soler and M.P. Safont Jordà (eds) *Intercultural Language Use and Language Learning* (pp. 79–100). Dordrecht: Springer.

Labov, W. (1972) *Sociolinguistic Patterns.* Oxford: Blackwell.

Lantolf, J.P. (2006) Sociocultural theory. State of the art. *Studies in Second Language Acquisition* 28, 67–109.

Leggarreta, D. (1977) Language choice in bilingual classrooms. *TESOL Quarterly* 11, 9–16.

Liebscher, G. and Dailey-O'Cain, J. (2005) Learner code-switching in the content-based foreign language classroom. *Modern Language Journal* 89, 234–247.

Lo, A. (1999) Codeswitching, speech community membership, and the construction of ethnic identity. *Journal of Sociolinguistics* 3, 461–479.

Macaro, E. (2001) Analysing student teachers' codeswitching in foreign language classrooms: Theories and decision making. *Modern Language Journal* 85, 531–548.

Majer, J. (2003) *Interactive Discourse in the Foreign Language Classroom.* Łódź: Wydawnictwo Uniwersytetu Łódzkiego.

Majer, J. (2006) Code-switching in classroom talk: A continuing controversy of language pedagogy. In J. Zybert (ed.) *Issues in Foreign Language Learning and Teaching* (pp. 124–146). Warszawa: Wydawnictwo Uniwersytetu Warszawskiego.

Majer, J. (2008) Negotiation of form in foreign-language classroom discourse. In M. Pawlak (ed.) *Investigating English Language Learning and Teaching* (pp. 79–94). Poznań-Kalisz: Adam Mickiewicz University.

Majer, J. (2009) A pedagogical evaluation of intra-sentential code-switching patterns in L2 classroom talk. *Research in Language* 7, 31–42.

Martin, P. (2003) Bilingual encounters in the classroom. In J.M. Dewaele, A. Housen and Li Wei (eds) *Bilingualism. Beyond Basic Principles. Festschrift in Honour of Hugo Baetens Beardsmore* (pp. 67–87). Clevedon: Multilingual Matters.

Martin-Jones, M. and Saxena, M. (2003) Bilingual resources and 'Funds of Knowledge' for teaching and learning in multi-ethnic classrooms in Britain. In A. Creese and P. Martin (eds) *Multilingual Classroom Ecologies. Inter-relationships, Interactions and Ideologies* (pp. 107–122). Clevedon: Multilingual Matters.

Matras, Y. (2009) *Language Contact*. Cambridge: Cambridge University Press.

Moore, D. (2002) Case study. Code-switching and learning in the classroom. *International Journal of Bilingual Education and Bilingualism* 5, 279–293.

Myers-Scotton, C. (2006) *Multiple Voices: An Introduction to Bilingualism*. Oxford: Blackwell.

Niżegorodcew, A. (1998) Uses of L1 in L2 acquisition/learning. In J. Arabski (ed.) *Studies in Foreign Language Learning and Teaching* (pp. 21–33). Katowice: Wydawnictwo Uniwersytetu Śląskiego.

Niżegorodcew, A. (2007) *Input for Instructed L2 Learners. The Relevance of Relevance*. Clevedon: Multilingual Matters.

Polio, C.G. and Duff, P.A. (1994) Teachers' language use in university FL classrooms: A qualitative analysis of English and TL alternation. *Modern Language Journal* 78, 313–326.

Py, B. (1992) Regards croisés sur les discours du bilingue et de l'apprenant ou retour sur le rôle de la langue maternelle dans l'acquisition d'une langue seconde. *LIDIL* 6, 9–25.

Romaine, S. (1995) *Bilingualism* (2nd edn). Oxford: Blackwell Publishing.

Sanz, C. (2008) Predicting enhanced L3 learning in bilingual contexts: The role of biliteracy. In C. Pérez-Vidal, M. Juan-Garau and A. Bel (eds) *A Portrait of the Young in the New Multilingual Spain* (pp. 220–240). Clevedon: Multilingual Matters.

Schweers, C.W., Jr. (1999) Using L1 in the L2 Classroom. *English Teaching Forum* 37, 6–13.

Scott, V.M. and de la Fuente, M.J. (2008) What's the problem? L2 learners' use of the L1 during consciousness-raising, form-focused tasks. *Modern Language Journal* 92, 100–113.

Seligson, P. (1997) *Helping Students to Speak*. London: Richmond Publishing.

Söderberg Arnfast, J. and Jørgensen J.N. (2003) Code-switching as a communication, learning, and social negotiation strategy in first-year learners of Danish. *International Journal of Applied Linguistics* 13, 23–53.

Üstünel, E. and Seedhouse, P. (2005) Why that, in that language, right now? Code-switching and pedagogical focus. *International Journal of Applied Linguistics* 15, 302–325.

van der Meij, H. and Zhao, X. (2010) Codeswitching in English courses in Chinese universities. *Modern Language Journal* 94, 396–411.

Willis, J. (1981) *Teaching English through English*. London: Longman.

Winford, D. (2003) *An Introduction to Contact Linguistics*. Oxford: Wiley-Blackwell.

Chapter 6

Speaking in English for Academic Purposes in the Light of Lingua Franca English and Sociocultural Theory

ANNA NIŻEGORODCEW

Introduction

Non-native academics speak and write more and more frequently in English as a language of international communication. Both writing and speaking in English for academic purposes (EAP) as a process which can be analysed has become a research subject of numerous studies (e.g. Zalewski, 2004). The term *English for academic purposes* usually refers to a genre of the English language as it is used, and consequently, taught to non-native higher education students preparing to study in English, according to English language native academic norms (in most cases British or American) (e.g. Dudley-Evans & St John, 1998; Gillet, 1996; Jordan, 1996).

In view of a rising interest in the study of non-native uses of English for international communication, also known as *lingua franca English* (ELF) (e.g. Grzega, 2005; House, 2003; Jenkins, 2007; Saraceni, 2008; Seidlhofer, 2006; Seidlhofer & Jenkins, 2008) and the developments of sociocultural second language acquisition (SLA) theory (e.g. Block, 2003; Lave & Wenger, 1991; Wenger, 1998; Young, 2009), it seems that speaking in EAP can also be perceived in the light of ELF theory and sociocultural approaches to SLA and use.

The aim of the present chapter, a contribution to a volume focused on speaking in a second and foreign language, is to propose a new view of the study of EAP use. It is proposed that it can be viewed not only from a pedagogical target language perspective but also from a pragmatic perspective, as a specific type of non-native discourse co-constructed in interaction.

Lingua Franca English

What can be observed in the last few years is a growth of scholarly interest in the status and function of English as an international language, that is ELF. Among the authors who have involved themselves in the defence of a separate status of ELF are Barbara Seidlhofer and Jennifer Jenkins. In opposition to Interlanguage theory (Selinker, 1972), they claim that comprehensible non-native English should be accepted in its own right as a language of international communication, and native speakers are not in a position to assess it by comparing it with their norms (Seidlhofer & Jenkins, 2008). Similarly, ELF theorists are not interested in the development of ELF towards the native target, since they argue that the criterion of intelligibility is enough to warrant ELF the status of language of international communication.

On the one hand, such a view seems to be politically correct in Europe, and indeed, as has been argued by House (2003), ELF as the main European language for communication is not a threat to multilingual Europe, where national languages are used in a different role – as languages for national identification. On the other hand, however, it could be claimed in the light of sociocultural theory that ELF speakers acquire a new identity or a new status as members of an 'academic community of practice' (Wenger, 1998). I would like to provide arguments that speaking in EAP strengthens the sense of a new identity.

According to Singleton and Aronin, 'English has (...) permeated the sense of identity of large number of non-native speakers to the extent that it is now "owned" by them' (Singleton & Aronin, 2007: 13) The authors further claim that this new identity of non-native users refers to their behaviour towards the English language, decisions they take to use it or not, and in what circumstances. In other words, the authors stress the role that English plays nowadays in non-native discourses. I believe that this claim can also be extended to EAP speakers in international settings.

English has become a relatively easy tool of international communication. Its apparent learning facility lies, on the one hand, in its grammatical system – its morpho-syntactic simplicity at the beginner level, and, on the other hand, in the approved teaching/learning approach associated with English language teaching – the Communicative Approach, in which the stress is put on more or less fluent communication, and not on the accuracy of language forms and meanings. It seems that one of the basic principles of the Communicative Approach – teaching language through communication (Widdowson, 1978) – has facilitated the process of paying attention rather to the function of language than its form.

The fundamental question about ELF is whether it should be treated as a universal variety of English, a variety limited to a particular region of the world (e.g. Europe), or alternatively, as the function of English used by speakers of other native languages (Saraceni, 2008: 25). In Saraceni's view:

> there has been too much emphasis on the *form* of English as a lingua franca and not enough on its function (...) questions that need to be

asked should address how people in the Expanding Circle[1] relate to English, what it represents to them, as it relocates itself from a foreign language to a lingua franca. (Saraceni, 2008: 26)

With reference to the ELF form, a distinction should be made between ELF on a low level and on an advanced level. On the low level, ELF may mean a simplified and/or distorted code used by non-native speakers who do not aspire to near-native proficiency and more formal registers. In this sense, ELF can even be compared with pidgin English. On the advanced level, however, ELF refers to the non-native use of standard English, allowing for certain deviations from the native norms, such as foreign accent, using more formal registers, using certain national idiosyncrasies and code-switching, rather than committing errors. Consequently, ELF as a variety of English should not be considered per se as a simplified and/or distorted variety of English. On the contrary, on the advanced level, it can be treated as an enriched variety of English. The enrichment refers to the new meanings being assimilated into English by its non-native users.

The process of borrowing English words by non-native speakers is another aspect of the English language appropriation process. In the present globalized world, borrowing of English words by other languages is facilitated because of the powerful influences exerted on other cultures by the globalized market economy, the internet, as well as the media and popular culture. Because of these influences, English words are omnipresent in other nations' daily lives, which is frequently resented in some countries and cultures as 'English linguistic imperialism' (Phillipson, 1992). In other countries, however, the process of English language appropriation is generally accepted and welcome. Reasons why some nations resent English and others welcome it has to do with negative attitudes based on the history or present political and cultural rivalry (e.g. in France), or, alternatively, with positive attitudes based on the English language being a counterbalance for the negative experiences with other languages and cultures (e.g. in Central and Eastern Europe – English as a counterbalance for Russian and German).

With regard to the definition of ELF as 'the function of English used by non-native speakers', it is a very broad definition indeed. However, such a broad definition allows for exploratory studies and detailed observations of *how* non-native speakers from different language and culture backgrounds use ELF for their specific purposes. According to Canagarajah (2007), ELF 'is intersubjectively constructed in each specific context of interaction. (...) Therefore, it is difficult to describe this language a priori' (2007: 925). What is stressed in this claim is a transient nature of ELF as a medium of spoken interaction among non-native users of English. From my perspective, however, what is most interesting is the intersubjectivity of using ELF. Such an approach is very close to the sociocultural theory of SLA and use.

Sociocultural Theory of SLA and Use

In sociocultural theory, using a second language in a particular sociocultural context is claimed to have an impact on the process of SLA in the sense of acquiring behavioural patterns of a given language community. While the psycholinguistic approach treats language acquisition as the internalization of a verbal code, sociocultural theory goes beyond language, and encompasses both non-verbal and verbal communication patterns. What is significant from our perspective is that SLA is viewed as a functional and regulatory process in attaining a new identity of a member of a 'community of practice' (Niżegorodcew, 2006; Wenger, 1998).

For instance, Smagieł (2008) researched the attitudes of young Polish immigrants in Great Britain and their influence on SLA. On the basis of a longitudinal study, she concluded that second language development is connected with a person's success in identifying with a second language community, which, in turn, was linked with his or her personality and experiences.

In this context, the concept of 'community of practice', as introduced by Wenger (1998), and 'situated learning' as 'legitimate peripheral participation' (Lave & Wenger, 1991) further elucidate the question of speaking in EAP as a gradual process of obtaining access to an expert academic community. Although the authors were concerned with speaking in English for Occupational Purposes (EOP) rather than EAP, the conclusions that they draw from their research can also apply to EAP. According to Wenger (Young, 2009:146):

> a community of practice is formed by three essential dimensions: (a) mutual engagement in activity with other members of the community, (b) an endeavor that is considered to be of relevance to all members of the community, and (c) a repertoire of language varieties, styles, and ways of making meaning that is shared by all members of the community

On the basis of situated learning theory, Young claims that what is learned by a newcomer to a community of practice is first of all 'local practices' and 'communicative styles' characteristic of the community. The newcomer is treated as a 'legitimated' participant, first on the 'periphery' of the community and then slowly 'moving though a series of increasingly expert participant statuses as the learner's knowledge and skills develop' (Young, 2009: 150). The question arises *how* this gradual process of becoming an expert participant happens. The author does not provide a clear answer in linguistic terms. He stresses the recurrent nature of practices that are goal-directed and have their value and meaning within the community.

Applying these theoretical considerations to spoken EAP contexts, what can be observed and interpreted as the non-native 'legitimate peripheral participation' of the speakers is their professional expert status being a supporting factor in moving them towards a fuller participation in EAP discourse, thanks to a repeated nature of discursive practices in clearly delineated institutional framework acting as a community, and being directed towards a common product goal. Moving a step further, it is illuminating to treat speaking in EAP from the perspective of complex systems theory (Larsen-Freeman & Cameron, 2008). According to the authors, 'when we consider two people engaged in talk, their "conversation" emerges from the dynamics of *how* [my emphasis] they talk to each other, while what they say reflects and constructs who they are as social beings' (2008: 163). Larsen-Freeman and Cameron claim that from the complex systems perspective, discourse is a self-organizing and co-adaptive process. As they comment, '[Language] learning is not the taking in of linguistic forms by learners, but the constant adaptation of their linguistic resources in the service of mean-ing-making in response to the affordances that emerge in the commu-nicative situation, which is, in turn, affected by learners' adaptability' (2008: 135). A similar approach to interactive discourse has been proposed by Clark as 'joint actions', when people coordinate with each other in conversations (Clark, 1996).

The complex systems perspective seems to account for the fact that cooperation and understanding is frequently reached although conversa-tions are fragmentary, and in the case of non-native participants, erroneous and incomplete. It also happens in speaking in EAP, where participation patterns emerge as speakers take into account various levels and dimensions of communication. According to Larsen-Freeman and Cameron (2008: 189), relatively stable patterns that emerge in speech can be called 'speech genres'. They are stable and reflecting traditional patterns, but also variable and changing through use. In the concluding remarks the authors claim that 'it is the variability of the system that shows that it has the potential for further change and development' (2008: 253). It seems plausible to propose that genre variability and change may occur because of non-native contributions.

Speaking in EAP in International Projects

The traditional, native norm approach to EAP treats the deviant non-native forms as errors or, at best, mistakes, that is, performance slips. However, it seems that the ever-increasing number of non-native EAP face-to-face and electronic communication has resulted in liberating the EAP speakers from following strictly native standards.

As has been said, ELF can be defined more by its function than by its form. It is my claim that the same, though narrower definition can also apply to spoken EAP. In this chapter's understanding of the term, speaking in EAP refers to the function of spoken English discourse used in international academic contexts by non-native participants. EAP can be more formal and difficult if the subject and purpose of communication require it or it can be less formal and easier for less sophisticated subjects and less complex purposes. Thus, it is not the academic subject by itself that defines EAP. As the term suggests, it is also the purpose for which English is used. The general purpose of speaking in EAP is obviously communicating with an academic audience, while more particular purposes involve making presentations, participating in discussions, negotiating issues and fulfilling other functions of academic discourse.

From what has been said above it follows that speaking in EAP in international projects can be viewed as a regulatory process in attaining the status of a member of an academic community of practice. The participation in the academic community of practice is dependent on common engagement in activities which are of relevance to all members of the community and on sharing a common repertoire of language varieties, styles and ways of making meaning. This common repertoire does not mean sharing a native speaker repertoire; it rather refers to the ELF repertoire, with all the above-mentioned reservations about the status of ELF as a language variety. Although moving from the 'legitimate periphery' towards the 'centre' of participation in academic communities of practice involves the development of linguistic and communicative skills, what is particularly stressed in this perspective is a common effort of a group of speakers to co-construct meanings, variability of their speech styles and goal-oriented language activities.

What Makes Oral Communication Successful: Observations Based on Face-to-Face and E-Mail Communication in International Projects

Participation in international academic projects made me reflect on the use of English in non-native spoken communication for academic purposes. In the projects in question, nine international partners used EAP in face-to-face and electronic communication, while each national team worked on its separate work packages to reach common goals. The projects involved academics from different European countries, with different national languages used both for everyday communication and as languages of academic instruction. A successful completion of the projects required the international partners to negotiate meanings and overcome difficulties through the medium of ELF.

Some of the partners spoke fluent English, whereas others had smaller or greater difficulties with expressing their meanings in English. However, all partners were given equal opportunities to take the floor, and nobody was downgraded owing to his or her lower proficiency in English. If there were problems concerning the intelligibility of what was said by one of the partners, others tried to clarify the meaning by asking additional questions. Everybody had the same rights and obligations with respect to their active spoken and email participation in the projects. The face-to-face sessions and email communication were organized and monitored by the project coordinators, whose proficiency in English and organizational skills were very high.

One of the factors to be taken into account in searching for what makes successful communication is the context known to all participants, as well as similar education and professional experience of the participants. In analysing spoken exchanges between the project participants, it is evident that their common European academic background facilitated mutual comprehension, even if the speakers made formal errors in English. Difficulties and misunderstandings were more numerous in the case of representatives of different fields of studies (e.g. sociology vs. modern languages), and academics coming from different educational systems (e.g. Western and Eastern Europe).

The most characteristic features of EAP spoken communication based on longitudinal observations (more than two years of observations in one of the projects) are as follows:

- Spoken EAP in the projects under observation was focused on tasks that were carefully described in written English documents beforehand. The written English of the documents was rather formal, resembling official European Union documents.
- While speaking, the participants modelled their English on the language of the written documents. It concerned, in particular, the terminology used in the projects. Also, some set phrases and expressions were repeatedly used in face-to-face and e-mail communication.
- Apart from the above observation, some participants used the terms taken from their national languages (in particular Russian and French terms), anglicizing them with English morphological endings and/or phonological features.
- Some of the participants spoke less than others, but their lack of proficiency in English did not seem to play a major role in taking part in spoken communication. One of the participants, whose proficiency in English was not very high, expressed her views

quite freely. Other members, with very strong foreign accents, took active part in discussions and did not hesitate to express their views. It seems that active participation in spoken EAP exchanges corresponded with the participants' experience with public speaking in English and personality features, as well as with the roles that they played in the projects. Those playing the roles of leaders and/or experts spoke more and more frequently.

- At the beginning of one of the projects, English was not considered as the only language of international communication, as it was used side by side with French. However, it was decided soon that English should be used as the only language of communication since some of the participants did not speak French at all.
- The participants did not expect one another to know their national languages, and they did not code-switch to them. The exception was the leader of one of the projects, whose French was better than his English, who frequently code-switched to French while speaking to French partners.
- While meeting in different European countries, the participants were interested in local customs, especially those referring to phrases used during meals (*bon appétit, cheers*). Generally, however, since they stayed in international hotels and worked full time, they had few opportunities to learn local languages.
- It seems that project participants from Eastern and Central Europe felt quite at ease using ELF. Some linguistic problems in using English were observed in South-Western Europeans, for whom English did not seem to be the primary language of international communication. On the other hand, for Northern Europeans, English was treated as a strongly established second language.
- The participants of the projects displayed their own idiosyncrasies in English language use that did not interfere with the messages that they were conveying. They also used their own distinctive styles, some of them being much more formal than others.
- It could be observed that the ELF the participants spoke had been learned at school rather than acquired in a target language setting. Consequently, the use of structures was accurate, vocabulary was rich and sophisticated (in the case of more proficient partners), but the spoken language sounded more like a written variety. It lacked informal expressions and, on some occasions, fluency. In the case of EAP, however, it served its academic purposes.
- It was interesting to observe how misunderstandings and arising conflicts were solved by the coordinators of the projects. In particular, one of the coordinators displayed considerable managerial and negotiating skills. She prevented open conflicts by patient

recapitulation of the tasks and reminding the participants of the deadlines and pending requirements.

- One of the principles of the longer project was informing all partners concerned about everything currently happening. In consequence, all emails (unless sent to particular persons) started with the form of address 'Dear All'.
- The main function of speaking in EAP was achieving the proposed goals of the projects. In other words, EAP was instrumental to the general objectives of the projects, which involved designing courses of studies in European universities.

Conclusions

In the international projects under consideration, spoken EAP was used in face-to-face and e-communication in order to achieve academic goals, the most important of them being designing academic courses. On the basis of a short literature survey, the conclusion was drawn that ELF can be understood both as a variety and a function of English. Since in the concept of EAP, language forms are subordinated to language functions, a pragmatic approach to EAP seems to be appropriate, especially when EAP is viewed not as a target language genre to be developed by non-native higher education students who have chosen to study in English, but as 'spoken English used in international academic contexts by non-native participants in order to achieve their academic purposes'. Some recent theoretical approaches to the study of SLA and second language use, such as sociocultural SLA theory, discursive practice theory, and complexity theory, seem to support the claim that speaking in EAP can be viewed as a regulatory process in identifying with an academic community of practice.

The question that was asked concerned successful oral communication in EAP. Being a participant of international educational projects, the author made longitudinal observations of face-to-face communications and analysed e-communication. The conclusions that were drawn from the observations and analyses refer both to the form and the function of EAP. In terms of proficiency, the participants' EAP was varied, from an intermediate to very advanced level. However, the individual proficiency levels were not assessed and did not affect the overall success of the project communication. The participants helped one another in reaching the project aims, and what was assessed were the goals of the projects rather than the linguistic competence of the participants.

To sum up, I believe that studying speaking in EAP in the light of ELF and sociocultural theory is useful since it broadens our theoretical and research perspectives. However, a pedagogical target language perspective cannot be disregarded by language teachers. The following remarks are devoted to teaching speaking in EAP.

Pedagogical Implications

Teachers must ask practical questions about the norms of the language to be taught and about recommended approaches to teaching spoken EAP. Clearly, there is a difference between familiarizing advanced students of English with standard non-native English and tolerating the non-standard English being used by these students. As claimed by Risager (2007: 197), non-standard forms can be taught for reception rather than production at an advanced stage. According to the author, language learners should be first acquainted with native norms of accuracy and appropriateness to be later able to consciously modify them. Interestingly, one of the proponents of the radical treatment of ELF as a variety of English, Jennifer Jenkins, admits that what she advocates refers to teaching recognition of ELF, and not necessarily its production (Seidlhofer & Jenkins, 2008).

It seems that in EAP courses, both native and non-native English teachers should have very clear guidelines which errors should be treated as definite errors to be corrected and which non-native deviations may be tolerated as ELF performance. Grzega claims that 'teachers should clearly distinguish several degrees of seriousness of errors/mistakes (in written texts as well as in spoken discourse)' (2005: 54). According to him, non-native standard English with elements of the lingua franca core is the least serious of deviations from the native norms. He provides lists of lingua franca core forms as they have been described for pronunciation by Jenkins (2007: 47) and for lexico-grammar by Seidlhofer (2006: 47).

However, what is listed as unproblematic for comprehension, such as for instance, not placing an article in front of nouns, may be quite consequential for EAP writers. Writers at the advanced levels of proficiency are stigmatized in more formal contexts by careless spelling and sloppy lexico-grammar. Certainly, written EAP is one of the most obvious contexts in which deviations from the native norms may have serious negative effects for non-native writers.

A question arises in what circumstances ELF non-standard forms can be used without negative consequences in speaking in EAP. It seems, as I have tried to demonstrate in this chapter, that in spoken EAP, non-native audiences are more tolerant of non-standard ELF forms, as long as the communicative discursive function of ELF is maintained. Consequently, while treating spoken EAP as ELF and putting stress on its communicative function, it would be desirable if EAP teachers made students aware of the factors that ensure greater intelligibility in spoken presentations and face-to-face communication, such as using active communicative strategies (e.g. appealing for clarification), relying on common knowledge and context and using non-verbal resources. In e-mail communication, quoting fragments of the interlocutor's mail seems to be an efficient strategy ensuring mutual understanding.

Last but not least, sociocultural aspects of speaking in EAP should be made explicit to the students. In particular, while organizing group work, teachers should make students aware of group dynamics, leadership, patterns of participation, turn-taking, presentation skills and so on. In view of sociocultural theory, students should be made aware that even if their English speaking skills are still at a low level, they are legitimate participants of the EAP community, in which their professional expertise and developing language skills will help them move from a periphery towards the centre.

Note

1. The Expanding Circle refers to the countries where English has been taught and learned as a foreign language.

References

Block, D. (2003) *The Social Turn in Second Language Acquisition.* Edinburgh: Edinburgh University Press.

Canagarajah, S. (2007) Lingua franca English, multilingual communities, and language acquisition. *The Modern Language Journal* 91, 923–939.

Clark, H. (1996) *Using Language.* Cambridge: Cambridge University Press.

Dudley-Evans, T. and St John, M. (1998) *Development in English for Specific Purposes: A Multi-disciplinary Approach.* Cambridge: Cambridge University Press.

Gillet, A. (1996) What's EAP? *IATEFL ESP SIG Newsletter* 6, 17–23.

Grzega, J. (2005) Reflections on concepts of English for Europe: British English, American English, Euro-English, Global English. *Journal of EuroLinguistix* 2, 44–64.

House, J. (2003) English as a lingua franca: A threat to multilingualism? *Journal of Sociolinguistics* 7, 556–578.

Jenkins, J. (2007) *English as a Lingua Franca: Attitude and Identity.* Oxford: Oxford University Press.

Jordan, B. (1996) There's more to EAP than meets the eye or ear. *IATEFL ESP SIG Newsletter* 7, 17–20.

Larsen-Freeman, D. and Cameron, L. (2008) *Complex Systems and Applied Linguistics.* Oxford: Oxford University Press.

Lave, J. and Wenger, E. (1991) *Situated Learning: Legitimate Peripheral Participation.* Cambridge: Cambridge University Press.

Niżegorodcew, A. (2006) Is SLA becoming a sociocultural approach? Paper presented at the 18th International Conference on Foreign/Second Language Acquisition, Szczyrk, May 2006.

Niżegorodcew, A. (2009) The sociocultural SLA world and second language acquisition in early childhood. In J. Arabski and A.Wojtaszek (ed.) *Language Learning Studies* (pp. 123–131). Katowice: Oficyna Wydawnicza WW.

Phillipson, R. (1992) *Linguistic Imperialism.* Oxford: Oxford University Press.

Risager, K. (2007) *Language and Culture Pedagogy*. Clevedon: Multilingual Matters.

Saraceni, M. (2008) English as a lingua franca: Between form and function. *English Today* 94, 20–26.

Seidlhofer, B. (2006) English as a lingua franca in the expanding circle: What it isn't. In R. Rubdy and M. Saraceni (eds) *English in the World: Global Rules, Global Roles* (pp. 40–50). London: Continuum.

Seidlhofer, B. and Jenkins, J. (2008) Reconciling multilingualism with English as a lingua franca: Realistic policy or wishful thinking? Panel discussion during the 15th World Congress of Applied Linguistics, Essen, August 2008.

Selinker, L. (1972) Interlanguage. *IRAL* 10, 209–231.

Singleton, D. and Aronin, L. (2007) The role of English in a multilingual world. In J. Arabski, D. Gabryś-Barker and A. Łyda (eds) *PASE Papers 2007: Studies in Language and Methodology of Teaching Foreign Languages* (pp. 11–21). Katowice: Para.

Smagieł, A. (2008) The acculturation process of Polish immigrants in the UK. Unpublished MA thesis, Jagiellonian University, Krakow.

Wenger, E. (1998) *Communities of Practice: Learning, Meaning and Identity*. Cambridge: Cambridge University Press.

Widdowson, H. (1978) *Teaching Language as Communication*. Oxford: Oxford University Press.

Young, R. (2009) *Discursive Practice in Language Learning and Teaching: Language Learning Monograph Series*. Chichester: Wiley-Blackwell.

Zalewski, J. (2004) *Epistemology of the Composing Process: Writing in English for General Academic Purposes*. Opole: Opole University Press.

Part 2

Speaking and Individual Variables

Near-Nativeness as a Function of Cognitive and Personality Factors: Three Case Studies of Highly Able Foreign Language Learners

ADRIANA BIEDROŃ

Introduction[1]

Reaching a near-native competence in speaking by a highly able foreign language learner is a function of many and varied factors, such as aptitude, intelligence, motivation, personality characteristics, learning experience, learning strategies and social environment. Research during the last 50 years has provided evidence that language aptitude is, besides motivation, the strongest predictor of foreign language learning success (Dörnyei, 2005). Special significance is attributed to the factor of memory, especially working memory, present in all complex cognitive functions, which constitutes an important component of contemporary foreign language aptitude models (Robinson, 2007; Skehan, 2002). Do, however, high abilities go hand in hand with a particular personality type, a style of coping with stress or locus of control? This chapter attempts to present and compare cognitive and personality factors in three case studies of highly able foreign language learners. All three learners are linguistically gifted and capable of communicating in foreign languages at a near-native level of proficiency. The first case study is of a 21-year-old student of mathematics who speaks four languages, including two languages at level C1. The second case study is of an English philology graduate – a secondary school teacher in the target language country. Her level of advancement was very highly evaluated by native speakers. The third case study is of a doctoral student – a polyglot speaking 11 languages, and proficient in four: Chinese, Arabic, English and German. The scores of the three case studies in aptitude tests – The Modern Language Aptitude Test (MLAT) (Carroll & Sapon, 2002) and the Language Ability Test (Wojtowicz, 2006) – are close to maximal. Memory test scores are also high, which indicates a capacious phonological loop, as well as an efficient central executive (Baddeley *et al.*, 1998). Nonetheless, the biographies, personalities, learning strategies and intelligence of the subjects are very different, which indicates the multiplicity of factors assisting high linguistic abilities.

High Foreign Language Abilities

Language aptitude is one of the individual difference variables that significantly contributes to success in foreign language learning (Dörnyei, 2005). There is evidence in support of the existence of exceptional foreign language learners (cf. Bongaerts *et al.*, 1997; Boxtel *et al.*, 2003; Ioup *et al.*, 1994; Morgan *et al.*, 2007; Moyer, 1999; Obler, 1989; Sawyer & Ranta, 2001; Schneiderman & Desmarais, 1988; Skehan, 1998); however, the criteria of choice, as well as research methodology, in the presented studies significantly differ.

An exceptional ability is defined as a specific complex of individual factors, emerging in early childhood in a few individuals (Callahan, 2000). The most frequently used criterion is high intelligence quotient (IQ): over 130 points. Other criteria include speed of learning, extended knowledge, early intellectual maturity and extraordinary achievements in some area, for example, science, arts or languages (Nęcka, 2003). Most researchers agree that high intellect does not guarantee a talent (cf. Skehan, 1998) and that high abilities are specific sets of individual cognitive, emotional, personal and even social features (cf. Corno *et al.*, 2002; Nęcka, 2003; Robinson, 2002, 2007). The hypothesis that abilities are not limited only to cognitive factors is reflected in contemporary psychological and second language acquisition (SLA) theories of abilities (cf. Ceci, 1996; Corno *et al.*, 2002; Perkins, 1995; Renzulli, 1986; Robinson, 2007; Sękowski, 2004; Snow *et al.*, 1996).

There is a marked paucity of research into linguistic talent or high ability and the term itself is vaguely defined. Linguistic talent is described as an exceptional ability to achieve native-like competence in a foreign language after puberty and relatively quickly (Ioup *et al.*, 1994; Skehan, 1998). A good predictor of the pace of learning, especially at the beginning stages, is a prognostic test of foreign language aptitude, the MLAT (Carroll & Sapon, 2002), which also indicates foreign language aptitude extremes (Ehrman, 1998).

Cognitive and Personality Features of Highly Able Foreign Language Learners

The relevant literature mentions an array of factors present in highly able foreign language learners (HAFLL):

(1) An extraordinary memory, especially working memory (Baddeley *et al.*, 1998; Harrington & Sawyer, 1992; Mackey *et al.*, 2002; Miyake & Friedman, 1998; Obler, 1989; Robinson, 2002; Skehan, 1998). Working

memory is necessary in all complex cognitive functions (Conway *et al.*, 2008). According to Skehan (1998), working memory is a prominent characteristic of HAFLL.

(2)   Above-average phonetic abilities, that is the ability to recognise and imitate language sounds (Bongaerts *et al.*, 1997; Ioup *et al.*, 1994; Moyer, 1999).

(3)   High intelligence, especially verbal intelligence. Analytical, reasoning and problem-solving abilities, and a fast rate of processing condition foreign language learning success, especially in a formal setting (Sasaki, 1996; Sternberg, 2002).

(4)   A high level of competence in a native language, including an extended lexicon both in speaking and in writing (Skehan, 1998; Sparks *et al.*, 1998).

(5)   Efficient language learning strategies. Evidence is provided that successful, advanced foreign language learners use more efficient, varied and complex strategies of learning, being able to adapt a strategy to a situation or a task (Droździał-Szelest, 2008; Griffiths, 2008; Pawlak, 2009).

Other features, usually associated with foreign language success, might accompany high language aptitude. These are an analytical learning style and a high tolerance of ambiguity (Ehrman & Oxford, 1995), an introverted-intuitive-thinking-judging personality type (Ehrman, 2008), internality of control (Dörnyei, 2005; Williams & Burden, 1997), high motivation (Dörnyei, 2005; Ushioda, 2008) and autonomous behaviour (Dörnyei, 2005; Little, 2004). Also, the personality trait of *Openness to experience*, that is intellectual curiosity, inventiveness, creativity, as well as *Conscientiousness*, indicating self-control, self-discipline, order, planning and perseverance, might characterise HAFLL (Dörnyei, 2005; McCrae & Costa, 2003). Moreover, emotional intelligence (Dewaele *et al.*, 2008), a task-oriented style of coping with stressful and upsetting situations (Szczepaniak *et al.*, 1996) and a low level of anxiety (Dewaele, 2007; Dewaele *et al.*, 2008; Ehrman, 2008) are likely to co-exist in HAFLL.

The literature presents group studies on exceptional foreign language speakers. They generally examine native-like attainment in L2 syntax (Boxtel *et al.*, 2003) or in pronunciation (Bongaerts *et al.*, 1997, 2000; Moyer, 1999). For pronunciation it has been shown that native-like attainment is possible to achieve for some late learners; however, all the reported cases of success referred to those learners whose L1 was typologically closely related to the L2. In the case of syntax, the conclusions are more ambiguous. In Moyer's study (1999), a learner of German was described as exceptional. The evaluation of his performance was consistently native across all tasks, despite the fact that he was first exposed to German at the age of 22, had been immersed for only 2 years and had received only a five-year instruction. His performance was evaluated as more native-like than that of native speakers. He had never learnt any languages before. He declared fascination with the language and its speakers and a very strong motivation to acculturate and to sound German. In a similar study by Bongaerts *et al.* (2000), a group of highly motivated and advanced foreign language learners was chosen specifically for their exceptional abilities by teachers who identified them as excellent speakers of L2 – English. The research provided evidence for their high proficiency – the selected subjects overlapped with native speaker controls with respect to their pronunciation skills.

The Study

Objective

The objective of this study was to describe the cognitive-affective features of three HAFLL – advanced speakers of foreign languages: foreign language aptitude, intelligence, working memory, learning styles and strategies, motivation, personality, psychological need, locus of control, stress coping style and emotional intelligence. All three subjects were near-native speakers of English. This qualitative study is part of larger-scale research aiming at a construction of a cognitive-affective profile of an HAFLL. The research procedure was conducted by two specialists: the linguistic tests by the author of this chapter and the psychological tests by a psychologist. The research complies with the qualitative and quantitative criteria of choice of a highly able learner proposed in literature (Hewston *et al.*, 2005; Skehan, 1998).

Instruments

The following instruments were used in the study:

(1) *Wechsler Adult Intelligence Scale – WAIS-R (PL)* – a Polish adaptation by Brzezinski *et al.* (1996). It consists of six verbal subtests – information, digit span, vocabulary, arithmetic, comprehension, similarities – and five performance subtests: picture completion, picture arrangement, block design, object assembly, digit symbol – coding. A general intelligence quotient, as well as verbal and non-verbal scale quotients, is obtained. At the second stage of analysis, scores for three indices: verbal comprehension, perceptual organisation, memory and resistance to distraction, are determined.

(2) *MLAT* (Carroll & Sapon, 2002). This is a language aptitude test designed to diagnose the rate of progress in a foreign language. The MLAT is a test entirely in English suitable for native and near-native speakers of English. It measures aptitude traits by five part scores: memory (parts I and V), phonetics (II), vocabulary (III) and grammar (IV).

(3) *Language Ability Test (Test Zdolności Językowych TZJ)* by Wojtowicz (2006). The test was constructed to diagnose foreign language aptitude. It includes three scales: Discourse, Vocabulary and Grammar.

(4) *Polish Reading Span (PRSPAN)* – a Polish adaptation of the American Reading Span (RSPAN) (Engle *et al.*, 1999), designed by the author of the study. In accordance with Daneman and Carpenter's (1980) classical reading span, the PRSPAN is a dual task that requires the participant to read a series of sentences and, simultaneously, to keep track of the last word displayed, so that the words can be recollected later.

(5) *The Revised NEO-Five Factor Inventory* (Costa & McCrae, 1992) – a Polish adaptation by Zawadzki *et al.* (1998) – is a psychological personality inventory; a 60-question measure of the Five Factor Model: Extraversion, Agreeableness, Conscientiousness, Neuroticism and Openness.

(6) *Adjective Check List (ACL)* (Gough & Heilbrun, 1980), a Polish adaptation by Juros *et al.* (1987), is an instrument that operationalises the concept of psychological need.

(7) *Coping Inventory for Stressful Situations (CISS)* (Endler & Parker, 1990), adapted by Szczepaniak *et al.* (1996). The inventory consists of three scales referring to coping styles: task-oriented style, emotional-oriented style and avoiding-oriented style.

(8) *Delta Questionnaire* by Drwal (1995) is a tool designed to examine the Locus of Control (LOC). The LOC scale comprises 14 statements accounting for controllability dimension in everyday situations. A high result in the controllability dimension (LOC) indicates externality of control.

(9) *Emotional Intelligence Questionnaire (INTE)* by Schutte *et al.* (1998) – a Polish adaptation by Ciechanowicz *et al.* (2000). This tool was constructed to investigate emotional intelligence, defined as the ability to recognise, understand and control one's own, as well as other people's emotions.

Four traditional SLA instruments were used: *Motivation and Strategies Questionnaire (MSQ)* (Ehrman, 1996); *Second Language Tolerance of Ambiguity Scale* (Ely, 1995); *Style Analysis Survey (SAS)* (Oxford, 1995) and *The Tyacke Profile* (Tyacke, 1998). Also, the subjects filled out a survey that included questions about biographical data.

Results

Dagmara

Dagmara is a 21-year-old student in her second year of a university-level course in mathematics. She has been learning four languages, which she has mastered to different levels of competence. English is a language that the subject mastered to a near-native level (C2 – CPE). She started to learn it when she was one year old. She started to learn German when she was 10, and achieved level C1. Her level in French after three years of learning was B1/2. A fast rate of progress in Spanish indicates her above-average aptitude; Dagmara, having participated in a 60-hour course at level A2, finished with a mark of 4.5 (on a 2–5 scale). At the moment of research, she was attending a 60-hour course at level B1. She has always received top marks for speaking. It should be noted that she has never been abroad. Moreover, a severe sight impairment makes it necessary for her to use a magnifying glass for reading. Dagmara learns foreign languages under various conditions, including being taught by parents, a private school and self-study (English), school (French and German) and a university course (Spanish). As she claims, the knowledge of one language decisively facilitates learning subsequent ones.

Motivation.   Dagmara declares a very high motivation with regard to foreign language learning; "I'm considering an interpreter's job", "Learning foreign languages brings me pleasure", "I can't imagine not being able to communicate abroad", and "I'm simply used to it – I have been learning languages since I was a child".

Educational background.   Dagmara studies mathematics. She is going to work in a branch of economics – finance.

Family background.   She started to speak very early, at the age of 10 months. She started to read when she was five. Her parents cared very much about her development, gave her educational toys and books, talked to her a lot, invented learning games and encouraged her to watch educational programmes in English. They read books to her in Polish and English.

Native language.   Dagmara has never had any problems with ortho-graphy and grammar, and was also very good at literature, always attaining top marks She reads a lot in Polish.

Preferred study conditions.   According to Dagmara, the first stages of learning should take place in a formal environment, at school or on a course, with a Polish teacher, which helps to structure knowledge. She does not consider being taught by a native speaker more efficient – on the contrary, she regards it as very chaotic. She thinks the same about learning abroad: 'It is, obviously, possible to learn to communicate in this way, but at the expense of the ability to write and understand rules in a language. Although staying among natives speakers is very good, it can by no means be a foundation for knowledge of a language.'

Learning strategies.   Dagmara prefers learning through reading and listening to texts in the target language. In her opinion, writing essays consolidates grammar rules and extends vocabulary. Her conviction is that a teacher is necessary in being taught speaking: she feels she needs a teacher 'who would talk to me, force me to formulate my thoughts and opinions. It is impossible to learn it from a recording'.

She has a very traditional view of learning grammar; doing exercises, analysing rules, learning declensions. She definitely chooses explicit instruction accompanied by various exercises. She is convinced of the necessity of correction of all mistakes in a written work. She is a perfectionist, characterised by an average ambiguity tolerance.

Dagmara has very complex and extended strategies of learning vocabulary. She uses both contextualised and decontextualised strategies. She particularly appreciates work with a text:

> I usually start with a list of words and the translation of all of them (including cases and plural forms). In the short run, such a list can be simply memorised, but I try to avoid this. I'd rather make up sentences or texts including the words. Reading texts full of new words (for example in textbooks) is very efficient. Another helpful method is to write a longer essay on a topic connected with the words I have to learn. In this way, I have to use them in my work.

She is also very concerned about her pronunciation, attributing much value to systematic practice. Summing up, she uses many learning strategies and believes that all methods are efficient in a particular context. She has a well-developed repertoire of metacognitive strategies: planning, monitoring of progress and systematic self-evaluation.

She possesses features of an autonomous learner, who knows her needs and takes responsibility for the process of learning.

Learning styles.   Global and intuitive styles prevail; auditory modality; preference for order and structure.

Self-efficacy and anxiety.   Dagmara believes that she is linguistically talented at an above-average level; however, she attributes her success to systematic effort. Her self-assessment is accurate; she attributes to herself such features as cautiousness, independence, planning, realism, and intellect. Both her language learning and communication anxiety levels are quite high.

Intelligence.   General intelligence quotient: 135 (very high); verbal scale: 143 (very high); non-verbal scale: 123 (high). The results indicate the very high intellectual potential of the subject. The profile of cognitive functions is unbalanced, with a large dominance of verbal over non-verbal abilities. It the interpretation of the psychologist, this is the result of a serious sight impairment. The profile of verbal abilities is harmonious and reaches the level of 18–19 points, which is high.

Verbal scale: information (general knowledge): 14; digit span (auditory memory): 19; vocabulary (vocabulary and the ability to define): 18; arithmetic (arithmetic reasoning, resistance to distraction, memory): 18; comprehension (a knowledge and interpretation of social norms): 18; similarities (abstract thinking, generalising, analogous reasoning): 16.

Non-verbal scale results are unbalanced: picture completion (visual perception of details, distinguishing important and unimportant details): 12; picture arrangement (causal reasoning, visual–motor coordination): 13; block design (organisation of visually perceived concrete material, visual–motor coordination, visual analysis and synthesis): 18; object assembly (visual–motor coordination, visual synthesis): 12, digit symbol – coding (visual memory, pace of visual–motor learning): 13. These scores are interpreted as a result of the sight impairment (a high result in block design indicates good coordination and synthesis – and Dagmara was able to see only the blocks well).

The WAIS-R verbal comprehension index is very high: 138; perceptual organisation is high: 124; memory and resistance to distraction is also very high: 142.

Working memory.   Dagmara was able to recollect 92% of the words. This is a very high result.

Language aptitude.   The subject gained very high scores in both aptitude tests. Her results in parts I, II and V of the MLAT investigating short-term memory and phonetic abilities were maximal; in part III (vocabulary), she gained 76% and in part IV (grammar sensitivity) 64%. Comparing her results to the percentile norms for the MLAT for College Freshmen Women, she has a rank of 99. These results indicate her high phonetic abilities and excellent phonemic memory. In the Language Ability Test (TZJ), her results are placed in the 10th sten.

Personality.   The most significant feature of Dagmara is openness to experience, which means intellectual curiosity, looking for new solutions, creativity, aesthetic sensitivity and unconventionality. The second strong characteristic is conscientiousness, that is strong will, persistence in reaching goals, thoroughness, dutifulness, reliability and thoughtfulness. Dagmara is an emotionally balanced person, calm, doing well in difficult, stressful situations; her emotional reactions are adjusted to situations in which she finds herself. She is an ambivert (a balance between extroversion and introversion); she can function well in independent tasks as well as cooperate in a group. She reveals a moderate need for external stimulation and an average ability to start new social contacts.

Her most important need is the need for achievement. She is a hard-working person, determined to reach her goals. Another strong need is that of dominance – she is ambitious, decisive, consistent, stubborn and competitive. The third well-developed need is the need for order. She keeps to once established plans and dislikes obstacles.

Her emotional intelligence is quite high. However, she may have problems in interpersonal contacts because of her insecurity, low self-confidence and low need for affiliation.

Locus of control.   Internal.

Stress copying style.   A task-oriented copying style decisively dominates. This means that Dagmara does not avoid confrontation; in a stressful situation, she establishes a plan and follows it.

To sum up, Dagmara is a person linguistically competent at an above-average level. She gained especially high results in the tests of short-term and working memory, which confirms the hypothesis of extraordinary memory abilities in linguistically talented learners. She is a very intelligent person, particularly with respect to verbal abilities. She also reveals analytical and logical thinking ability, as well as a high level of phonetic ability. Dagmara is an autonomous, mature, self-aware and strategically competent learner and a talented foreign language speaker.

Joanna

Joanna is a 33-year-old Polish woman, who, at the time of the research, had lived in her target language country for seven years. She is an English philology graduate. She finished her studies with top marks. Nowadays, she uses the English language almost exclusively, both at home and at work. Joanna is an ESL teacher in a secondary school in the United States. The language level of the subject – a recorded excerpt of speech – was very highly evaluated by three independent native speakers. The average score was 9 points on a 10-point scale; the language level was assessed as near-native. The psychologist noted a process of supplanting the native language of the subject – Polish – by the language that she uses regularly – English. Joanna often resorts to English terms when defining words, and, as was concluded by the psychologist and as she herself declares, she thinks in English. This is quite an interesting phenomenon, bearing in mind that Joanna started to learn English relatively late – after 14; apart from short trips, she had never been abroad, and she emigrated as an adult.

Motivation.   As expected, Joanna's motivation is very high – her ultimate target is full assimilation in the target language country. What is more, she likes learning languages, which gives her a great deal of satisfaction.

Educational background.   MA in English philology.

Family background.   Joanna started to speak at the age of 2.5 and read in the first class of primary school. She is an only child and her parents had always been closely interested in her development and education; however, they virtually know no foreign languages. Nowadays, her husband and children are English-speaking, and English is her everyday communication language.

Native language.   She was always very good at Polish and never had problems with Polish orthography.

Preferred study conditions.   Joanna naturally chooses immersion as the most efficient method of learning.

Learning strategies.   Joanna strongly opts for a communicative approach in foreign language learning, which is probably a result of not only emigration but also a course in methodology during her studies, emphasising this method as the most efficient, as well as her occupation. Learning a foreign language is easy for her and the easiest skills are, not surprisingly, speaking and listening. As she declares, she does not have special preferences for learning grammar and vocabulary, as she acquires these subsystems naturally.

Learning styles.   Joanna has both very specific learning preferences and learning styles. Modality is definitely visual, with very high extroversion; intuitive and global styles prevail, spontaneity and organisation are in balance. Ambiguity tolerance is quite high. She rightly perceives herself as impulsive, spontaneous, emotional and practical at the same time.

Self-efficacy and anxiety.   She accurately evaluates her language aptitude as high. She declares no anxiety in learning and using a language.

Intelligence.   General intelligence quotient: 113 (above average); verbal scale: 112 (above average); non-verbal scale: 113 (above average). Joanna represents a moderately above-average intelligence; the profile of verbal abilities is balanced, whereas the profile of non-verbal abilities is not.

The WAIS-R verbal comprehension index is above average: 116; perceptual organisation is average: 108; memory and resistance to distraction is above average: 113.

Language aptitude.   The subject gained very high scores in the MLAT. Her results in parts I, II and V of the MLAT investigating short-term memory and phonetic abilities were maximal; in part III (vocabulary), she scored 90% and in part IV (grammar sensitivity) 76%. Her score ranks in the 99 percentile. In the Language Ability Test (TZJ), her results are placed in the ninth sten (84%). The lowest scores she gained were for 'grammar' and 'vocabulary': 73% and 83%, respectively. These results indicate the dominant language of the subject – English.

Working memory.   Seventy-five per cent of the recollected words. It is quite a high result.

Personality.   Joanna is a very emotionally stable person, characterised by well-developed emotion control. Her most significant characteristic is extraversion, that is high need for external stimulation, activity, sociability and ease in establishing personal contacts. She is open and direct in communicating needs and feelings, and can also be self-centred. Her second important feature is openness to experience. She is also quite a conscientious person, persistent and systematic.

Her most developed need is that for autonomy. She is independent, self-confident, stubborn and resolute. A need for change is also noticeable. Joanna is perceptive, spontaneous and quick in her reactions. Emotional intelligence is average.

Locus of control.   Decisively internal. She believes that she holds responsibility for all life events.

Stress copying style.   Task-oriented style prevails; however, avoiding style is also present. This means that she usually establishes strategies of action, but she also tends to procrastinate.

To sum up, Joanna is a very highly able foreign language learner, who gains high scores in memory tests performed on verbal material, but lower scores on numerical material. Phonetic and analytical abilities are high. Generally, Joanna had a score of 90% of correct answers in the MLAT, which is an outstanding result in comparison to the results presented by Ehrman (1998). In Ehrman's study, the average total for students best at speaking (14 persons nominated from 295 intensive course participants) was 151.2. Joanna's total was 173. In the third part (vocabulary), which is most predictive for speaking, the results were 33 in Ehrman's study and 45 in the case of Joanna. Joanna is a prototypical extrovert, open to new experience, self-confident, liking changes and active.

Maria

Maria is a 26-year-old assistant in the Chinese Language Department. She is a doctoral student of the Chinese language and a fifth-year student of Arabic philology. She is a polyglot, able to communicate in 11 languages. Her native language is Polish. Her L2 is Chinese, which she mastered to level C2. Her native-like proficiency at speaking was confirmed by both native and non-native co-workers, speakers of the Chinese language. She is also advanced in English (Certificate in Advanced English), German (C1) and Arabic (C1). Her declared knowledge of other languages – Swedish, Italian, Japanese, Croatian, Russian, Hebrew and Turkish (A2/ B2) – was confirmed by positive (good and very good) marks in her student grade book and in school reports.

Maria learns languages virtually under all conditions: by herself, at private lessons and on courses, at school, on university courses, during a scholarship abroad. Learning foreign languages is her hobby and passion. She acquires each subsequent language with greater ease, which is probably the result of aptitude, persistence and motivation. As she claims, she finds learning Slavic languages most difficult because of their similarity to Polish. Learning new writing systems is not difficult for her.

Motivation.   Maria's motivation is very high. She gives many reasons for learning foreign languages: interest, hobby, profession, aptitude, curiosity and a need for new challenges.

Educational background.   Maria is a doctoral student of Chinese and a fifth-year student of Arabic philology.

Family background.   She started to speak very early, but she cannot provide the exact date. She began to read and write in her native language when she was four. At the age of five, she was fluent in these skills. Her parents and grandparents do not know any foreign languages, but they strongly stimulated her development, giving her 'adult' books, games, puzzles and construction toys and answered all her questions.

Native language.   She was a very good student and never had problems with Polish grammar.

Preferred study conditions.   Maria strongly believes that a professional foreign language user should first have a strong formal educational background and then master a foreign language in the natural environment, not neglecting formal instruction at any stage of learning (dictionary work, grammar instruction with a handbook). Maria had plenty of possibilities to test her speaking skills in the target language country: Chinese during a one-year scholarship in China, Arabic during a few 1-month stays in Saudi Arabia and Italian and German during stays in Italy and Austria.

Learning strategies.   Maria is a typical individualistic learner who prefers formal methods, explicit grammar instruction accompanied by a lot of exercises and memorizing lists of words. She chooses to learn by reading and usually learns words in context. She likes to use her favourite proverbs and idioms in different languages. She considers her strategies efficient; however, she underlines the role of communication with native speakers. The preference for formal instruction might be the result of methods preferred by oriental teachers (Grammar-translation and audiolingualism), as well as the introverted personality type represented by Maria.

Maria is a perfectionist. Especially in the field of phonetics she strives to achieve native-like level. She prides herself on being taken for a native speaker of Chinese – a tone language, especially difficult for a European.

Learning styles.   There is no dominant style or modality. Tolerance of ambiguity is average. She perceives herself as a hard-working, well-organized, careful, thoughtful, reliable, analytical and orderly person. Psychological tests confirmed these observations.

Self-efficacy and anxiety. Maria evaluates her linguistic aptitude as very high: 'Comparing myself to others I realise that learning foreign languages comes faster and with greater ease to me, which I consider a real gift from nature. I think my linguistic abilities are high and I am not going to waste them.' Her level of foreign language learning anxiety is relatively low, but her performance anxiety is moderate.

Intelligence. General intelligence quotient: 124 (high); verbal scale: 127 (high); non-verbal scale: 118 (above average). Maria has a large intellectual potential, but particular subtests scores are very different. Very well-developed verbal reasoning (128), very rich vocabulary (18) and a very high score in memory and resistance to distraction index (130) outline Maria's cognitive profile. Her perceptual organisation index is much lower: 113.

Language aptitude. The subject gained very high scores in both the MLAT and the Language Ability Test (TZJ). Her score in part I of the MLAT is 93%, whereas in parts II and V it is 100%. In part III, she scored 68% and in part IV 66%. Her score ranks in the 99 percentile. In the Language Ability Test (TZJ), she answered all the questions correctly.

Working memory. In the PRSAN, Maria achieved an outstanding result of 100% of recollected words.

Personality. Maria is a very introverted and serious person keeping distance in interpersonal contacts. She is a reflective individual who prefers to work alone. She is emotionally balanced, calm, doing well in difficult, stressful situations, and her emotional reactions are adequate to a situation. Maria's other significant trait is high conscientiousness. She is a person characterised by strong will, persistent in completing personal goals, meticulous, dutiful, reliable and thoughtful. Her openness to experience is average – she is practical, keeping balance between conservative values and fascination with the new. Her interests might be unconventional. Her agreeableness is low – she can be sceptical, competitive, often aggressive in personal relationship.

She reveals a high need for achievement, which indicates that she is hard-working and goal-directed. Other highly developed needs are for persistence, order and autonomy. This indicates that the subject is hard-working, effortful, persistent in achieving her goals, keeping to the plan, independent, autonomous, stubborn and indifferent to the feelings of others. Her need for aggression is also high. She tends to be competitive rather than cooperative. The emotional intelligence quotient of the subject is average.

Locus of control.   Maria displays a medium level of internal control. She generally believes in her control over life situations; however, she might search for reasons for her failures outside herself.

Stress copying style.   In stressful situations, she chooses mainly a task-oriented coping style. She concentrates on the task, searches for methods which would hasten finding a solution to the problem. She treats stress as a challenge.

To sum up, Maria is an example of a very highly able foreign language learner, whose most striking cognitive feature is outstanding memory. Her short-term memory (digit-symbol coding, digit span, MLAT I and V), as well as working memory (the PRSPAN, backwards digit span), results provide evidence for her possession of an efficient central executive and capacious phonological loop. Her analytical and phonetic abilities are also well developed. Maria, similarly to Dagmara, prefers traditional learning methods. She is an introverted, very hard-working, intelligent and autonomous foreign language learner.

Conclusions

All three subjects are HAFLL and very proficient foreign language speakers. Two of them, Dagmara and Maria, are very intelligent, with a dominance of verbal intelligence, which was revealed in early speaking and reading at the age of five. They are characterised by a very good memory and high phonetic abilities. As far as personality features are concerned, they are both orderly, autonomous, controlling, consistent and analytical. They prefer individual work and traditional methods of learning. The third person, Joanna, displays a diametrically different cognitive-emotional profile. Her intelligence is only above average; her memory is good, but only with respect to verbal material. She is extroverted, sociable and cooperative. These characteristics enabled her to achieve near-native fluency in speaking. Joanna definitely prefers group work, communicative exercises and immersion. Such differentiation is probably a result of personality, but also of a teaching method promoted by a teacher. All three learners are very conscientious, well-organised and hard-working; they have the feeling of control over a situation and cope well with stress. These positive features might be connected with their professions: Maria and Joanna are teachers, whereas Dagmara studies mathematics and is going to work in finance. In line with Dörnyei's suggestion (2005), two of the subjects, Dagmara and Joanna, display high openness to experience, which means high intellectual curiosity. All three learners are very highly motivated and interested in the target language and the target language culture. They can be described as mature, autonomous, persistent, ambitious and competitive. It is probably these factors in connection with high aptitude that determined their success as fluent foreign language speakers.

Note

1. The Polish Ministry of Science and Higher Education supported preparation of this research project in 2009 and 2010.

References

Baddeley, A., Gathercole, S. and Papagno, C. (1998) The phonological loop as a language acquisition device. *Psychological Review* 105, 158–173.

Bongaerts, T., van Summeren, C., Planken, B. and Schils, E. (1997) Age and ultimate attainment in the pronunciation of a foreign language. *Studies in Second Language Acquisition* 19, 447–465.

Bongaerts, T., Mennen, S. and van der Silk, F (2000) Authenticity of pronunciation in naturalistic second language acquisition. The case of very advanced late learners if Dutch as a second language. *Studia Linguistica* 54, 298–308.

Boxtel, van S., Bongaerts, T. and Coppen, A.P. (2003) Native-like attainment in L2 syntax. *EUROSLA Yearbook* 3, 157–181.

Brzezinski, J., Gaul, M., Hornowska, E., Machowski, A. and Zakrzewska, M. (1996) *Skala Inteligencji D. Wechslera dla Dorosłych. Wersja Zrewidowana. WAIS-R (Pl). Podręcznik.* Warszawa: Pracownia Testów Psychologicznych PTP.

Callahan, C.M. (2000) Intelligence and giftedness. In R.J. Sternberg (ed.) *Handbook of Intelligence* (pp.159–176). Cambridge, New York: Cambridge University Press.

Carroll, J.B. and Sapon, S. (2002) *Modern Language Aptitude Test. MLAT. Manual 2002 Edition.* N. Bethesda, MD: Second Language Testing, Inc.

Ceci, S.J. (1996) *On Intelligence. A Bio-Ecological Treatise on Intellectual Development* (2nd edn). Cambridge, MA: Harvard University Press.

Ciechanowicz, A., Jaworowska, A. and Matczak, A. (2000) *Kwestionariusz Inteligencji Emocjonalnej INTE. Podręcznik.* Warszawa: Pracownia Testów Psychologicznych PTP.

Conway, A.R.A., Jarrold, Ch., Kane, M.J., Miyake, A. and Towse, J.N. (2008) Variation in working memory. An introduction. In A.R.A. Conway, Ch. Jarrold, M.J. Kane, A. Miyake and J.N. Towse (eds) *Variation in Working Memory* (pp. 3–17). Oxford: Oxford University Press.

Corno, L., Cronbach, L.J., Kupermintz, H., Lohman, D.F., Mandinach, E.B., Porteus, A.W. and Talbert, J.E. (2002) *Remaking the Concept of Aptitude: Extending the Legacy of Richard E. Snow.* Mahwah, NJ: Erlbaum.

Costa, P.T., Jr. and McCrae, R.R. (1992) *Revised NEO Personality Inventory (NEO-PI-R) and NEO Five-Factor Inventory (NEO-FFI) Manual.* Odessa, FL: Psychological Assessment Resources.

Daneman, M. and Carpenter, P. (1980) Individual differences in working memory and reading. *Journal of Verbal Learning and Verbal Behavior* 19, 450–466.

Dewaele, J.M. (2007) The effect of multilingualism, sociobiographical, and situational factors on communicative anxiety and foreign language anxiety of mature language learners. *International Journal of Bilingualism* 11, 391–409.

Dewaele, J.M., Petrides, K.V. and Furnham, A. (2008) Effects of trait Emotional Intelligence and sociobiographical variables on communicative anxiety and foreign language anxiety among adult multilinguals. A review and empirical investigation. *Language Learning* 58, 911–960.

Dörnyei, Z. (2005) *The Psychology of the Language Learner*. Mahwah, NJ: Erlbaum.
Droździał-Szelest, K. (2008) *Trening strategiczny na lekcji języka obcego – mit czy rzeczywistość?* In M. Pawlak (ed.) *Autonomia w Nauce Języka Obcego – Co Osiągnęliśmy i Dokąd Zmierzamy* (pp. 405–415). Poznań: Wydawnictwo UAM.
Drwal, R.Ł. (1995) *Adaptacja Kwestionariuszy Osobowości. Wybrane Techniki i Zagadnienia*. Warszawa: Wydawnictwo Naukowe PWN.
Ehrman, M.E. (1996) *Understanding Second Language Learning Difficulties*. Thousand Oaks, CA: Sage.
Ehrman, M.E. (1998) The Modern Language Aptitude Test for predicting learning success and advising students. *Applied Language Learning* 9, 31–70.
Ehrman, M.E. (2008) Personality and good language learners. In C. Griffiths (ed.) *Lessons from Good Language Learners* (pp. 83–99). Cambridge: Cambridge University Press.
Ehrman, M.E. and Oxford, R.L. (1995) Cognition plus: Correlates of language learning success. *Modern Language Journal* 7, 67–89.
Ely, Ch.M. (1995) Second Language Tolerance of Ambiguity Scale. In J. Reid (ed.) *Learning Styles in EFL/ESL Classroom* (pp. 216–217). Boston: Heinle & Heinle.
Endler, N.S. and Parker J.D.A. (1990) *Coping Inventory for Stressful Situations. CISSManual*. Toronto: Multi-Health Systems.
Engle, R.W., Laughlin, J.E., Tuholski, S.W. and Conway, A.R.A. (1999) Working memory, short-term memory, and general fluid intelligence: A latent-variable approach. *Journal of Experimental Psychology: General* 128, 309–331.
Gough, H.G. and Heilbrun, A.B. (1980) *The Adjective Check List. Manual 1980 Edition*. Palo Alto, CA: Consulting Psychologists Press, Inc.
Griffiths, C. (2008) Strategies and good language learners. In C. Griffiths (ed.) *Lessons from Good Language Learners* (pp. 83–98). Cambridge: Cambridge University Press.
Harrington, M. and Sawyer, M. (1992) L2 working memory capacity and L2 reading skill. *Studies in Second Language Acquisition* 14, 25–38.
Hewston, R., Campbell, R.J., Eyre, D., Muijs, R.D., Neelands, J.G. and Robinson, W. (2005) A baseline review of the literature on effective pedagogies for gifted and talented students. *Occasional Paper* 5. Coventry: The University of Warwick.
Ioup, G., Boustagui, E., El Tigi, M. and Moselle, M. (1994) Re-examining the CPH. A case study of successful adult SLA in a naturalistic environment. *Studies in Second Language Acquisition* 16, 73–98.
Juros, A., Oleś, P. and Wujec, Z. (1987) *Analiza Wyboru Przymiotników do Opisu Siebie-Test ACL. Badania Porównawcze*. Lublin: Towarzystwo Naukowe KUL.
Little, D. (2004) Autonomy and autonomous learners. In M. Byram (ed.) *Routlege Encyclopedia of Language Teaching and Learning* (pp. 69–72). London: Routlege.
Mackey, A., Philip, J., Egi, T., Fujii, A. and Tatsumi, T. (2002) Individual differences in working memory, noticing interactional feedback and L2 development. In P. Robinson (ed.) *Individual Differences and Instructed Language Learning* (pp. 181–209). Philadelphia: John Benjamins.
McCrae, R.R. and Costa, P.T. (2003) *Personality in Adulthood: A Five-Factor Theory Perspective* (2nd edn). New York: Guilford Press.
Miyake, A. and Friedman, N.P. (1998) Individual differences in second language proficiency: Working memory as language aptitude. In A. Healy and L. Bourne (eds) *Foreign Language Learning* (pp. 339–364). Mahwah, NJ: Erlbaum.
Morgan, G., Smith, N., Tsimpli, I. and Woll, B. (2007) Classifier learning and modality in a polyglot savant. *Lingua* 117, 1339–1353.
Moyer, A. (1999) Ultimate attainment in L2 phonology. *Studies in Second Language Acquisition* 21, 81–108.

Nęcka, E. (2003) *Inteligencja. Geneza, Struktura, Funkcje.* Gdańsk: Gdańskie Wydawnictwo Psychologiczne.

Obler, L. (1989) Exceptional second language learners. In S. Gass, C. Madden, D. Preston and L. Selinker (eds) *Variation in Second Language Acquisition: Psycholinguistic Issues* (pp. 141–159). Clevedon: Multilingual Matters.

Oxford, R.L. (1995) Style Analysis Survey. In J. Reid (ed.) *Learning Styles in EFL/ ESL Classroom* (pp. 208–215). Boston: Heinle & Heinle.

Pawlak, M. (2009) Instructional mode and the use of grammar learning strategies. In M. Pawlak (ed.) *Studies in Pedagogy and Fine Arts. New Perspectives on Individual Differences in Language Learning and Teaching* (Vol. 8, pp. 267–290). Poznań-Kalisz: Faculty of Pedagogy and Fine Arts in Kalisz. Adam Mickiewicz University in Poznań.

Perkins, D.N. (1995) *Outsmarting IQ: The Emerging Science of Learnable Intelligence.* New York: Free Press.

Renzulli, J. (1986) The three-ring conception of giftedness: A developmental model for creative productivity. In R. J. Sternberg and J.E. Davidson (eds) *Conceptions of Giftedness* (pp. 53–93). Cambridge-London: Cambridge University Press.

Robinson, P. (2002) Learning conditions, aptitude complexes and SLA: A framework for research and pedagogy. In P. Robinson (ed.) *Individual Differences and Instructed Language Learning* (pp. 113–133). Philadelphia: John Benjamins.

Robinson P. (2007) Aptitudes, abilities, contexts, and practice. In R.M. DeKeyser (ed.) *Practice in Second Language* (pp. 256–286). Cambridge: Cambridge University Press.

Sasaki, M. (1996) *Second Language Proficiency, Foreign Language Aptitude, and Intelligence. Quantitative and Qualitative Analyses.* New York: Peter Lang.

Sawyer, M. and Ranta, L. (2001) Aptitude, individual differences, and instructional design. In P. Robinson (ed.) *Cognition and Second Language Instruction* (pp. 319–354). Cambridge: Cambridge University Press.

Schneiderman, E.I. and Desmarais, C. (1988) The talented language learner: Some preliminary findings. *Second Language Research* 4, 91–109.

Schutte, N.S., Malouff, J.M., Hall, L.E., Haggerty, D.J., Cooper, J.T., Golden, C.J. and Dornheim, L. (1998) Development and validation of a measure of emotional intelligence. *Personality and Individual Differences* 25, 167–177.

Sękowski, A.E. (ed.) (2004) *Psychologia Zdolności. Współczesne Kierunki Badań.* Warszawa: Wydawnictwo Naukowe PWN.

Skehan, P. (1998) *A Cognitive Approach to Language Learning.* Oxford: Oxford University Press.

Skehan, P. (2002) Theorising and updating aptitude. In P. Robinson (ed.) *Individual Differences and Instructed Language Learning* (pp. 69–95). Philadelphia: John Benjamins.

Snow, R.E., Corno, L. and Jackson, D.N. (1996) Individual differences in affective and conative functions. In D.C. Berliner and R.C. Calfee (eds) *Handbook of Educational Psychology* (pp. 243–310). New York: Macmillan.

Sparks, R.L., Artzer, M., Ganschow, L., Siebenhar, D., Plageman, M. and Patton, J. (1998) Differences in native-language skills, foreign-language aptitude, and foreign language grades among high-, average-, and low proficiency foreign language learners: Two studies. *Language Testing* 15, 181–216

Sternberg, R.J. (2002) The theory of Successful Intelligence and its implications for language aptitude testing. In P. Robinson (ed.) *Individual Differences and Instructed Language Learning* (pp. 13–43). Philadelphia: John Benjamins

Szczepaniak, P., Strelau, J. and Wrześniewski, K. (1996) Diagnoza stylów radzenia sobie ze stresem za pomocą polskiej wersji kwestionariusza CISS Endlera i Parkera. *Przegląd Psychologiczny* 1, 187–210.

Tyacke, M. (1998) The Tyacke Profile. In J.M. Reid (ed.) *Understanding Learning Styles in the Second Language Classroom* (p. 167). Upper Saddle River, NJ: Prentice-Hall.

Ushioda, E. (2008) Motivation and good language learners. In C. Griffiths (ed.) *Lessons From Good Language Learners* (pp. 19–34). Cambridge: Cambridge University Press.

Williams, M. and Burden, R.L. (1997) *Psychology for Language Teachers: A Social Constructivist Approach.* Cambridge: Cambridge University Press.

Wojtowicz, M. (2006) *Test Zdolności Językowych TZJ.* Warszawa: Pracownia Testów Psychologicznych PTP.

Zawadzki, B., Strelau, J., Szczepaniak, P. and Śliwińska, M. (1998) *Test osobowości NEO FFI. Podręcznik.* Warszawa: Pracownia Testów Psychologicznych.

Chapter 8

"I Am Good at Speaking, But I Failed My Phonetics Class" – Pronunciation and Speaking in Advanced Learners of English

EWA WANIEK-KLIMCZAK

Introduction

The relationship between pronunciation and speaking has been long established in the English as a Foreign Language (EFL) tradition with reference to 'comfortable intelligibility' – the pronunciation which enables the interlocutors to communicate without major effort (see e.g. Celce-Murcia *et al.*, 1996; Dalton & Seidlhofer, 1994; Kenworthy, 1987). The targeted degree of 'comfort' depends on individual needs of the students and the context for language usage; however, the focus is on reaching communicative goals and consequently, it is fluency rather than accuracy that becomes the primary objective. If one adopts the viewpoint advocated by the proponents of English as a lingua franca (e.g. Jenkins, 2000), fluency becomes not only the main but also the only goal of pronunciation teaching, as the acceptance of variable non-native English pronunciations beyond the limited set of phonetic features included in the 'lingua franca core' means that there is no model in relation to which accuracy could be taught. The above discussion suggests that the teaching of practical English phonetics understood as a traditional pronunciation class devoted to a target-like development of this element of the language system might be viewed as outdated and pointless. Nevertheless, the need for such courses continues in the context of a more advanced, specialized language training, and they are offered at an academic level throughout Europe. From the perspective of the communicative approach to language teaching, practical phonetics courses can be viewed as more intensive pronunciation boxes included in many English as a Foreign Language textbooks. As with the pronunciation boxes, the courses focus on the elements of the language system and promote accuracy as well as fluency, with the aim of developing the speaking skill.

The connection between speaking and pronunciation seems equally obvious and natural: in human communication, speaking relies on pronunciation of sound sequences. Learning to speak a language means learning how to pronounce words, just like learning to write a language means learning how to represent words with different letters or sign shapes. Both ways of using a language require practice to become reliable communication tools, with spelling and handwriting corresponding to the sound structure and pronunciation. While the comparison holds for young learners, adults can be expected to be concerned much more with spelling and sound structure than with the actual letter or sound shape. In practice then, it is only in the case of those adults who have a special interest in the additional language they learn or use that pronunciation accuracy will be felt to be needed. Studies conducted among students in Poland (Janicka *et al.*, 2005; Waniek-Klimczak, 2002) prove that students majoring in English tend to aim at native-like pronunciation. In contrast, students with a similar proficiency level not planning to use English as their main professional interest seem less likely to make this choice (Waniek-Klimczak & Klimczak, 2005). Interestingly, even in the English-majoring group it is the fluency, ease of communication and confidence in speech that are mentioned as more important than native-like accent.

The choice of the target accent and the degree to which a student wishes to identify with the target speech community, although connected with the development of the speaking skill, have long been regarded as independent aspects of second/foreign language acquisition. Numerous factors affecting the degree of a foreign accent have been found, both linguistic and extra-linguistic, including the age of language onset, motivation and language experience (for an overview, see e.g. Major, 2001; Piske *et al.*, 2001). While the majority of these factors affect all aspects of second language acquisition, the affective variables, including such characteristics as inhibition and ego-permeability, seem to be particularly strongly related to speaking and pronunciation. Although often questioned, the early experiments involving small dosages of alcohol (Guoira *et al.*, 1972), hypnosis (Schumann *et al.*, 1978) and valium (Guoira *et al.*, 1980) as factors lowering inhibition and increasing permeability of ego boundaries provided initial support for the intuitive belief that lowered inhibition improves pronunciation. Other personality variables, such as self-esteem, risk taking or tolerance of ambiguity, contribute to the relative success in the acquisition and use of speaking in a foreign language. The difficulty has been well expressed by Hughes: 'to learn to communicate expertly in another language a speaker must change and expand identity as he or she learns the cultural, social, and even political factors, which go into language choices, needed to speak appropriately with a new "voice"' (2002: 9).

In the process of second language acquisition, pronunciation and speaking, although inherently linked, may indeed take different routes. The identity issue, so strongly stressed by the researchers advocating the acceptance of a foreign accent in English as a lingua franca, cannot be ignored in pronunciation instruction. The individual choices that students make with respect to the target variety of English need to be recognized, and even if the lingua franca core proposed by Jenkins (2000) is not accepted as a viable option (see contributions by Dziubalska-Kołaczyk & Przedlacka, 2005, for a discussion of this issue), the question of the degree of native-like pronunciation the students want to achieve remains open. Specifying the target as 'comfortable intelligibility' brings pronunciation teaching closer to the development of the speaking skill; however, the vagueness of the term does not make it a realistic goal in a phonetics class. One could argue that a separate pronunciation class as such is not needed in English instruction unless there is a special reason for it.

The situation further explored in this chapter could be well referred to as a special case in the sense that the context for teaching English described and investigated in the study is restricted to students at a relatively advanced proficiency level, who have chosen English as their major at the first level of tertiary university education (BA level). The choice of the target group is not accidental: students majoring in English seem to be one of the best researched EFL student group in Poland with respect to pronunciation attitudes (Janicka *et al.*, 2005; Krzyżyński, 1988; Sobkowiak, 2002; Waniek-Klimczak, 2002). While the studies differ in their aims and scope and results vary in relation to the type of questions asked and research methods employed, they bring solid evidence that pronunciation is an important issue for the students and native-like pronunciation in particular remains an attractive, viable goal. Similar results of the study conducted in Austria (Dalton-Puffer *et al.*, 1997) lend further support to relatively conservative pronunciation attitudes in the students majoring in English in non-English–speaking countries. As the majority of these students can be expected to become translators or EFL teachers, their attitudes and success in reaching the goals will largely determine their future careers.

For the purpose of this chapter, success will be understood in the most straightforward school terms as a grade given at the end of the course. For the discussion of the relationship between speaking and pronunciation, the grades in these courses will be discussed in comparison to two other courses taken by the same group of students: writing and practical grammar. The courses develop either productive skills or elements of the language system, and the fact that they are offered and graded separately creates a unique opportunity for analysis. What could be expected as the most straightforward relationship would be a positive correlation between practical phonetics/speaking and practical grammar/writing, with the positive relationship between both elements of the system and the two productive skills certainly hoped for. Undoubtedly, however, success in the use of the two channels – speaking and writing – as well as the two elements of the system may correspond to different personality variables. Exploring the relationship between selected affective variables and success in speaking/pronunciation, we will expect to find patterns explaining the causes of frustration in a student who is good at speaking but fails his or her pronunciation class. The discrepancy may seem a simple case of an apparent lack of consistency in the grading systems. This chapter argues that the case is far from simple: as the difference in the grading criteria reflects the focus of the course, it can be interpreted as symptomatic of a more general accuracy – fluency, skill – system dichotomy. Investigating the relationship between pronunciation and speaking in an academic setting, the study reported here explores the aspect of the debate which is believed to be vital for the development of English proficiency in future teachers or translators, or more generally – users of English for professional purposes.

The Study

The study investigates the relationship between pronunciation and speaking on the basis of the results of the courses completed by 50 undergraduate students majoring in English at the University of Łódź, Poland. In order to be admitted to the programme, the students need to pass the state secondary school final exam in English and Polish at an above-average level, which in the case of English is assumed to correspond to at least the upper-intermediate level of language proficiency. The university courses are organized into two semesters, with 15 weeks in each semester and at the time of the survey the participants had successfully completed the first semester and were beginning the second one.

The study was conducted in three stages: firstly, a pronunciation and speaking attitude survey was conducted; secondly, the first-semester final grades in practical English courses were correlated and finally, group and individual student personality traits were checked and correlated with the grades. The study used two instruments: the first one was a questionnaire based on the format used in an earlier study (Waniek-Klimczak & Klimczak, 2005) and regularly employed by the author in her teaching practice and the second one was a Language Learning Attitudes Questionnaire available online from the Summer Institute of Linguistics (www.sil.org).

The analysis is based on the second and third stages: first-semester course results are checked for correlation and then compared with the results of the Language Learning Attitude Questionnaire. Before the analysis, group characteristics checked on the basis of the survey of pronunciation learning attitudes are discussed. The survey aimed to verify a background assumption that fluency in speaking and accuracy in pronunciation are recognized as important goals by the respondents. It is only if this condition is fulfilled that we can claim that the grading system based on pronunciation accuracy in the case of practical phonetics class and fluency in the case of speaking class reflects students' success in reaching their learning goals. The third part of the study explores the possible reasons for the assumed discrepancy between success in pronunciation and speaking by looking at the affective characteristics of the students and correlating the grades with the value for such factors as self-image, inhibition, risk-taking, ego-permeability and ambiguity tolerance as estimated on the basis of the results of the Language Learning Attitudes Questionnaire.

Pronunciation learning attitudes: A survey

The aim of the survey was to learn about students' attitudes towards learning the pronunciation of English as one of the elements of the language system and speaking as one of the skills. It was based on a questionnaire administered to 50 students, randomly selected from the group of 132 first-year students of English. Following the English major curriculum, the students participated in the practical English classes, comprising speaking, writing, practical phonetics and practical grammar. At the time when the survey was carried out, they had completed one semester, with 30 hours per semester for each class. Apart from the practical English classes, the students were required to take a number of literature and linguistics courses conducted in English.

The questionnaire elicited answers aiming at establishing the students' attitudes and priorities in learning speaking and pronunciation of English, with the scale or multiple-choice format, supplemented by a comment option. The responses justify the following group character-istics of the students:

(1) Speaking is the most important and at the same time the most difficult skill for the students; the second most difficult is writing, which also marginally wins as second most useful (see Figure 8.1). While the two productive skills are rated the highest on both accounts, it is speaking that is believed to be by far the most important and difficult skill.

(2) When asked about the importance of the sub-skills, students chose vocabulary and pronunciation as almost equally important, with grammar rated much lower (Figure 8.2).

(3) When asked about the priorities in pronunciation learning, the respondents chose (in order of frequency of appearance) fluency, individual sounds, word stress, intonation and finally the rhythm of speech.

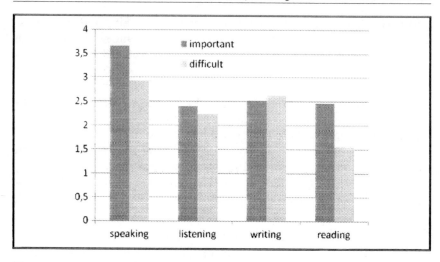

Figure 8.1 Mean ratings for importance and difficulty of individual skills (scale 1–4)

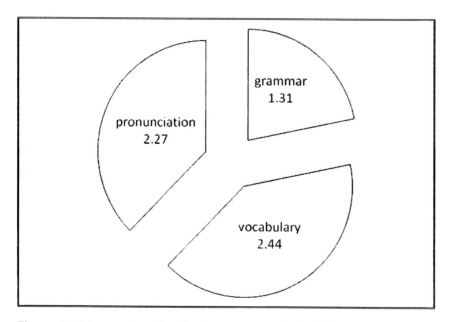

Figure 8.2 Mean ratings for the importance of sub-skills within speaking (scale 1–3)

(4) A vast majority of the students believe that a single model of pronunciation should be taught (80%), and the model most frequently chosen was standard English (76%), followed by General American (22%). As many as 74% of the respondents would want to achieve native-like pronunciation; however, when asked to name the most important goals that they want to achieve in learning speaking, they provided the following answers: 'I want to speak fluently, with advanced vocabulary', 'I want to be easily understood', 'I don't want to have a strong Polish accent', 'I don't want to sound funny', 'I want to speak without serious mistakes'.

The results show that the overall profile of the respondents fits the pattern described in earlier studies investigating the attitudes of the students majoring in English (Janicka *et al.*, 2005; Sobkowiak, 2002; Waniek-Klimczak, 2002; Waniek-Klimczak & Klimczak, 2005). Not surprisingly, the students do recognize the importance of the model accent and the majority of them declare native-like pronunciation to be the ultimate goal, even when they are aware that it might be very difficult, if not impossible, to reach the aim. When given more options in specifying the goals, however, students do mention ease of communication and comfortable intelligibility, with fluency rated much higher than individual sounds as pronunciation priority. Consequently, it seems legitimate to argue that while fluency remains the main objective, the students are also accuracy-conscious and recognize the need for its development.

Speaking and pronunciation: The relationship between the grades

The academic system followed by the students requires them to take a number of compulsory courses not only in English literature and linguistics but also general English, referred to as 'practical English'. At the time the study was conducted, during the first year of studies, the students took two courses focusing on the development of productive skills, speaking and writing, and two courses developing the sub-systems: practical phonetics and practical grammar. Without going into details of the grading system adopted in each type of the course, we will assume here that, following general course outlines, the productive skill classes focused on the development of communicative abilities through different channels, while the sub-system courses were mostly concerned with accuracy in the production of the elements of the language system: pronunciation in the case of phonetics and grammatical structures in the case of practical grammar.

Given that all courses are designed to increase the level of language proficiency in the students, both students and teachers tend to assume that a relatively high level of correspondence in the grades will reflect individual student's success in achieving this task. On the other hand, however, the fluency–accuracy focus difference may be expected to lead to inevitable discrepancies between the two types of courses, hence a possible source of considerable frustration that I heard many times during the past 20 years of my teaching. Indeed, when checked for regularity by means of correlation (Table 8.1), the grades reflect the dichotomy, but only in the case of the pronunciation versus speaking class. It is in these courses that the lack of correspondence in the grades yields statistically insignificant results, with all the other courses showing a positive correlation in the grades. The correlation between the grades points to a high degree of agreement between the teachers and a symmetrical development of language proficiency in the students, with both speaking and pronunciation correlating regularly with writing and grammar, but not with each other.

The correspondence between grades in such courses as pronunciation and writing, pronunciation and grammar or speaking and writing and speaking and grammar suggests that it is not the grading system that is at fault here. If it is not a deficiency in the grading system, the sources of the lack of correspondence or weaker/stronger correspondence between the grades may be suggestive of the nature of the learning process in individual students. Let us notice here that the degree of regularity in the correspondence between pronunciation and writing is weaker than between pronunciation and grammar, suggesting a possible affinity between the two accuracy-oriented courses and the development of the sub-systems. The detailed relationship between the individual course grades would need to be further investigated before any other conclusions could be drawn; at this point suffice it to say that the lack of regular correspondence between pronunciation and speaking as the only irregularity in practical English classes seems highly suggestive.

There is clearly something very specific about pronunciation and speaking. The intricate relationship supported by numerous foreign accent studies has been aptly put by Hughes 'The human voice and the

Table 8.1 The results of correlation between the grades for the four courses ($N = 50$)

	Pronunciation	*Speaking*	*Writing*	*Grammar*
Pronunciation		0.156	0.28*	0.38**
Speaking			0.34*	0.44**
Writing				0.46*

*Corresponds to the chance probability level smaller than 5%.
**Corresponds to the chance probability level smaller than 1%.

faculty of speech are inherently bound up with the projection of the self into the world' (2002: 8). Looking for possible sources of the difference in the grades and an apparent conflict in the process of the development of language proficiency in EFL, we will explore a possible effect of selected affective variables.

The effect of affective variables on speaking and pronunciation

The third part of the study explores the values of selected affective variables on the general success of the students and the grades in pronunciation and speaking as elements of practical English courses. The correlation study is based on the data supplied by the survey conducted with the use of a Language Learning Attitude Questionnaire available from the Summer Institute of Linguistics (Language Learning Attitudes Questionnaire, www.sil.org). The same group of students who participated in the previous parts of the study were asked to fill in the forms. The questionnaire includes 27 statements and participants were asked to react to them by choosing one of five answers on the Likert scale (strongly agree – agree – neither – disagree – strongly disagree). The answers are then rated and interpreted as suggestive of the value for five affective variables: self-image, inhibition, risk-taking, ego-permeability and ambiguity tolerance. In all cases except for ambiguity tolerance, the higher the scores, the more a particular trait is present; in the case of ambiguity tolerance, however, the lower the score, the stronger the trait. The students filled in the questionnaire on one setting, and then calculated the scores for each variable themselves; after the task, during an informal discussion, the students reacted to the results, with general agreement rather than surprise or disbelief. In fact, many students reported having used the questionnaire for self-scoring before.

The results were first analysed for the whole group. As can be seen in Table 8.2, the attitudinal profile of the students proves them generally

Table 8.2 The results of the Scoring Your Attitudes Questionnaire; score interpretation: 0–15 low, 16–35 average, 36–47 above average, 48–64 high ($N = 50$)

Affective factor	*Mean value*	*Standard deviation*
Self-image	33 average	4.7
Inhibition	31 average	9.4
Risk-taking	41 above average	8.3
Ego-permeability	39 above average	6.6
Ambiguity tolerance	43 above average	5.8

Table 8.3 The results of Pearson correlation for the relationship between personality factors and grades $(N = 50)$; $p = 0.01 = 0.23$; $p = 0.05 = 0.27$; $p = 0.01 = 0.35$

	Pronunciation	Speaking	Writing	Grammar
Self-image	0.09	− 0.06	− 0.19	0.03
Inhibition	0.06	− 0.23	− **0.33***	0.14
Risk-taking	− 0.22	− 0.06	0.10	− 0.22
Ego-permeability	0.2	0.05	0.05	− 0.05
Ambiguity tolerance	0.1	**0.31***	0.01	− **0.42****

*Corresponds to the chance probability level smaller than 5%.
**Corresponds to the chance probability level smaller than 1%.

well suited for the type of studies they chose. While none of the variables was lower than average, the group tendency was to score above average or close to that level. A particularly high score on ambiguity tolerance, however, suggests that the students tend to value accuracy above average. As illustrated by standard deviation figures, there is relatively more agreement among the group on self-image and ambiguity tolerance score than on other traits, with inhibition varying to the largest extent.

At the final stage of the study, individual scores of the students for each variable were correlated with their grades in four practical English courses. The results (Table 8.3) show that while the degree of regularity in the correspondence differs to a considerable degree, it is only the score in pronunciation that shows a weak correspondence to ego-personality (positive relationship) and risk-taking (negative correlation). Speaking, on the other hand, proves to correlate with low ambiguity tolerance and lack of inhibition. In the case of other courses, there is no surprise in writing, similarly to speaking, showing negative correlation with inhibition. A highly significant negative correlation between the grades in practical grammar and low ambiguity tolerance would need further analysis to be explained.

Discussion

When built on the basis of the Language Learning Attitudes Questionnaire, the profile of a successful foreign language student could be expected to include a high level of self-image, risk-taking, ego-permeability and ambiguity tolerance, with low inhibition (see e.g. the discussion of personality factors in Brown, 2007, or Johnson, 2001). The group results tabulated in Table 8.2 prove not all expectations to be true in the case of the investigated students. The most striking difference can be observed in the case of ambiguity tolerance: here future language specialists, teachers or translators tend to agree to such statements as 'I want to have everything worked out in my own head before I answer' or 'There is a right and a wrong way to do almost everything, and I think it's my duty to figure out which is which and do it right', which makes them clearly strong on accuracy. The tendency for accuracy then and a clear right–wrong distinction as the basic attitude to language and linguistic norms may be responsible for a high level of self-criticism leading to a rather surprisingly low group score on self-image. No wonder then that when asked how they would like to speak English, they say 'fluently', adding 'without major mistakes', but they also say 'I don't want to sound funny to native speakers of English'.

With respect to goals in pronunciation learning, the students declare that they would like to speak like native speakers of English and most of them believe that a consistent native-speaker model should be used in teaching English. They select fluency as the main objective in their learning, but add individual sounds and word stress. When asked in a closed question format if they would like to speak like native speakers they say 'yes', but when asked to add comments, they mention speaking without a strong Polish accent. In fact, a few students also say: 'I would like not to be afraid to speak English (I still am)'. Does that mean that the group of students who chose English as their major at the undergraduate level differ from study-based prototypical successful language students? They must have been successful in their English classes before choosing the university (they needed good grades on their final exams to be admitted). As there was no questionnaire conducted at the beginning of their studies, there is no way to check whether their attitudes changed with the language experience at the university. Is there a possibility that the university experience makes them less like other successful language students? Or is it a sign of increased awareness of the amount of work that needs to be done before the students will feel satisfied with the level of 'comfort' in their oral performance? While the answer to these questions would require further study, the mixed profile of the students suggests possible directions for the exploration of the relationship between success in speaking and pronunciation.

Speaking, the most important and most difficult skill in students' views, is certain to be in the centre of their attention. Compared with the secondary school experience, the students are likely to receive considerably more oral input in English and to have more opportunities to use speaking in various literature and linguistic courses. The practical English class in speaking will be just one of many occasions to develop and practice this skill. A high degree of correlation between speaking, writing and practical grammar further supports a symmetrical development of language proficiency in the students. It is only practical phonetics that does not follow. Obviously, the lack of significant correlation does not mean that all students good at speaking receive lower grades in pronunciation; the situation may be also reversed, that is highly successful pronunciation students may be less successful in their speaking.

The lack of correlation in the grades corresponds to the tendency for different personality traits to be most regularly correlated with each of the grades. In the case of pronunciation, a positive effect of a higher level of ego-permeability (weak positive correlation) can be both expected and predicted to have a positive effect in the development of speaking as well. However, negative risk-taking is more surprising and suggests a possible conflict between the strategies needed for success in speaking and success in pronunciation. In both cases, the correlation level is very weak (just below 10% probability value); however, the direction of difference seems extremely interesting. Further research would be needed to verify this discrepancy with a higher certainty level; however, even at this point, the difference in success between pronunciation and speaking can be claimed to be related to the difference in risk-taking. Another trait significantly correlated with speaking, but not pronunciation, is ambiguity tolerance, a characteristic clearly needed for successful communication. Finally, two traits that correlate in an irregular, but reverse, way are self-image and inhibition. Especially inhibition, with its significant negative correlation with speaking could be expected to be also needed to be lowered for successful pronunciation.

The overall profile of an advanced student majoring in English and successful in speaking will include low inhibition and low ambiguity tolerance; to be successful in pronunciation, the student needs to have permeable ego boundaries and no tendency for risk-taking. While these results depend on the interpretation of the traits assumed by the instrument adopted for the study and the way they have been operationalized may have affected the findings, the reactions of the participants with whom I discussed the results seems to support this interpretation. Highly concerned with accuracy as the element that they believe they need to succeed in the professional use of English, they value fluency as the most important communication component. In order to be fully successful, they seem to need guidance and encouragement that would boost their self-image, lower inhibition and ego-boundaries and also decrease rather than increase the tendency for risk-taking.

Conclusion

Speaking and pronunciation, a skill and a sub-skill, although inherently related, prove to follow slightly different paths in the development of language proficiency in EFL. From the perspective of instructed learning, the most apparent difference is in the fluency–accuracy focus which may result in a different degree of success depending on personality and attitude variables. The study reported here found that Polish students majoring in English chose fluency as the main goal in their language studies; however, they also value accuracy as corresponding to the pronunciation of sounds and words. However, this well-balanced attitude does not correspond to equal success in speaking and pronunciation, as measured by the grades students received in their practical English speaking and practical phonetics classes. The lack of correlation between the grades is partly explained by the difference in personality traits found to be most needed for success in the two courses: high ego-permeability/low risk-taking for pronunciation and low inhibition/low ambiguity-tolerance in speaking. The key difference between speaking and pronunciation is in risk-taking, negatively correlated with pronunciation. Advising a student who is good at speaking but failed her phonetics class, we can say: concentrate on accuracy and take fewer risks in your pronunciation class, but don't let the pronunciation instruction increase your inhibition! Reaching the level of comfortable intelligibility is a matter of defining the comfort. However, setting the standards of comfort too high may be detrimental to the communicative ability.

References

Brown, H.D. (2007) *Principles of Language Learning and Teaching*. Harlow: Pearson Education.

Celce-Murcia, M., Brinton, D.M. and Goodwin, J.M. (1996) *Teaching Pronunciation*. Cambridge: Cambridge University Press.

Dalton, Ch. and Seidlhofer, B. (1994) *Pronunciation*. Oxford: Oxford University Press.

Dalton-Puffer, Ch., Kaltenboeck, G. and Smit, U. (1997) Learner attitudes and L2 pronunciation in Austria. *World Englishes* 16, 115–127.

Dziubalska-Kołaczyk, K and Przedlacka, J. (eds) (2005) *English Pronunciation Models: A Changing Scene*. Frankfurt: Peter Lang.

Guoira, A.Z., Acton, W.R., Erard, R. and Strickland, F.W. (1980) The effect of Benzodiazepine (Valium) on permeability of language ego boundaries. *Langugae Learning* 30, 351–363.

Guoira, A.Z., Beit-Hallahmi, B., Brannon, R.C., Dull, C.Y. and Scovel, T. (1972) The effect of experimentally induced changes in ego states on pronunciation ability in a second language: An exploratory study. *Comprehensive Psychiatry* 13, 139–150.

Hughes, R. (2002) *Teaching and Researching Speaking*. Harlow: Person Education.

Janicka, K., Kul, M. and Weckwerth, J. (2005) Polish students' attitudes to native English accents as models for EFL pronunciation. In K. Dziubalska-Kołaczyk and J. Przedlacka (eds) *English Pronunciation Models: A Changing Scene*. (pp. 251–292). Frankfurt: Peter Lang.

Jenkins, J. (2000) *The Phonology of English as an International Language*. Oxford: Oxford University Press.

Johnson, K. (2001) *An Introduction to Foreign Language Learning and Teaching*. Harlow: Pearson Education.

Kenworthy, J. (1987) *Teaching English Pronunciation*. London: Longman.

Krzyżyński, J. (1988) Folk linguistics and its influence on the attitudes and motivation of learners of English as a foreign language. *Glottodidactica* 19, 107–113.

Major, R. (2001) *Foreign Accent: The Ontogeny and Phylogeny of Second Language Phonology*. Mahwah, NJ: Erlbaum.

Piske, T., MacKay, I.R.A. and Flege J.E. (2001) Factors affecting degree of foreign accent in an L2: A review. *Journal of Phonetics* 29, 191–215.

Schumann, J.H., Holroyd, J., Campbell, R.N. and Ward, F.A. (1978) Improvement of foreign language pronunciation under hypnosis. *Language Learning* 28, 143–148.

Sobkowiak, W. (2002) English speech in Polish eyes: What university students think about English pronunciation teaching and learning. In E. Waniek-Klimczak and J.P. Melia (eds) *Accents and Speech in Teaching English Phonetics and Phonology: EFL Perspective* (pp. 177–196). Frankfurt: Peter Lang.

Waniek-Klimczak, E. (2002) Context for teaching English phonetics and phonology. In E. Waniek-Klimczak and J.P. Melia (eds) *Accents and Speech in Teaching English Phonetics and Phonology: EFL Perspective* (pp. 139–152). Frankfurt: Peter Lang.

Waniek-Klimczak, E. and Klimczak, K. (2005) Target in speech development: Learners' views. In K. Dziubalska-Kołaczyk and J. Przedlacka (eds) *English Pronunciation Models: A Changing Scene* (pp. 229– 249). Frankfurt: Peter Lang.

www.sil.org. Language Learning Attitudes Questionnaire (accessed January 22, 2009).

Chapter 9

Oral Skills Awareness of Advanced EFL Learners

KRYSTYNA DROŹDZIAŁ-SZELEST

Introduction

Oral proficiency or an ability to be able to communicate efficiently in English with both its native and non-native speakers is perceived by a great majority of language learners all over the world as an ultimate goal of their learning. At the same time, however, many of them seem to be unaware of the simple fact that speaking in a way that is both accurate and appropriate is probably the most difficult skill to develop as it involves mastery of different aspects of linguistic and non-linguistic features of language.

Therefore, the first question that needs to be answered is what it means to be a successful foreign language speaker. It is practically impossible to answer this question without referring to what native speakers know about their mother tongue and how they use this knowledge in communication. Customarily, native speakers' command of the language is described in terms of 'communicative competence', that is in Hymes' words, 'that aspect of our competence that enables us to convey and interpret messages and to negotiate meanings interpersonally within specific contexts' (cited in Brown, 1994: 227). The concept of communicative competence, later developed by Canale and Swain (1980), is perceived as consisting of four components, namely grammatical competence, discourse competence, sociolinguistic competence and strategic competence, each of which, in turn, encompasses a number of component features responsible for the persons' ability to interact with other speakers of the language. The extent to which speakers have mastered these component features is responsible for their differential success with communication (cf. Brown, 1994: 227–228). Within the last few years, special attention has been given to sociolinguistic and strategic components, although some researchers believe that strategic competence 'is, perhaps, the most important of all the communicative competence elements', as it allows speakers to 'compensate for imperfect knowledge of linguistic, sociolinguistic, and discourse rules'. As Shumin (2002: 208) explains, 'With reference to speaking, strategic competence refers to the ability to know when and how to take the floor, how to keep a conversation going, how to terminate the conversation, and how to clear up communication breakdown as well as comprehension problems'.

It goes without saying that native speakers' knowledge about language is very complex; it includes both the knowledge about how the system of language works and the knowledge how to use it in a given situation, as language is not used in a vacuum. In the words of Hammerly (1985: 55), 'the ability to express oneself in a socially appropriate manner applies to all levels of formality, from an intimate tête-à-tête to the most formal presentation before a large audience; very *few native speakers* have the ability to communicate competently in all possible situations'. Accordingly, speaking is a process during which speakers rely on all the available information (background and linguistic) to create messages that will be understandable and meaningful to the intended audience. What is more, the processes involved in speech production in the native language are mostly subconscious.

When it comes to a foreign or second language, there seems to be a general consensus that complete competence (i.e. native-like proficiency) is very rarely, if at all, attained by language learners; nevertheless, it is often used as a point of reference in the process of assessing second/foreign language achievement (cf. Stern, 1983: 346). Non-native speakers, even at an advanced level, usually manage to develop partial communicative competence, when compared with native speakers of that language, which is not surprising given the fact that the conditions under which they develop the language are quite different. Just as different native speakers develop different skills and sub-skills, so do non-native speakers, learners of English as a second or foreign language; however, among different learners at different stages of learning, foreign language competence (including oral proficiency) ranges from zero to native-like proficiency.

At this point it seems useful to refer to Rubin and Thompson (1994: 15–18), who, following the system used by the American Council on the Teaching of Foreign Languages, present the Inverted Pyramid of Language Proficiency, which may serve as a point of reference when trying to evaluate learners' speaking ability (S). The pyramid consists of six levels, ranging from Novice (S 0) or Prefunctional Level to that of Educated Native Speaker Level (S 5). According to Rubin and Thompson (1994:17), the so-called Limited Working Proficiency Level (S 2) is 'the highest level of proficiency attained by persons who have studied the language formally without having had an opportunity to live in the country or in a community where it is spoken'. In the case of some learners, however, it is actually quite realistic to attain the Superior (S 3) or Professional Proficiency Level which makes it possible to fulfil the responsibilities of their job or academic requirements. As Rubin and Thompson explain, 'experience shows that this level is rarely attainable without an extended stay in the country where the language is spoken'. The Distinguished Proficiency (S 4) or Near Native Proficiency Level requires 'many years of study and an extended stay in the country where the language is spoken. As a rule, very few learners can attain such a high level' (1994: 18). The levels are distinguished on the basis of the degree of *fluency, grammatical accuracy, 'precision of vocabulary'* and *idiomaticity.*

Rubin and Thompson's view presented above echoes the one expressed by Hammerly who stated that 'a fairy advanced degree of second language competence of native-like *quality* is attainable within excellent language programs; but the attainment of second language competence of native-like *scope* requires much unconscious acquisition beyond the best language program' (1985: 54). A similar claim was made by Shumin, who, referring to adult English as a Foreign Language (EFL) learners, said that they 'are relatively poor at spoken English, especially regarding fluency, control of idiomatic expressions, and understanding of cultural pragmatics. Few can achieve native-like proficiency in oral communication' (2002: 204).

As has been stated at the beginning of this chapter, in spite of all the problems involved, it is quite clear that language learners can actually develop speaking skills in a classroom context, allowing them to express intended meanings in ways that are comprehensible to their interlocutors, both native and non-native speakers. On the other hand, however, many of them (as well as other parties involved in language education as well) seem to be unaware of the true nature of the skill, which may be partially responsible for the fact that their oral proficiency usually stays short in comparison with that of native speakers.

A useful frame of reference helping learners fully realize what it means to be orally proficient in a foreign or second language as well as assess their abilities can be found in the publication of the Council of Europe – *Common European Framework of Reference for Languages*, where the skill of speaking is first described in terms of different levels of achievement (A–C levels), and then subdivided into *spoken interaction* and *spoken production* (2001: 23; 26). Furthermore, several 'qualitative aspects of spoken language use' are specified for each level, including range, accuracy, fluency, interaction and coherence (2001: Table 3, 28–29). In oral production, 'the language user produces an oral text which is received by an audience of one or more listeners', for instance, a monologue (describing experience or taking part in a debate), making an announcement, addressing audiences (2001: 58–59). In interactive activities (conversations, informal discussions, formal discussions and meetings, interviewing etc.), 'the language user acts alternately as speaker and listener with one or more interlocutors so as to construct conjointly, through the negotiation of meaning following the co-operative principle, conversational discourse' (2001: 73). Thus, from the point of view of communication, the following linguistic competences will be important: *lexical* (vocabulary range and control), *grammatical* (accuracy), *semantic* (deals with the learners' awareness and control of the organization of meaning) and *phonological* (2001: 109). In addition, *sociolinguistic appropriateness* (i.e. politeness conventions, register differences), *discourse competence* and an *ability to deal with communication* problems and so on will play an important role.

Recently, it has been suggested that the key factor in developing an ability to use the language efficiently is awareness, defined as an understanding of what language is and how it is used in communication, or, in other words, how it conveys the meanings and expresses our thoughts. It involves being conscious of the many units of language and the way they are put together, but also keeping in mind the fact that 'meaning does not come ready-made or "packaged" in words and sentences, but is constructed by speakers and hearers through the process of interpretation, in the context in which the language is used' (van Lier, 1995: 39). Proponents of the concept of language awareness assume that some level of consciousness about linguistic use, knowledge and learning on the part of learners is beneficial if they want to become skilful communicators.

> They need to know that many different forms can be used to perform a function and also that a single form can often serve a variety of functions. They must be able to choose from among these the most appropriate form, given the social context and the roles of the interlocutors. They must also be able to manage the process of negotiating meaning with their interlocutors. Communication is a process; knowledge of the forms of language is insufficient. (Larsen-Freeman, 2000: 128)

Rubin and Thompson emphasize that all native speakers communicate without thinking about the process; however,

> in order to accelerate the learning of another language, we need to become more aware of the knowledge and skills we bring to the process. By identifying and recognizing what we already know, we can more effectively guide our learning and be able to take shortcut or recognize where we have gone wrong in expressing ourselves or in interpreting others' messages. (1994: 30)

Background to the Study

In recent years, a lot of attention within the language learning field has been given to the importance of strategies and strategy training, which has found its reflection in numerous publications on the subject. As far as speaking is concerned, the research has primarily focused on strategies for talking or communication strategies. In the literature we can find different taxonomies of such strategies and accounts of how they are used by foreign language learners as well as descriptions of strategy training programmes (cf. Oxford's (1990) list of 'strategies useful for speaking', Rubin and Thompson's (1994: 100–109) discussion of 'strategies for developing speaking skills' or Weaver *et al.*'s (1994, cited in Cohen 1998: 153–156) list of strategies used before, during and after speaking). It is very rarely, however, that the researchers try to investigate other aspects of speaking, such as, for instance, learners' awareness of what being a good foreign language speaker involves, how to assess one's speaking ability or how to improve one's oral proficiency.

To fill in the gap, the present chapter reports on the results of a small-scale study attempting to investigate the degree of oral skills awareness demonstrated by advanced learners of English, on the assumption that awareness is a key factor determining further development of their oral proficiency skills. The study was conducted at the beginning of the academic year 2009/2010 and its subjects were students of English philology at Adam Mickiewicz University in Poznań, attending the first-year MA programme. Originally, the purpose of this relatively informal study was to provide the author, the students' MA theses supervisor, with more information concerning their ability to participate in the programme in terms of their language proficiency.

It has to be explained at this point that the students were admitted to the programme on the basis of the recruitment procedure, a part of which was an oral interview with the future supervisor of their theses. During the interview, in addition to the students' subject knowledge and their academic potential, their global language proficiency was assessed, with the emphasis on their ability to carry out a communicative exchange related to their subject area. That part of evaluation was carried out by an experienced EFL teacher whose only task was listening to the candidates and taking notes concerning their use of language in terms of fluency and accuracy. The rationale for such a procedure is to eliminate the candidates whose language may not be at a sufficient level guaranteeing successful completion of an MA thesis in English. Other factors taken into consideration included the students' grade point average on the completion of the BA course, and their final diploma examination mark. The candidates were mostly graduates of BA courses at teacher training colleges, as well as English philology departments at the state and private universities from all over Poland.

Subjects and Instruments of Data Collection

As has been already mentioned, the subjects of the study were English philology students enrolled in the first year of an MA programme at the

School of English. There are 14 students in the original seminar group; however, only 13 students, 10 women and 3 men, participated in the study, as one female student was absent on the day the questionnaire was administered. The students were from 22 to 26 years old, and had been learning English for an average of more than 13 years, with the shortest time of study being 10 years and the longest 17. All but one said that they had attended additional classes, either in the form of organized language courses or some kind of private lessons. As explained elsewhere, they had all graduated from teacher training colleges or similar institutions, with BA diplomas allowing them to teach English at different levels of state and private education. During their studies, they used English as the language of instruction, which means that in addition to receiving instruction in English and having to speak English in class, all their written work – homework assignments, semester works, as well as exams and diploma papers – was written in English.

In addition, nine students reported having visited an English-speaking country, mainly for work purposes; five students had taken part in various European student exchange programmes in Turkey (one), Spain (three), and Estonia (one), with proficiency in English being the major requirement. The programmes involved teaching practice or some kind of voluntary work. One of the students, after completing her BA studies, went back to Turkey to teach English, but unfortunately, because of some administrative problems, had to leave after a few months. It may come as a surprise that four students had never been to an English-speaking country; however, they, nevertheless, reported having had contacts with both native and non-native speakers of that language. The students who spent some time in an English-speaking country did not report having any problems with communicating in English. Given such learning experience, it can be safely assumed that the subjects qualify as advanced and successful/good learners of English. What is more, being graduates of BA programmes preparing them for the teaching profession, they could be expected to have a better understanding of what it means to know a language and what it involves to be a language learner.

The data were obtained by means of a questionnaire administered during one of the seminar meetings at the beginning of the academic year, thus ensuring that the students returned all the copies. Keeping in mind the students' level of proficiency, both the instructions and the survey items were in English, but the participants were told that they could respond in English or in Polish, according to their preferences. It was assumed that the students might prefer to resort to the native language to avoid any possible misunderstanding. Although such a solution may be surprising given the respondents' level of proficiency in English, it is often used to minimize the risk of their failing to answer some questions or answering them imprecisely in the target language.

As it turned out, only one respondent chose to address some of the questions in Polish; otherwise, she used a mixture of the two languages or just English.

The questionnaire consisted of three parts, with the first one aiming at obtaining background information about the subjects. It contained questions concerning the respondents' age, length of the study and their out-of-school encounters with English. Also, the students were asked about their visits to English-speaking countries and problems that they had experienced communicating with native speakers. The second part of the questionnaire contained open-ended questions relating to the students' views and beliefs concerning the speaking skill, their perception of themselves as speakers of English and their assessment of their speaking ability in terms of accuracy and fluency. The last part focused on communication strategies that the students employ when engaging in speaking. Here, the students' task was simply to indicate which of the strategies listed they use before, while and after speaking. The list of strategies used was taken from Neuburg and Harris (2003: 96–97).

The responses provided by the subjects were subjected to qualitative and quantitative analysis, with the aim of finding some patterns in the data, allowing for drawing some more general conclusions. It has to be stressed, however, that because of the fairly informal nature of the study, any conclusions must be highly speculative. After analyzing the students' responses, the author decided to compare the results concerning their self-assessment of oral proficiency with the notes taken by the 'language observer' during the interview. In addition, the students' grades assessing their language performance were looked at.

Findings of the Study

As the data concerning the students' background have already been discussed in the section above, this section will focus first on the responses provided to the open-ended questions seeking the students' views on various aspects of oral proficiency.

The first question searched the students' opinion about whether *speaking emerges/develops on its own or whether it has to be learned/taught.* Generally, the students (11) expressed an opinion that the development of speaking takes place as a combined result of both processes. They emphasized that even though, initially, speaking may appear naturally as a result of exposure to the language, it has 'to be helped a bit', especially, as in a foreign language learning context the students may not have enough contacts with the language outside the classroom. They also stressed the role of teachers in creating opportunities for using the language and for motivating the students. In order to develop our speaking ability we need to speak; the more we speak, the faster the development; in other words, we become good speakers through speaking. It was also pointed out that it was actually possible to learn certain techniques or tricks, as they were called, to be used in communication to make it more effective. On the other hand, however, we cannot force people to develop speaking. Two students claimed that in contrast to grammar or vocabulary, there is no particular way to teach speaking as such. It simply emerges as the time goes by; however, it can be facilitated by 'providing the students with rich input and stimulating them to speak'. The students pointed out, however, that without learning/being taught vocabulary and grammar, as well as some patterns of interaction, the development of speaking may be impeded, that is it may stop at a very basic level. Not having enough exposure to the target language, learners need to be guided how to behave in terms of communicative interaction, that is 'how to use the L2 properly'. The remaining two students, who stated that speaking has to be learned/taught, focused on the role of the teacher and the classroom as crucial factors in providing the guidance and creating opportunities for speaking; as one of them commented, 'students need to have an opportunity to open their mouth'. On the whole, an opinion prevailed that both teaching and learning are necessary to shape speaking, as the initial knowledge will not be enough to develop 'proper speaking'. The students have to make an effort as well, as being a good speaker requires some work.

In the next question, the students were asked whether *they are good at speaking to other people* and to *explain how they feel about speaking English*. It did not come as a surprise that most of the respondents (nine) believed that they were good speakers, or even more, good communicators. They had had quite a lot of speaking practice, both with native and non-native speakers, inside Poland and abroad, and the feedback they received from their interlocutors had always been favourable. As they stressed, they liked speaking, as it allowed them to establish and maintain contact with other people. On the whole, they felt confident when speaking and they enjoyed engaging in conversations with others. Some students further explained that their attitude depended on such factors as the length of the speaking time, the topic, and familiarity with relevant vocabulary, as well as their interlocutors. As one of the respondents stated, it is easier to talk to somebody we know. Another one emphasized the importance of speaking in a 'natural environment'.

A couple of the students reported feeling stressed, insecure and ashamed of themselves during speaking classes at the School of English, where there is strong emphasis on accuracy. They added that their confidence usually disappeared when they were evaluated as, for instance, during the exams, or when they spoke to someone more proficient, academic teachers, for instance.

Two female students, in particular, had a very positive picture of themselves as speakers of English. They described themselves as talkative and open, capable of establishing a good rapport with their interlocutors. In addition, they stated that they liked speaking and they did not have any problems as far as communicating was concerned. In their opinion, it did not really matter whether they spoke Polish or English. Both of them had already started working as teachers of English, which may partially account for their beliefs. In the opinion of the present author, based on the classroom performance of these students, their assessment is fully justified; they are very good at speaking, responsive and pleasant to listen to. They demonstrate a high level of proficiency grammar- and vocabulary-wise, and their pronunciation can also be described as very good, with distinguished traces of, respectively, British and American English.

Among the students there were some, however, who did not have such a high opinion about their speaking ability. One male respondent claimed to be 'somewhere in the middle', giving his insufficient knowledge of vocabulary as the main reason. Another one explained that she was not a confident speaker of Polish either; she described herself as a very reflective person, probably an example of a careful learner, who had to plan her utterances in advance, and often felt embarrassed when speaking. However, she also added that when she felt that she had something interesting to contribute to the discussion, her confidence increased and she was quite likely to become more talkative. What she said could be easily noticed in class; very often she was just a listener, but on a number of occasions she let herself be known as a very confident and even passionate speaker. Two learners made a point of feeling proud of being able to communicate efficiently in a language other than their native. Most respondents emphasized that they liked English, the very sound of it, and they took pleasure from being able to speak it. On the whole, they had a positive picture of themselves as speakers of English.

When it comes to the next question, that is *if it matters whether they speak to native or non-native speakers*, the respondents were divided in their opinions. Only one person stated that it did not matter to her at all; at the same time she added that, in her opinion, native speakers (henceforth NSs) did not pay much attention to mistakes, whereas non-native speakers (henceforth NNSs) were less tolerant in that respect. It turned out later that she actually meant non-native (Polish) teachers of English. Twelve respondents were convinced that it did make a difference whom they talked to. Four respondents found it more difficult to talk to NSs, explaining that they felt stressed and were afraid of making mistakes. In their opinion, it was much easier in the case of NNSs because 'we know we are all learners and making mistakes is natural'. Another concern was the use of vocabulary. The respondents felt that they could have problems with understanding NSs because of the latter's choice of vocabulary (in terms of the levels of formality and sophistication), which might be unknown to the learners. The respondents believed that such problems did not appear in conversations with NNSs, because the vocabulary was usually at a comparable level.

Generally, the respondents claimed to pay more attention to accuracy when talking to NSs, especially with respect to pronunciation, and they complained about the level of anxiety and frustration experienced. At the same time, one person declared that he liked listening to NSs because of their expertise in the use of English. Another one added that NSs provide a model for speaking in terms of grammar and vocabulary, and contacts with them are a good opportunity 'to be exposed to a meaningful context'. As one of the students put it, 'On the one hand it is nice talking to a native speaker, but on the other hand I sometimes feel intimidated because of my poor vocabulary and accent'. The respondents were convinced that NSs 'may detect any mistake', 'can notice each and every mistake in grammar' or even that they (NSs) would correct the mistakes made by their non-native interlocutors. On the whole, six students felt more at ease when talking to NNSs who were described as more friendly and understanding, and being at the same level, non-judgmental. Nonetheless, some students admitted that in spite of everything they enjoyed speaking to NSs and often asked them for correction and advice.

Some respondents, however, expressed a different opinion. One person wrote that when talking to NSs, 'it is not necessary to pay attention to grammar, as they are more lenient', and 'since even NSs make mistakes, I don't feel nervous'. The respondent admitted though that even so she tried to be more careful about pronunciation and collocations. Another student expressed a similar concern, stating that she did not think about grammar mistakes, 'as they (i.e. NSs) don't notice them', yet she confessed to 'feeling stupid' when in more 'private situations' she was not able to use 'modern, everyday language'.

The next question aimed at finding out *which of the two, fluency or accuracy, the respondents focus on when speaking*. The analysis of their answers clearly indicates that most of them were preoccupied with accuracy (eight), especially, as they explained, since they had begun studying at the School of English. The main reason given was that they did not want to make mistakes and that 'accuracy was important'. One respondent claimed that when she focused on fluency only, she made a lot of mistakes. Another one expressed an opinion that 'the better the accuracy, the more focus on fluency, and then grammar competence comes sort of naturally'. One male respondent explained that he used to focus on accuracy, especially in the area of grammar and pronunciation, but now as he could see his fluency getting better, he started focussing on it. The students' major concerns seemed to be grammar and pronunciation. They emphasized the importance of correct speech; they did not want to make mistakes which would make them feel stupid. The students believed that they did not have major problems with fluency and they did not have to focus on it. One student was convinced that, as far as she was concerned, accuracy came 'quite naturally in everyday conversations'.

Three respondents emphasized the importance of being able to get a message across, especially when talking to NSs; at the same time, they expressed concern about correct pronunciation. Two respondents stated that they pay attention to both accuracy and fluency, but, as one of them put it, 'controlling accuracy is more challenging'. Another one explained that the focus depended on the context and the goal of communication; when talking with friends, she claimed to be paying more attention to fluency, whereas, for instance, during the exams she tried to take care of both accuracy and fluency.

In the following question, the respondents were supposed *to assess their speaking ability with reference to (a) accuracy (vocabulary, grammar, pronunciation, style, stress, intonation etc.) and (b) fluency (clarity of meaning, spontaneity etc.).* Unfortunately, their responses were rather sketchy and they did not provide too much additional information. As far as accuracy is concerned, it came as no surprise that the students' biggest problems were pronunciation and intonation (mentioned by nine respondents), and vocabulary, especially in the area of collocations (five respondents). With regard to vocabulary, the students were also concerned about the discrepancy between their receptive and productive vocabulary. Otherwise, the students' perception of accuracy, especially in terms of the use of grammar, was quite favourable even though some students reported having problems when trying to use some more complex structures. On the whole, the students did not report any problems with fluency; if they did appear, they related to the so-called tough topics or situations when the students had to speak for a longer period of time. In addition, as some explained, the fluency depended on the familiarity with the subject and the audience. Nevertheless, many students emphasized the need to work on fluency as well as the fact that when they focused too much on accuracy, fluency suffered.[1]

Answering the question *Do you ever experience fear or anxiety when speaking English,* practically all the respondents gave a positive answer; however, their explanations differed. Five felt anxious 'when speaking in public', for instance giving presentations or making speeches in front of their peers in class, five experienced anxiety during exams, especially the ones assessing their language proficiency, three referred to the situations in which they had to talk to their teachers (professors); other instances included talking to people at a higher language proficiency level, being evaluated, talking to native speakers (for instance, one respondent expressed a fear that he might sound impolite because of incorrect intonation) and not knowing what to say.

The students were also asked whether *they ever/still practise their speaking* and *how and when they do it*. As the answers were rather vague (the students listed 'mentally making up sentences', speaking to oneself, practising with a friend, 'gathering vocabulary', reading aloud, singing etc.), it may be assumed that most of them did not engage in any kind of deliberate, planned practice. A possible explanation may be that since English is the language of instruction at the School of English, and, additionally, the students have to attend obligatory practical English classes, including conversation/spoken English class, they do not feel the need for any extra practice. Another reason may be that some students teach different courses, which provides another opportunity for some kind of involuntary practice. There were two respondents though who reported involving themselves in deliberate speaking practice when working on their language proficiency. One student had weekly appointments with a trained phonetician, during which she discussed different topics. As she said, she valued this kind of practice a lot. Another female respondent attended a remedial phonetics course and, additionally, practised with an online language programme. She did that to prepare for the practical English exam to be taken at the end of the academic year.

Even though the students seemed not to feel the need for extra practice, they did prepare for their spoken English/conversation classes, as revealed by their responses to the question about *how they prepare for a discussion class* (the idea comes from the study described in Kawai (2008: 224)). Nine respondents mentioned reading and gathering information on the subject, including internet sources; 12 listed checking or revising relevant vocabulary, including idioms and phrases, adding that they also checked pronunciation of the new words. A few stated that they looked for grammatical structures to be used in a given context. Some respondents talked about brainstorming ideas with friends, collecting arguments for and against, as well as thinking about how to support these arguments by writing a plan or putting down the main points and going over them a couple of times in order to add more information, 'saying things aloud' or even acting out a discussion. The students also talked about 'trying to predict arguments or trying to find out about other people's views on the subject'.

When asked about *possible difficulties that might appear during the discussion*, they reported running out of ideas (five), vocabulary problems (six) – referring to the lack of significant vocabulary (in the case of 'specific topic'), forgetting the words and problems with pronunciation. Some students worried about not being able to support their arguments (four) or to refute (two) somebody else's arguments, or that they might have problems understanding somebody's point of view. One person was concerned with the fact that her preoccupation with accuracy might interfere with presenting her arguments clearly or that she might have problems with finding good counterarguments.

Among the ways of trying to overcome the above-mentioned difficulties, the respondents repeated the ones mentioned before, when addressing the question about preparing for a discussion class. They emphasized the importance of advance preparation in the form of gathering information (data, facts, ideas), thinking about and preparing good examples, planning in advance the line of argumentation and defending it, practising speaking in a group of friends to overcome shyness and preparing vocabulary lists.

Overall, on the basis of the above analysis alone, it can be concluded that the respondents appear to be quite well aware of their oral proficiency, including its different components. They seem to be quite able to identify their strong as well as weak points, and to find solutions to their problems. Nevertheless, being their teacher and meeting them on a weekly basis, the author has to admit that the level of awareness is not as high as the results of the questionnaire might suggest.

Thus, it is justifiable at this point to refer to the assessment of the students' performance carried out by 'the language observer' during the introductory interview. As was explained above, the would-be students were evaluated in terms of fluency/communicative effectiveness and accuracy, including pronunciation, grammar and vocabulary. Although all the respondents were judged as communicatively competent, there were actually quite a lot of differences as far as their accuracy and fluency were concerned, which, by the way, is a testimony to varying language teaching standards across Poland.[2] Among the language problems noted down by the interviewer, the most serious one seemed to be the students' *pronunciation* (mostly problems with vowels, weak forms, stress, final devoicing), which in some cases was described as poor (three instances) or even 'Polish', meaning really hopeless (two cases). On the other hand, two students were identified as having very distinct British English or American English pronunciation, respectively. *No major problems with grammar* (syntax) were observed, except for occasional errors in the use of articles and slips of the tongue of different kind, which was, in general, judged as fair. The same can be said about vocabulary, although numerous *problems with collocations* were noted. When it comes to fluency and communicative ability, *most students were judged as fluent and communicative*; according to the 'language observer', they were responsive, willing to talk, eager to answer questions and, on the whole, did quite well, often making up for other deficiencies. One female student was described as having problems with longer answers; another one spoke very fast, which at times resulted in blurred pronunciation. Yet another one was described as trying but shy, repetitive and not loud enough; only one student's communicative ability was described as a border case – she was not very cooperative, did not seem to have much to say and spoke in broken unfinished sentences.

Altogether, the students' proficiency in English was judged as *good* (four students), *fair* (six students) and *rather poor, but sufficient for the purpose* (three). For the sake of clarity, it has to be added that the respondents were quite well prepared for the interview in terms of content knowledge; that is they could talk without any problems about EFL methodology using appropriate register and they could relate their knowledge to personal experience, their diploma papers and research conducted for that purpose, as well as their prospective MA theses. In general, the students displayed a sound knowledge of the field as well as an ability to express their own ideas on the topics under discussion. In addition, they were able to clarify occasional misunderstandings when questioned by the interviewer, as well as ask for clarification themselves. They did not seem to have any problems with maintaining conversation, changing its course and so on. Except for occasional problems, most of them turned out to be quite successful, alert and willing communicators.

As far as the respondents' assessment is concerned, it becomes apparent that it is sometimes slightly at odds with the one provided by the 'language observer'. There are no major differences as far as accuracy is concerned, except for pronunciation. Although, on the whole, the students were very critical of their pronunciation, and they described it as the biggest problem, some of them did not seem to be aware of the true nature of the problem. It concerns two students in particular, whose pronunciation was judged as 'Polish' and who described it as just *poor* and *needing improvement.* The students in question attributed their problems to the lack of basic knowledge (pronunciation was not taught at all or was not taught 'properly'). One student blamed her 'poor' pronunciation on being forced to transfer from a British to an American English group. In this context, it is quite interesting to note that two students whose pronunciation was assessed as quite good perceived it as still needing major improvement, especially in the area of stress and intonation.

When it comes to fluency, again, it seems that both the respondents and 'the language observer' agreed in their assessment, except for two cases. One respondent, who was described as 'communicative, trying but shy', expressed doubts about her communicative ability, explaining that she had serious problems with expressing her thoughts, which at times resulted in her producing illogical and unclear utterances. Another one, whose performance was summed up in the words 'not much to say, unfinished/broken sentences', actually described her fluency as good;

she also added that the more she spoke, the more it [the fluency] progressed.

The final part of the questionnaire[3] was administered with the purpose of finding out whether the respondents were able to identify speaking strategies that they employed in communication. The strategies were divided into three groups: before speaking, while speaking and after speaking. Among the most frequently indicated strategies were the following (the numbers in parentheses refer to the number of times a given strategy was indicated):

(1) 'I use "hesitation techniques" ("fillers") like *Well... /now let me see,* etc. to give myself time to think not only about what to say but also how to say it' *(12)*;

(2) 'If I find I do not know the words for what I want to say, I change the way I was going to say something' *(11)*;

(3) 'I describe what something looks like, what you can use it for... (circumlocution)' *(11)*;

(4) 'I listen for words and expressions that I have just heard the native speaker say and try to use them myself' (10);

(5) 'I plan how to cope with a speaking task by thinking about what to say... looking key words up in a dictionary, or thinking of an easier way of saying it' (10);

(6) 'I use a word that has roughly the same meaning...' *(10)*;

(7) 'I use "set phrases" that I am confident with to give myself time to think of how to say something I am less sure of' (9);

(8) 'I use mime, gestures, facial expressions or I point at something to show what I mean' (9);

(9) 'I think about politeness forms, cultural conventions etc. so as to avoid giving offence' (9).

As can be seen, points 1–4 and 6–9 are examples of *while speaking strategies*, whereas point 5 refers to one of *before speaking strategies*. *After speaking strategies*, that is 'writing down unknown words or grammatical rules and looking them up in a dictionary' or 'thinking about why some of the used strategies did not work and what could be done next time' were indicated by seven respondents. None of the respondents indicated the strategy of *foreignizing* ('I make up words by saying the mother tongue word but with the foreign accent'). Only four students identified the strategy 'I show I need help by pausing, a puzzled expression etc.' or the strategy of 'encouraging the native speaker to do the talking by asking questions like "What do you think?"'. There were some differences between the respondents with regard to the type and the number of the strategies indicated, but this issue is beyond the scope of this chapter.

On the basis of the analysis of this part of the questionnaire, it can be stated that the respondents are quite well aware of the speaking strategies that they employ. What is more, the strategies reported by them are compatible with their earlier comments about their speaking abilities.

Conclusions, Implications and Directions for Future Research

As the results of the study reveal, the respondents, advanced EFL learners, on the whole, demonstrate a relatively high degree of awareness with reference to their oral proficiency. To start with, having reached a relatively high level of language proficiency, they understand the complex nature of the speaking skill and realize that its development hinges on the combined efforts of the teacher and a foreign language learner, and that it takes time. They also appear to be aware that being a good foreign language speaker and a skilful communicator requires much more than just knowing the rules of grammar, as language is not used in a vacuum. The students have used English to communicate with both its native and other non-native speakers and, as a result, are in a position to understand how different factors influence communication.

On the whole, the students are also able to assess their own speaking abilities, although, as the results of the research project suggest, their assessment is not always realistic and well founded. Such a situation can be partially explained by the lack of relevant feedback from the students' teachers at the earlier stages of language instruction, on the one hand, and the positive affective feedback from their interlocutors in various kinds of out-of-school context, on the other. Even though the students recognize the value of practice, they do not seem to feel the need to work on their oral proficiency outside the school context, which is a bit worrying.

On the basis of their responses, it is also evident that they recognize the importance of sociolinguistic factors, as the lack of knowledge in this area may seriously impede communication; it is not clear though what steps they take to make up for their deficiencies in that area. They are conscious of numerous problems that may appear during communication, and, as indicated by their responses, they can make use of relevant strategies. It is a bit disconcerting though that the students do not seem to be making much use of the *after speaking strategies*, which could help them improve their communicative ability.

Judging by the slight discrepancy between the students' assessment of their oral proficiency and the one conduced by the 'language observer', it can be said that the students' awareness in some areas leaves much to be desired and that there is a room for improvement. If, as it is suggested, awareness is a key factor in developing learners' communicative ability, raising their awareness about some aspects of the English language in general, and oral proficiency in particular, is worth trying. One way of doing it would be modifying practical English syllabuses for spoken language in the philology departments to include, among others, language awareness and learning awareness training, which, on the one hand, could help students become more conscious of their wants and needs as far as effective communication in a foreign language is concerned, and, on the other, would better prepare them for their profession. Keeping in mind the fact that students do not resort to using *after speaking strategies,* which play an important role in the process of refining the speaking skill, it also seems advisable to include training in the area of selected communication strategies.

It should be remembered, however, that because of the small size of the group and the informal nature of the study described in this chapter, any conclusions must be highly tentative. At the same time it is hoped that its results will suggest some directions for further research in this area. We seem to have quite enough knowledge concerning the development of the speaking skill and the use of communication strategies. What we do need now is more information about, for instance, what learners know about the process of communication and how they assess their knowledge and abilities in that respect. Thus, more studies investigating learners' awareness at different levels of language proficiency are necessary in order to help them attain high levels of oral competence, which is an important goal for a majority of foreign language learners.

Notes

1. The students' responses to this particular question will be compared with the assessment of their fluency and accuracy carried out by 'the language observer' during the interview.
2. All but one graduated with a high grade point average (4.0–4.5; one student graduated with 3.5), with their practical English grades being within the same range.
3. The questionnaire investigating learners' speaking strategies comes from Neuburg and Harris (2003: 4–5).

References

Brown, H.D. (1994) *Principles of Language Learning and Teaching* (3rd edn). Englewood Cliffs, NJ: Prentice-Hall Regents.

Canale, M. and Swain, M. (1980) Theoretical bases of communicative approaches to teaching and testing. *Applied Linguistics* 1, 1–47.

Cohen, A.D. (1998) *Strategies in Learning and Using a Second Language.* London: Longman.

Council of Europe (2001) *Common European Framework of Reference for Languages: Learning, Teaching, Assessment.* Cambridge: Cambridge University Press.

Hammerly, H. (1985) *An Integrated Theory of Language Teaching*. Blaine: Second Language Publications.

Kawai, Y. (2008) Speaking and good language learners. In C. Griffiths (ed.) *Lessons from Good Language Learners* (pp. 218–230). Cambridge: Cambridge University Press.

Larsen-Freeman, D. (2000) *Techniques and Principles in Language Teaching* (2nd edn). Oxford: Oxford University Press.

Neuburg, R. and Harris, V. (2003) *Learning My Way. A Handbook on Language Learning Strategies*. Kaunas: Technologija. (Socrates Grundtvig)

Oxford, R. (1990) *Language Learning Strategies: What Every Teacher Should Know*. Boston: Heinle & Heinle.

Shumin, K. (2002) Factors to consider: Developing adult EFL students' speaking abilities. In J.C. Richards and W.A. Renandya (eds) *Methodology in Language Teaching. An Anthology of Current Practice* (pp. 204–211). Cambridge: Cambridge University Press.

Rubin, J. and Thompson, I. (1994) *How to Be a More Successful Language Learner* (2nd edn). Boston: Heinle & Heinle Publishers.

Stern, H.H. (1983) *Fundamental Concepts of Language Teaching*. Oxford: Oxford University Press.

Van Lier, L. (1995) *Introducing Language Awareness*. London: Penguin.

Weaver, S.J., Alcaya, C., Lybeck, K. and Mougel, P. (1994) Speaking strategies: a list compiled by teachers in the experimental sections of the strategies-based instruction experiment. Unpublished document, National Language Resource Center, University of Minnesota, Minneapolis.

Chapter 10

Pronunciation Learning Strategies – Identification and Classification

ANETA CAŁKA

Introduction

Speaking a foreign language is a very complex skill, including vocabulary, grammar, pronunciation, fluency, the ability to structure talk or even non-verbal abilities. Among these elements, pronunciation is one of the most difficult ones, especially if the learner aims at acquiring nativelike pronunciation. Reaching this aim may require years of hard work and even then some learners may not be successful. Failure in pronunciation acquisition may be caused by various factors, such as age, aptitude, personality, inappropriate attitude, weak motivation as well as application of ineffective learning strategies.

Research on the so-called good language learners has shown that successful learners use a wide repertoire of learning strategies and have the ability to select appropriate strategies for a given learning situation or task. Assuming that training weaker students in language learning strategies (LLS) may help them acquire a second language, researchers have carried out experiments aiming at examining the effects of such training. Results of these experiments have varied, but most of them have been positive. It can be assumed that introducing a similar training in the use of pronunciation learning strategies (PLS) could help less effective learners master L2 pronunciation.

Few studies on PLS have been carried out so far. They have resulted in identification and description of some PLS (e.g. Droździał-Szelest, 1997; Eckstein, 2007; Naiman *et al.*, 1978; Osborne, 2003; Pawlak, 2006, 2008; Peterson, 2000; Rivers, 1979) and in classification of PLS (Eckstein, 2007; Peterson, 2000) as well as provided evidence that applying effective PLS improves pronunciation skills (Eckstein, 2007) and training students in their use has positive effects (Bukowski, 2004; Varasarin, 2007). There is, however, a need for further, more detailed exploration of the subject.

The aim of the present chapter is to contribute to fulfilling this need by reporting the results of a study aiming at identifying PLS used by advanced learners of English, proposing a detailed classification of PLS and making suggestions concerning training learners in PLS use. The chapter begins with a discussion of some important issues connected with defining learning strategies and an attempt to define PLS. This is followed by a short description of existing PLS typologies and the author's proposal of PLS classification. Finally, the research project, its outcomes and conclusions are presented.

Definitions of Learning Strategies

Defining learning strategies is not easy. Researchers often disagree with one another on the characteristic features of strategies and terminological nuances. They are at odds, for example, as to whether strategies are observable or unobservable, consciously or subconsciously applied and so on. Notions such as learning strategies, tactics, techniques, processes, tasks and so on have often been used interchangeably, although nowadays most researchers differentiate between strategies and processes (which are more general and complex), tactics or techniques (which refer to more concrete behaviours) (cf. Grenfell & Macaro, 2007).

There is general agreement that the aim of using LLS is to improve the learner's language competencies as well as facilitate and accelerate the process of language acquisition. Most definitions of LLS emphasise an active role of the learner, who should control the process of learning by choosing the ways of achieving goals set by himself. Thus using learning strategies is strictly connected with learner autonomy. Oxford defines learning strategies as 'specific actions taken by the learner to make learning easier, faster, more enjoyable, more self-directed, more effective, and more transferable to new situations' (1990: 8). This definition seems to include all the features of LLS mentioned above. The learner involves himself actively in the process of learning by self-directing his knowledge, plans and undertakes actions aiming at increasing the effectiveness of his learning, applies facilitators and overcomes difficulties. Moreover, Oxford's definition implies that strategies are universal (transferable to new learning situations) and that applying them brings satisfaction from the achieved goal or from overcoming a learning problem. On the basis of Oxford's definition of learning strategies, PLS can be defined as specific actions taken by the learner to make learning pronunciation easier, faster, more enjoyable, more self-directed, more effective and more transferable to new situations.

Classifications of PLS

In the state-of-the-art literature, references to two taxonomies of PLS can be found: by Peterson (2000) and by Eckstein (2007). Peterson's (2000: 26–27) taxonomy was designed on the basis of Oxford's (1990) classification. She distinguishes 12 strategies and 43 tactics. Her taxonomy is very comprehensive and includes strategies identified by herself as well as by Naiman *et al.* (1978) and Rivers (1979). Some of the tactics she lists, however, could be assigned to more than one group of strategies. For example, using phonetic symbols (a memory tactic according to Peterson) could also be classified as a cognitive strategy of using resources (a dictionary) or as a strategy of organising your knowledge (making notes). What is more, it is possible to complete Peterson's taxonomy with more strategies and tactics, especially within memory or compensation sets of strategies.

Eckstein (2007: 35) used Kolb's (1984) learning construct as the basis of his classification. He distinguishes 28 PLS connected with a given stage of pronunciation acquisition: input/practice, noticing/feedback, hypothesis forming, hypothesis testing, and adds an extra category – motivational strategies (Eckstein, 2007: 76). According to Eckstein, his organisation of PLS helps to meet learners' needs at a given pronunciation acquisition level and facilitates pronunciation automaticity. However, his taxonomy differs a lot from generic strategy classifications designed by other researchers, which makes it hard to make comparisons or references between them. Also, Eckstein's taxonomy could be completed with more memory and affective strategies.

For the reasons mentioned above, the author of the present chapter has decided to make an attempt to design a new taxonomy. The taxonomy is presented in Table 10.1. It has been created on the basis of Oxford's (1990) and Peterson's (2000) classifications. Next to each tactic there is a number of the relevant statement of the questionnaire (see the Appendix) which served as the main research tool of the study described below. Following Oxford (1990) and Peterson (2000), the strategies are divided into *direct* (memory, cognitive and compensation strategies) and *indirect* (metacognitive, affective and social strategies) strategies.

Research Project

Participants and data collection procedures

The research project described below constituted the first stage of a broader investigation into the effects of instruction in PLS. It was conducted among first-year students of English at two private teacher training colleges in Olsztyn in October 2008. Its aim was to identify the PLS the students had been using before completing a course in practical phonetics in order to plan and implement appropriate training.

The subjects of the study included 74 part-time and full-time students (11 males and 63 females). They ranged in age from 19 to 44 years, with a mean age of 24 years. On average, the subjects had been learning English for about eight years prior to the experiment. Some of them, especially part-time students, had had breaks in their education. Almost half of the

Table 10.1 Proposed classification of PLS

Direct strategies	
Group of Strategies	***Tactics***
Memory strategies	
A. Representing sounds in memory	(1) Grouping (3) (2) Making up songs, rhymes, sentences, etc., to memorise pronunciation (11) (3) Making associations: • *Visual* – associating the pronunciation of a word with the place where one has seen its transcription (7); associating sounds with mental or actual pictures (2); visualising transcription of a given word (6) • *Auditory* – associating the pronunciation of a word or sound with words or sounds existing in other languages, nature (1) • *Visual-auditory* – associating the pronunciation of a word or sound with a situation in which one has heard it (8) (4) using phonetic symbols or one's own code (5)
B. Reviewing well	(1) Regular revisions of new words' pronunciation (12)
C. Employing action	(1) Using mechanical techniques, e.g. using flash cards (13) (2) Making notes: creating posters, vocabulary lists with transcription, highlighting, etc. (4)
D. Rote-learning	(1) Repeating a word (aloud or silently) several times over (9) (2) Listening to a recorded list of words several times over to memorise their pronunciation (10)
Cognitive strategies	
A. Practising pronunciation	(1) Formally practising with sounds: • Phonetic drills (14) • Repeating after target language (TL) speakers (15) • Repeating simultaneously with TL speakers (16) • Repeating simultaneously with TL speakers, imitating their voice, gestures, etc. (17) • Imitating mouth movements made by TL speakers (20) • Listening to recordings to identify the pronunciation of new words (practising perception) (34)

Table 10.1 (*Continued*)

Direct strategies		
Group of Strategies		**Tactics**

		• Reading aloud, reciting, acting out dialogues, etc. (25, 26)
		• Whispering in order to 'feel' articulation better (27)
		• Exercising speech organs (22)
		• Observing speech organs in the mirror when speaking the TL (21)
		• Talking to oneself in the TL (24)
		• Rehearsing (23)
		• Completing various phonetic exercises (32)
		• Doing transcription exercises (33)
		(2) Practising naturalistically with a clear communicative aim:
		  • Using media (18)
		  • Speaking with foreigners in the TL (19)

B. Receiving and sending messages on pronunciation	(1)	Using resources, e.g. pronunciation dictionaries, books, websites on phonetics and phonology (28, 29)
C. Analysing and reasoning	(1) (2)	Reasoning deductively: forming and using pronunciation rules, testing hypotheses (30) Analysing contrastively: comparing TL sounds with sounds existing in other languages (31), imitating TL native speakers speaking the learner's mother tongue in order to feel the differences between the languages (36) and analysing pronunciation mistakes they make (37)
D. Creating structure for input and output	(1)	Taking notes: using phonetic symbols or one's own code to write down the pronunciation of new words (33); taking notes on pronunciation rules and information on phonetics and phonology (35)
Compensation strategies		
A. Guessing intelligently	(1)	Guessing the pronunciation of new words (e.g. on the basis of their spelling) (38)
B. Overcoming limitations in pronunciation	(1) (2) (3)	Using L1 pronunciation if the word in the TL and in the L1 is spelled in a similar way (40) Using proximal articulation (41) Avoiding words whose pronunciation one does not know (39)

Table 10.1 (*Continued*)

Indirect strategies	
Strategies group	**Tactics**
Metacognitive strategies	
A. Centring one's learning	(1) Revising theoretical knowledge on phonetics before doing a pronunciation task (47) (2) Paying attention to pronunciation – in general (directed attention) (43); or concentrating on a given phonetic feature (selective attention) (44)
B. Arranging and planning one's learning	(1) Searching information on pronunciation learning (45) (2) Organising learning (46) (3) Setting short and long time aims (49) (4) Planning for a language task (50) (5) Seeking practice opportunities (42) (6) Planning pronunciation learning (selecting materials, exercises, strategies, etc.) (48)
C. Evaluating one's learning	(1) Self-monitoring (51) (2) Self-evaluation (recording oneself to evaluate one's pronunciation) (52)
Affective strategies	
A. Lowering anxiety	(1) Using relaxation techniques, e.g. breathing, laughter, music (53)
B. Encouraging oneself	(1) Encouraging oneself to work on pronunciation (55) or to speak in the TL (54) (2) Rewarding oneself for success or effort put in pronunciation learning (56)
C. Taking one's emotional temperature	(1) Listening to one's body (57) (2) Having a sense of humour about one's mispronunciations (58) (3) Analysing one's feelings connected with pronunciation learning (59) (4) Discussing feelings with others (60)
Social strategies	
A. Asking questions	(1) Asking for help (62) (2) Asking for correction (61)
B. Cooperating with others	(1) Cooperating with peers and/or advanced users of the TL (63) (2) Peer tutoring (64)

respondents (31) claimed that they had not learnt English pronunciation prior to the experiment. Twenty-four students had stayed in English-speaking countries for two months to five years and had contacts with native speakers of English. Other respondents had learnt English only at school or attended English courses.

The preliminary identification of PLS used by the subjects was done on the basis of their answers to an open question: 'How did you learn English pronunciation before entering the college?' Detailed data on the types of strategies and frequency of their use were collected by means of a questionnaire (see the Appendix) designed on the basis of Oxford's Strategy Inventory for Language Learning (SILL) (1990: 293–296). The questionnaire consisted of 65 statements written in Polish in order to avoid confusion and misunderstandings. The respondents were asked to specify how often they applied a given way of learning pronunciation, using a five-point Likert scale, with 1 – never or almost never, 2 – rarely, 3 – sometimes, 4 – usually, 5 – always or almost always. The questionnaire was divided into five parts: A – memory strategies, B – cognitive strategies, C – compensation strategies, D – metacognitive strategies, E – affective strategies, F – social strategies. The last question was open-ended so that the participants could add any ways of pronunciation learning not mentioned in the questionnaire. The analysis involved determining the strategies and tactics listed in response to the open-ended item as well as calculating the means and standard deviations for each of the PLS included in the questionnaire.

Results

Preliminary identification of PLS showed that the subjects who had been learning pronunciation prior to the course used cognitive and metacognitive strategies. Most of them employed practising pronunciation, either formally by repeating (18 subjects), reading aloud (1 subject), or naturalistically by using the media (9 subjects) and speaking with foreigners (4 subjects). Another cognitive strategy applied by the participants was receiving and sending messages by using resources. Three respondents knew phonetic symbols and looked up pronunciation of new words in a dictionary, one had taught himself from the coursebook *Wymowa angielska dla wszystkich* (*English Pronunciation for Everybody*) and one had learnt pronunciation by using an interactive computer program. Using a pronunciation coursebook or a computer program is also connected with completing pronunciation exercises, which is an example of formal practising. That is why this tactic was added in parentheses in Table 10.2, which shows details on the identified PLS. One metacognitive strategy was identified, paying attention to pronunciation when listening to people speaking English (7 cases).

Table 10.2 Results for preliminary identification of PLS

Strategies	Tactics	Number of students
Cognitive strategies		
Practising pronunciation	(1) Practising formally with sounds • Repeating • (Completing phonetic exercises) • Reading aloud (2) Practising naturalistically with a clear communicative aim • Using media • Speaking with foreigners in the TL	18 (2) 1 9 4
Receiving and sending messages on pronunciation	Using resources to improve pronunciation • Using dictionaries • Using pronunciation coursebooks • Using computer programs to learn pronunciation	3 1 1
Metacognitive strategies		
Paying attention	Paying directed attention • Listening to people speaking English (live or recordings)	7

Since some of the subjects could have had difficulties in specifying their ways of learning pronunciation, another research tool was used. The author designed a questionnaire examining the frequency of use of particular strategies (see the Appendix) with the hope that completing it would make it easier for the students to state what PLS they were acquainted with. Table 10.3 shows the results of the questionnaire. The statements in each set of strategies are organised from most to least popular by means of all respondents' scores, and the means and standard deviations are also provided. In many cases the latter turned out to be high, which proves that there was a lot of variation in the participants' responses.

Let us first focus on the reported frequency of use of direct strategies. Among memory strategies, the most popular behaviour was rote learning, which is generally considered to be of low efficiency. At the same time, this was the most frequently applied strategy among all strategies examined in the study. Many subjects also memorised words by associating them with the situation in which they had heard them or by using phonetic symbols (or own code) to write down their pronunciation. The least popular tactics were listening to a recorded list of words several times over and using flash cards. Within cognitive

Table 10.3 Questionnaire results

Strategies group	Questionnaire statement number	Mean frequency of use	Standard deviation	Strategies group	Questionnaire statement number	Mean frequency of use	Standard deviation
Memory strategies	9	4.51	0.81	Compensation strategies	41	3.89	1.07
	8	3.7	1.13		38	3.77	1.13
	5	3.4	1.34		40	2.84	1.36
	7	3.27	1.34		39	2.62	1.29
	4	2.93	1.49	Metacognitive strategies	43	4.34	0.85
	12	2.89	1.14		50	4.19	0.9
	6	2.8	1.18		51	3.88	0.94
	3	2.76	1.2		46	3.74	1.1
	1	2.74	1.28		45	3.49	1.16
	2	2.46	1.18		49	3.19	1.24
	11	2.15	1.07		42	3.16	1.07
	13	1.7	1.08		44	2.84	1.33
	10	1.57	0.95		48	2.57	1.28

Table 10.3 (*Continued*)

Strategies group	Questionnaire statement number	Mean frequency of use	Standard deviation	Strategies group	Questionnaire statement number	Mean frequency of use	Standard deviation
Cognitive strategies	15	4.07	0.96	Affective strategies	47	2.26	1.38
	28	3.77	1.32		52	1.46	0.85
	18	3.76	0.98		58	3.99	1.12
	26	3.76	0.95		54	3.74	1.07
	24	3.53	1.02		55	3.31	1.08
	23	3.3	1.31		53	2.99	1.27
	19	3.22	1.56		57	2.68	1.34
	14	3.18	1.2		59	2.16	1.27
	16	2.72	1.29	Social strategies	60	2.09	1.15
	31	2.57	1.19		56	1.85	1.17
	25	2.55	1.28		62	3.99	1.03
	30	2.39	1.17		61	3.41	1.35
	37	2.14	1.32		64	2.42	1.26
	17	2.05	1.26		63	1.97	1.05

Table 10.3 (*Continued*)

Strategies group	Questionnaire statement number	Mean frequency of use	Standard deviation	Strategies group	Questionnaire statement number	Mean frequency of use	Standard deviation
	20	2.04	1.14	Open statement	65	1.59	1.24
	34	1.91	1.17				
	22	1.72	1.12				
	33	1.7	0.96				
	35	1.69	1.13				
	27	1.62	1.02				
	32	1.49	0.9				
	36	1.49	0.86				
	21	1.46	0.7				
	29	1.32	0.81				

strategies, repeating after target language (TL) speakers was most frequently used. Other strategies often applied were using resources (a dictionary) and reading aloud. The subjects rarely or almost never imitated TL native speakers speaking Polish to feel the difference between the two languages or completed phonetics exercises. They almost never observed their speech organs in the mirror while speaking English or searched for information on phonetics and phonology in books or websites. The latter was the least frequent tactic among all strategies examined in the study. In the case of lack of ability to produce a given TL sound, the subjects relied on proximal articulation. If they did not know how to pronounce a word, they applied intelligent guessing rather than avoiding the word or using Polish pronunciation.

When it comes to indirect PLS, among metacognitive strategies, paying attention to pronunciation was a fairly frequently used tactic. Behaviours such as looking up the pronunciation of new words in a dictionary and practising their pronunciation when preparing for oral assignments were also popular. Planning learning or revising theoretical information on phonetics prior to doing practical exercises appeared to be rarely used. The respondents admitted that they never or almost never applied self-evaluation. The most often used tactic among affective strategies was having a sense of humour about one's mispronunciations. The subjects also often encouraged themselves to speak English even if they were afraid of making pronunciation mistakes or encouraged themselves to work hard on their pronunciation. They rarely analysed their feelings connected with pronunciation learning and/or talked about them with others. The least frequent behaviour was rewarding oneself for success or effort put in pronunciation learning. Finally, the most popular social strategy was asking questions, especially the tactic of asking for help. The second most popular behaviour was asking for correction of the learner's mispronunciations. Peer tutoring and cooperation were rarely used by the participants in the study.

The last statement, the open-ended one, was completed only by 12 respondents. Ten of them mentioned singing in English, a behaviour that could be classified as a strategy of practising naturalistically. One student pointed to speaking aloud in order to improve pronunciation, which was actually included in the questionnaire (Statement 24). Yet another subject did not specify what 'other ways' of learning pronunciation she applied.

Conclusions

The research results presented above showed that the subjects used strategies belonging to all the groups of PLS, but did not apply a wide repertoire of tactics. They chose one or two favourite ones and relied on them when working on their pronunciation. Moreover, the tactics which the students selected were not very creative.

The most popular memory strategy was rote learning, a behaviour that brings short-time effects. Therefore there is a need to instruct L2 students in the use of memory tactics which guarantee long-time effects, such as grouping, making associations and putting words into context in order to memorise their pronunciation. The most often applied cognitive tactics were repeating, reading aloud and using a dictionary to check the pronunciation of unknown words. Surprisingly, the students rarely used modern technology, such as computer programs, the internet and dictaphones. Such tools facilitate information acquisition thanks to combining sound and vision, offering attractive ways of learning pronunciation, such as games and quizzes, and enabling access to authentic recordings. Rare use of other tactics, such as mirror practice, searching for theoretical information on English phonetics and phonology, is probably connected with the fact that most of the respondents had just started formal pronunciation instruction and were not aware of their gaps of knowledge in the subject. Compensation strategies were quite often used by the respondents. Many learners use them subconsciously when they lack the necessary knowledge or abilities. Undoubtedly, it is useful to train students in the use of such strategies, for they facilitate communication. However, if the learner's goal is acquiring nativelike pronunciation, their application should be limited. It would be disadvantageous to use proximal articulation, guessing or avoidance *instead* of putting effort into improving one's pronunciation. Therefore, the instructor should draw his or her learners' attention to situations in which using compensation strategies is desirable and in which it is not. As far as metacognitive strategies are concerned, it seems important to instruct the students how to plan pronunciation learning and how to evaluate themselves. These abilities help learners assess their strong and weak points and set goals which they should aim at if they want to be successful pronunciation learners. Metacognitive strategies also enable learners to take control of and responsibility for their learning, thanks to which they become more independent and autonomous.

Appendix

Questionnaire examining the frequency of use of PLS, designed on the basis of Oxford's (1990: 293–296) SILL.

Please read the statements below and mark the response (1, 2, 3, 4 or 5) that tells how often you apply a given way of learning English pronunciation.

1 – Never or almost never
2 – Rarely
3 – Sometimes
4 – Usually
5 – Always or almost always

PART A

1. In order to memorise the pronunciation of a given word I try to associate it with the pronunciation of a different word (in another language I know) or with some sounds (e.g. animal sounds, sounds of machines, devices, etc.).	1 2 3 4 5
2. I memorise the pronunciation of a given word by associating it with an image or a picture (in mind or in actual drawing).	1 2 3 4 5
3. I group words that sound similar in order to memorise their pronunciation.	1 2 3 4 5
4. I use visual aids to memorise the pronunciation of new words (e.g. posters with transcription of new words, and marking phonetic symbols with various colours).	1 2 3 4 5
5. In order to memorise the pronunciation of a given word I use phonetic symbols or my own code to write down its pronunciation.	1 2 3 4 5
6. I memorise the pronunciation of a given word by visualising its transcription.	1 2 3 4 5
7. I memorise the pronunciation of new words by remembering the location of their transcription on the page, board, etc.	1 2 3 4 5
8. I memorise the pronunciation of new words when I associate them with a situation in which I have heard them.	1 2 3 4 5
9. I repeat a word several times over (aloud or in my mind) to memorise its pronunciation.	1 2 3 4 5

10. I record words whose pronunciation I want to memorise and listen to the recording several times over.	1 2 3 4 5
11. I memorise the pronunciation of a given word by putting it into context (a sentence, a story, a rhyme, etc.)	1 2 3 4 5
12. I review the pronunciation of recently learnt words regularly.	1 2 3 4 5
13. I use flash cards which I put from 'I want to learn' pile to 'I have learnt' pile.	1 2 3 4 5

If you use other ways of memorising pronunciation than those mentioned above, please add them to the questionnaire at point 65.

PART B

14. I practise pronunciation by repeating sounds, words, sentences, etc., several times in the same way or in different ways (changing speed, dividing words into syllables, etc.).	1 2 3 4 5
15. I repeat sounds, words, sentences, etc., after English speakers.	1 2 3 4 5
16. I repeat sounds, words, sentences, etc., simultaneously with English speakers.	1 2 3 4 5
17. I repeat sounds, words, sentences, etc., simultaneously with English speakers, imitating their gestures and facial expressions.	1 2 3 4 5
18. I listen to the radio and/or watch TV in English.	1 2 3 4 5
19. I speak to foreigners in English.	1 2 3 4 5
20. I imitate mouth movements made by English speakers.	1 2 3 4 5
21. I observe the movements of articulators in the mirror when speaking English.	1 2 3 4 5
22. I do exercises recommended by speech therapists in order to make my tongue, lips and jaw more flexible.	1 2 3 4 5

23. Before I say something aloud, I practise saying a given word, sentence, etc., in my mind.	1 2 3 4 5
24. I practise my pronunciation by speaking to myself in English.	1 2 3 4 5
25. I practise my pronunciation by reciting texts and/or acting out dialogues.	1 2 3 4 5
26. I practise reading aloud, paying particular attention to my pronunciation.	1 2 3 4 5
27. I practise whispering to focus on the feeling of articulation.	1 2 3 4 5
28. I look up the pronunciation of unknown words in a dictionary.	1 2 3 4 5
29. I search for information on phonetics and phonology in books, on the internet, etc.	1 2 3 4 5
30. I try to identify and use pronunciation rules.	1 2 3 4 5
31. I analyse the differences between English pronunciation and the pronunciation of other languages.	1 2 3 4 5
32. I complete various phonetic exercises which I find in coursebooks, computer programs and on internet sites.	1 2 3 4 5
33. I use phonetic symbols.	1 2 3 4 5
34. I listen to recordings several times in order to identify the pronunciation of unknown words (perception practice).	1 2 3 4 5
35. I make notes on interesting phonetic problems.	1 2 3 4 5
36. I imitate native speakers of English, speaking Polish in order to feel the difference between the two languages better.	1 2 3 4 5
37. I pay attention to pronunciation errors made by native speakers of English-speaking Polish.	1 2 3 4 5

PART C

38. If I do not know how to pronounce a given word, I guess its pronunciation.	1 2 3 4 5
39. If I do not know how to pronounce a given word, I avoid using it.	1 2 3 4 5
40. If I do not know how to pronounce a given word and its spelling is similar to a Polish word, I use Polish pronunciation hoping that I will be understood.	1 2 3 4 5
41. If I cannot produce a given English sound, I produce a sound as similar to it as possible.	1 2 3 4 5

PART D

42. I try to find as many different ways of practising my English pronunciation as I can.	1 2 3 4 5
43. I pay attention to pronunciation when someone is speaking English.	1 2 3 4 5
44. I choose a phonetic problem (e.g. a given sound, word stress, intonation, etc.) and pay attention to it when someone is speaking English.	1 2 3 4 5
45. I try to find out how to improve my pronunciation.	1 2 3 4 5
46. I care for appropriate learning conditions so that my work on pronunciation is as efficient as possible.	1 2 3 4 5
47. Before practising a given pronunciation feature I revise appropriate theoretical knowledge.	1 2 3 4 5
48. I plan pronunciation learning – I set the time of learning, select materials, strategies, etc.	1 2 3 4 5
49. I have clear goals for improving my pronunciation.	1 2 3 4 5
50. When I prepare a talk in English, I look up the pronunciation of new words in a dictionary and practise their pronunciation.	1 2 3 4 5

51. I notice my pronunciation problems and try to overcome them.	1 2 3 4 5
52. I evaluate my progress in pronunciation by recording myself and comparing my pronunciation to the pronunciation of native speakers of English.	1 2 3 4 5

PART E

53. I try to relax whenever I feel afraid of reading aloud or speaking in English.	1 2 3 4 5
54. I encourage myself to speak English even when I am afraid that my pronunciation is not good.	1 2 3 4 5
55. I encourage myself to work on pronunciation even when I think that something is too difficult for me or when I do not feel like learning.	1 2 3 4 5
56. I give myself a reward or treat when I have worked hard on pronunciation.	1 2 3 4 5
57. I notice if I am tense or nervous when I am learning English pronunciation or speaking English and I try to relax.	1 2 3 4 5
58. I use a sense of humour about my mispronunciations.	1 2 3 4 5
59. I analyse my feelings connected with learning pronunciation.	1 2 3 4 5
60. I talk to someone else about how I feel when I am learning pronunciation.	1 2 3 4 5

PART F

61. I ask English speakers to correct my pronunciation when I speak.	1 2 3 4 5
62. I ask others for help if I do not know how to pronounce a given sound or word.	1 2 3 4 5

| 63. I learn pronunciation with other students, friends. | 1 2 3 4 5 |
| 64. I help others in learning pronunciation. | 1 2 3 4 5 |

OTHER

| 65. I use other way(s) of learning pronunciation (*Explain what you do*)... | 1 2 3 4 5 |

References

Bukowski, D. (2004) On the training of metacognitive and socio-affective strategies – some implications for teaching and learning English phonetics. In W. Sobkowiak and E. Waniek-Klimczak, E. (eds) *Dydaktyka fonetyki języka obcego w Polsce. Zeszyty Naukowe Państwowej Wyższej Szkoły Zawodowej w Koninie nr 1/2004* (pp. 20–27). Konin: Wydawnictwo Państwowej Wyższej Szkoły Zawodowej w Koninie.

Droździał-Szelest, K. (1997) *Language Learning Strategies in the Process of Acquiring a Foreign Language*. Poznań: Morivex.

Eckstein, G.T. (2007) A correlation of pronunciation learning strategies with spontaneous English pronunciation of adult ESL learners. MA thesis, Brigham Young University. Retrieved February 20, 2009, from: On WWW at http://contentdm.lib.byu.edu/ETD/image/etd1973.pdf.

Grenfell, M. and Macaro, E. (2007) Claims and critiques. In A.D. Cohen and E. Macaro (eds) *Language Learner Strategies: Thirty Years of Research and Practice* (pp. 9–28). Oxford: Oxford University Press.

Kolb, D.A. (1984) *Experiential Learning: Experience as the Source of Learning and Development*. Englewood Cliffs, NJ: Prentice-Hall.

Naiman, N., Fröhlich, M., Stern, H.H. and Todesco, A. (1978) *The Good Language Learner: A Report*. Research in Education Series 7. Ontario, Canada: Ontario Institute for Studies in Education.

Osborne, A. (2003) Pronunciation strategies of advanced ESOL learners. *IRAL* 41,131–143.

Oxford, R., (1990) *Language Learning Strategies: What Every Teacher Should Know*. Boston, MA: Heinle & Heinle.

Pawlak, M. (2006) 'On the use of pronunciation learning strategies by Polish foreign language learners'. In W. Sobkowiak and E. Waniek-Klimczak (eds) *Dydaktyka fonetyki języka obcego w Polsce* (pp. 121–135). Konin: Wydawnictwo Państwowej Wyższej Szkoły Zawodowej w Koninie.

Pawlak, M. (2008) Another look at the use of pronunciation learning strategies: An advanced learner's perspective. In E. Waniek-Klimczak (ed.) *Issues in Accents of English* (pp. 304–322). Newcastle upon Tyne, UK: Cambridge Schools Publishing.

Peterson S. S. (2000) *Pronunciation Learning Strategies: A First Look* (Unpublished research report, ERIC Document Reproduction Service ED 450599; FL 026618).

Retrieved June 10, 2006, from: On WWW at http://www.eric.ed.gov/ERIC Docs/data/ericdocs2sql/content_storage_01/0000019b/80/16/de/81.pdf.

Rivers, W. (1979) Learning a sixth language: An adult's learner diary. *Canadian Modern Language Review* 36, 67–82.

Varasarin, P. (2007) An action research study on pronunciation training, language learning strategies and speaking confidence. PhD dissertation, Victoria University. Retrieved March 15, 2009, from: On WWW at http://wallaby.vu.edu.au/adt-VVUT/uploads/approved/adt-VVUT20070911.162030/public/01 front.pdf.

Chapter 11
Metaphonetic Awareness in the Production of Speech

MAGDALENA WREMBEL

Consciousness in Foreign Language Learning

Defining the term

The discussion on the relationships between different types of knowledge involved in the process of foreign language acquisition is often based on the underlying problem of consciousness. There have been several attempts in the literature to identify this notion, particularly from a broad perspective of language awareness. van Lier (1998), for instance, proposes a broad view of consciousness reaching beyond a common practice of associating this term only with explicit knowledge of grammatical rules and formal analyses. To the traditional cognitive treatment of consciousness, van Lier adds a less prominent perspective that focuses on the social context. Within the cognitive perspective, several levels of consciousness are commonly identified including the following:

Level 1: Global ('intransitive') consciousness – being alive and awake. It is the most basic level that is a prerequisite for any learning.
Level 2: Awareness ('transitive' consciousness) – perceptual activity of objects and events embracing attention, focus and vigilance. This level is gradable.
Level 3: Metaconsciousness – being aware of the activity of the mind. It involves language awareness and metalinguistic awareness of formal linguistic properties.
Level 4: Voluntary action, reflective processes – deliberate and purposeful action
 (cf. van Lier, 1998: 131).

This hierarchy of consciousness levels indicates that each one presupposes the preceding one(s). Such a rationalist perspective which associates consciousness with thoughts and feelings of an individual prevails in most discussions of the issue in question.

A less popular approach, however, views consciousness as a social construct operating through social interactions. Drawing attention to the etymology of this term, and particularly to the prefix *con-*, Toulmin

(1982) suggests that it means 'jointly knowing'. From this perspective, consciousness is defined as the objectively observable organisation of behaviour that is imposed on humans through participation in socio-cultural practices. Along the same lines, Chafe considers consciousness 'as the crucial interface between the conscious organism and its environment' (1994: 38). This conscious interaction is possible thanks to various modes of human communication, the most important of which being language. Therefore, consciousness is commonly considered to be intimately connected with language since it is through language that our consciousness is constructed and language is seen as the essence of human social interaction. Recapitulating, both consciousness and language can be approached either from primarily cognitive (i.e. intrapersonal) or from social (i.e. interpersonal) perspectives.

The role of consciousness

The role of consciousness in foreign language acquisition has been widely debated and there seems to be no consensus on it, with a prevalent view being that of scepticism. The strongest arguments against any role of consciousness were originally put forward by behaviourists who considered this notion to be subjective, meaningless and epipheno-menal (i.e. playing no causal role in human life). With the decline of behaviourism, the issue of consciousness and its role in language learning was subject to a serious reconsideration and some mainstream cognitive frameworks have started to consider awareness as necessary for learning. Nonetheless, many of the most influential authorities in the field of second language acquisition (SLA) firmly believe that language learning is essentially unconscious; what is acquired is implicit mental grammar, and conscious learning is of little use in the actual language production and comprehension (cf., e.g. Chomsky, 1959, 1980; Krashen, 1981).

One of the theoretical frameworks that advocate the role of conscious-ness as a necessary condition for foreign language learning is that of Białystok (1994) and Białystok and Ryan (1985). The proposed model considers learning to be a process of developing analysed knowledge and control over that knowledge. Thus, the earlier notion of the explicit/implicit dichotomy is presented in terms of two intersecting continua that reflect the degree to which given rules are controlled or analysed. Analysed knowledge is defined as conscious as opposed to intuitive knowledge. In the process of language development, knowledge becomes more analysed, complex and abstract. Moreover, implicit knowledge becomes explicit and can be subject to conscious analysis. The control component, in turn, can be defined in terms of its functions, namely selecting and coordinating items of information and knowledge as well as enabling this performance to become automatic. In addition, control involves the access procedures for the representation of knowledge and it is responsible for the development of selective attention in relation to relevant aspects of representation. The two components are required for different types of processing; analysed knowledge is responsible for accuracy, whereas control is responsible for fluency. Furthermore, Białystok posits a claim that learners will perform differently on tasks which make high demands on analysed knowledge or control as a function of their learning experience.

Another vocal proposal of a conscious mechanism underlying language learning, based on recent psychological research, was put forward by Schmidt (1990: 131), who distinguished three types of consciousness, including (1) consciousness as awareness, (2) consciousness as intention and (3) consciousness as knowledge. The first sense was further subdivided according to different levels of awareness, ranging from 'perception' (not always conscious) via 'noticing' (involving focal awareness) and, finally, 'understanding' (i.e. conscious analysis).

Schmidt (1990) addressed the major issues in SLA related to the role of consciousness in input processing, namely (1) whether conscious awareness is necessary for language learning at the level of noticing ('subliminal learning' issue), (2) whether learning requires from learners to consciously pay attention (i.e. 'incidental learning' issue) and (3) whether conscious understanding is indispensable (implicit vs explicit learning). He concluded that subliminal learning is impossible, stressing that some degree of consciousness is indispensable for 'noticing'. This process consists in learners' comparison between the observed input and their own production at a particular stage of development of the interlanguage system. *Conscious noticing* is thus a precondition for the input to become intake and be stored in temporary memory. Conversely, incidental learning appears to be possible and effective; however, Schmidt indicates that paying attention may be a very helpful factor. Finally, although Schmidt claims that there is evidence for a facilitative effect of conscious understanding, he does not preclude completely implicit language learning. On the whole, however, he tends to emphasise the role of consciousness and awareness in the process of language learning.

Metalinguistic Awareness

Levels of language awareness

One of the most persistent problems with the notion of consciousness, from the perspective of second language learning, is the distinction between *intuitive language awareness* and *metalinguistic knowledge*. To reflect this discrepancy, Gombert (1992) distinguishes between *epilinguistic* and *metalinguistic awareness*. Epilinguistic awareness is unconscious, spontaneous and contextualised and thus can be exemplified by the instances of self-repair in speech performance. Metalinguistic awareness, on the other hand, is decontextualised, conscious and intentional and involves, for instance, language analysis in the classroom or conscious reflection on language properties.

Similarly, van Lier (1998) refers to *practical/narrative* and *academic/ technical control*, pointing out that the latter applies specialised technical vocabulary and involves explicit usage of linguistic structures, whereas the former does not. Furthermore, van Lier proposes a model of multiple layers of language awareness (see Figure 11.1). In the course of learning, transformations from Level 2 to Level 3(a) and from Level 3(a) to Level 3(b) are possible and constitute natural results of learning. He suggests, however, that all the levels of language awareness persist even as language knowledge becomes more sophisticated and reaches the metalingustic form.

Functions of metaphonetic awareness

Since the scope of the present contribution concerns phonetic performance in speech, an attempt is made to translate the previously discussed role of conscious awareness in second language learning into the specific realm of L2 phonological acquisition.

From the perspective of the presented discussion, the notion of metaphonetic awareness is understood by the present author as pertaining to the explicit dimension of L2 knowledge in the form of conscious analytic awareness of the formal properties of the target language, and specifically its phonetics and phonology. This explicit dimension embraces both declarative forms (i.e. knowledge of facts) as well as

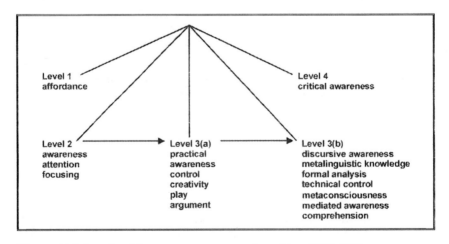

Figure 11.1 Levels of language awareness (van Lier, 1998: 136)

some degree of procedural knowledge, as in my broader conceptualisation of the term it would also entail conscious knowledge of learning and production strategies in L2 speech, which fall within the scope of the procedural aspect. Consequently, metaphonetic awareness requires a high degree of analysed knowledge, that is abstract structured knowledge of phonetics and phonology, as well as a considerable level of processing control, that is intentional focus on phonetic forms and articulatory gestures during speech performance.

Adopting Ellis' (1994) stipulations on the functioning of explicit knowledge, it is, therefore, postulated by the present author that metaphonetic awareness may function in a threefold manner as the following (see Wrembel, 2005, for a more detailed discussion of the proposed metacompetence model):

(1) Facilitator of intake operating at the level of perception and helping input to become conscious intake. It consists in conscious noticing of specific characteristics of L2 sounds by attracting learners' attention to those linguistic features they have learnt about through formal explicit instruction.

(2) Acquisition facilitator as metacompetence is predicted to have the potential to facilitate the process of acquisition and form adequate representations by deciphering underlying intentions and preventing the mapping into L1 system.

(3) Monitoring device exercising control of the output as conscious L2 competence helps to provide reflective feedback on the production. Moreover, metaphonetic competence is a means of empowering L2 learners and enhancing their autonomy by equipping them with necessary tools for self-monitoring and self-correction.

Research on metalinguistic awareness

The recent upsurge of interest in metalinguistic awareness has been particularly triggered by a growing concern about declining standards of students' language achievements and dissatisfaction with their knowledge about language. As a result of this, several research attempts have been made to examine the nature of metalinguistic awareness and the relationship between metalinguistic awareness and learner competence in the sense of language proficiency.

Alderson *et al.* (1997) investigated this relationship on the basis of a battery of tests for metalinguistic knowledge and language aptitude, yet the results pointed to a weak correlation between these variables. On the other hand, findings from some previous studies including Białystok (1982) or Gass (1988) demonstrated that higher levels of metalinguistic awareness are concomitant with improvements in L2 proficiency. Furthermore, Renou (2001) conducted a study which was based on the assumption that linguistic and metalinguistic proficiencies consist of two components, that is analysed knowledge and control over that knowledge (cf. Białystok & Ryan, 1985). Renou used grammaticality judgements as a measure of metalinguistic awareness as she compared communicative versus grammar approach to L2 learning. Her findings indicate that increases in metalinguistic awareness were associated with increases in language proficiency. The interface between metalinguistic task performance and oral production in a second language was also examined by White and Ranta (2002). The findings revealed that metalinguistic instruction correlated significantly with higher levels of performance on a metalinguistic task as well as oral production.

To the best of my knowledge, the majority of studies to date on the role of metalinguistic awareness in fostering language proficiency has focused on grammatical proficiency as well as the knowledge of metalinguistic terminology. My previous long-term empirical study (cf. Wrembel, 2005) was fairly innovative in this respect since it explored the impact of analysed phonological knowledge and metalinguistic awareness on second language pronunciation performance. The results demonstrated that meta-awareness raising and conscious acquisition of explicit knowledge contribute to the development of L2 phonological competence. The present study aims at complementing the earlier investigation by tapping into learners' self-perception of metaphonetic awareness in spontaneous L2 speech production.

Experiment

The present experiment consisted in a preliminary investigation into strategies of conscious control over foreign language pronunciation in the production of L2 speech conducted with the application of think aloud protocols. The study aimed to elicit the participants' self-reflection on the means of monitoring their English pronunciation during spontaneous speech as well as to identify strategies for raising phonetic awareness.

Think aloud protocols

The study was based on an introspective method called think aloud protocols (TAPs), that is verbalised reports aimed at disclosing the participants' intuition and mental processes when performing a given task. In spite of the initial criticism that this instrument triggered when first applied in psychological experiments in the 20th century, it is now widely used in research on human information processing (Ericsson & Simon, 1984), on meta-awareness in multilingualism (e.g. Jessner, 2006) or on pronunciation-monitoring strategies (Osborne, 2003). According to Ericsson and Simon (1984), the process of verbalisation of cognitive processes in TAPs can be traced at three different levels of thought processing:

- the level of verbalisation (articulation of oral encodings);
- the level of description or explication of the content;
- the level of explanation of thoughts and ideas or emotional reactions to the assigned task.

Cohen (1996), in turn, claims that verbal reports reflect the following aspects:

- self-report, that is learners' descriptions and general statements about their learning process;
- self-observation, that is inspections of specific language behaviour (both introspective and retrospective);
- self-revelation, that is disclosure of the thought process.

TAPs differ from self-report interviews and questionnaires since they attempt to elicit introspective data at the moment or near the moment of the learning event (Jessner, 2006), and therefore this method was selected for the purpose of the present experiment.

Participants and procedure

The participants of the study included 15 first-year students of the School of English at Adam Mickiewicz University, Poznań, Poland. Their mean age was 19.5 years, and their proficiency level of English was between intermediate and upper-intermediate.

The study consisted of two parts: the first one involved introspective TAPs, whereas the second part consisted in retrospective protocols based on self-repair and commentaries. Recording 1 was a spontaneous oral presentation in English based on six general questions on meta-awareness and pronunciation monitoring. The respondents were seated in front of the computer screen with a recording program on and addressed the questions that were presented in a written form, trying to verbalise all the thoughts and reflections that came to their minds. The sessions were conducted on individual basis. The researcher did not intervene in any way in the process of self-reflection.

In the second part of the experiment, a 30-second-long fragment of Recording 1 was played back and the participant was asked for comments and self-correction. The samples were recorded as 16-bit mono files at a sampling frequency of 16,000 Hz using CoolEdit96 software. Recording 1 lasted on average 3.16 seconds, whereas Recording 2 lasted 0.49 seconds.

The support questions that the participants were supposed to address when performing their verbal protocols involved the following:

(1) How do you try to monitor your English pronunciation?
(2) Do you consciously think about it during spontaneous speech/
     during pronunciation classes?
(3) What helps you monitor your oral production?
(4) Which strategies of practicing and monitoring your pronunciation
     do you use?
(5) Which aspects of pronunciation are you able to monitor the most
     during oral production?
(6) What helps you develop your phonetic awareness?

Results

The data generated by means of the conducted TAPs were mostly of a
quantitative nature. The first part of the experiment consisted in
introspective TAPs that were aimed at investigating the participants'
metaphonetic awareness as well as their ability to analyse and consciously monitor the phonetic output during spontaneous L2 speech.

In response to Question 1 on how they try to monitor their English
pronunciation, the subjects stated that it is difficult because it seems
unnatural to them. On the other hand, several subjects admitted that
they attempt to do so and that it is a question of practice, and with time
it becomes more achievable. Several participants referred to the awareness of the phonological rules that they have learnt in the course of their
studies. However, some admitted that although they seem to know
theoretically how to pronounce a given word, in practice, they
fail to articulate it correctly. Others stressed their conscious efforts to
remain intelligible for the interlocutor by speaking clearly and at a slower
rate.

Question 2 aimed at exploring whether the subjects consciously think
about pronunciation during spontaneous speech or during their pronunciation classes. The spontaneous speech condition usually triggered
negative responses as the subjects admitted that they are mostly unable
to monitor pronunciation, however hard they try, since they mainly focus
on other aspects of speech such as the content and grammatical
correctness. Nonetheless, when addressing the second part of the
question, the subjects frequently declared that they pay particular
attention to monitoring their speech with respect to phonetic accuracy
during pronunciation classes. This focus on form was described as
requiring a lot of effort and involving a slower rate of speech.

Question 3 on what helps them monitor their oral production
triggered the following responses:

• peer correction when communicating in English outside class (an
  aspect indicated unanimously by all the respondents);
• teacher correction in class;

- recording of one's speech and critical self-evaluation;
- slower rate of speech;
- speaking aloud to oneself;
- practice in front of the mirror, controlling mimics;
- stress management.

The following question was aimed at eliciting the strategies that used to practice and monitor their pronunciation. The participants declared that they regularly record and listen to their own speech, imitate model texts recorded by native speakers, repeat problematic words aloud often with kinaesthetic reinforcement and check transcription in dictionaries. Other enumerated strategies involved exposure to spoken language and conscious reflection on committed pronunciation errors.

Question 5 investigated the aspects of pronunciation that the participants are able to monitor the most during oral production. The subjects declared that they consciously try to control especially the quality and quantity of vowels and diphthongs, some problematic consonants, word stress, fluency and those aspects which their teacher draw their attention to.

In response to Question 6 on what helps them develop their phonetic awareness, the participants pointed particularly to classes of practical phonetics, their declarative knowledge of rules, feedback from other listeners and conscious analysis of modal oral texts.

Quantitative analysis of Recording 1 revealed that the instances of self-repair and self-correction were observed in 10 out of 15 participants (1 to 4 times per person, a total of 22 self-corrections). At the segmental level, there were 17 instances of self-correction involving vowels (9 times) and consonants (8 times). At the suprasegmental level, self-correction occurred 5 times and involved word stress placement. There was only one case of a direct question, that is a request for confirmation of a phonetic form.

The second part of the experiment consisted in retrospective oral protocols recorded after listening to a 30-second-long fragment of the previous recording of their spontaneous speech. The analysis of Recording 2 revealed the amount and type of self-corrections and retrospective commentaries voiced by the participants. In total, 47 instances of comments and self-corrections were observed ($M = 3$) and they involved the following aspects of the participants' phonetic performance:

(1) vowel quality (10);
(2) vowel length (7);
(3) consonantal errors (7);
(4) lack of fluency, fillers (6);
(5) unclear articulation (5);

(6) lack of self-confidence (3);
(7) mispronunciation of a whole word (2);
(8) intonation (2);
(9) rate of speech (2);
(10) final obstruent devoicing (1).

Discussion

The results of TAPs provide evidence for a significant level of metaphonetic awareness among the participants during their spontaneous spoken performance. The elements of epilinguistic awareness were evidenced by spontaneous self-correction. Metalinguistic awareness proved to be fairly well developed as the participants exhibited an awareness of their own specific phonetic problems and an ability to analyse their own speech in retrospection. Moreover, the meta-awareness was also demonstrated through the application of strategies for improving foreign language pronunciation. The following strategies of pronunciation modification were declared as being regularly used by the participants:

(1) Metacognitive strategies
  (a) self-monitoring (during L2 speech performance);
  (b) self-evaluation (listening to recordings of once own spoken performance);
  (c) selective/guided attention (while listening to phonetic properties of L2 speech).
(2) Socioaffective
  (a) interactions with peers (group practice of pronunciation);
  (b) peer correction.
(3) Cognitive
  (a) practical pronunciation exercises (drills, imitation);
  (b) reference materials (e.g. referring to pronunciation dictionaries).

Furthermore, TAPs proved to be a fairly efficient means of investigating the participants' metaphonetic awareness as well as their ability to analyse and consciously monitor the phonetic output during spontaneous L2 speech.

On the whole, the level of metaphonetic awareness was evaluated from the analysis versus control perspective (cf. Białystok & Ryan, 1985). With respect to the former, the subjects demonstrated a rather high degree of analysed knowledge that was evidenced by elicited aspects of formalised phonetic knowledge, instances of self-repair and explicit statements of pronunciation strategies applied by the subjects. However, the level of control was much lower as the participants experienced problems with focusing on phonetic form during their L2 speech, thus processing control proved often insufficient.

Pedagogical Implications

Following recent trends in pronunciation pedagogy, the present author advocates the idea of developing metaphonetic awareness through a gradual introduction of stages of conscious control of the process of speech production. It is, therefore, proposed that the consecutive stages of monitoring of phonetic coding should involve as follows:

(1) analytic conscious listening practice;
(2) imitation;
(3) shadowing (delayed imitation of the target text);
(4) text reading;
(5) rote learning – reciting texts from memory;
(6) acting out scenes and dialogues;
(7) prepared oral presentations;
(8) spontaneous speeches;

Moreover, it is suggested that some guidelines for self-monitoring of speech performance should be applied, as proposed by Morley (1994: 87), including the following:

- using strong, vigorous speech;
- taking time to slow your rate of speech and vary tempo;
- using controlled speed and pausing by phrase groups;
- using clear emphasis;
- establishing the rhythmic stress–unstress pattern of English including reductions and contractions;
- linking words into phrase groups across word boundaries;
- using lively, expressive voice qualities.

Furthermore, drawing on Sharwood Smith's (1990) suggestion of different manifestations of language consciousness raising, I proposed a schema of techniques for developing metaphonetic awareness (see Table 11.1). This schematic presentation is based on different degrees of explicitness on the one hand and elaboration on the other. Alphabetic ordering of sections corresponds to the proposed order of incorporating respective types of techniques into a pronunciation syllabus allowing, however, for a cyclic re-occurrence of specific practices (for a detailed discussion of the proposed techniques, see Wrembel, 2006).

The presented metaphonetic awareness framework strives to empower learners by equipping them with self-monitoring and self-correction

Table 11.1 Techniques for raising metaphonetic awareness in speech production

B Articulatory control	D Multimedia learning aids
Articulatory warm-up exercises Drama voice techniques Articulatory setting exercises: • voice quality • imitation and oral mimicry	Animated views of the articulators Video close-ups of the mouth Computerised displays of speech patterns Spectrograms
A Basic awareness raising	**C Informed teaching techniques**
Relaxation, breathing, visualisation Sensitisation: • perceptual tuning in Awareness raising activities: • discussions • questionnaires • metaphonetic trivia • concern for pronunciation	Theoretical foundations (rules) Contrastive information Pitch-contour notation Guided ear-training – analytic listening Self-monitoring techniques

Elaboration →

Explicitness (covert–overt)

strategies so that they may be involved consciously in the speech modification process. In practice, it entails helping L2 learners to develop self-rehearsal techniques (e.g. talking to oneself, audio- or videotaping presentations or rehearsing in small groups) as well as providing them with procedures for self-diagnosis.

In conclusion, there seems to be a general consensus that the ultimate goal of learning is achieving a stage at which L2 learners can use the target language in a spontaneous, unreflecting manner. It remains, however, an area of contention among different approaches to SLA research how this goal can be achieved. The present proposal of promoting metalinguistic awareness in the area of L2 phonetic performance is in line with the call for consciousness raising in second language learning expressed by several authorities in the field of SLA (cf. Schmidt, 1990; Sharwood Smith, 1990). Therefore, the present author maintains that through developing metaphonetic awareness based on (1) constructing some explicit representation of phonetic/phonological knowledge, (2) providing metacognitive training in the form of pronunciation strategy instruction and (3) introducing practical techniques based on consecutive steps of increased speech monitoring, one can considerably increase conscious phonetic control over the process of foreign speech production.

References

Alderson, J., Clapham, C. and Steel, D. (1997) Metalinguistic knowledge, language aptitude and language proficiency. *Language Teaching Research* 1, 93–121.

Białystok, E. (1982) On the relationship between knowing and using linguistic forms. *Applied Linguistics* 3, 181–206.

Białystok, E. (1994) Analysis and control in the development of second language proficiency. *Studies in Second Language Acquisition* 16, 157–168.

Białystok, E. and Ryan, E. (1985) Toward a definition of metalinguistic skill. *Merrill-Palmer Quarterly* 31, 229–251.

Chafe, W. (1994) *Discourse, Consciousness, and Time.* Chicago: University of Chicago Press.

Chomsky, N. (1959) Review of *Verbal Behaviour* by B.F. Skinner. *Language* 35, 26–58.

Chomsky, N. (1980) *Rules and Representations.* New York: Columbia University Press.

Cohen, A. (1996) Verbal reports as a source of insights into second language learner strategies. *Applied Language Learning* 7, 5–24.

Ellis, R. (1994) *The Study of Second Language Acquisition.* Oxford: Oxford University Press.

Ericsson, A. and Simon, H. (1984) *Protocol Analysis: Verbal Reports as Data.* Cambridge, MA: MIT Press.

Gass, S. (1988) Integrating research areas: A framework for second language studies. *Applied Linguistics* 9, 198–217.

Gombert, J.E. (1992) *Metalinguistic Development.* New York: Harvester Wheatsheaf.

Jessner, U. (2006) *Linguistic Awareness in Multilinguals: English as a Third Language.* Edinburgh: Edinburgh University Press.

Krashen S. (1981) *Second Language Acquisition and Second Language Learning.* Oxford: Pergamon Institute.

Morley, J. (1994) *Pronunciation Pedagogy and Theory: New Views, New Directions.* Alexandria: TESOL.

Osborne, A. (2003) Pronunciation strategies of advanced ESOL learners. *IRAL* 41, 131–143.

Renou, J. (2001) An examination of the relationship between metalinguistic awareness and second-language proficiency of adult learners of French. *Language Awareness* 10, 248–267.

Schmidt, R. (1990) The role of consciousness in second language learning. *Applied Linguistics* 11, 129–158.

Sharwood Smith, M. (1990) Consciousness-raising and the second language learner. *Applied Linguistics* 11, 159–168.

Toulmin, S. (1982) The genealogy of 'consciousness'. In P.F. Secord (ed.) *Explaining Human Behaviour: Consciousness, Human Action, and Social Structure* (pp. 53–70). Beverly Hills, CA: Sage.

van Lier, L. (1998) The relationship between consciousness, interaction and language Learning. *Language Awareness* 7, 128–145.

White, J. and Ranta, L. (2002) Examining the interface between metalinguistic task performance and oral production in a second language. *Language Awareness* 11, 259–289.

Wrembel, M. (2005) Phonological metacompetence in the acquisition of second language phonetics. PhD thesis, Adam Mickiewicz University.

Wrembel, M. (2006) Consciousness in pronunciation teaching and learning. In *IATEFL Poland Newsletter, Post-Conference Edition No 26* (pp. 11–20). Warszawa: IATEFL.

Chapter 12
Foreign Language Speaking Anxiety from the Perspective of Polish Students of German Studies

KRZYSZTOF NERLICKI

Introduction

The impact of individual factors on language acquisition has had a prominent place in scientific research for more than 30 years. The need for this kind of investigation arose as a result of pedagogic observation and experience, which suggest that learning is not only determined by biological and cognitive factors but also depends on students' individual characteristics (e.g. ability, motivation, learning style and personality), their foreign language learning beliefs, their previous learning experience and, finally, the surroundings in which they learn. From among these aspects, foreign language learning and speaking anxiety in foreign language speaking have attracted a significant amount of scholarly attention. During the past three decades, attitudes towards language teaching have changed from the traditional grammar translation and audio-lingual methods and have instead gravitated towards communicative language teaching. It has been observed, however, that the pedagogic focus on the practical use of language might in fact result many times in an increase of anxiety. This anxiety is visible especially, but not only, when students speak in a foreign language.

The extensive English literature on this subject mainly concerns the anxiety of learning English as a foreign language. Research results have been published for various ethnic groups, particularly numerous are those studies that are devoted to Chinese, Japanese and Korean students, also in comparison with other Anglophone countries. Little research has been conducted in central and eastern European countries (e.g. Piechurska-Kuciel, 2008; Turula, 2006; Zybert, 2006) and in relation to other foreign languages, such as German (Nerlicki, 2007, 2009). The goal of the current chapter is to present the opinions of Polish students of Germanic studies on their anxiety when speaking German. The key assumption, based on the literature and my own research, is that many sources of foreign language speaking anxiety come into being *before* the actual processes of speaking. They are a product of students' foreign language learning experiences and beliefs. Their nature is often hypothetical, and they are based on the simple assumption that something can go wrong in oral communication. Actual problems on the cognitive plane during speech production are frequently the result of such anxieties. They might increase whilst speaking and, as a result, negatively affect the entire utterance. It is easy to see when comparing the results of different studies that many causes of anxiety are characterized by a particular universalism. One should, therefore, consider what induces it. Is this anxiety merely a product of similar character traits among those who suffer from it? Are similar social conditions in the organization of foreign language teaching a source of this anxiety? Is it that despite the years that have passed, we still have not freed ourselves from considering language teaching and learning to be a study of its system (e.g. its grammatical and lexical aspects) which does not always translate into practical use? Has this given rise in some teachers and, more importantly, students to a more or less unconscious system of beliefs that determine the actual goals in terms of how foreign languages should be taught and learned? Or finally, should we accept that anxiety is an inescapable part of communicative language teaching, and therefore we should only deal with its effects as quickly as possible? And if so, how should we do this? In the context of the presented study of Polish students, the current chapter and its pedagogical implications are hoped to contribute to the research that is being carried out worldwide.

Anxiety in Foreign Language Learning: A Brief Overview of Relevant Research

As was mentioned before, scholarly interest in foreign language anxiety began as early as the late 1960s and developed during the 1970s, 1980s and 1990s. This is related to the fact that the (sometimes purely theoretical) models of language acquisition which were proposed at that time began taking into consideration the interrelations between the biological, cognitive factors in language learning and the affective and social ones. I would like to mention here Krashen's affective filter hypothesis, Schumann's acculturation model and Gardner's socio-educational model. Their proponents paid special attention to the psycho-socio-cultural context of language learning, which might have a significant influence on students' performance (Lim, 2004: 42). It was in this context that the impact of anxiety on language learning aroused interest. This kind of research extended the investigation into the characteristics of the so-called good language learner that had begun in the mid-1970s. Only a few studies (e.g. Kleinmann, 1977) managed to show weak positive correlation between anxiety and learning achieve-ment. In relation to the learning situation, a distinction was introduced between *facilitating* and *debilitating anxiety*. It was assumed that anxiety can act as a substantial obstacle to performing specific communication tasks. The essence of the influence of anxiety on the communication tasks students perform is the level of difficulty of these tasks and, undoubtedly, the time students need to complete them. MacIntyre (1995: 92), adducing Eysenck's (1979) research, claims that an increase in the level of anxiety is directly proportional to the size of the compensation required for the completion of a given task (e.g. in an oral performance, the student must recall lexico-grammatical structures before the actual language production). When completing easy (but time-pressured) tasks, students do not need to compensate for possible gaps in their competence, and so the anxiety does not yet enter the phase of negative influence. Moreover, according to the Yerkes–Dodson law, low-level anxiety can in fact support the learning process (which has been termed facilitating anxiety). With difficult tasks (communicative situations), students enter into a phase of negative influence of anxiety which, as a result of its increased force, renders the achievement of the intended goal impossible.

Naturally, foreign language anxiety is not an isolated factor. Lim (2004) points out that while it can stimulate positive emotions in students with higher IQs, in those with lower IQs, even a simple task leads to, for example, a decrease in motivation and anxiety as a side effect. Researchers, basing their analysis primarily on psychological works, were aware that the substance of the appearing anxiety should be considered in the context both of individual aspects (both emotional and cognitive, which are connected with, among other aspects, the level of difficulty of the tasks given to the students) and of environmental aspects (modes of learning: at school vs outside of it, native vs non-native surroundings, etc.). Hence, it was acknowledged that negative emotions in foreign language learning should be classified first of all as so-called *social anxiety* (cf. MacIntyre, 1995). According to MacIntyre, social anxiety results primarily from social and communicative factors induced by the processes of learning and using a foreign language, eventually negatively affecting cognition (e.g. distracting self-directed cognition, expectations of failure and a decrease in cognitive processing ability) and students' actions (e.g. increases in arousal of the sympathetic nervous system, inhibited actions, attempts to escape the situation, and also, in physiology, stammering and blushing) (MacIntyre, 1995: 91, 93; Woodrow, 2006: 310). Because of its complex functions in the process of language acquisition and foreign language utterance production, researchers lean towards recognizing the cognitive plane as being the most negatively affected. The kind of influence varies depending on the manner of information processing: (1) in the phase of input reception, (2) its combination with other information or (3) during output production (e.g. MacIntyre & Gardner, 1994). In general, *trait, situation-specific* and *state anxiety* are distinguished. Trait anxiety is related to the personality of the student. It is understood as a tendency towards timid reactions; it is stable in time and essentially invariable. Situation-specific anxiety is a form of trait anxiety. It is connected with particular situations. It, too, is stable in time, but does not have to be constant. State anxiety surfaces in a given unforeseen moment as a reaction to something (MacIntyre & Gardner, 1991: 90). MacIntyre and Gardner believe that anxieties in foreign language learning are mainly situation-specific, for 'individuals feel different levels of anxiety depending on how they appraise and perceive given situations' (Lim, 2004).

Within this short presentation of the current state of research into foreign language anxiety, it is worth mentioning a debate whose theoretical empirical basis can be reduced to one crucial question: Is anxiety the cause or the consequence of the negative results in language study? Sparks and Ganschow (1991) took the position that difficulties in foreign language learning do not result from anxiety but from cognitive problems in L1 processing. These assumptions were based on the study of L1 reading and writing competence in children, which was conducted in the mid-1980s by, among others, Vellutino and Scanlon (1986, after Ganschow & Sparks, 1996). They found that people who read and write comparatively little have problems in processing information on the phono-orthographic plane and, to a lesser degree, on the semantic plane. According to researchers, the poor performance of this type of students is likely to be the cause of the negative emotions that appear. The Linguistic Coding Differences Hypothesis put forward by Sparks and Ganschow assumes that the causal connection is directed from cognitive problems in language processing to the arising anxieties (e.g. Ganschow & Sparks, 1996; Sparks & Ganschow, 1993). Sparks and Ganschow (1995) are sceptical about the assumption that anxiety is the cause of poor results of study and offer examples of people with high levels of anxiety who did not necessarily perform poorly at oral exercises. Gardner, Horwitz, MacIntyre and others adopt a different standpoint. Horwitz (2000) emphasizes that cognitive deficiency in L1 processing might indeed negatively affect L2 study and, as a consequence, give rise to anxiety. There are, however, many students who manifest speaking anxiety without any L1 deficiency having been identified. Many arguments have been produced to prove that the Sparks and Ganschow hypothesis is only correct to a limited degree. Horwitz (2000) found that many foreign language teachers are anxious to speak in a foreign language; this in itself contradicts Sparks and Ganschow's hypothesis, as it is doubtful that people with cognitive problems would want to become language teachers, not to mention the limited likelihood of them finishing a course of linguistic studies. Tittle (1997) adduces the research carried out by

Beck (1967), which shows that affective factors are strictly determined by the individual's perception of events and experiences. People with social anxiety, which includes foreign language anxiety, regard learning and communication situations as stressful even if in reality they are not. The more difficult the specific situations appear in students' beliefs, the higher the stress they induce. Lim (2004) cites Pekrun's (1984) study which demonstrates that anxiety is actually the product of students' assumptions that the results of their future actions will be negative (the so-called *expectancy-value theory of anxiety*): '(...) anxiety occurs when learners expect negative events and when they value highly the outcome of the events' (Lim, 2004: 44). In his other research, Lim (2003, after Lim, 2004) observes that anxiety appears in people susceptible to this kind of emotions when they perform highly complex and important tasks (e.g. tests) and when their locus of control is low.

Therefore, anxiety leads to difficulties in linguistic production; it increases negative external and personal evaluation; and at the same time, it also strengthens the students' conviction that they are incapable of coping with given learning or communicative actions. This can be schematically presented as in Figure 12.1. Looking at this scheme, it is impossible to rule out Sparks and Ganschow's hypothesis that it is cognitive difficulties that might account for poor performance or negative personal or external evaluation, and these in turn lead to greater anxiety. However, if we take into account research findings showing that anxiety arises quite frequently in students who are successful in study (Horwitz, 2000) and who often strive for linguistic perfection (Bailey, 1983), then anxiety indeed appears to be the main cause of the failures that occur from time to time. Phillips (1991) believes that language aptitude alone is not always sufficient to guarantee success in language study. It is often the case that foreign language beliefs, and not real learning or communicative situations, have much more influence on the development of anxiety. Phillips (1991) refers to the research by Guiora and colleagues (e.g. Guoira *et al.*, 1972), who believe that self-image and self-expression are closely

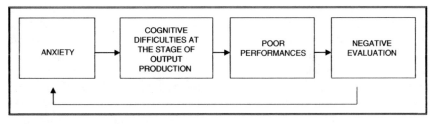

Figure 12.1 Circular dependencies between anxiety, cognitive processes, students' performances and evaluation.

correlated to the so-called language ego. This refers in particular to the development of strong awareness in students that language learning is a major challenge, and the use of language (including their own mother tongue) is not always free of errors. Hence, '(...) an adult language learner must develop a new ego for each foreign language learned and must be willing to appear foolish because errors are inevitable during the language learning process' (Phillips, 1991: 3).

Before describing the remaining causes of anxiety in foreign language learning, it is worthwhile noting that many past studies used standard questionnaires. Among them, the Foreign Language Classroom Anxiety Scale (FLCAS) has gained particular popularity (Horwitz *et al.*, 1986). The questionnaire is composed of 33 items and measures three types of anxiety: *communication apprehension anxiety, test anxiety* and *fear of negative evaluation*. MacIntyre (1995) observes that many points measure typical situation-specific anxiety, that is situations in which students believe that they react or would react nervously. Horwitz *et al.* (1986) found that about a third of the interviewed students suffered from foreign language learning anxiety. Besides FLCAS, other versions of standard question-naires have been created to measure various anxieties in foreign language study, including the Foreign Language Reading Anxiety Scale and Foreign Writing Anxiety (after Pichette, 2009). Other research instruments that have been used include interviews, learning diaries and journals, and students' observations. Many studies have attempted to establish a relationship between the manifested levels of anxiety and, for example, results in oral and written tests of various skills. They have explored, among others, the correlation between anxiety and vocabulary learning (MacIntyre & Gardner, 1989), the influence of anxiety on listening comprehension skills (Kim, 2000, after Lim, 2004), the correla-tion between anxiety and the skill of reading (Saito *et al.*, 1999) and the influence of anxiety on writing (Cheng, 2004).[1]

In relation to the speaking skill, researchers draw attention to the fact that students are often overly ambitious, believing that they will soon be able to speak fluently (Lim, 2004). The most numerous causes of negative classroom emotions are – as enumerated by the students themselves – giving an oral presentation, performing a role play in front of the class, contributing to a formal discussion, answering a teacher's question, speaking informally to the teacher and taking part in a group discussion. Outside of the classroom, anxieties arise in such situations as answering the lecturer's questions, asking the lecturer questions, taking part in a conversation with more than one native speaker (NS), answering the NS's questions and starting a conversation with an NS (Woodrow, 2006; cf. also Young, 1990). An important role in the emergence of, but also in overcoming anxieties, can be played by the teacher's personality, and the way the work is organized during class and the group itself. Cohen and

Norst (1980) demonstrated that students are first and foremost concerned with the positive traits in the teacher's personality, while his or her competence is a secondary consideration. Palacios' research (1998, after Lim, 2004) revealed that teachers who often talk to students about their problems in foreign language learning can thus reduce the appearance of negative emotions. Students mostly do not like classes in which the audio-lingual method of linguistic drills is preferred, or speaking in front of the class (Young, 1991). They are also not happy about being asked questions as though they were in school (Koch & Terrell, 1991). Nevertheless, Phillips (1991) established that creating friendly conditions for the study of a foreign language often conflicts with the development of communicative competence. Paradoxically, too numerous speaking exercises can intensify anxiety. Many researchers emphasize that students quite frequently compare their own linguistic competence to that of other students. Timid students tend to underestimate their abilities (MacIntyre *et al.*, 1997), and do not like to ask publicly for an explanation of a problem in order to avoid becoming an attention-seeker (Stroud & Wee, 2006: 301). In their study of Chinese students, Yan and Horwitz (2008) pointed to the impact of social factors (e.g. the fact that they come from different regions of China, different educational systems or finally differences in the economic development of various provinces) on self-perception and thereby on the formation of anxieties. It is not difficult to guess that students from outside big cities considered themselves to be less competent. These attitudes were also connected with their parents' foreign language learning beliefs and their social status. As the researchers observed, this problem is important when students begin their studies before stronger social links have had time to emerge within the group.

Research Project

Research objectives

Previous research has shown that students specialising in a given language (referred to as philology students in the Polish educational context) are not free from foreign language speaking anxiety. The questions we need to address are therefore as follows: How do they perceive the phenomenon? Where is the source of their anxiety? Is it a direct consequence of communicative problems, or is it that they hypothetically assume, on the basis of their own foreign language learning experience and beliefs, that difficulties will arise, and this reinforces the sense of anxiety? Is it possible to say that the patterns found in language-conscious advanced students, when compared with other groups, follow some universal model on the causes of anxiety, regardless of the context of language teaching and learning processes?

Participants

The research project was conducted in the winter semester 2007/2008 and 2008/2009 on a group of 83 first and second year students (73 females, 10 males) of German studies at the Koszalin University of Technology (first year group) and the University of Szczecin (second year group). Three-year BA studies candidates are expected to have an intermediate knowledge of German, so that they can participate with relative ease in classes that are taught in this language. In recent years, however, the linguistic level of candidates has been constantly dropping, with many students having substantial gaps in their linguistic and communicative competence, especially with respect to the skill of speaking. On the other hand, it has been observed that students feel a strong need for a reflective attitude in language study and wish to discuss their learning and communicative problems. The choice of first and second year students of German studies was made in order to determine their opinions on foreign language oral communication, to develop their learning awareness and to adapt the pedagogic actions to their experiences and expectations.

Research method

The research instruments used in the study included dialogue journals and diaries. Research in foreign language acquisition has employed this method for many years. As an example, the works of Bailey (1991) and Peyton (2000) should be mentioned here. Peyton (2000: 3) defines dialogue journals as follows:

> Dialogue journals are written conversations in which a learner and teacher (or other writing partner) communicate regularly (daily, weekly, or on a schedule that fits the educational setting) over a semester, school year, or course. Learners write as much as they choose on a wide range of topics and in a variety of genres and styles. The teachers write back regularly, responding to questions and comments, introducing new topics, or asking questions. The teacher is primarily a participant in an ongoing, written conversation with the learner rather than an evaluator who corrects and comments on the quality of the learner's writing.

Journals should be regarded as a research tool on the one hand and as an instrument which can develop and support learning and communicative awareness in students on the other hand. They were used in the examined group for a written exchange of opinions between students and the present author on their (mainly school) experiences in relation to the evolution of their foreign language speaking skill. The dialogues were conducted in Polish, German or both languages, according to students' choice. The issue of anxiety was explored by means of the following questions: Are you afraid to speak in German? If yes, when and in front of whom? Can you say why? How are you trying to control the anxiety? What do you feel when you speak German with Germans? What do you feel when you speak German with Poles (other students, teachers)? It should be emphasized that students mentioned their anxiety when discussing other topics, including (1) school experience which influenced the development of the skill of speaking, (2) attitudes towards foreign language errors and their correction by the teacher, (3) linguistic situations when students want to say something in German but do not know how to express it, (4) individual preferences on using the language in monologues and conversation and (5) when comparing their own and other students' competence.

Findings and discussion

The collected qualitative data show that Polish students of Germanic studies do not differ from other learners with regard to their opinions on foreign language speaking anxiety. Given the space limitations of the present chapter, I would like to focus primarily on the problems directly and indirectly related to information processing on the cognitive plane during oral utterance production. The following conclusion can be drawn from the analysed discussions: factors which lead to problems on the cognitive plane and often contribute to the development of foreign language speaking anxiety appear *before* or *during* the processes of utterance production. However, the collected empirical data suggest that foreign language anxiety is strongly determined by factors which are present *before* oral communication (and which are known to students), while problems on the cognitive plane are either a consequence of them or contribute to greater anxiety. Those factors that appear *before* the production of an oral utterance are surely strongly related to the students' personalities (trait anxiety), their previous learning experience, conditions dictated by the communicative situation (teacher, native speaker, other students, monologue vs dialogue communication, etc.) and their personal foreign language learning beliefs. Let us now examine and discuss a few examples[2]:

Student A: My problem is that I'm afraid to speak because I always subconsciously feel that my oral performance will be incorrect. Grammatically or otherwise. But I am aware that it would be better for me if I could nevertheless try and take the risk, and learn from my mistakes in this way. I think that fear of criticism is important, too, or the feeling of embarrassment in front of the group.
Student B: I think that the fact that I'm afraid to speak German in public is more a result of the fact that I try to be as 'hypercorrect' as

possible. It's embarrassing to speak my mind in front of people who possess greater knowledge than I do. I think this tips the scales.

Student C: I prefer to write than to speak German. The reason for this is that when I speak German, I'm afraid that I'll make a mistake. (...) I'd like to use German fluently... But I must overcome my internal fear of making grammatical mistakes, or in pronunciation, because otherwise I won't achieve perfection in speaking.

Student D: I'm very much afraid of speaking German, especially at the university, when the teacher and the other students await my speaking performance during class, and they're all only focused on me. I know that they'll catch even the slightest mistake or fault. I try to force myself to stop fear from paralysing me (...).

Student E: When I talk to Germans, I'm very stressed. As I mentioned before, it's caused by the fact that I might make linguistic mistakes. I think then that the German will laugh at me and won't understand what I wanted to say. It's not always like that. The last time I spoke to Germans and couldn't understand what they wanted to tell me, they tried to explain it to me using other words. I think that in the beginning everyone's afraid to talk to people who speak German perfectly.

Teacher: Do you like to talk to Germans for a long time?

Student E: When I talk to Germans, I'm afraid that they won't understand what I wanted to say because of some grammatical or phonetic errors that I will make. I'm also afraid that it'll be difficult for me to understand them. That's why I try to speak briefly when talking to Germans. When I speak German with Poles, I feel more secure because I know that if I can't explain something in German, I'll have the possibility of explaining it in Polish.

Student F: During the conversation, the teacher played the role of the corrector (...). Our conversations weren't spontaneous. Every utterance was first prepared, written down and checked many times to make sure it's all correct.

Student G: I'm most afraid of speaking German in front of Poles who know the language very well. I don't feel this in the presence of Germans who understand that I'm not German and mistakes are something normal for them.

The above cases show that students' oral productions and possible problems on the cognitive plane are determined by factors that arise from their previous experience and/or their foreign language learning beliefs. It is interesting that many of these arguments, which result in negative emotions, are only based on hypothetical assumptions. These assumptions primarily concern the possibility of making a mistake and the resulting reaction of the people around them. This, moreover, is also hypothetical in many cases. Student A subconsciously feels that her oral performance will be incorrect. She is afraid of the criticism of those around her, although she admits elsewhere that she has never been criticized, for example, by other students. Student E is afraid of conversing with native speakers because they can spot her every mistake. She thinks that they might ridicule her for this reason. Again, the assumption is purely hypothetical in this case. The result of such an opinion is the production of short utterances or ending them as quickly as possible in order to avoid exposure to a possible negative experience. This can be observed particularly clearly in the first year students of Germanic studies; their fear of foreigners is of a purely hypothetical nature, since many of them have never spoken to Germans before. In Case B, the student is driven by her pursuit of hypercorrectness. She admits, however, that the fear is determined by the influence of those around her and because she compares herself to other, particularly better, students. A similar argument is used in Example C. Thus, writing is a more secure way of communication in a foreign language. It should be pointed out that many students consider written language to be a safer form of foreign language performance, unlike in their mother tongue. This is mainly due to the fact that they can think over their utterance more thoroughly and correct any possible mistakes. The question of speaking anxiety crops up in numerous arguments for writing and against speaking. Student D does not see communicative partners in her surroundings, but people who are watching for her mistakes and competence gaps, and who are less interested in what she is saying. A specific posture is adopted towards Polish teachers of German (Examples F and G). Students do not treat teachers as their communicative partners, which, I believe, is based chiefly on their school experience. They rather tend to attribute to them the function of judges of correctness. In fact, it is difficult not to gain this impression when watching many a foreign language class. An overly strong focus on form leads students (and some teachers) to the conviction that only linguistic correctness guarantees successful communication. As it is a long and arduous process to attain correctness, a lack of satisfactory results intensifies negative emotions.

It can be deduced from the students' opinions that there are essentially only two causes of anxiety *during* the process of speaking and that the anxiety itself is a consequence of the problems on the cognitive plane during speech production. These causes are the following: gaps in linguistic competence and error correction initiated by the teacher through which the course of the utterance is broken. Students attribute their competence gaps primarily to lexis: their insufficient knowledge of vocabulary or difficulties in retrieving it from long-term memory (the connection between the gaps and the grammar is weaker in their opinion). In such moments, students lose focus and often employ reduction strategies; they attempt to finish speaking as quickly as possible. The phenomenon intensifies when students want to or are asked to say something spontaneously, without prior preparation, especially in a conversation with the teacher or a native speaker. Lack of fluency in speaking performance and the reaction of those around them (sometimes even the usual expectation for a continuation of the utterance) are other factors which do not help to facilitate the cognitive processes and intensify foreign language speaking anxiety.

> **Student H:** Speaking German is difficult for me because of gaps in my vocabulary. It happens that I forget even the simplest words during speaking, not to mention the more difficult ones. (...) When I'm expected to talk without preparation, it's connected with interrupted utterances, spoken word by word. I still can't get rid of being slightly stressed; if what I'm going to say is correct, if it makes sense.

Student H emphasizes cognitive problems connected with vocabulary, but in the final phase of his statement, we can observe factors that probably determine more than one of his utterances even *before* they begin ('if what I'm going to say is correct, if it makes sense').

> **Teacher:** When speaking, is it more difficult to control vocabulary or grammar?
> **Student I:** I think that when speaking, it's more difficult to control vocabulary than grammar! Before I start saying something, I compose in my mind what it should be like to be grammatically correct. Sometimes during an utterance, I lose the word order somewhere and than the verb's not in the correct place, but what I'm more terrified by is the lack of vocabulary. Sometimes when I have to speak my mind on some subject without prior preparation, I realize that I'm at a loss for words and then I get anxious and 'jam'. I don't know if it's because my vocabulary is poor, or maybe it's that the fear of speaking has this kind of effect on me?!

The student finds it difficult to determine whether narrow vocabulary hinders his cognition and intensifies his anxiety or whether it is the speaking anxiety that causes all the problems. This shows that it is not always easy to capture the phenomenon of anxiety in the causal model.

As I mentioned earlier, anxiety *during* speaking also appears when students are corrected on the spot through an interruption of their oral performance. Many respondents (on average half of the examined population) did not like this form of correction. It might seem that at the moment of error correction, students' cognitive resources shift toward the information on the mistake they made (the so-called focus on form). However, some students commented that this kind of correction is ineffective in their case as they are trying to focus on what they still want to say. Unfortunately, an interruption of the utterance only makes them lose the trail of thoughts and they try to quickly end the utterance; it may also render them incapable of continuing it at all.

> **Student J:** I don't like it when somebody corrects me while I'm speaking. I lose the thread then. (...) When somebody interrupts me, I concentrate instead on what I'm going to say later, not on remembering the mistakes. As a consequence, I make the same mistakes again after some time.
>
> **Student K:** I have nothing against being corrected because I'm aware that I make mistakes. Personally, I prefer to be corrected after I finish speaking. When I start saying something, I'd like to say what I planned. When somebody interrupts and corrects me, I begin to loose my thought, I get confused (...) and hurry to the end of what I'm saying as fast as I can, not paying attention to grammar any more.

It should be remarked here that students who do not like this form of correction, most often link its results with a smaller or greater speaking anxiety. This does not occur, or is very rare, in students who prefer this form of correction and do not like to be corrected after they finish speaking. Teachers' emotional reactions are closely connected with error correction. Awareness of the fact that the teacher will react badly to a mistake, results in anxiety not only at the moment when negative feedback is given but before other oral activities.

> **Student L:** The teacher didn't like it when we made mistakes. He thought that after a few lessons we should master complex grammatical structures. He was getting very upset. It was indescribable! When I made a mistake, he instantly corrected me. I often forgot what else I was going to say. I hated it! Such behaviour had a negative effect on me. I would often lose motivation to continue studying (...) Now I'm constantly afraid of speaking German with people who know the language better than me, that they'll be correcting me. I try to overcome this by only building those structures that I'm sure are correct.

The above opinion shows how negative evaluation during speaking became a lasting experience connected with anxiety, which, in a similar manner to the aforementioned cases, surfaces before the process of speaking begins. Student L undoubtedly tries to intentionally get around this problem, but he does that by not taking a risk and only using those linguistic structures that he considers to be absolutely correct.

The examples quoted above demonstrate that Polish students of Germanic studies do not differ essentially from other learners in their assessment of the causes of foreign language speaking anxiety (e.g. Ewald, 2007). Their previous foreign language learning experience and beliefs influence the formation of speaking anxiety to a large degree. Indeed, the presented examples of anxiety show that negative emotions are not a direct consequence of cognitive problems in a given communicative situation, but that they instead can be the cause of anxiety resulting from the students' attitude towards speaking. In many cases, we could see that students are afraid to speak because they fear possible linguistic mistakes and the negative reaction that might ensue from those around them. It is my belief that this situation largely results from language teaching that is still primarily directed towards formal correctness, the attainment of which is a long process. In rare cases, the majority of which concerned fear of talking to native speakers of the language, the students said that they were afraid that they would not be able to reach some communicative goal. The problem was only limited to the assumption that errors might occur. Surely, determining formal correctness or incorrectness facilitates the task of teachers when they evaluate their students' oral competence. It should be considered, however, whether the accuracy-based model of teaching and learning does not create a conviction in students that foreign language communication is exclusively determined by correctness. Even positive reactions coming from teachers during correction do not guarantee that anxiety will not surface in students. Obviously, error correction should not be discarded. The presented research, however, shows that students are in most cases incapable of risk-taking; it is possible that they are not encouraged enough to do this during class. They do not take a risk because they know from their own experience, but also from their formed beliefs, that what they want to say does not guarantee formal correctness, and this is what they most firmly associate with the achievement of communicative goals. It can be further concluded, as a result of comparing students' opinions on foreign language speaking anxiety with their evaluation of school classes, that developing speaking skills is in many cases reduced to a minimum in schools or that it follows the traditional model: the teacher's question – a short answer – feedback. Oral presentations are usually based on prior preparation at home (of some story, for example), and this is often limited to the memorization of certain phrases. Spontaneous communication, especially in the form of conversation, takes the shape of short dialogue sequences which do not require any greater cognitive effort. Naturally, it would be difficult to question this form of school teaching; it is, after all, but a small part of the constant formation of linguistic competence which also takes place outside of school. What should be considered, though, is the degree to which much language teaching and learning, which undoubtedly cannot eliminate formal instruction, constitutes a contradiction of the principles of the communicative approach. A glance at children learning their mother tongue is enough: they make mistakes for years, naturally and unconsciously taking a communicative risk because this is the essence of language acquisition. The process is similar in adults. Do any of us reflect on how many lesser or greater linguistic mistakes we make every day?

Conclusions

Coming back to the question posed at the beginning of this chapter, whether anxiety (which surfaces at different levels) is a common phenomenon, it needs to be said that it cannot be completely avoided, if for no other reason than students' traits of character or the communicative situations we find ourselves in. We are aware of them from mother tongue communication, too (e.g. fear of conversation with a superior). Striving for immediate success in learning a foreign language is natural, but not necessarily easily achievable. The problem of foreign language speaking anxiety should therefore become a subject of conscious discussion in a foreign language classroom. Students should know that anxiety is not an isolated phenomenon. Many students, who engaged in discussions with the author of this paper through dialogue journals, admitted that the awareness that other people also wrestle with such problems was the first step towards overcoming their own fear. It is not something bad from a pedagogical point of view when the teacher, who himself or herself feels anxiety, can describe it and seek its causes in front of students. The teacher cannot pretend to be perfect as he or she is not, being sure to have experienced similar difficulties when studying the target language. Through such sincere discussion, the distance between the teacher and the students will surely be reduced, but this will not negatively affect his or her authority. It is through increased language, learning and communicative awareness that students will acquire the courage to talk about their problems.

Notes

1. See an overview in Horwitz (2010).
2. Translated from Polish or German.

References

Bailey, K.M. (1983) Competitiveness and anxiety in adult second language learning. In H.W. Seliger and M.H. Long (eds) *Classroom Oriented Research in Second Language Acquisition* (pp. 67–103). Rowley, MA: Newbury House.
Bailey, K.M. (1991) Diary studies of classroom language learning: The doubting game and the believing game. In E. Sadtono (ed.) *Language Acquisition and the Second/Foreign Language Classroom*. Anthology Series 28 [online]. ERIC Reproduction Document Service No. ED 367 166. Singapore: SEAMEO.
Beck, A.T. (1967) *Depression: Causes and Treatment*. Philadelphia: University of Pennsylvania.

Cheng, Y-S. (2004) A measure of foreign language writing anxiety: Scale development and preliminary validation. *Journal of Second Language Writing* 13, 313–335.

Cohen, Y. and Norst, M.J. (1980) Fear, dependence and loss of self-esteem: Affective barriers in second language learning among adults. *RELC Journal* 20, 61–77.

Ewald, J.D. (2007) Foreign language learning anxiety in upper-level classes: Involving students as researchers. *Foreign Language Annals* 40, 122–142.

Eysenck, M.W. (1979) Anxiety, learning and memory: A reconceptualization. *Journal of Research in Personality* 13, 363–385.

Ganschow, L. and Sparks, R.L. (1996) Anxiety about foreign language learning among high school women. *Modern Language Journal* 80, 199–212.

Guiora, A.Z., Beit-Hallahmi, B., Brannon, R.C.L., Dull, C.Y. and Scovel, T. (1972) The effects of experimentally induced changes in ego states on pronunciation ability in a second language: An exploratory study. *Comprehensive Psychiatry* 73, 421–428.

Horwitz, E.K. (2000) Horwitz comments: It ain't over 'til It's over: On foreign language anxiety, first language deficits, and the confounding of variables. *Modern Language Journal* 84, 256–259.

Horwitz, E.K. (2010) Foreign and second language anxiety. *Language Teaching* 43, 154–167.

Horwitz, E.K., Horwitz, M.B. and Cope, J. (1986) Foreign language classroom anxiety. *Modern Language Journal* 70, 125–132.

Kim, J-H. (2000) Foreign language listening anxiety: A study of Korean students learning English. Unpublished doctoral dissertation, The University of Texas at Austin.

Kleinmann, H.H. (1977) Avoidance behaviour in adult second language. *Language Learning* 27, 93–107.

Koch, A.S. and Terrell, T.D. (1991) Affective reactions of foreign language students to natural approach activities and teaching techniques. In E.K. Horwitz and D.J. Young (eds) *Language Anxiety: From Theory and Practice to Classroom Implications* (pp. 108–126). Englewood Cliffs, NJ: Prentice-Hall.

Lim, H-Y. (2003) Theoretical relationships between anxiety and motivation in second/foreign language learning. *Texas Papers in Foreign Language Education* 8, 33–52.

Lim, H-Y. (2004) Effects of task values, attributions, and cultural constructs on foreign language use anxiety among International Teaching Assistants. PhD thesis, University of Texas at Austin.

MacIntyre, P.D. (1995) How does anxiety affect second language learning? A reply to Sparks and Ganschow. *Modern Language Journal* 79, 90–99.

MacIntyre, P.D. and Gardner, R.C. (1989) Anxiety and second-language learning: Toward a theoretical clarification. *Language Learning* 39, 251–275.

MacIntyre, P.D. and Gardner, R.C. (1991) Methods and results in the study of anxiety and language learning: A review of the literature. *Language Learning* 41, 85–117.

MacIntyre, P.D. and Gardner, R.C. (1994) The subtle effects of language anxiety on cognitive processing in the second language. *Language Learning* 44, 283–305.

MacIntyre, P.D., Noels, K.A. and Clément, R. (1997) Biases in self-ratings of second language proficiency: The role of language anxiety. *Language Learning* 47, 265–287.

Nerlicki, K. (2007) Angstgefühle und deren mögliche Auswirkungen auf das Lernen von Fremdsprachen. Fokus: Studienanfänger/innen in der Germanistik – eine Fallstudie. *Convivium. Germanistisches Jahrbuch Polen*, 227–261.

Nerlicki, K. (2009) Über Sprechängste polnischer Germanistikstudenten im Kontakt mit deutschen Muttersprachlern, polnischen Lehrern und anderen Lernern. In A. Mrożewska (ed.) *Philologische Ostsee-Studien* (pp. 91–112). Koszalin: Wydawnictwo Uczelniane Politechniki Koszalińskiej.

Palacios, L.M. (1998) Foreign language anxiety and classroom environment: A study of Spanish university students. Unpublished doctoral dissertation, The University of Texas at Austin.

Pekrun, R. (1984) An expectancy-value model of anxiety. In H.M. van der Ploeg, R. Schwarzer and C.D. Spielberger (eds) *Advances in Test Anxiety Research* (Vol. 3, pp. 63–72). Hillsdale, NJ: Erlbaum.

Peyton, J.K. (2000) Dialogue journals: Interactive writing to develop language and literacy [online]. ERIC Reproduction Document Service No. ED 450 614.

Phillips, E.M. (1991) Anxiety and oral competence: Classroom dilemma. *The French Review* 65, 1–14.

Pichette, F. (2009) Second language anxiety and distance language learning. *Foreign Language Annals* 42, 77–93.

Piechurska-Kuciel, E. (2008) *Language Anxiety in Secondary Grammar School Students*. Opole: Wydawnictwo Uniwersytetu Opolskiego.

Saito, Y., Horwitz, E.K. and Garza, Th.J. (1999) Foreign language reading anxiety. *Modern Language Journal* 83, 202–218.

Sparks, R.L. and Ganschow, L. (1991) Foreign language learning differences: Affective or native language aptitude? *Modern Language Journal* 17, 2–16.

Sparks, R.L. and Ganschow, L. (1993) Searching for the cognitive locus of foreign language learning difficulties: Linking first and second language learning. *Modern Language Journal* 77, 289–302.

Sparks, R.L. and Ganschow, L. (1995) A strong inference to causal factors in foreign language learning: A response to MacIntyre. *Modern Language Journal* 79, 235–244.

Stroud, Ch. and Wee, L. (2006) Anxiety and identity in the language classroom. *RELC Journal* 37, 299–307.

Tittle, M. (1997) The effects of foreign and second language students' irrational beliefs and anxiety on classroom achievement [online]. ERIC Reproduction Document Service No. ED 411 674.

Turula, A. (2006) *Language Anxiety and Classroom Dynamics: A Study of the Adult Beginner*. Bielsko-Biała, Poland: Wydawnictwo ATH.

Vellutino, F. and Scanlon, D. (1986) Linguistic coding and metalinguistic awareness: Their relationship to verbal and code acquisition in poor and normal readers. In D. Yaden and S. Templeton (eds) *Metalinguistic Awareness and Beginning Literacy* (pp. 115–141) Portsmouth, NH: Heinemann.

Woodrow, L. (2006) Anxiety and speaking English as a second language. *RELC Journal* 37, 308–328.

Yan, X. and Horwitz, E. (2008) Learners' perceptions of how anxiety interacts with personal and instructional factors to influence their achievement in English: A qualitative analysis of EFL learners in China. *Language Learning* 58, 151–183.

Young, D.J. (1990) An investigation of students' perspectives on anxiety and speaking. *Foreign Language Annals* 23, 539–553.

Young, D.J. (1991) Creating a low-anxiety classroom environment: What does language anxiety research suggest? *The Modern Language Journal* 75, 426–439.

Zybert, J. (2006) Learning anxiety in the language classroom. *Glottodidactica* XXXII, 123–137.

Chapter 13

The Relationship between Language Anxiety and the Development of the Speaking Skill: Results of a Longitudinal Study

EWA PIECHURSKA-KUCIEL

Introduction

The aim of this chapter is to present the role of language anxiety in producing communication barriers when using a foreign language (FL). For this purpose the issue of language anxiety together with its relationship to the speaking skill is outlined. Subsequently, an empirical study devoted to the relationship between language anxiety and self-assessment of the speaking skill, observed over the length of secondary grammar school education, is described. And finally, the research results are discussed along with their possible implications for FL classroom procedures.

Theoretical Background

Learning an FL is a 'deeply unsettling psychological proposition' (Guiora, 1983: 3). It requires, among others, the communication of messages that are at the same time conversationally appropriate and personally meaningful by using phonological, semantic and syntactic systems that might still be unfamiliar (Horwitz, 1996). Consequently, FL learning can bring about an array of negative consequences, such as threatening one's self-concept or lowering self-esteem. It is thus integrated with the production of language anxiety, a negative emotion specific to the second language learning process, which in turn significantly obstructs the development of the speaking skill.

Language anxiety: Definition, origins and effects

In the field of psychology, *anxiety* is described as an emotion often produced in response to stress; it is a normal reaction like anger or joy. Its task is to prepare the individual for action in dangerous situations. For the purpose of this chapter, anxiety is broadly defined as a socio-psycho-biologic phenomenon experienced as a foreboding dread or threat resulting from the individual's appraisal of a situation and their capacity to deal with it (Pekrun, 1992).

Traditionally, conceptual (general) anxiety is divided into *state* and *trait* anxiety. The *state* type denotes subjective and conscious feelings of apprehension and tension accompanied by stimulation or activation of the autonomous nervous system (Spielberger, 1966). In other words, it is a transitory condition of unpleasant, consciously perceived feelings of tension, apprehension and nervousness that vary in intensity and fluctuate in time as a reaction to circumstances perceived as threatening (Novy & Nelson, 1995). *Trait anxiety*, meanwhile, refers to a motif or acquired behavioural disposition because of which a human being perceives a wide variety of objectively unthreatening situations as threatening, causing their disproportional overreaction to such situations (Spielberger, 1966). It follows that trait anxiety is viewed as an individual's predisposition to be anxious.

For the sake of clarity, the above typology must be supplemented with yet another anxiety type connecting individual reactions with specific sorts of situations. For this purpose, to complement the existing typology, *situation-specific* anxiety is introduced (Ellis, 1994). It signifies a stable trait that defines the likelihood of becoming anxious in particular situations or a single context, such as public speaking, testing or driving. Naturally, along with dispositional apprehension (trait anxiety), situations can make individuals anxious.

One such class of situations is learning or using an FL. Accordingly, for the sake of describing affective processes in the field of second language acquisition (SLA), a kind of anxiety conceptually different from other anxiety types has been introduced, namely *foreign language anxiety* or *language anxiety*. Horwitz *et al.* (1986: 128), in their revolutionary study, propose to define it as 'a distinct complex of self-perceptions, beliefs, feelings, and behaviors related to classroom language learning arising from the uniqueness of the language learning process'. Their definition stresses the importance of the formal language learning context for producing self-centred thoughts, feelings of inadequacy and fear of failure. Language anxiety may also be seen as 'the worry and negative emotional reaction aroused when learning or using a second language' (MacIntyre, 1999: 27). For the purpose of this chapter, the term is understood as the unique feelings of tension and apprehension experienced in the SLA process in the classroom context, arising from the necessity to learn and use an FL that has not been fully mastered. It is characterised by task-irrelevant cognitions and a variety of physiological responses, such as increased heart rate.

Language anxiety and the speaking skill

Speaking has intuitively gained the status of a key skill, and language learners are often referred to as 'speakers' of that target language (Ur, 2000: 120). Moreover, as Horwitz and Young (1991) propose, the most anxiety-provoking situation is speaking in front of peers and teachers. The skill is also said to be extremely difficult to develop, especially in the classroom environment. Learners who fail to learn how to speak in a second/foreign language, in spite of successful acquisition of other skills, often complain of having a 'mental block' (Horwitz *et al.*, 1986: 125), hindering them from succeeding in learning a second/foreign language. Their feelings of nervousness, stress and anxiety are a significant obstacle in the development of language proficiency, especially their performance abilities, such as speaking. Not surprisingly then, it is argued that these particular feelings of anxiety specifically associated with learning and speaking an FL distinguish learning L2 from learning other skills or subjects.

Generally, it is speculated that language anxiety mainly refers to oral communication (Cheng *et al.*, 1999). It is proposed that it is mostly grounded in the speaking and listening skills (Horwitz *et al.*, 1986), which may take the form of free speech or sound, and linguistic structure discrimination. As far as the cognitive processes involved in listening, writing and reading are concerned, they seem to be differently related to anxiety, because they do not require the same performance characteristics, as in the case of speaking (Vargas Batista, 2009). This is the reason why it is speaking that has gained most attention, because it 'seems to be the most threatening aspect of foreign language learning' (Horwitz *et al.*, 1986: 23).

The connection between language anxiety and the speaking skill can be best explained by an analysis of the foundations of language anxiety, which are rooted in psychological characteristics of the FL learner. They constitute the general anxieties underpinning the theoretical model of language anxiety: *communication apprehension, test anxiety* and *fear of negative evaluation anxiety* (MacIntyre & Gardner, 1989). These anxiety types constitute forms of performance anxiety because language anxiety mainly deals with performance evaluation within academic and social contexts (Cha, 2006). Hence, the phenomenon is inseparably connected with the speaking skill, involving the demonstration of language abilities.

Communication apprehension (also known as stage fright, communication anxiety or performance anxiety) generally refers to a type of anxiety experienced in interpersonal communicative settings (Horwitz, 2002). It is defined as the level of fear associated with real or anticipated communicative outcomes with another person or group of people or 'the fear or anxiety an individual feels about orally communicating' (Daly, 1991: 3). As the educational environment promotes orality as 'a necessary, positive personal characteristic' (Daly, 1991: 7), learners may feel that they have little control of the communicative situation, as their performance is constantly monitored by both their teacher and peers (Horwitz *et al.*, 1986). As a result, communication apprehension seems to be augmented in relation to the learner's negative self-perceptions caused by the inability to understand others and make oneself understood (MacIntyre & Gardner, 1989), especially when using a language that has not fully been mastered. The impact of communication apprehension on language anxiety refers to a fear of making mistakes, intense feelings of self-consciousness or a desire to be perfect when speaking. Learners who fear communicating in the classroom deprive themselves of chances to practise their speaking skills and tend to be convinced that they have little influence on the communicative situation. Their teacher and other peers, by constantly inspecting the learner's oral performance, worsen the situation. In addition, personal convictions about not being understood or not being able to understand provoke strong feelings of communication avoidance (Horwitz *et al.*, 1986).

Test anxiety is defined as 'a situation-specific form of trait anxiety' (Zohar, 1998: 330) that pushes an individual to react to threatening situations with psychological, physiological and behavioural responses that are sometimes debilitating. Therefore, test anxiety is usually connected with emotional reactions accompanying situations where one's performance (e.g. speaking) is being measured or assessed (McDonald, 2001). The necessity to perform in the presence of others (e.g. peers and the teacher) induces strong feelings of anxiety. There are also other negative effects of test anxiety in the FL class, such as fear of making mistakes, intense feelings of self-consciousness or a desire to be perfect when speaking. Finally, there is learners' inappropriate perception of FL production in terms of tests – they fear performing in the FL, instead of approaching the communication act as 'an opportunity for communication' (Horwitz *et al.*, 1986: 128).

The third theoretical concept underpinning the construct of language anxiety is *fear of negative evaluation*, also called social–evaluative anxiety. This is characterised as 'an apprehension about others' evaluations, avoidance of evaluative situations, and the expectation that others would evaluate oneself negatively' (Watson & Friend, 1969: 450) and is considered valid for any potential evaluative situation where social anxiety may mediate (Wells *et al.*, 1995). This apprehension about others' evaluations, or avoidance of evaluative situations, associated with being evaluated unfavourably while anticipating or participating in a social situation, also applies to studying an FL in a formal language classroom. Consequently, it is proposed that students who fear negative evaluation are likely to experience elevated levels of language anxiety, especially in respect to their self-perception of speaking abilities (Kitano, 2001). The social relationships created in this condition may be viewed as stressful, because they are imposed on learners who are pushed to interact in spite of their unwillingness. In effect, in such a negative environment mounting anxiety about FL communication is produced. Students' heightened concern with their FL competence, especially performance, gives way to their attempts to diminish the possibility of negative evaluations, such as minimal interactions or passivity and withdrawal.

Description of the Research Project

Rationale for the study

The three theoretical constructs underpinning the phenomenon of language anxiety create a portrait of an anxious FL learner who is excessively concerned with the impression they make with their communication efforts. Cognitions about their own behaviour are negative and full of self-derogatory comments and doubts, and focusing on this rather than on the task (MacIntyre & Gardner, 1989) produces deficits in performance, that is speaking. This assigns the speaking skill a dominant role in comparison to the remaining macro-skills (listening, writing and reading).

The main purpose of the study is to analyse the relationship between self-assessment of the speaking skill and language anxiety levels measured over the length of secondary grammar school education. It is expected that students with high language anxiety levels fear speaking in class. In this way they deprive themselves of opportunities to practise the FL; hence, their self-assessment of speaking is low. Nevertheless, when they gain more knowledge, they are able to identify more positive emotions in the SLA process, and their language anxiety levels decrease. At the same time, their self-assessment of speaking turns more positive because of their growing mastery of the FL. For this purpose the following hypothesis is proposed:

> **H**: *Self-assessment of the speaking skill is negatively correlated with language anxiety.*

Method

The aim of this research is to investigate the development of self-assessment of the speaking skill over the length of secondary grammar school against the background of language anxiety levels.

Participants

The study informants were 393 (266 girls and 127 boys) students from the six secondary grammar schools in Opole, located in south-western Poland. At the beginning of the study, when they entered secondary grammar school education, their average age was 16.7 years (minimum 15 and maximum 18). They came from 17 classes (natural groups) where English was taught as the second compulsory FL (from beginner to intermediate level), 3–5 hours a week. German or French was their primary compulsory FL, taught more intensively up to the advanced level.

Instruments

The primary instrument applied in the study was a questionnaire. It included the *Foreign Language Classroom Anxiety Scale* (Horwitz *et al.*, 1986), whose purpose is to assess the degree to which students feel anxious during language classes. Sample items on the scale are as follows: *I can feel my heart pounding when I'm going to be called on in language class* or *I keep thinking that the other students are better at languages than I am*. All positive items were key-reversed so that a high score on the scale represented a high anxiety level. The minimum number of points that could be obtained on the scale was 33, while the maximum was 165. The scale's reliability was assessed in terms of the Cronbach alpha coefficient of 0.94. The participants also disclosed information about their self-assessment of the speaking skill on a Likert scale (1 – *very poor*, 2 – *poor*, 3 – *sufficient*, 4 – *good*, 5 – *very good*, 6 – *excellent*).

Procedure

The research is quantitative and longitudinal, with three measurements taken at different points of time (*time-series* design). The cyclical components were language anxiety levels and self-assessment of the speaking skill measured every year. This permitted an investigation into the effect of time and growing proficiency on the language anxiety results.

The data collection procedure took place in three waves over the length of the participants' secondary grammar school education:

- Year 1 (December 2002)
- Year 2 (December 2003)
- Year 3 (January 2005)

At each point of measurement, the students were asked to complete the same questionnaire, giving sincere answers without taking excessive time to think.

Analyses

The data were computed by means of the statistical program called STATISTICA. The main operations were *means* (arithmetic average) and *standard deviation*, *SD* (which shows how far individuals vary from the mean). Among other descriptive statistics there were also parametric correlations (*Pearson's product-moment correlation r*), serving the purpose of assessing the degree of relationship between variables. The non-parametric correlation (*Spearman's rank-order correlation R*) measures the relationship between variables when one of them is ordinal (language anxiety vs self-assessment of the speaking skill). The inferential statistical procedures applied in the study aimed at computing the probability of obtaining a particular pattern of data. Among them was *the correlated t-test*, showing differences between measurements of the same variable (e.g. language anxiety levels) in the same group of subjects (the within-group variation). Finally, in this study *the Wilcoxon Signed-Rank Test* (a non-parametric alternative to the *t*-test) was used to measure differences in the same group of subjects in the measurement of self-assessment of the speaking skill, placed on the ordinal scale (a Likert scale, which extends between 1–6).

Results

The main results of the study show that the mean self-assessment of the speaking skill was lowest in Year 1, with a tendency for a slight increase gradually in Years 2 and 3. As far as the mean scores of language anxiety levels are concerned, the highest result was observed in Year 1, decreasing towards the end of secondary grammar school (see Table 13.1 for detailed results).

In the next step, the development of self-assessment of speaking was analysed by comparing the results obtained in each year. It turned out that a significant drop was observed only after Year 1. However, such a decrease was not found towards the end of secondary grammar school education. As far as language anxiety levels are concerned, their significant and regular reduction was noted in all the measurements (see Table 13.2 for detailed computations). Finally, there is a relationship between self-assessment of the speaking skill and language anxiety levels over the length of secondary grammar school education. In the case of the 3 years, there were similar correlations: -0.56^{***} in Year 1, -0.60^{***} in Year 2 and -0.57^{***} in Year 3.

Table 13.1 Means and standard deviations of self-assessment of speaking and language anxiety levels

	Self-assessment of speaking		*Language anxiety*	
	Mean	*SD*	*Mean*	*SD*
Year 1	3.60	0.99	86.85	24.10
Year 2	3.76	0.92	82.75	23.30
Year 3	3.79	0.92	80.70	24.29

Table 13.2 Within-group comparisons of self-assessment of the speaking skill and language anxiety levels over the length of secondary grammar school

	Self-assessment of speaking Z	*Language anxiety t(392)*
Year 1 × Year 2	3.84[***]	4.90[***]
Year 2 × Year 3	.46	2.44[*]

Note: [*]$p \leq 0.05$; [**]$p < 0.01$; [***]$p < 0.001$

Discussion

The main purpose of the study was to corroborate the hypothesis that *self-assessment of the speaking skill is negatively correlated with language anxiety*. The research results show that the hypothesis can be fully accepted.

In order to justify the above result, the concept of self-assessment of FL skills first needs to be addressed. Hereby it is understood as an ability to estimate in a reliable manner one's own knowledge and performance required in FL oral production. The reliability assumption is made on the basis of studies on self-assessment, revealing that there is quite a strong agreement overall between teachers and students in their assessments (Sullivan & Hall, 1997). It can therefore be inferred that the participants' self-assessment of their speaking skill is likely to render reliable information about the level of their oral ability. The relationship between self-assessment and anxiety has already been explored by the research on psychological and personality traits of a self-rater (AlFallay, 2004), showing that self-assessing abilities are affected by many factors, anxiety being among them.

The speaking skill is a 'multilevel, hierarchical skill, in which high-level plans, in the form of speaker intentions, are realised through the process of formulation and articulation' (Bygate, 2001a: 27). Because of its complexity, it is extremely difficult to acquire for a non-native speaker and a highly anxiety-provoking aspect of learning an FL (cf. Horwitz *et al.*, 1986: 23). However, in present-day FL pedagogy, its role is crucial because of the idea that one must talk in order to learn (Skehan, 1989). It follows that the requirement for the active use of spoken language can be extremely stressful, placing the nascent second language communicator in a most perilous situation, which strongly connects the skill with the production of negative emotions in the FL class.

The specificity of the speaking skill is likely to induce anxiety reactions, especially in the FL learning situation. First of all, speech production involves particular characteristics, such as conceptualisation, formulation, articulation and self-monitoring (Bygate, 2001b). *Conceptualisation*, connected with planning the message content, is also connected with the ability to self-correct. Consequently, problems drawing on background knowledge, or knowledge about the topic, may produce anxiety reactions, obstructing the communication process. In the FL language learning process, the requirement to rely on one's knowledge of the language, accompanied by background knowledge, may seriously threaten uninhibited language development. The next feature of the speaking skill, *formulation*, consists in finding the words and expressions to convey the meaning, as well as preparing the sound patterns. Successful readiness to perform in the FL may require the performer, or the language learner, to have a positive self-image and beliefs about own capabilities. In a situation when the FL user is unsure about their ability to deal with the formulation obligations, a communication problem is likely to occur. *Articulation*, on the other hand, involving motor control of articulatory organs that may involve different arrangements than in mother tongue use, further aggravates any potential difficulties involved in the FL speech act. Incorrect pronunciation or incoherent communication attempts are likely to cumulate, leading to more negative emotions identified in the FL learning process. Finally, the last feature of speech production, *self-monitoring*, or being able to recognise and self-correct mistakes, also brings about negative emotions, especially in reference to the FL use. Self-correction requires time, focus on form and knowledge of rules. Unfortunately, speech is usually produced 'online'; hence, these requirements may not always be fulfilled, especially in the case of less proficient learners who are not yet able to control all aspects of speech production. This is the reason why they often have to sacrifice accuracy for the sake of fluency, or vice versa.

It should be observed that the strong relationship between language anxiety levels and self-assessment of FL speaking abilities is identified in all the three measurements taken during secondary grammar school education. At the beginning of the participants' school experience, language anxiety levels are highest, which can be attributed to the learners' unfamiliarity with the FL learning process in the new environment, teacher expectations or peer behaviour. At this point the learner experiences maximum discomfort, worry and negativity in connection with their language development prospects. As a result, their assessment of the FL speaking ability is lowest. This finding confirms the models of the language anxiety development proposed by MacIntyre and Gardner (1989), who also argue that after this culminating point, when learners' proficiency and experience in the FL increase, anxiety starts declining consistently. More positive experiences and increased achievement give way to the decline of negative emotions. Not surprisingly, the participants' self-assessment significantly rises, confirming the strong bonds between language anxiety and speaking.

The relationship between anxiety and self-assessment of the speaking skill can also be described on the basis of another model proposed by MacIntyre and Gardner (1994). According to this model, general cognitive processes involved in language acquisition pass through the three stages: *input* (the new material is first approached and coded), *processing* (the existing knowledge and the new material are connected and stored) and *output* (the acquired material is demonstrated or retrieved). Processing problems at each stage are claimed to be caused by respective anxiety types, that is input anxiety, processing anxiety and output anxiety. As far as language demonstration or production is concerned, it is output anxiety that comes into play, affecting the quality of language performance in a negative manner. Aside from insufficient language command, the disruption of the retrieval of information, the newness of the language learning situation or the ambiguity of feedback from the teacher and peers, accompanied by any processing difficulties taking place at the previous stages, augment the negative feelings identified at the level of language production.

Finally, it ought to be stressed that the participants of the study were followed throughout the whole length of their secondary grammar school education. At the beginning of the research they had faced school transition, after their graduation from junior high school, so they were still unfamiliar with the demands of the new environment. Apart from that, they had to learn to comply with new norms and regularities, requiring them to behave in unusual, more adult ways (Piechurska-Kuciel, 2008). These factors were likely to cause strong negative emotions that might have impeded their SLA process in this new setting. The students' negative reactions could also be increased by the uneven proficiency level of the learners, who had had diverse linguistic backgrounds and varying FL experience. Consequently, both beginner and more proficient students might have been seriously threatened at the prospect of using L2 in class, though for different reasons. The former desperately needed language experience, while the latter might be intimidated by the newness of the surroundings. Nevertheless, the optimistic research finding is that all students learn to manage to control their FL language learning process – in the consecutive years they self-assess their speaking ability at a significantly higher level, while their language anxiety diminishes. The result can be attributed to their growing proficiency, which, in effect, allows for identifying more positive emotions with their language acquisition process and for decreasing levels of negative emotions, such as language anxiety.

Overall, it can be concluded that anxiety is justly considered a major obstacle in developing an FL, especially speaking skills. With language anxiety being one of the best predictors of FL success, the strong relationship between anxiety and proficiency appears to be an undisputable finding. Automatic language production expected in well-developed FL users calls for long and intensive language practice as well as for successful management of negative emotions.

Implications and Limitations of the Study

Language anxiety, with its serious negative impact on the FL learning process, constitutes an important field of SLA study that is worthy of thorough investigation. It is generally believed that language acquisition cannot take place in a high-anxiety context (Oxford, 1999). For that reason, it is the role of the teacher to provide a non-threatening environment, which is helpful in alleviating language anxiety feelings. Obviously, students' heightened concern with their FL competence, especially performance, results in their attempts to diminish the possibility of negative evaluations by performing minimal interactions or exhibiting passivity or withdrawal. It follows that such behaviours should be eliminated, because they deprive students of chances to develop their FL mastery. There is an excellent opportunity for alleviating the learner's negative self-perceptions – caused by the inability to understand others and make oneself understood – by providing more language experience in a preferably low-anxiety environment.

Providing a stress-free environment that allows for expanding the speaking skill can be accomplished by teaching anxious students to recognise the most common anxiety symptoms, as their awareness of the body reactions allows for gaining control over their emotions. Anxious students can also be advised to organise a study plan for the calendar year in order to cater for more effective study time. As well, it is important to apply cooperative learning, which creates opportunities for students to know their peers better. This can enable them to feel less stressed in their presence and count on one another's help. It should also be noted that a warm and friendly teacher who is genuinely interested in students' problems may be the key to obtaining positive learning effects. Also, an interesting way of helping students learn is applying a teaching approach that aids remembering and concentration, even among those with learning disabilities, called multisensory language instruction. As for the FL teaching practices aimed at lowering students' levels of language anxiety, they are outlined in a comprehensive manner in Young (1999), which includes practical guidelines for teaching the speaking skill in a non-threatening manner (Phillips, 1999) (see Piechurska-Kuciel, 2008, for more ideas).

This study has some limitations that should be addressed. The main drawback derives from the variable of the self-assessment of the speaking skill. It would be desirable to opt for more objective and controlled data, like a number of points gained in an oral exam or aggregated data from school records (final grades and grades obtained on oral tests). This way a significant degree of confounding connected with the operational definition of the variable could be eliminated. The research would also benefit from including control variables that could explain the interplay between language anxiety and self-assessment of the speaking skill, like the participants' gender or place of residence. Their inclusion could shed more light on the social implications of the relationship under scrutiny.

References

AlFallay, I. (2004) The role of some selected psychological and personality traits of the rater in the accuracy of self- and peer-assessment. *System* 32, 407–425.

Bygate, M. (2001a) Speaking. In R. Kaplan (ed.) *The Oxford Handbook of Applied Linguistics* (pp. 27–38). Oxford: Oxford University Press.

Bygate, M. (2001b) Speaking. In R. Carter and D. Nunan (eds) *The Cambridge Guide to Teaching English to Speakers of Other Languages* (pp. 14–20). Cambridge: Cambridge University Press.

Cha, H. (2006) *Korean elementary ESOL students' English language anxiety and defense mechanism in the ESOL and mainstream classes: Theoretical and pedagogical implications for TESOL*. PhD dissertation, The Florida State University College of Education. Retrieved October 10, 2009, from: On WWW at http://etd.lib.fsu.edu/theses/available/etd-04022006-035500/.

Cheng, Y-S, Horwitz, E.K. and Schallert, D.L. (1999) Language anxiety: Differentiating writing and speaking components. *Language Learning* 49, 417–446.

Daly, J.A. (1991) Understanding communication apprehension: An introduction for language educators. In E. Horwitz and D. Young (eds) *Language Anxiety: From Theory and Research to Classroom Implications* (pp. 3–13). Englewood Cliffs, NJ: Prentice-Hall.

Ellis, R. (1994) *The Study of Second Language Acquisition*. Oxford: Oxford University Press.

Guiora, A.Z. (1983) The dialectic of language acquisition. *Language Learning* 33, 3–12.

Horwitz, B. (2002) Introduction and overview: The hidden communication problem. In B. Horwitz (ed.) *Communication Apprehension: Origins and Management* (pp. 1–25). Albany, NY: Singular/Thomson Learning.

Horwitz, E.K. (1986) Preliminary evidence for the reliability and validity of a foreign language anxiety scale. *TESOL Quarterly* 20 (3), 559–562.

Horwitz, E.K. (1996) Student affective reactions and the teaching and learning of foreign languages. *International Journal of Educational Research* 23, 573–579.

Horwitz, E.K., Horwitz, M.B. and Cope, J. (1986) Foreign language classroom anxiety. *Modern Language Journal* 70, 125–132.

Horwitz, E.K. and Young, D.J. (1991) Afterword. In E.K. Horwitz and D.J. Young (eds) *Language Anxiety: From Theory and Research to Classroom Implications* (pp. 177–178). Englewood Cliffs, NJ: Prentice-Hall.

Kitano, K. (2001) Anxiety in the college Japanese language classroom. *Modern Language Journal* 85, 549–566.

MacIntyre, P.D. (1999) Language anxiety: A review of the research for language teachers. In D.J. Young (ed.) *Affect in Foreign Language and Second Language*

Learning: A Practical Guide to Creating a Low-Anxiety Classroom Atmosphere (pp. 24–45). Boston: McGraw-Hill.

MacIntyre, P.D. and Gardner, R.C. (1989) Anxiety and second language learning: Toward a theoretical clarification. *Language Learning* 39, 251–275.

MacIntyre, P.D. and Gardner, R.C. (1994) The effects of induced anxiety on three stages of cognitive processing in computerized vocabulary learning. *Studies in Second Language Acquisition* 16, 1–17.

McDonald, A. (2001) The prevalence and effects of test anxiety in school children. *Educational Psychology* 21, 89–102.

Novy, D.M. and Nelson, D.V. (1995) Psychometric comparability of the English- and Spanish-language versions of the State-Trait Anxiety Inventory. *Hispanic Journal of Behavioural Sciences* 17, 209–225.

Oxford, R.L. (1999) Anxiety and the language learner: New insights. In J. Arnold (ed.) *Affect in Language Learning* (pp. 58–67). Cambridge: Cambridge University Press.

Pekrun, R. (1992) Expectancy-value theory of anxiety: Overview and implications. In D. Forgays and T. Sosnowski (eds) *Anxiety: Recent Developments in Cognitive, Psychological and Health Research* (pp. 23–39). Washington, DC: Hemisphere.

Phillips, E.M. (1999) Decreasing language anxiety: Practical techniques for oral activities. In D.J. Young (ed.) *Affect in Foreign Language and Second Language Learning: A Practical Guide to Creating a Low-Anxiety Classroom* (pp. 124–143). Boston: McGraw-Hill.

Piechurska-Kuciel, E. (2008) *Language Anxiety in Secondary Grammar School Students*. Opole: Wydawnictwo Uniwersytetu Opolskiego.

Skehan, P. (1989) *Individual Differences in Second-Language Learning*. London: Edward Arnold.

Spielberger, C.D. (1966) Theory and research of anxiety. In C. D. Spielberger (ed.) *Anxiety and Behaviour* (pp. 3–25). New York: Academic Press.

Sullivan, K. and Hall, C. (1997) Introducing students to self-assessment. *Assessment and Evaluation in Higher Education* 22, 289–305.

Vargas Batista, G.M. (2009) *Teaching units to lower language anxiety for 8th and 9th grade ESL students in Puerto Rico*. MA dissertation, University of Puerto Rico. Retrieved July 22, 2007, from http://proquest.umi.com/pqdlink?did=10378 88001&Fmt=7&clientI d=79356&RQT=309&VName=PQD.

Watson, D. and Friend, R. (1969) Measurement of social-evaluative anxiety. *Journal of Consulting and Clinical Psychology* 33, 448–457.

Wells, A., Clark, D.M., Salkovskis, P., Ludgate, J., Hackmann, A. and Gelder, M. (1995) Social phobia: The role of in-situation safety behaviors in maintaining anxiety and negative beliefs. *Behavior Therapy* 26, 153–161.

Young, D.J. (ed.) (1999) *Affect in Foreign Language and Second Language Learning: A Practical Guide to Creating a Low-Anxiety Classroom*. Boston: McGraw-Hill.

Ur, P. (2000) *A Course in Language Teaching: Practice and Theory*. Cambridge: Cambridge University Press.

Zohar, D. (1998) An additive model of test anxiety role of exam-specific expectations. *Journal of Educational Psychology* 90, 330–340.

Part 3
Research into Instructed Acquisition of Speaking

Chapter 14

On the Authenticity of Communication in the Foreign Language Classroom

SEBASTIAN PIOTROWSKI

Introduction

The growth of interest in communication in the foreign language classroom and outside it, observable in research on foreign language acquisition since the 1970s, went hand in hand with the functionalists' challenge of Chomsky's generative language model. Scholars in ethnography of communication (Gumperz & Hymes, 1972) and symbolic interactionism (Goffman, 1974) played a special role in this development. Drawing on the concept of context of situation (Malinowski, 1923), which belongs to the field of social anthropology, they emphatically stated that language cannot be treated as a set of correct sentences, existing independently of any specific interlocutor or situation. The rejection of a decontextualised approach to language teaching/learning is common today among acquisitionists as well as among methodologists. Embracing the ethnographic and ecological perspectives is becoming an increasingly popular practice (e.g. Cambra Giné, 2003; de Salins, 1992; Pallotti, 2002) in research on foreign language acquisition in formal settings. Consequently, there is fairly common agreement that language is learnt through communication and that the success or failure of our language learning depends largely on how the communication proceeds. This general assumption underlies, among other things, Long's (1985) *interaction hypothesis* and Swain's (1985, 2005) *output hypothesis*. According to Majer (2003), it is through interactive communication that the learner develops all kinds of competence: sociolinguistic, pragmatic, discursive and strategic. The rediscovery of Vygotsky's (1978) works on language acquisition in children (the *zone of proximal development hypothesis*) points to considerable interest of researchers in the role of cooperation between interlocutors in the acquisition process. Thus, the centre of gravity has visibly shifted from product-oriented research towards process-oriented research. It is also in this context that we should consider the undertaking of detailed analyses of interaction, communication and their accompanying strategies – in the process of

215

acquisition taking place in natural as well as institutional setting (Pawlak, 2009a).

Numerous studies show that communication in the foreign language classroom bears only a little resemblance to that which takes place in natural settings – that it lacks authenticity (understood here as interlocutors' involvement in communication). It has been observed that most teacher–learner interactions follow the question–answer–evaluation pattern, that the teacher markedly dominates and manages the interaction and that there is a significant prevalence of display questions – that is questions that the teacher knows answers to but pretends not to know them. Yet, on the other hand, it is difficult to pinpoint features pertaining only to communication in the foreign language classroom and at the same time not pertaining to communication in natural settings.

In the present chapter we will approach the issue of communicative authenticity in terms of selected features of communication in the foreign language classroom, though not exclusively specific to it (*focus on meaning, form, process*). We will also attempt to answer the question of to what extent this authenticity differs from that which characterises communication in natural settings (Majer, 1998, 2003), that is in situations when the language of communication is not, at the same time, the object of learning by the interlocutors involved in that communication. Finally, assuming that authentic target language communication that consists in using the language in context and goes beyond mere production of decontextualised formulas contributes towards developing the learner's exolingual competence (Piotrowski, 2005) and personal communicative competence (Wilczyńska, 2002), we shall try to indicate potential areas of classroom interaction in which that authentic communication could occur. The reflections and analyses presented below are based on explorative qualitative research, conforming to the classroom-centred research perspective, which Allwright (1983: 191) defined as follows: 'It simply tries to investigate what happens inside the classroom when learners and teachers come together'.

For the purposes of the study, which was conducted in five Polish secondary schools, 148 lessons of French as a foreign language were recorded live (Polish was the first language for all the teachers and learners recorded). All the samples of class interaction quoted in the present chapter come from these data. The following transcription code has been used:

E	teacher
A, M, J, B, JU, KA, MM	learners
Ax	an unidentified learner

+ , + + , + + +	pauses according to length
?	rising intonation
...?...	an unintelligible fragment
[xxxx]	a comment on the transcription
[...]	an omitted fragment of transcription
/xxx/	a phonemic transcription
xxxx	a fragment in the first language
xxx	a gloss in English
XXX	emphatic pronunciation

Features of Communication in the Foreign Language Classroom

Communication in the foreign language classroom is undoubtedly a type of exolingual communication (e.g. Piotrowski, 2005; Porquier, 1984; Porquier & Py, 2004) – that is to say, it occurs in situations in which interlocutors, out of choice or necessity, use a language other than their first language (they may possibly share the first language). The term 'exolingual communication' – indirectly drawing on the concept of languages in contact (Weinreich, 1967), which describes interethnic communication – was initially employed to convey the specificity of communicative situations between native speakers of a language and immigrants who learnt the language in natural settings, without the aid of institutional education.

Thus understood, exolingual communication is characterised, above all, by a clearly perceptible asymmetry of competence between inter-locutors as far as the language of communication is concerned and by the employment of strategies that enable verbal communication despite the limited language competence of some/one of the interlocutors. In other words, exolingual communication is asymmetrical communication, requiring of its participants a constant adjustment to one another and to the situation; it is communication fraught with obstacles that force its participants to stop once in a while in order to overcome these obstacles in the course of so-called *side sequences*.

Transferring the concept of exolingual communication to the field of institutional foreign language teaching and learning, we usually have a situation in which the teacher and the learners share a common first language but, within the framework of a didactic contract (either implicit or explicit), they decide to use a foreign language in the classroom. Of course, exolingual communication may have and often does have bilingual features. In natural settings, an interlocutor using a *basic variety* of interlanguage (Klein & Perdue, 1997), which differs considerably from the target language, frequently either intersperses their discourse with first language items or creates neologisms based on their first language. In formal settings, resorting to that language is more natural if the teacher and the learners share a common first language (as they do in our data). This may result in exolingual communication changing into de facto bilingual endolingual communication, pivoted on the first language rather than on the target language (Piotrowski, 2009).

Another essential feature of exolingual communication in the classroom is its plurifocalisation (e.g. Bange, 1992; Ellis, 1984; Piotrowski, 2006), which consists in the interlocutors' attention being directed not only to the meaning of utterances but also to their form, or even to the very process of performing a specific task (cf. Points 3, 4 and 5 below). On the one hand, this stems from the fact that asymmetry of competence in the target language causes inevitable comprehension problems; on the other hand, the education context induces interlocutors to monitor the correctness of their utterances constantly.

Focus on Meaning

The focus of interlocutors' attention on the meaning of utterance is a characteristic feature of endolingual (as well as exolingual) communication occurring in natural settings. Focus on meaning implies that interlocutors engage in communication without paying much attention to the code of utterances. The situation of foreign language learners in formal settings is, of course, different: learners are fully aware that the meeting with the teacher is not a social one and that virtually every language activity is connected with specific tasks subject to evaluation. Understandably, such circumstances make it difficult – though possible, as shown in the data sample below – to concentrate exclusively on the meaning of utterance:

(1) [task: to speak on the subject of fashion]

    1.   E   bon le sujet de la leçon d'aujourd'hui c'est 'Parler de la mode'

                [E writes the subject on the blackboard]

                ok the subject of today's lesson: "Talking about fashion"

    [...]

    2.   E   Joanna tu parles de la mode avec tes amis?

                Joanna do you talk about fashion with your friends?

    3.   A   non *no*

4.   E   non pourquoi? est-ce que tu ne t'intéresses pas à la mode?

           no? why not? aren't you interested in fashion?

5.   A   je pense qu'il y a des choses plus intéressantes

           I think there are more exciting things

6.   E   ah bon tu penses qu'il y a des choses plus intéressantes que la mode oui? c'est vrai

           you think there are more exciting things than fashion? well, it is true

The learner's utterances 3 and 5 leave no doubt that she is fully involved in communication. The teacher's reaction, especially utterance 6, reveals a certain surprise at the boldness of the learner's utterance, full of determination. The interlocutors' attention is in this case fully concentrated on the meaning of utterances, at least as far as the observable layer of discourse is concerned, and the learner's utterances, formally and pragmatically appropriate, obscure the asymmetry of competence between the interlocutors. Still, the analysis of our data reveals that authentic utterances of learners, with focus on meaning, are extremely rare, and it is utterances with double focus – that is on both form and meaning – that constitute the norm.

Focus on Form

The inevitable asymmetry of competence in the target language results in the interlocutors' attention being focused on both the form and the meaning of utterances. However, while in natural communication focus on form is usually aimed at finding a way to overcome a communication problem, in the foreign language classroom this focus often has the character of evaluation or correction on the teacher's part and self-evaluation on the learner's part, and the possible communication problem is pushed into the background. This is shown in the following data sample:

(2) [task: to prepare a dialogue and act one's part]

1.   E   allez-y je vous en prie Justine et Maciek on vous écoute

           let's go Justine and Maciek we are listening to you

2.   M   **a to jako dialog tak?**

           it's supposed to be a dialogue right?

3.   E   uhm *yes*

4. M   euh... bonjour madame je voudrais me renseigner s'il y a
         quelque circuit organisé pour des châteaux?

         good morning, could you tell me if there are any tours of the
         castles?

5. J   je vous propose /yn/ programme sur l'été tourisme l'été /
         pʀopoze/ un circuit intéressant vous partez le matin en
         autocar sur la Vendée puis...?... et enfin nous arrivons
         au château Colbert après le le déjeuner dans ce château
         nous visiterons...?... /lə/ Cholet

         I suggest the summer tourist programme departure in the
         morning by bus to Vendee then...?... we finally arrive at Colbert
         Castle after visiting the castle there is sightseeing of /lə/ Cholet

6. E   Cholet...

[...]

7. M   j'ai écouté qu'il y a un petit qu'il /ʀesevwa/ qu'on /
         ʀesevwa/ un petit cadeau dans ce château

         I've heard there is a small present that you get a small present
         in that castle

8. E   encore une fois + Maciek

         once again Maciek

9. M   j'ai écouté...

         I've heard...

10. E   j'ai entendu dire j'ai entendu dire que

         I've heard that I've heard that

11. M   **czy słyszałem?**

         did I hear?

12. E   uhm j'ai entendu j'ai entendu dire que [E writes the
         expression on the blackboard]

         I've heard that I've heard that

13. M   euh... qui que pour les touristes il y a un petit cadeau

         that for tourists there is a small present

14. E   uhm qu'il y a un petit cadeau pour les participants + pour
         les participants?

         that there is a small present for participants

15. M   **dla uczestników**

         for participants

16. E   uhm *yes*

17. J   oui c'est vrai vous avez vous avez même un petit
           mouchoir

           yes that's true you get a handkerchief

In the above excerpt from a task, in which learners are expected to act
out a dialogue, we may observe utterances typical of exolingual
communication in the classroom, with marked focus on form, causing
the dialogue to break off every now and then. In natural settings,
communication frequently breaks down as well, and interlocutors'
attention may be focused on the very form of utterances, but this usually
happens in moments that are problematic from the point of view of
communicative success. The situation is different in the above episode, in
which dialogue breaks down when the teacher has decided that the
learner's utterance needs immediate correction. The teacher's interventions, directing attention to form (6, 8, 10, 12, 14), completely prevent the
learners from getting involved in the parts they are acting and deprive
the dialogue of communicative authenticity. In addition, the strongly
marked focus on form transforms what was originally intended as a role-
play into an evaluation task of a metalinguistic character. Interventions of
a third party, in this case a teacher a priori not involved in the dialogue,
destabilise dialogue structure and undermine the status of interlocutors.
In this manner, the final utterance (17) appears to be up in the air, leaving
it uncertain whether it is addressed to partner M, role-playing the
dialogue with J, to the teacher-evaluator, who has become an active
participant of the scene being acted out, or to both of them.

Focus on form, even strongly marked and manifesting itself as an
extensive side sequence, does not necessarily mean that the performed
task – particularly a communicative task – will lack authenticity.
Nonetheless, for the sake of retaining some form of authenticity, it is
essential that the focus should be initiated by a learner involved in
performing a specific task. If the focus is initiated by the teacher acting in
the capacity of an evaluator, the task takes on a metalinguistic character,
and its authenticity (understood here as involvement on the part of
learners-performers) is strongly reduced. Besides, if imposed by a person
not directly involved in the task, focus on form may be ineffective from
the point of view of language acquisition. For example, after a long side
sequence initiated by the teacher, with focus on the expression *j'ai
entendu dire que*, the learner resumes the task but does not incorporate the
expression into her own utterance (13). Thus, the work on language input
that the teacher expects in this case, that is another use of the corrected
form by the learner, fails to take place, which considerably diminishes the
chance of coding the item properly.

Focus on the Process of Task Performance

Classroom communication is also characterised by learners' focus on the process of task performance. Unlike in typical focus on form, where a fragment of the code is subjected to more or less extensive negotiation involving both interlocutors, here we deal with the learner's own verbalised reflection on the task being performed.

(3) [task: to present everyday activities]

    1. B   je me lève à six heures je fais ma toilette à /seʀ/ six heures /ʒu/ habille

            I get up at six wash myself and dress

    2. E   je m'habille

            I get dressed

    3. B   /ʒu/ prends mon petit déjeuner **nie chwileczkę pięć to jest** cinq **więc dobrze powiedziałam**

            I have breakfast no wait a minute five is cinq *so I was right*

    4. E   qu'est-ce que tu fais à cinq heures?

            and what do you do at five?

In this case, focus on task performance process takes on the form of a metalinguistic comment in the mother tongue. Interestingly, the item *cinq* (*five*), referred to in the comment, does not appear anywhere earlier in the discourse. It is therefore possible to conclude that the number *five* is a point of reference on the dial of a clock that the learner mentally arranges for herself. As in typical side sequences with focus on form, the basic activity (here: presenting everyday activities) is temporarily suspended, but instead of negotiations apropos of the problematic item a unilateral metalinguistic comment follows, combined with self-evaluation.

The learner's marked focus on the very process of task performance is also visible in the sample below:

(4) [task: to make a sentence using appropriate pronouns]

    1. E   ils vous avaient prêté de l'argent? ils vous avaient prêté de l'argent? + ils vous avaient prêté de l'argent? Justyna?

            did they lend you money did they lend you money did they lend you money Justyna?

    2. JU   non ils ne leur en...

            no they didn't lend them...

3. E   attention ils VOUS avaient prêté de l'argent?
        be careful did they lend YOU money?

4. JU non nous ne...
        no we didn't...

5. E   ils + vous + avaient + prêté de l'argent
        did they lend you money?

6. JU non ils ne vous... **gubię się**
        no they didn't lend us... I'm confused

7. E   je répète la question "ils vous avaient prêté de l'argent?"
        I repeat the question did they lend you money?

8. JU ils ne nous en + avaient pas prêté
        no they didn't lend it to us

9. E   voilà *ok*

The metalinguistic comment *Gubię się* (*I'm confused*) reflects the difficulty that the learner has in constructing sentences with appropriately chosen and correctly placed pronouns. The main activity (constructing a sentence) is briefly suspended, giving way to the metalinguistic comment which may also be interpreted as a certain kind of strategy: *I'm confused* may amount to an implicit call for help, addressed to a more competent interlocutor (the teacher or another learner); it may also function as a pause that will allow a learner to summon up the necessary resources and resume the task on his or her own.

Moreover, focus on the process of task performance shows that metacognitive activity plays an important role in the foreign language classroom. Such an activity finds concrete expression precisely in the metalinguistic comments through which learners regulate and evaluate their own utterances. For the learner, every utterance in a foreign language is a task demanding increased mental effort (Gaonac'h, 1990), which accounts for the clear signs of learners' monitoring of their own utterances.

Metalinguistic comments do occur in utterances of native speakers of a language, enabling them to regulate utterances, for example, when looking for an appropriate term. But in the classroom they take a much more condensed form, giving an external observer the impression that communication is taking place on two distinct levels: the level of communication as such and the level of verbalised reflection on communication (i.e. metacommunication). This impression, as the cited examples demonstrate, is reinforced by the fact that metalinguistic comments are formulated in the mother tongue, whereas tasks are performed in the foreign language.

Authentic Metacommunication in a Foreign Language

The marked prevalence of focus on form and task performance process shows that communication concerning the target language itself has an important place in the foreign language classroom. That metacommunication, beside the metalinguistic comments mentioned above (see Point 5), accounts for a substantial part of classroom communication, constituted, among other things, by the learners' questions concerning forms and procedures, the teacher's commands and instructions concerning tasks, comments concerning the organisation of the lesson and remarks concerning conduct. The examples cited below (5 and 6) show that this area has high communicative potential:

(5)

    1. E   **zaproponujcie komuś tą konstrukcją si plus** imparfait **zwiedzanie Paryża**

              use the si plus imparfait *construction to suggest sightseeing of Paris to somebody*

    2. Ax   et si on visitait Paris?

              how about sightseeing Paris?

(6)

    1. E   on a déjà parlé de vêtements élégants au théâtre ça va? c'est tout alors?

              we have already talked about elegant clothes to wear to the theatre haven't we? so that's all?

    2. Ax   **ja mam pytanie sorko to ostatnie to** /eleʒɑ̃/ **czy**...

              I have a question miss about this last one, is this word /eleʒɑ̃/

              ...

    3. E   élégants [E writes the word on the blackboard]+ + **jeśli po "g" jest "a" "o" "u"** on prononce toujours **"g" jeżeli jest "e" "i"** c'est toujours **"ʒ"** ça va?

              if "g" comes before "a" "o" "u" we always pronounce it as "g" if there is "e" "i" it is always "ʒ" ok?

Metalinguistic instructions and questions are probably the most typical utterances in the foreign language classroom. Talking about the foreign language is an indispensable and essential element of the foreign language teaching and learning process in an institutional setting and may play an important role in instructed acquisition, provided that it is done in the foreign language. Metalinguistic questions, instructions and comments tend to be simple, short constructions, and formulating them in the foreign language may start at a very early stage of teaching/learning. Metacommunication in a foreign language may also play the role of training for communication in natural settings because it is authentic, since the teacher's instructions are really instructions to be followed and learners' questions are really questions that the askers do not know answers to.

Can a Language Task be Authentic?

As regards tasks performed in class, we cannot say that some tasks are more or less authentic than others but rather that their performance is more or less authentic. A task that is communicative by definition may transform into a typically metalinguistic one during performance (see Example 2, where dialogue de facto transforms into a task that consists in practising isolated forms of the language code) – or vice versa, as the following episode demonstrates:

(7) [task: a list of everyday activities, E writes on the blackboard: lire; the learners are to translate into their first language individual terms given in the target language by the teacher]

1.	E	un journal?
		magazine?
2.	EL	**czasopismo**
		magazine
3.	E	**myjemy się**
		we wash ourselves
4.	KA	**nie szkoda wody**
		no, it's a waste of water
[...]		
5.	E	**zapomnieliśmy o kolacji**
		we forgot about supper
6.	MM	**my nie jemy kolacji**
		we don't have supper

Thanks to the introduction – on the learners' initiative – of certain elements of irony (utterances 4 and 6 – MM jokes about her current dieting), a typically metalinguistic task consisting in translation of terms becomes an area of authentic, spontaneous, fully involved communication – which, admittedly, proceeds in the first language. Modifying the observed communication practice towards a more frequent use of the target language (by learners as well as by teachers) may foster authentic target language communication in the foreign language classroom.

Concluding Remarks

The analysis of selected inherent features of classroom communication indicates that the formal aspects of language are given priority, while meaning-oriented foreign language utterances that engage interlocutors are rather an exception. Foreign language communication in the classroom differs considerably from that which proceeds in natural settings, and this is so for at least two objective reasons:

(1) as exolingual communication, classroom communication demands that interlocutors constantly direct attention to comprehension problems, with the reservation that, in the context under discussion here, the strategy of resorting to the mother tongue is usually employed as a remedy; the usefulness of this strategy, as Pawlak rightly points out (2009b), will turn out to be rather limited in natural settings, in contact with native speakers of a foreign language;

(2) as an example of communication in an institutional setting, communication in the foreign language classroom has all the features of educational discourse, strongly focused on form and search for correctness during the performance of tasks regardless of the type of these tasks; this results in pushing meaning-related issues to the background (contrary to what is the case in natural settings, when message meaning tends to be of prime importance).

The above features of communication in the classroom do not necessarily make it impossible for authentic meaning-focused communication to occur there, but this would demand modifying the existing communication practice and particularly reducing the use of the first language to the minimum because

(1) systematic use of the mother tongue results in learners communicating at a level that is below their actual competence, for example in asking the simplest metalinguistic questions (Piotrowski, 2008);

(2) teachers' use of the mother tongue results in the potential of metacommunication being left unexploited – and, after all, formulating commands and instructions in the target language may provide useful practice in authentic communication resembling that which takes place in natural settings.

Thus, the authenticity of communication in the classroom is not determined by task type, method, or even the kind of texts (Badio, 2009) or other teaching aids used, but by whether the communication ritual implemented in a specific context fosters authentic foreign language interaction. That ritual is largely shaped by the teacher himself or herself, who establishes and implements the frequently unwritten rules that determine the functioning of interlocutors in interaction (e.g. Lantolf & Genung, 2000; Smuk, 2009). Although communication in natural settings is the point of reference when it comes to authentic communication, this does not mean that interactions in the classroom should copy informal interactions. This would simply be impossible, since the classroom has its own specificity (Jankowska, 2008). Yet, communication in the foreign language classroom should train learners to communicate also – or even primarily – outside the classroom (in natural exolingual situations), which makes it so essential to develop such communication rituals that enable involved communication not only in the first language but primarily in the target language.

References

Allwright, R.L. (1983) Classroom-centered research on language teaching and learning: A brief historical overview. *TESOL Quarterly* 17 (2), 191–204.

Badio, J. (2009) Ponowne spojrzenie na problem autentyczności w nauczaniu języka obcego. In M. Pawlak, M. Derenowski and B. Wolski (eds) *Problemy współczesnej dydaktyki języków obcych* (pp. 87–94). Poznań-Kalisz: UAM.

Bange, P. (1992) A propos de la communication et de l'apprentissage en L2, notamment dans ses formes institutionnelles. *Acquisition et Interaction en Langue Etrangère* 1, 53–85.

Cambra Giné, M. (2003) *Une approche ethnographique de la classe de langue.* Paris: Didier.

de Salins, G.D. (1992) *Une introduction à l'ethnographie de la communication. Pour la formation à l'enseignement du français langue étrangère.* Paris: Didier.

Ellis, R. (1984) *Classroom Second Language Development: A Study of Classroom Interaction and Language Acquisition.* Oxford: Pergamon Press.

Gaonac'h, D. (1990) Les stratégies attentionnelles dans l'utilisation d'une langue étrangère. In D. Gaonac'h (ed.) *Acquisition et utilisation d'une langue étrangère. L'approche cognitive* (pp. 41–49). Paris: Hachette.

Goffman, E. (1974) *Frame Analysis : An Essay on the Organization of Experience.* New York: Harper & Row.

Gumperz, J.J. and Hymes, D. (eds) (1972) *Directions in Sociolinguistics: The Ethnography of Communication.* New York: Holt, Rinehart and Winston.

Jankowska, A. (2008) "Prawdziwa" komunikacja w klasie – czy jest możliwa? In M. Jodłowiec and A. Niżegorodcew (eds) *W stronę nowoczesnego nauczania języków obcych* (pp. 239–248). Kraków: Tertium.

Klein, W. and Perdue, C. (1997) The basic variety (or: Couldn't natural languages be much simpler?). *Second Language Research* 13, 301–348.

Lantolf, J.P. and Genung, P.B. (2000) L'acquisition scolaire d'une langue étrangère vue dans la perspective de la théorie de l'activité: une étude de cas. *Acquisition et Interaction en Langue Etrangère* 12, 99–122.

Long, M. (1985) Input and second language acquisition theory. In S. Gass and C. Madden (eds) *Input in Second Language Acquisition* (pp. 377–393). Rowley, MA: Newbury House.

Majer, J. (1998) Poles apart? Bridging the gap between naturalistic and pedagogic discourse. In P.J. Melia (ed.) *Innovations and Outcomes in English Language Teacher Education* (pp. 145–163). Warszawa: The British Council Poland.

Majer, J. (2003) *Interactive Discourse in the Foreign Language Classroom*. Łódź: Wydawnictwo Uniwersytetu Łódzkiego.

Malinowski, B. (1923) The problem of meaning in primitive languages. In C.K. Ogden and I.A. Richards (eds) *The Meaning of Meaning* (pp. 296–336). New York: Harcourt, Brace and Company.

Pallotti, G. (2002) La classe dans une perspective écologique de l'acquisition. *Acquisition et Interaction en Langue Etrangère* 16, 165–197.

Pawlak, M. (ed.) (2009a) Metody badań w językoznawstwie stosowanym. *Neofilolog* 32, 65–83.

Pawlak, M. (2009b) Rola nauczyciela w kształtowaniu procesów interakcyjnych podczas lekcji języka obcego. In M. Pawlak, A. Mystkowska-Wiertelak and Agnieszka Pietrzykowska (eds) *Nauczyciel języków obcych dziś i jutro* (pp. 311–337). Poznań Kalisz: Adam Mickiewicz University Press.

Piotrowski, S. (2005) Kompetencja egzolingwalna w klasie języka drugiego. In K. Karpińska Szaj (ed.) *Nauka języków obcych w dobie integracji europejskiej* (pp. 241–248). Łask: Oficyna Wydawnicza Leksem.

Piotrowski, S. (2006) *Gestion des tâches et mode d'accès à la langue. L'apprentissage du français en milieu institutionnel polonais*. Lublin: Towarzystwo Naukowe KUL.

Piotrowski, S. (2008) La métalangue en classe de langue étrangère. In J. Florczak and M. Gajos (eds) *Językoznawstwo a dydaktyka języków obcych. Teoria i praktyka* (pp. 99– 106). Warszawa: Piktor.

Piotrowski, S. (2009) Strategie w akwizycji języka obcego w środowisku instytucjonalnym. In J. Nijakowska (ed.) *Język – Poznanie – Zachowanie. Perspektywy i Wyzwania w studiach nad przyswajaniem języka obcego* (pp. 190–201). Łódź: Wydawnictwo Uniwersytetu Łódzkiego.

Porquier, R. (1984) Communication exolingue et apprentissage des langues. In *Acquisition d'une langue étrangère III* (pp. 17–47). Paris-Neuchâtel: Presses Universitaires de Vincennes-Centre de linguistique appliquée.

Porquier, R. and Py, B. (2004) *Apprentissage d'une langue étrangère: contextes et discours*. Paris: Didier.

Smuk, M. (2009) Od psychoterapii do dydaktyki – o autentyczności nauczyciela. In M. Pawlak, M. Derenowski and B. Wolski (eds) *Problemy współczesnej dydaktyki języków obcych* (pp. 95–104). Poznań-Kalisz: Adam Mickiewicz University Press.

Swain, M. (1985) Communicative competence: Some roles of comprehensible input and comprehensible output in its development. In S. Gass and C. Madden (eds) *Input in Second Language Acquisition* (pp. 235–253). Rowley, MA: Newbury House.

Swain, M. (2005) The output hypothesis: Theory and research. In E. Hinkel (ed.) *Handbook of Research in Second Language Acquisition* (pp. 471–483). Mahwah, NJ: Erlbaum.

Vygotsky, L.S. (1978) *Mind in Society: The Development of Higher Psychological Processes.* Cambridge: Harvard University Press.

Weinreich, U. (1967) *Languages in Contact: Findings and Problems.* The Hague: Mouton.

Wilczyńska, W. (2002) Podmiotowość i autonomia jako wyznaczniki osobistej kompetencji komunikacyjnej. In W. Wilczyńska (ed.) *Autonomizacja w dydaktyce języków obcych. Doskonalenie się w komunikacji Ustnej* (pp. 51–67). Poznań: Adam Mickiewicz University Press.

Chapter 15

Ways to Proficiency in Spoken English as a Foreign Language – Tracing Individual Development

IRENA CZWENAR

Introduction

The usual way of measuring linguistic development in the practice of language teaching is through the application of batteries of language tests addressing various subsystems and skills. Oral proficiency testing invariably involves assessment of the students' performance in an oral interview carried out by a group of examiners, at least one of whom acts as a rater.

Since proficiency is a complex construct, the measurement of its development must involve an explicit identification of its perceived dimensions. The aspects of oral proficiency which were addressed in the present study include the qualitative aspects of *fluency, linguistic accuracy* and *complexity*. Although the choice of proficiency dimensions, that is marking criteria, varies across existing examination formats, the three aspects of proficiency examined in this study feature in the widely accepted standardised assessment frameworks (cf. *ACTEFL Examination Guidelines*, 1999; Council of Europe, 2001). Besides, in second language acquisition (SLA) research there is a tradition of measuring the quality of performance in terms of fluency, accuracy and complexity (cf. Larsen-Freeman, 2006; Robinson, 2001; Skehan & Foster, 1999; Tarone, 1980).

Spoken Language Characteristics

The present section briefly describes the most important features of the spoken language. These particular linguistic features, which reflect various aspects of the speech production process, are as follows:

(1) Speech is delivered via the oral/auditory channel, which means that it is produced by interlocutors talking face to face in a particular context. This inevitably affects the way in which speakers 'package' information and the language choices they make.
(2) Spoken language is typically dynamic and interactive; discourse develops as a result of interaction between the speakers and between the speakers and the context.

(3) Most speech is produced spontaneously, with no possibility of planning or rehearsing in advance. The real-time 'online' processing makes it sensitive to the constraints of short-term memory.

The above properties have profound implications for the organisation and quality of the subsystems of the spoken language, that is grammar, lexicon and phonology. In most general terms, the syntax of the spoken language tends to be fragmented and relatively simple; phrasal and clausal structures are less elaborated than those typical of the written genres. A similar lack of elaboration characterises spoken vocabulary, which is of a narrower range and more repetitive than the vocabulary used in the written language. Spontaneous, unprepared talk abounds in hesitation phenomena, including repetitions, reformulations, silent and filled pauses.

The grammar of the spoken language

In structural terms, spoken discourse does not resemble a hierarchy, and *subordination* and *embedding* are far less frequent than in the written mode. The most common pattern of clause combination in spoken language is the linking of clauses in a sequential way, with clauses being added one after another (which is a result of real-time processing). Because the processes of conceptualisation, formulation and articulation of a message run in parallel (cf. Levelt, 1989), speakers have no time to work out complex patterns of the main and subordinate clauses. Thus, clause subordination is rare in informal spoken English; the prevailing clause-linking device is coordination, with conjunctions such as *and*, *but*, *or*. There are examples of clause subordination by means of *because* and *so*, but these two connectors often act more like coordinating than subordinating conjunctions. Subordinate clauses often occupy complete speaker turns, in which case they do not appear to be overtly connected to any specific main clause. Very often, they refer to and complement the other speaker's turn. Clausal blends, that is syntactic structures which are completed differently from the way in which they were begun, are also typical in spoken English (cf. Carter & McCarthy, 2006). Some of the most common structural features characterising the grammar of the spoken language are given below:

(1) Clauses and phrases tend to be linked through chaining or coordination.
(2) There is a high incidence of subordinate clauses which do not appear to be connected to any particular main clauses.
(3) Grammatical structures are far less complex than in the written language. Post-modification is rare.
(4) Many constructions are incomplete or simply abandoned by the speaker.

Lexical properties of the spoken language

The specificity of spoken language vocabulary is closely associated with the nature of speech and cognitive, psychological and social factors underlying the processes of speech production. It is important to note at this point that certain aspects of spoken vocabulary may be present in one spoken genre or text type, yet not necessarily observable in another. Therefore, the properties of spoken language vocabulary discussed in this section should be seen as representing informal, conversational register, rather than applying to the spoken language in general. The choice of this particular variety of spoken English is motivated by the intention to highlight those aspects of lexis which are the most salient characteristics of the kind of spoken discourse investigated in the present study. The general characteristics of informal conversational vocabulary, in terms of its complexity, range and frequency of individual words, based on the findings of corpus-based research (cf. Biber *et al.*, 1999; Carter & McCarthy, 1997), include the following:

(1) Speakers avoid 'lexical and syntactic elaboration'; as a result they rarely use complex and sophisticated words (Biber *et al.*, 1999).
(2) A fair amount of conversational lexis serves interpersonal and interactional purposes rather than transactional ones.
(3) Spoken language is characterised by a high occurrence of prefabricated lexical expressions, often idiomatic in structure and meaning.
(4) Many 'words' cannot be classified in terms of traditional grammar; for example *now* may be used to refer to time, but also as a discourse marker, used to close down a topic or phase of a conversation.

Avoidance of 'lexical and syntactic elaboration' is reflected in a relatively low level of *lexical density* (cf. Biber *et al.*, 1999). Another statistical measure of the vocabulary profile of a text is *lexical variation* (McCarthy, 1990; Schmitt, 2000). This parameter makes use of the distinction between *types* and *tokens*; repetitions of the same word are treated as one type, while each occurrence of a word is a token. A text in which many tokens are repeated has a relatively low number of types, and consequently, its lexical variation expressed as *the type/token (T/T) ratio* is low. The two measures reflect slightly different dimensions of vocabulary statistics. A text containing numerous repetitions of content words may be characterised by a high lexical density and a low lexical variation at the same time.

The effects of processing constraints on the quality of speech

Spoken language is rarely prepared in advance and rehearsed. The 'online' production of speech means that the processes of planning and execution of utterances run in parallel. As well as encoding his or her own utterances, the interlocutor has to decode the language produced by the other participant(s) in interaction. The most obvious outcome of the difficulties involved in the encoding and decoding of messages is the occurrence of dysfluency phenomena in the form of *pauses, repeats* and *reformulations*. Processing constraints also have an impact on the length and complexity of syntactic structures the speaker is able to produce, since the possibilities of planning utterances ahead of the actual production are severely affected by the limitations of the human working memory (reported to have a span of five to seven words). By the same token, the size of the syntactic structure which can be held incomplete in memory until the next planning phase begins is reduced. Another consequence of this mode of production is the fact that structures occupying initial and middle positions of a clause are relatively simple when compared with those occupying final positions (Biber *et al.*, 1999).

The Study

Participants and procedures

The aim of the study reported in this chapter was to identify properties which characterise the spoken English of non-native speaking students of English. The aspects of spoken English, which will be discussed below, include the following:

(1) fluency of oral performance;
(2) grammatical and lexical accuracy, counted as the number of errors;
(3) lexical variation measured by means of the T/T ratio;
(4) grammatical complexity represented by the number of structural units, such as dependent clauses and phrases.

The study was conducted at the English Philology Department on students attending a three-year bachelor degree programme in English. On entering the college, the students typically represent the level of proficiency in English comparable to that of Cambridge First Certificate candidates. Graduates are expected to have attained the level of proficiency corresponding to CAE (Certificate in Advanced English) and to be nearing the level of CPE (Certificate of Proficiency in English). The students' achievement is measured by means of various types of language tests addressing language subsystems and skills. Oral proficiency is assessed on the basis of the student's performance in an oral interview by a group of examiners using descriptive assessment criteria, which are then averaged to give the final grade. The same questions keep recurring as the students take their final examinations: Do the students improve their oral proficiency skills in the course of college training? If they do, how much progress do they make every year? Can the students' performance on oral tasks be measured in a more objective way than through assessment issued by a group of raters? Can we isolate the crucial components of their oral performance in order to provide clearer evidence of improvement?

The present study was undertaken in response to the above general considerations and its ultimate aim was to develop a structured way of grasping the sense of progress and development of oral proficiency of upper-intermediate and advanced students of English. Owing to the lack of a general index of foreign language acquisition (Ellis, 1994) and to the complexity of language, it is impossible to capture the sense of progress by examining improvement in a single component of proficiency (Skehan & Foster, 1997). Therefore, the specific aims of the study were to investigate the gains in oral fluency, accuracy and complexity of the spoken language production of the students.

The method of investigation adopted in the study involved longitudinal monitoring of the students' progress in oral proficiency. To this end, the students were interviewed in a set of oral tasks applied serially over a period of three years. The interviews were conducted on a one-to-one basis. The interview questions, which were predetermined in advance, were open-ended in order to elicit longer responses from the students. The rationale behind using open-ended questions was to obtain a substantial amount of 'natural-sounding' spoken language data. After pilot testing of the format, the first interview was introduced in the first weeks of instruction; this point is referred to as 'Year 0'. The consecutive interviews were repeated in the final weeks of Year One, Year Two and Year Three. This way, eight of the nine subjects took part in a series of four interviews and one subject participated in three interviews, so that the procedure eventually yielded 35 interviews.

The interview schedule was built around three tasks, in which the interview format resembled the procedure formerly used in CFC examinations. The tasks elicited transactional language in the form of long turns. The same tasks were repeated on every application of the interview. The following tasks were used:

(1) The interviewee responded to questions about her hometown, family, interests and future plans.
(2) On the basis of a visual prompt, the interviewee compared and contrasted two situations, adding her personal reflections on the problem.
(3) The interviewee expressed her opinion on a wider issue of successful language learning.

All the interviews were tape-recorded and transcribed for later analyses. The transcripts were saved in an electronic form, thus producing a mini-corpus of learner spoken English containing 24,500 words. The data were subsequently coded and analysed in terms of fluency, accuracy and complexity measures. The prevailing methods of data analyses were quantitative.

Fluency was operationalised in terms of three temporal measures: (a) *rate of speech*, defined as the number of words per minute; (b) *frequency of pauses*, that is the number of silent and filled pauses per 100 words; (c) *mean length of a pause*. The temporal parameters were measured by means of spectral analysis tools available from the Praat electronic package (Boersma & Weenink, 2004). The measure of accuracy used in this study was *the number of errors per 100 words*. In order to perform the error count consistently, a distinction between error *type* and *token* was recognised, as suggested by Lennon (1991). Thus, errors which were identical at the level of lexical realisation were treated as tokens of the same type. The procedure of error count included only error types. Linguistic complexity was examined at the lexical and grammatical levels. The main measure of lexical complexity was *lexical variation* operationalised as the T/T ratio. *Grammatical complexity* was described in terms of syntactic sophistication at the phrase and clause levels. As a point of reference, a taxonomy of phrasal and clausal units was drawn up, adapted from the wide range of descriptive categories provided by Miller and Weinert (1998) and Biber *et al.* (1999). For each set of the data, *the mean score* was calculated to illustrate the group's average on the given parameter in successive years. Moreover, *the standard deviation* (SD) for each set of results was calculated to show the degree of dispersion in the group.

Results and discussion

Fluency

Each of the fluency measures used in the study reflects a different aspect of fluent speech production, yet all these parameters are inextricably linked to one another. The rate of speech is taken to reflect the speed and automaticity of speech production. An increase in the rate of speech is thus considered to indicate improvement in fluency. The frequency and distribution of pauses show how much information the speaker is able to encode in a single act of planning a message. The falling trend in the frequency of pausing is thus indicative of better performance. The mean length of a pause shows how much time the speaker needs to encode the next message. The falling trend in the mean length of a pause is interpreted as evidence for improvement. In order to render the degree of progress in a more transparent way, the results displayed in this section will be limited to one measure of fluency, that is the rate of speech.

As can be seen from Table 15.1, improvement in the rate of speech over the three-year period is indicated by the mean score, which increased from 103.06 words per minute in Year 0 to 110.69 in Year 3. However,

Table 15.1 Scores obtained for the rate of speech (number of words per minute)

Student	Year 0	Year 1	Year 2	Year 3
A	115.7	116.5	115.9	123.8
B	123.5	122.2	141.9	158.6
C	96.2	75.4	75	82.3
D	86.54	92.1	113.6	113.2
E	106.8	98.4	103.1	105.9
F	111.4	102.2	100.3	116.8
G	102.7	–	121.5	102.3
H	107.7	88.5	106.3	106.3
I	77	83.3	78.6	87
M	103.06	97.33	106.24	110.69
SD	13.67	14.97	19.54	21.06

there is a certain degree of inter-individual variation; the SD value, which illustrates dispersion within the group, is on the increase as well. This implies that the rate of improvement for individual students varies, meaning that while some students made considerable progress (A, B, D, F, I), others showed a slower rate of improvement or stability (E, G, H) or even regression (C).

Figure 15.1 communicates the above scores in a visual format, which offers a better opportunity for drawing comparisons between the speakers. For example it shows the substantial difference in the rate of speech produced by Student B and Student C. Also, the lines in the graph – ascending or descending in turns – show the extent of fluctuation in the rate of speech for more than half the students. Only three of them (A, B, D) improved their speech rate consistently over the years.

Accuracy

The measure of accuracy used in the study was *the number of errors per 100 words*. This general measure of accuracy is reported to have been used in research of learner language before (cf. Ellis & Barkhuizen, 2005). Erroneous utterances were identified in terms of *extent* (cf. Lennon, 1991). All the instances of error were cross-checked against the British National Corpus data for greater reliability and consistence with native speech norms. Instances of error immediately self-corrected by the speakers were excluded from the count. Two broad categories of error were

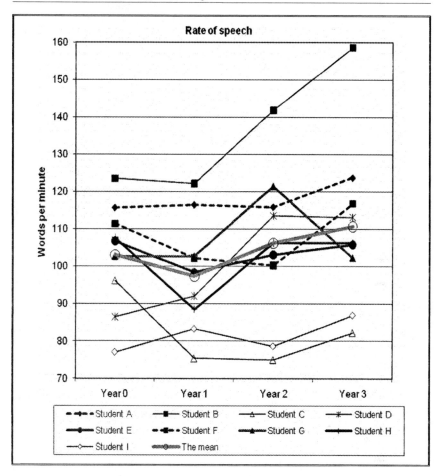

Figure 15.1 Rate of speech: within-group variation

adopted: grammatical and lexical. The problem of error embedding was resolved by calculating an erroneous sequence of language containing an embedded error as 1 token. The details of the scores for accuracy are displayed in Table 15.2 and Figure 15.2.

The mean score in accuracy for the group improved over time in that the number of errors per 100 words had fallen from 5.74 to 4.1. The dispersion within the group decreased, as indicated by the decline in the SD value from 1.52 to 1.09. Considerable improvement had taken place in the case of Students B and I, where the reduction of frequency of error was more than 50%. Only one student (D) obtained a raw score which indicated a higher frequency of error at the final point of measurement than at the onset of the study. And although her final score was not

Table 15.2 Errors per 100 words (number of errors divided by the total number of words, divided by 100)

Student	Year 0	Year 1	Year 2	Year 3
A	7.99	5.11	4.98	5.36
B	5.35	2.60	3.79	2.48
C	3.98	4.43	3.62	3.03
D	3.84	5.06	4.81	4.21
E	6.46	4.02	4.56	5.20
F	3.56	3.54	3.78	3.13
G	6.11	–	4.86	5.50
H	7.63	6.93	8.77	4.77
I	6.74	6.04	3.77	3.23
M	5.74	4.72	4.77	4.10
SD	1.52	1.27	1.51	1.09

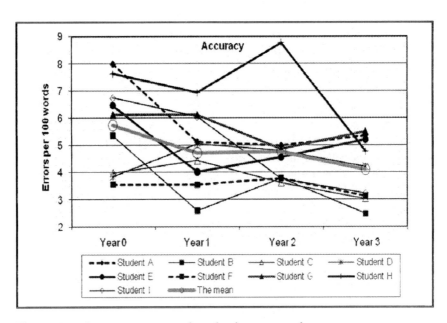

Figure 15.2 Accuracy measured as the frequency of error

markedly different from the mean, there was no improvement in comparison with her initial score. The other students showed moderate progress on this measure, even though the rate of improvement fluctuated from year to year.

Lexical complexity

The parameter used for measuring lexical complexity was the *T/T ratio*, taken to be an index of lexical variation or richness. It is arrived at by dividing the total number of different words, that is types, by the total number of words in a text (tokens). This measure is known to be affected by the length of the text, that is to say, the longer the text is, the lower the T/T ratio. Because the texts produced by the students in the study vary in length, it was necessary to obtain a standardised ratio. Therefore the actual scores were obtained with the help of Wordsmith Tools software (Scott, 1998), which allowed to divide each text into segments of equal size (400 words) and calculate the mean score for all the segments.

As can be seen from the figures in Table 15.3 and the graph in Figure 15.3, there was a steady increase in the mean score for the T/T ratio. However, individual results show a high degree of fluctuation in lexical complexity over the years. At the same time, the SD value is at its lowest in Year 1 but remains relatively constant during the following years, which suggests that the students demonstrated similar tendencies – rising or falling – to use rich vocabulary at successive points of measurement. It can be inferred from Table 15.3 that almost all the students followed the same route of lexical complexity development over the years, the exceptions being Student A, who evidently underperformed on this measure in Year 1; Student D, who obtained the highest score in the group in Year 2; and Student G, whose score in Year 3 exceeded the mean by a large margin.

Grammatical complexity

The grammatical complexity measure presented below, that is, the amount of clausal subordination, was defined as the number of dependent clauses, both finite and non-finite, per 100 words. The study actually used one more measure of grammatical complexity – the number of complex phrases per 100 words – but given the limited scope of the chapter the latter will not be presented graphically. The notion of *complexity*, as applied in this analysis, is used in compliance with the standards defined for spoken English, that is, any clauses which were incomplete were discarded from the count. Clauses containing errors within the verb phrase boundaries were ignored. The scores obtained for grammatical complexity are shown in Table 15.4 and Figure 15.4.

As can be seen from the data, all the students improved their performance in the use of subordination and most students improved

Table 15.3 Lexical variation calculated as the T/T ratio

Student	Year 0	Year 1	Year 2	Year 3
A	40.00	34.75	41.25	41.50
B	36.75	40.25	41.00	40.33
C	36.50	42.00	41.38	42.50
D	40.87	42.75	45.50	42.25
E	39.25	41.00	40.50	41.25
F	39.75	39.25	38.00	40.50
G	40.00	–	40.00	47.75
H	37.00	38.70	35.75	39.50
I	41.50	43.00	41.13	44.50
M	39.07	40.21	40.50	42.23
SD	1.75	2.53	2.50	2.39

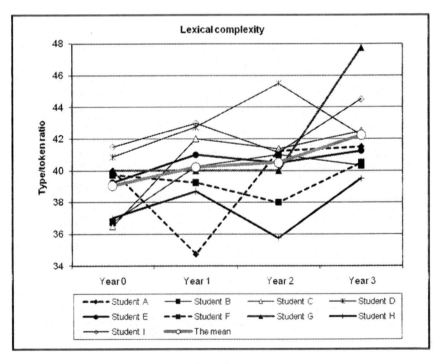

Figure 15.3 Lexical complexity: The T/T ratio

Table 15.4 Grammatical complexity (dependent clauses per 100 words)

Student	Year 0	Year 1	Year 2	Year 3
A	3.27	5.49	5.63	5.21
B	4.74	5.20	5.46	5.73
C	4.14	5.22	6.41	5.81
D	4.32	4.57	4.29	4.81
E	3.23	4.02	3.54	4.97
F	3.36	4.67	4.86	5.68
G	2.32	–	3.68	5.35
H	2.79	4.25	3.83	4.37
I	3.54	3.69	4.51	4.99
M	3.52	4.64	4.69	5.21
SD	0.67	0.60	0.97	0.43

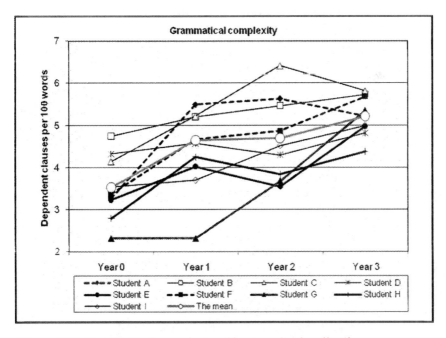

Figure 15.4 Grammatical complexity: The use of subordination

consistently throughout the years. The SD index reached its lowest value in Year 3, which indicates less variation along this measure in the group performance at the final stage of language instruction. Even though in some cases there was a falling trend in the final year (Students A and C), the end results were markedly better than they were at the initial stage. Therefore, we can observe a gradual rise in the value of the mean score obtained in the consecutive years of the study. Figure 15.4 demonstrates this growing tendency clearly.

Conclusion

The findings of the study allow us to infer that sustainable development of oral proficiency in the foreign language is not ensured for every member of the same student group, despite the fact that they are all involved in the same language teaching programme. However, in spite of the differences in the levels of fluency, accuracy and complexity achieved by individual students, the central tendencies for each measure, as shown by the mean score, are positive. The fact that some of the students improved one aspect of oral proficiency while neglecting another may indicate that their linguistic systems had not stabilised sufficiently; that is they were still at the phase of restructuring. The finding that some aspects of language proficiency may improve while other aspects regress is supported by similar evidence from studies of linguistic development reported in the SLA literature (cf. Larsen-Freeman, 2006).

With respect to fluency development, the findings showed that some of its temporal aspects improved over time while others remained at the same level. The sets of data obtained at successive points of measurement demonstrated an upward trend for the rate of speech and frequency of pauses, as indicated by the mean score. However, the mean length of the pause remained relatively constant throughout the years. The results also showed greater accuracy in the use of lexical items and grammatical structures in the students' oral performance. As regards complexity, the results showed a marked increase in the index of lexical complexity (the T/T ratio) and in both indices of grammatical complexity (dependent clauses and complex phrases counted per 100 running words).

As regards individual improvement, fluency, accuracy and complexity levels did not improve in equal proportions in the consecutive years, and development along one or two of these dimensions seems to have taken place at the expense of another. A plausible pattern that emerges from the data obtained is that of conflicting priorities in individual paths of linguistic development; an enhancement in one of the aspects of proficiency seems to exert an inhibitory effect on the development of another/other dimension(s).

A variety of factors may contribute to the shaping of individual paths of development. An important variable which significantly contributes to language improvement is the sum of linguistic experience of the learner. Individual student profiles sketched on the basis of information provided via questionnaires (not discussed in this chapter) suggest that the subjects of the study had rather limited experience of using English for real communication in naturalistic settings. Even though the students were offered ample opportunities to engage in communicative activities, their learning experience was nevertheless situated in the language classroom context. The length of language learning experience preceding admission to the college does not seem to have affected the students' proficiency level in English. As a matter of fact, the best results have been reported for those students who had learnt English for a relatively short period of time (e.g. Students B and F) before entering the college. The same students were found to be able to make better use of the available resources for language enhancement and take every opportunity to improve their English. This observation emphasises the role of learner autonomy and responsibility for one's own learning.

References

ACTFL Proficiency Guidelines (1999) New York: American Council on the Teaching of Foreign Languages.

Biber, J., Johansson, S. and Leech, G. (1999) *Longman Grammar of Spoken and Written English*. Harlow: Longman.

Boersma, P. and Weenink, D. (2004) Praat: Doing phonetics by computer. (Version 4.2.17) [Computer program]. Retrieved September 29, 2004, from http://www.praat.org/

Carter, R. and McCarthy, M. (1997) Written and spoken vocabulary. In N. Schmitt and M. McCarthy (eds) *Vocabulary: Description, Acquisition and Pedagogy* (pp. 20–39). Cambridge: Cambridge University Press.

Carter, R. and McCarthy, M. (2006) *Cambridge Grammar of English: A Comprehensive Guide; Spoken and Written English Grammar and Usage*. Cambridge: Cambridge University Press.

Council of Europe (2001) *Common European Framework of Reference for Languages: Learning, Teaching, Assessment*. Cambridge: Cambridge University Press.

Ellis, R. (1994) *The Study of Second Language Acquisition*. Oxford: Oxford University Press.

Ellis, R. and Barkhuizen, G. (2005) *Analysing Learner Language*. Oxford: Oxford University Press.

Larsen-Freeman, D. (2006) The emergence of complexity, fluency, and accuracy in the oral and written production of five Chinese learners of English. *Applied Linguistics* 27, 590–619.

Lennon, P. (1991) Error: Some problems of definition, identification, and distinction. *Applied Linguistics* 12, 180–195.

Levelt, W.J.M. (1989) *Speaking: From Intention to Articulation.* Cambridge, MA: MIT Press.

McCarthy, M. (1990) *Vocabulary.* Oxford: Oxford University Press.

Miller, J. and Weinert, R. (1998) *Spontaneous Spoken Language: Syntax and Discourse.* Oxford: Clarendon Press.

Robinson, P. (2001) Task complexity, task difficulty, and task production: Exploring interactions in a componential framework. *Applied Linguistics* 22, 27–57.

Schmitt, N. (2000) *Vocabulary in Language Teaching.* Cambridge: Cambridge University Press.

Scott, M. (1998) *WordSmith Tools,* Version 3.0. Oxford: Oxford University Press.

Skehan, P. and Foster, P. (1997) Task type and task processing conditions as influences on foreign language performance. *Language Teaching Research* 1, 185–211.

Skehan, P. and Foster, P. (1999) The influence of task structure and processing conditions on narrative retellings. *Language Learning* 49, 93–120.

Tarone, E. (1980) Communication strategies, foreigner talk and repair in interlanguage. *Language Learning* 30, 417–431.

Chapter 16

Task Repetition as a Way of Enhancing Oral Communication in a Foreign Language

ANNA MYSTKOWSKA-WIERTELAK

Introduction

None of the language skills occupy such a peculiar position in language pedagogy as speech production. It seems justifiable to say that the ultimate goal of most endeavors aimed at learning a foreign language is to be able to speak fluently expressing the intended meaning with ease and confidence. Many teachers and learners would probably attest that the evaluation of one's command of a foreign language concerns, first and foremost, the appraisal of the ability to communicate. Thus, teaching how to speak turns out to be one of the biggest challenges teachers face. Not only do they need to equip their students with structures and lexical items, but also they teach ways of dealing with psychological limitations and inhibitions. Moreover, the impressive list of teachers' responsibilities comprises developing sociolinguistic competence to ensure effective communication and also teaching pronunciation, since not only the content but also the form of an utterance plays a role in the way the message is received. On the basis of speech sounds reaching our ears we tend to judge the speaker's personality, attitude, background or even status. We are also inclined to create and project the picture of ourselves onto others: changes of the tempo and intonation as well as pauses and modulation enable us to build the texture of the utterance which supports or enhances what we say (Luoma, 2004: 10). Realizing the complexity and demands inherent in developing oral fluency, teachers have long been trying to find new ways and techniques that could be employed with view to assisting learners in the painstaking task of learning how to speak. The account of an experiment conducted by the present author describes one such attempt.

Speech Production

In order to understand the mechanisms involved in developing speaking skills, it is useful to consider the nature and conditions of speech production. The theoretical framework in L2 speech production research that most linguists refer to (cf. Bygate, 1996, 2001; Bygate *et al.*, 2001; Ellis, 2005, 2008; Hughes, 2002; Luoma, 2004) is the one proposed by Levelt (1989), which was originally meant for monolingual communication. Later, it was applied to the analysis of the speech of bilinguals and L2 learners by de Bot (1992) and Kormos (2006). Levelt (1989) believed that speech production can be described through the functioning of a number of relatively autonomous processes: conceptualization of the message, formulation of the language representation and articulation. At the level of conceptualization the speaker plans the content of the utterance by drawing from their knowledge of the world or the topic, the information about a specific situation or type of discourse or interaction. The message is still at the preverbal stage, but it contains all the data needed to convert it into language. The subsequent stage of formulation involves finding the words and phrases in the mental lexicon of the speaker. Each word consists of two types of data: *lemma*, containing information about the meaning and syntax, and *lexeme*, delineating its morphological and phonological profile. The process of retrieving of lexical items is thus connected with grammatical encoding, which leads to the origination of the *surface structure* – a string of lemmas composed of phrases of different kind. This, in turn, undergoes phonological encoding that results in a phonetic or articulatory plan, which Levelt calls *internal speech* (Ellis, 2005: 12). The mechanisms comprised in the third process – articulation – are responsible for converting chunks of internal speech into actual speech, which entails motor control of the speech apparatus. The three processes described above are regulated by ongoing self-monitoring that checks whether the information at the preverbal stage reflects the actual intentions of the speaker, controls the stage of grammatical and phonological encoding and inspects the final utterance originated in the course of the whole process. Since all these processes proceed simultaneously, the eventual success depends on the degree of their automaticity. Levelt (1989) pointed out that conceptualization and monitoring function under controlled processing, whereas formulation and articulation are mainly automatic.

De Bot (1992) employed Levelt's model to account for speech production in an L2 and pointed out that formulation is governed by two separate processing systems, L1 and L2 specific, whose independence does not exclude interconnections. Taking into account L1 interference in the production of L2 sounds, de Bot doubts there exist separate systems responsible for articulation (1992: 17). The processes of formulation and articulation may not engage L1 speakers' attention; however, L2 learners need to employ their conscious processors to accomplish the same goal, which not infrequently leads to problems in production. L2 learners find it exceedingly difficult to cope with the demands posed by the mechanisms involved in speech production on their working memory

(Ellis, 2005: 13). Given the tenets of Levelt's model, Ellis (2005: 14) concedes that 'rehearsal (...) may provide learners with an opportunity to attend to all three components (...) so it would seem reasonable to assume that this type of pre-task planning will lead to all-round improvements when that task is repeated, as found by Bygate (1996)'.

Aspects of Language Production

Skehan (1998) distinguishes three aspects of production: fluency – the ability of the speaker to mobilize the system to express meaning in real time; accuracy – the capacity to conform to the target language norms; complexity – the application of complex, sophisticated forms. Each of the aspects corresponds to a different system of language. Fluency relies on the data stored in the memory-based system from which prefabricated chunks of language can be drawn and which also provides communication strategies if problems need to be dealt with. Although both accuracy and complexity entail syntactic processing and draw on the rule-based system, they differ considerably with respect to the level of control and willingness to take risk: while accuracy reflects the speaker's need to manage the resources and refrain from making mistakes, complexity is indicative of the drive to experiment with language (Ellis, 2005: 15). Given the limited nature of human processing capacity, L2 learners have to reach a kind of compromise between the three aspects: more attention directed to one of them may result in the deterioration of the others (Skehan, 1998).

The emphasis on any of the three aspects also depends on the context in which the utterance is generated. A whole array of speech characteristics imprint importantly on the produced language. First, speaking is reciprocal – speakers need to adapt the language they produce to verbal and non-verbal reactions of the audience. Most conversations take place *here and now,* which forces the speaker to make decisions concerning both the content and the form of an utterance online, not having time for corrections or checking. Thus, oral production is less predictable than writing. Moreover, rarely does symmetry characterize interlocutors' rights in the conversation, for example topic initiation, asking questions or closing the conversation. Furthermore, the form of an utterance will also depend on its type and content as well as social distance between the speakers.

A question arises as to how learners of a foreign language can be assisted in the burdensome task of learning to speak if directing their attention to one of the aspects will most likely negatively affect the remaining two (Skehan, 1998). Simultaneous focus on all three aspects seems to pose an overwhelming challenge: increased emphasis on fluency might lead to overreliance on ready-made expressions and insensitivity to the application of grammatical rules; greater pressure on grammatical accuracy will affect fluency and discourage learners from experimenting with language, while too much experimentation with new words and structures might result in the production of inaccurate forms and hinder fluency (Ellis, 2005: 16). It seems justifiable to say that type of task learners are confronted with, depending on the emphasis on any of the aspects, will directly influence their development (Bygate, 2001: 17). The results obtained in a number of studies (e.g. Bygate, 1999; Foster & Skehan, 1996; Skehan & Foster, 1997; Yuan & Ellis, 2003) corroborate the assumption that the three aspects of language production are not only separate concepts but also compete with one another, given the limited processing capacity (Ellis, 2008: 491).

The Effects of Speech Planning on L2 Production

Ellis (2005, 2008) distinguishes two types of task-based planning: *pretask planning* and *within-task planning*. Pretask planning is further divided into *rehearsal* and *strategic planning*. The former refers to an opportunity learners receive to perform the task at least twice, with the first performance treated as a preparation for the one that follows. In strategic planning, learners examine the content and determine how to express it. What differs strategic planning from other pretask activities, such as brainstorming, searching the dictionary or inspecting the model for production, is the fact that the content needs to be provided to the learners (Ellis, 2005: 3). Within-task planning can be further divided depending on whether learners performing a task do it under time pressure or not. An unpressured performance allows learners to plan their production carefully online, which results in the so-called *planned language use*, whereas pressured performance requires brisk planning which leads to *unplanned language use*. The two types of language use, according to Ochs (1979), differ considerably with respect to the extent to which targetlike forms are used: while unplanned language use is characterized by the appearance of non-standard forms acquired in early stages of acquisition, planned language use displays the application of more complex forms. Generally, the two types of planning, being separate in character, do not exclude each other within the same task (Ellis, 2008: 493–494).

Planning may affect both the content and the choice of language forms employed to express this content. Ellis (2005: 17) believes that planning allows learners to draw from their L2 knowledge through controlled processing and it also promotes selective attention, leaving enough time for monitoring. The impact of pretask planning and unpressured online planning on task performance is, however, different: pretask planning enables learners to conceptualize the message content and facilitates controlled processing and selective attention to form, while unpressured online planning influences the choices made at the level of formulation, since it allows controlled processing and monitoring, leaving out the dimension of conceptualization.

Research on Task Planning

Research on rehearsal has shown that repeated performance of the same task positively affects all the three aspects of speech production. Bygate (1996) compared the production of the same learner who described a short *Tom and Jerry* cartoon on two occasions. The benefits of task repetition were manifested in the increased complexity of the presentation on the second occasion: more lexical verbs were used as well as irregular past tense forms, more sophisticated lexical items appeared together with a wider range of cohesive devices. Moreover, the number of inaccurate lexical collocations turned out to decrease, while self-correcting repetitions were observed more frequently. Another study reported by Bygate (2001) attempted to investigate the impact of practicing of a particular type of task on the second performance of the same task as well as the performance of a new task of the same type. As expected, the repetition of the same task resulted in greater fluency and complexity. Disconcertingly, no transfer of practice effect was observed in the case of the new task.

Analogous were the results reported by Gass *et al.* (1999) with reference to the study whose aim was to investigate the use of L2 Spanish in tasks that included the same or different content. The general proficiency, accuracy and lexical complexity improved only when the participants were involved in the task with the same content and no such effect was noted for the new task. Another task rehearsal study was presented by Lynch and McLean (2000, 2001). The students taking part in the experiment prepared a poster and a presentation on the basis of an academic article they read; then, they stood next to their posters and answered questions of other group members who asked them to explain and clarify the ideas herein included. Since the group consisted of a big number of students, identical or similar questions were asked, giving the authors the chance to present one idea many times. The researchers proved that repetition generally contributed to improved fluency and accuracy. The type of benefit depended on the students' proficiency level: at the higher level the positive influence was manifested in increased clarity and economy, while at a lower level grammatical accuracy and pronunciation improved the most (Ellis, 2005: 19). Bygate and Samuda (2005) reported case studies of three learners who were required to repeat a narrative and it turned out that task repetition facilitated progress from a chaotic reports to a well-organized and lucid story. As can be inferred from the above-mentioned research, repetition of the same task has an advantageous effect on learners' performance. According to Bygate (1999), learners first concentrate on the message content, and having identified basic language to encode it, engage in selecting and monitoring of suitable words and phrases. In the course of task repetition, learners are granted the opportunity to ease the burden of simultaneous focus on the three competing aspects of speech production and can allocate an increased amount of processing ability to formulation, articulation and monitoring.

The Study

Although the project uses similar procedures of data collection and analysis as those employed by Bygate (1996), it cannot be considered a replication study because of a different task design and the involvement of a greater number of participants. The above-mentioned research projects, probably apart from the one by Lynch and McLean (2000, 2001), are laboratory studies having little in common with classroom reality. As many practitioners will probably attest, most learners expect from their teacher not only expertise in the target language but also a varied and balanced diet of motivating and engaging topics, tasks and activities. A question arises whether the repetition of exactly the same task is likely to satisfy their expectations. The study described below is an attempt to engage students in a task involving repetition; however, much effort was made to ensure the activity was, nevertheless, still attractive and stimulating. The study was a part of an ordinary class of the second year of master degree studies at the faculty of English philology. The conversations and presentations of four students working in one group were recorded and transcribed, and a detailed analysis concerned the language produced only by two of the group members.

Task design

The task the students were asked to perform referred to the statement included in the Speaking section of *Masterclass Proficiency*: 'Advertising should be banned as it persuades people to buy goods they don't want or need with money they don't possess'. Before the students began to explain whether they agree or disagree with the supposition, they took part in a short introductory session that consisted in listening to a recorded material, introducing necessary lexis, evaluating photographs being part of an advertising campaign.

The task consisted of three stages: first, Students A and B were asked to prepare a list of arguments supporting the above statement, while Students C and D worked on a list of arguments against it. Then, new pairs were created: Students A and C and Students B and D exchanged

Table 16.1 Indicators of task performance

	Repertoire/complexity	*Accuracy*	*Fluency*
Vocabulary	Range (type/token ratio)	Selection Collocation	Repetition
Discourse	Range of connectors		
Grammar	Verb forms Syntactic complexity	Errors	

Source: Adapted from Bygate (1996: 140)

arguments for and against. In the third part, one of the tasks students were asked was to make a presentation in an open forum which is a summary of the discussions they have had so far, incorporating arguments of both sides. Knowing it from the start, they listened attentively to the ideas of the opposing side so that they could use them in their own summary.

Table 16.1 presents the specific features of oral language that were analyzed. *Repertoire* or *complexity* concerns the range of language features used by the speaker, such as the variety of vocabulary items, called *type/token ratio* and understood as the total number of different words used (types) divided by the total number of words in a text (tokens); the variety of discourse connectors (*cohesion ratio*); the choice of verb forms and syntactic complexity. *Accuracy* refers to the choice of words and collocations as well the presence of errors. The third factor, *fluency*, refers to the amount and type of repetition. Pause length and frequency can also be indicative of the feature; however, they were not referred to in the present study. Two types of repetitions were identified: verbatim repetition when the speaker hesitates, buying time to search for an appropriate lexical item or grammatical form; and substitutive repetition which takes place when the learner comes up with a corrected word or structure.

Research findings

The interaction of four students in one group was recorded and then transcribed. Only the samples provided by Beata, on two occasions, and Magda, on three occasions, were analyzed.

It needs to be noted that the analysis concerns only two students and as such cannot be considered as representative of other learners. The results obtained by Beata are presented in Table 16.2. Unlike in the experiment conducted by Bygate (1996), the number of words on the second occasion increased, since the second trial involved not only the presentation of the student's own opinions and arguments but also the incorporation of the ideas delivered by the interlocutor in the pair. Both participants made very few errors, which is quite understandable, taking into account their

Table 16.2 The results obtained by Beata during the first and second stages of the task

	Time 1	*Time 2*
Total number of words	127	241
Errors	1	–
Verb form selection	7	11
To be	–	3
Gerund	5	4
Infinitive	5	6
Modal	1	–
Passives	3	3
Conditional	24	31
Tenses	–	1
Present	–	1
Past		
Future		
Subordinate clauses	3	14
Lexis	39	36
Type/token ratio	–	–
Cohesive devices		
Collocations	1	2
Inappropriate	7	15
Appropriate		
Disfluencies	1	2
Verbatim repetitions	–	1
Substitutive repetitions		

proficiency level – C1/C2. In the case of Beata, no errors were noted on Time 2.

Bygate (1996) in his experiment placed much emphasis on the analysis of the application of different verb forms, claiming that they occupy a very special position in the speaker's performance. Quoting Ellis (1987) and Crookes (1989), he claims that the choice of a verb form depends on the amount of time learners can spend planning their utterance: when learners were allowed more planning time, their utterances showed greater accuracy, particularly concerning the use of irregular verb forms. In the case of tasks involving repetition, the planning time prior to the first performance adds up to the planning before the second and third, and it applies to the planning performed by the speaker themselves or their partners in the group within which they cooperate.

As can be seen in Table 16.1, the allocation of more planning time not always resulted in a quantitative change of the application of particular structures, and thus, the number of conditional forms remained the same on both occasions. What is more, a passive structure disappeared in Beata's second performance, probably because extra planning time enabled her to identify the agent of that particular action, rendering the passive voice unnecessary. Contrary to the expectations, not a drop but an increase in the use of *to be* forms was observed (57%). The drop would have testified to the growing complexity of the production, since substituting precise verbs for the common *to be* entails greater sophistication of the linguistic repertoire. Nevertheless, some positive changes were observed: gerund forms, nonexistent on the first occasion, appeared; more modal verbs and infinitive forms were used; present tense forms were employed more frequently (an increase of 29%) and, in the second presentation, necessary contexts for the use of past and future tense forms were created. Beata's second sample proved to be grammatically more complex since the number of compound sentences increased dramatically, the increase being of the order of 460%.

The next set of data describes the selection of lexical items. Taking into account the fact that much time was allocated to content planning at Time 1, it was assumed that the second attempt would allow the choice of more precise or sophisticated vocabulary, an indicator of which may be the calculation of the type/token ratio. The higher the proportion of different words (types) to the total number of words in the text (tokens), the more varied the language is, including more adjectives and adverbs, and less repetitions. Surprisingly, no such improvement was observed in the case of Beata, whose ratio at Time 1 was 39 and amounted to 36 at Time 2. What needs to be taken into account and might be viewed as a weakness of the present study, however, is the fact that Beata's performance at Time 2 considerably exceeded Time 1 in length, thus making the two results difficult to compare. The following measure was to reflect the range of cohesive devices, words such as *so, because, first, finally*. In the original study, the *cohesion ratio* was calculated as a proportion of the number of clauses, and since no such devices were present in Beata's performance on both occasions, no such calculation was conducted here.

The measure of lexical collocation was meant to indicate the extent to which the learner was capable of collocating words appropriately to express the intended meaning. First, inappropriate collocations were calculated on both occasions and it turned out that Beata selected the wrong collocation once at Time 1 and twice on Time 2. Seven appropriate collocations were identified at Time 1 and 15 at Time 2, which seems to reveal that the speaker's selection of vocabulary approximated that of a native speaker's on the second occasion more than on the first.

Another indicator of the speaker's growing ability to control the language they produce is the appearance of repetitions. Bygate (1996: 144) believes that verbatim repetitions which concern grammatical structures at Time 1 take place to buy extra time to find a proper word or form. At Time 2, when the conceptualization has been accomplished, the time and attention can be used to find a more suitable grammatical form or a more precise word. This may lead to substitutive repetition. Neither verbatim nor substitutive repetitions were frequent in the discourse produced by Beata at both times. Nevertheless, some slight differences were noted. At Time 1, verbatim repetitions took place only once and twice on the second occasion. No substitutive repetitions were reported at Time 1 and one such repetition was noted at Time 2.

Table 16.3 reports the results obtained by Magda on three occasions since she was the one to take part in Stage 3 of the experiment and make a summary of the discussions conducted in pairs. The total number of words Magda used in her first and second presentations was very similar, 164 and 168, respectively. At Time 3 the number of words reached 223, which was caused by the task specificity, since it required the student to report the arguments for and against the thesis included in the task on advertising. The number of errors was bigger on the second occasion (5), but on the third occasion it equaled that of the first attempt (3). It seems that the extra time Magda could enjoy, given more planning time at Time 3, allowed her to refine the language she used.

As far as verb forms are concerned, there is no clear indication of gradual refinement. In some cases the numbers drop on the second occasion, only to increase on the third, or, as in the case of *to be*, increase considerably at Time 2 but decrease at Time 3. As for the application of different grammatical tenses, present simple was used 15, 14 and again 15 times at the three subsequent measures. The present continuous tense appeared three times at Time 2 and two times at Time 3. Magda chose to express her opinions in the past tense only once at Time 1; she did not need the form at Time 2, but at Time 3 the number of applications of past tense forms rose to 5 instances. More in agreement with the initial expectations were the results concerning the use of subordinate clauses, with 3 at Time 1, 9 at Time 2 and 10 at Time 3.

The set of data referring to vocabulary variation within the text shows no difference between Time 1 and Time 2 (44). At Time 3 the ratio was smaller (37), although this time the performance was longer. The rising tendency in the use of cohesive devices was not retained on the third occasion. The improvement in the use of inappropriate collocations was observed between the first two attempts, 2 cases and 1 case, respectively. Unfortunately, the summary included 4 inappropriately collocated expressions. The factor responsible for the increase in this respect was the need to perform in an open forum, which might have increased

Table 16.3 The results obtained by Magda during the first, second and third stages of the task

	Time 1	*Time 2*	*Time 3*
Total number of words	164	168	223
Errors	3	5	3
Verb form selection			
To be	5	12	7
Gerund	1	5	1
Infinitive	3	3	3
Modal	10	3	6
Passives	2	3	3
Conditional	3	–	2
Tenses			
Present (continuous)	15	14 (3)	15 (2)
Past	1	–	5
Future	–	–	–
Subordinate clauses	3	9	10
Lexis			
Type/token ratio	44	44	37
Cohesive devices	3	6	4
Collocations			
Inappropriate	2	1	4
Appropriate	12	11	18
Disfluencies			
Verbatim repetitions	2	–	1
Substitutive repetitions	2	2	6

anxiety, putting greater pressure on the processing ability of the speaker. Similar scores concerning appropriate collocations were reported at Time 1 and Time 2, and at Time 3, as many as 18 expressions were classified as appropriate, proving that the speaker's choice of vocabulary was more nativelike on the third occasion.

Verbatim repetitions, giving the speaker time to retrieve appropriate lexical items, were not frequent – 2 at Time 1 and 1 at Time 3 – whereas no such repetitions were recorded at Time 2. Substitutive repetitions or self-corrections, indicative of a shift of attention from conceptualization to the formulation of the utterance, happened twice on the first two occasions. At her third attempt, Magda, having planned her presentation at the two proceeding stages, attempted at self-correcting 6 times, which testifies to the fact that she could use the extra time to improve the fluency of her speech.

Conclusions

Less conclusive than that of Bygate (1996), the results of the present study suggest that task repetition can assist learners in the development of accuracy, repertoire and fluency. The findings show that being preoccupied with planning the content of the message, learners sometimes fail to identify the optimal means to express it. Another attempt at the same content enables them to allocate their attentional resources to the formulation phase: selection of words and phrases and correct grammatical forms.

Promising as the results may be, it needs to be remembered that they concern only two students and, as such, cannot be generalized without being confirmed in a larger group of learners, thus making the present project a pilot study for further research, allowing the researcher to eliminate its weaknesses and inconsistencies. Nevertheless, the following tentative conclusions can be drawn: task repetition may enable learners to shift their attention from the conceptualization to formulation of the utterance. Thus, learners may improve their accuracy and increase the range of words and forms in the course of tasks that necessitate repetition of the same or a very similar task. It seems that encouraging students to embark on the same activity at least twice might have beneficial effects on the growth of their interlanguage and the development of fluency. Still, the question remains as to how to make it attractive and challenging.

References

Bygate, M. (1996) Effects of task repetition: Appraising the developing language of learners. In J. Willis and D. Willis (eds) *Challenge and Change in Language Teaching* (pp. 136–146). Oxford: Macmillan Heineman.

Bygate, M. (1999) Tasks and the context for the framing, re-framing and unframing of language. *System* 27, 33–48.

Bygate, M. (2001) Effects of task repetition on the structure and control of language. In M. Bygate, P. Skehan and M. Swain (eds) *Task-Based Learning: Language Teaching, Learning and Assessment* (pp. 23–48). London: Longman.

Bygate, M. and Samuda, V. (2005) Integrative planning through the use of task repetition. In R. Ellis (ed.) *Planning and Task Performance in a Second Language* (pp. 37–76). Amsterdam: John Benjamins.

Bygate, M., Skehan, P. and Swain, M. (eds) (2001) *Task-Based Learning: Language Teaching, Learning and Assessment*. London: Longman.

Crookes, G. (1989) Planning and interlanguage variation. *Studies in Second Language Acquisition* 11, 267–283.

de Bot, K. (1992) A bilingual production model: Levelt's "speaking" model adapted. *Applied Linguistics* 13, 1–24.

Ellis, R. (1987) Interlanguage variability in narrative discourse: Style shifting in the use of the past tense. *Studies in Second Language Acquisition* 9, 12–20.

Ellis, R. (2005) Planning and task-based performance: Theory and research. In R. Ellis (ed.) *Planning and Task Performance in a Second Language* (pp. 3–36). Amsterdam: Benjamins.

Ellis, R. (2008) *The Study of Second Language Acquisition*. Oxford: Oxford University Press.

Foster, P. and Skehan, P. (1996) The influence of planning on performance in task-based learning. *Studies in Second Language Acquisition* 18, 299–324.

Gass, S., Mackey, A., Alvarez-Torres, M. and Fernández-García, M. (1999) The effects of task repetition on linguistic output. *Language Learning* 49, 549–581.

Hughes, R. (2002) *Teaching and Researching Speaking*. Harlow: Longman.

Kormos, J. (2006) *Speech Production and Second Language Acquisition*. Mahwah, NJ: Erlbaum.

Levelt, W. (1989) *Speaking: From Intention to Articulation*. Cambridge, MA: MIT Press.

Luoma, S. (2004) *Assessing Speaking*. Cambridge: Cambridge University Press.

Lynch, T. and MacLean, J. (2000) Exploring the effects of task repetition and recycling for classroom language learning. *Language Teaching Research* 4, 221–250.

Lynch, T. and MacLean, J. (2001) Effects of immediate repetition on learners' performance. In M. Bygate, P. Skehan and M. Swain (eds) *Researching Pedagogic Tasks, Second Language Learning, Teaching and Testing* (pp. 141–162). Harlow: Longman.

Ochs, E. (1979) Planned and unplanned discourse. In T. Givón (ed.) *Syntax and Semanatics, Volume 12: Discourse and Semantics* (pp. 57–78). New York: Academic Press.

Skehan, P. (1998) *A Cognitive Approach to Language Learning*. Oxford: Oxford University Press.

Skehan, P. and Foster, P. (1997) The influence of planning and post-task activities on accuracy and complexity in task-based learning. *Language Teaching Research* 1, 185–211.

Yuan, F. and Ellis, R. (2003) The effects of pretask and online planning on fluency, complexity and accuracy in L2 monologic oral production. *Applied Linguistics* 24, 1–27.

Chapter 17

The Use of the Internet and Instant Messengers in Assisting the Acquisition of Speaking Skills in English Lessons

MARIUSZ KRUK

Introduction

The development of speaking skills is a demanding task for both language teachers and students in view of the fact that it requires a great deal of involvement, perseverance and effort. This task is especially difficult in the Polish educational context where foreign language instruction is usually limited to two or three classes a week. Thus, it is particularly important to plan lessons properly in order to motivate students to speak the target language. Moreover, it is crucial to promote learner autonomy in order to enable students to use their potential as well as to show them how to develop the target language on their own after compulsory school lessons. In addition, it seems to be warranted to implement computer technology and the internet, in particular in teaching speaking skills, since the online environment provides authenticity and facilitates learner autonomy. The aim of this chapter is to report on the findings of a quasi-experimental study, the aim of which was to examine the extent to which the use of internet resources and instant messengers affects the development of speaking skills related to particular language functions in comparison with traditional instruction.

Using Computers for Communication

Literature provides ample information related to language materials and activities available on the internet in order to develop speaking skills among learners of different levels of proficiency (e.g. Beatty, 2003; Erben *et al.*, 2009; Krajka, 2007; Teeler & Gray, 2000; Windeatt *et al.*, 2000). The use of a variety of materials in teaching speaking such as texts, graphics, and audio and video recordings can at the same time contribute to the development of other language skills and subsystems such as reading, listening, pronunciation or vocabulary. It should be pointed out that some computer applications designed with the purpose of online communication in the form of text messages can be implemented in language classes in order to practice speaking skills. Examples of such computer software include *IRC* or *Gadu-Gadu* (for *Windows* operating systems) and their *Linux* operating system equivalents *XChat* and *Kadu* (see also Erben *et al.*, 2009). Moreover, there are quite a few applications of this type that do not require installation on the user's hard disk drive (e.g. *Yahoo! Messenger for the Web* available at http://webmessenger. yahoo.com), and various features of some websites allow users to quickly leave messages on web pages without any form of registration (e.g. *shoutbox*). In addition, several computer applications (e.g. *Skype*) allow their users to communicate not only in the form of text messages but also by voice (Krajka, 2007; Mullen *et al.*, 2009).

As mentioned above, online conversations are frequently carried out in the form of text messages and take place *synchronously* (i.e. with all users logged on and chatting at the same time) or *asynchronously* (i.e. with a delayed message system such as electronic mail) (Warschauer & Healey, 1998). According to Lamy and Hampel (2007: 115), a synchronous conversation is similar to face-to-face one and, thus, perfect to practice speaking in the target language. It should be noted, however, that such conversations (i.e. carried out by means of online communication tools) have no characteristics typical of traditional ones (i.e. no gestures or body language, no facial expressions or, in most cases, voice).

Despite the fact that online communication is frequently carried out in the form of text, it shares a lot of features with spoken rather than written discourse (Górska, 2007). Moreover, online communication is similar to spoken conversation in view of the fact that it is spontaneous and unplanned as is the case with written discourse. In addition, online communication is similar to that conducted over the telephone in which speakers cannot see each other and voice/sound is replaced by letters on the computer screen. Such electronic discourse replaces face-to-face communication by writing, and writing in turn replaces voices (Davis & Brewer, 1997: 2). It could be argued that computer-mediated communication has many characteristics of speech such as 'repetition, direct address, dysfluencies, and markers of personal involvement' (Davis & Brewer, 1997: 113). Therefore, agreement, solidarity, humor, irony, anger and so forth can be represented by certain punctuation signs and emoticons or smilies (MacDonald & Perry, 2007). It should be noted, however, that electronic discourse differs from face-to-face communication in turn-taking, in which interruptions and overlaps are not possible (Davis & Brewer, 1997: 3). In spite of the fact that online interaction is not subjected to the turn-taking rules that apply to face-to-face communication, it can be compensated by a face-to-face equivalent of everyone in a discussion talking simultaneously (e.g. during *IRC* style chat room where users cannot see each other's comments until they have been posted) (Payne & Whitney, 2002: 24). It could be argued that such types of conversation practice can be useful in large foreign language classes, in particular where a large number of students make it almost impossible to develop speaking skills effectively.

As can be seen from the above, the development of speaking skills by means of computer technology can be an interesting and useful way of preparing language learners to speak the target language. At the same time, however, it cannot, for obvious reasons, replace face-to-face conversation.

Research Project

The subjects were 46 grade 2 Polish senior high school students attending two parallel classes of specialized (experimental group) and vocational (control group) senior high school. The experimental group consisted of 28 learners, 5 girls and 23 boys, and the control group comprised 18 students, all of whom were boys. All the students had been taught by the author of this chapter since the beginning of their education in the school. Furthermore, the curricular policy of the school provided both the experimental and control students with two 45-minute English lessons per week and divided experimental learners into two groups, each of which consisted of 14 students for their English language lessons in line with the alphabetical order. Judging by the marks the learners had been awarded at the end of the first grade or the ability to solve language activities, the two classes were comparable in terms of the learners' overall proficiency level. On the whole, the learners in both groups could be best described as weak but it has to be remembered that they also comprised a few more successful students.

The following data collection instruments were used: a background questionnaire, oral tests, an evaluation sheet and, in the experimental group only, observation, the learners' logs, individual interviews and an internet English forum. Moreover, all the data collection instruments were designed and presented to the students in Polish. In addition, the background questionnaire and the evaluation sheet were filled out by the subjects anonymously. Finally, the data were subjected to both qualitative and quantitative analyses.

Before the experiment got under way, the students were requested to fill out the background questionnaire and they were asked to perform the oral test. The test was always performed in dyads, which were formed at random. Each pair of learners received two different role cards which contained instructions and prompts written in Polish to conduct a short conversation at the travel agent's, with one student being the travel agent and the other the customer. The students were always provided with the opportunity to read the task and rehearse before the recording, and then each pair stood in front of a microphone and role-played. Once each pair of students had completed the task, they received another set of role cards and were requested to perform the task once again. This time, however, they were asked to swap the roles. In addition, the students' utterances were recorded on a laptop computer running *Windows XP* and by means of an omnidirectional desktop microphone and a computer program called *PolderbitS Sound Recorder and Editor*. The recordings were saved on the computer's hard disk in the form of an uncompressed sound file (*.wav).

The results of the whole test, administered before the treatment and after it, were each time subjected to quantitative analysis. In addition, the students in the experimental group were requested to complete their logs after each lesson. The logs were designed in such a way that they contained nine prompts in the form of statements or questions, such as 'In a few words write about what you have done during the lesson', 'What have you learned during the lesson?' 'Write about what was the easiest thing(s) to learn. Explain why', 'Write about the most difficult thing(s) to learn. Explain why', 'What could you do better next time?' or 'What did you like most and what you did not like?' The subjects were also encouraged to self-assess their own learning and assign their own homework. Moreover, the learner logs were produced by the participants of the study electronically in the form of text documents (mostly *Microsoft Office Word* documents) and sent to the researcher by e-mail after each lesson.

As regards the place of instruction, the lessons in the experimental group were conducted in the computer classroom and the classes in the control group took place in a regular classroom. When it comes to the computer classroom, it was equipped with 14 multimedia desktop computers running *Linux Suse 11.0* operating system and the 2 MB broadband connection to the internet. In addition, there was a multimedia projector and a laptop computer running *Windows XP* operating system used by the teacher during the lessons in the experimental group. As far as the lessons are concerned, they were related to the topic *In a travel agent's* and the students were provided with opportunities to practice formal requests typically used in formal conversations and encouraged to speak English. At the beginning of the first lesson, the experimental subjects were asked to do a number of interactive exercises related to formal requests, most of which were created by the teacher by means of the computer program called *Hot Potatoes* and included such exercises as matching questions with answers, matching English sentences with their Polish equivalents and writing a sentence by putting the words in the correct order. Additionally, the learners were given two multiple choice exercises connected with making and answering polite requests (http://www.kaleidovox.hu/enalap.html?loc=linkek/envocen.htm).At the end of the lesson, the students were instructed to start talking with each other by means of the online web messenger *Yahoo! Messenger for the Web* in order to familiarize themselves with the program as well as to practice the introduced words and expressions. As for the other lesson, the students were asked to pretend to be a customer and a travel agent in an attempt to make conversations in the travel company via the *Yahoo! Messenger for the Web*. Furthermore, the learners had the opportunity to use online dictionaries and find relevant information on top winter and summer resorts to be used during the conversations (http://skiing. about.com/od/skiresorts/u/wheretoski.htm, http://www.luxist.com/2006/05/08/top-ten-summer-resorts/). During the activity, the learners logged on to the instant messenger and talked to each other about holidays abroad, asking questions and providing answers related to the weather, places to see, leisure activities and sports, and so on. It should be pointed out that the students were asked to swap roles or change partners once the conversations were over as well as to start new ones.

With regard to the speaking activities in the control group, they were also related to the same topic and their purpose was identical as in the case of the experimental group, the only exception being that coursebook materials were used. Therefore, the first out of two such classes commenced with an activity which required the learners to listen to a recording and complete several sentences, that is examples of formal requests. Then the students read the whole sentences so that the teacher could verify whether they had been completed correctly. During the next phase of the lesson, the students were instructed to work in pairs and act out a role-play at the travel agent's following the stages presented in the coursebook. As for the second lesson, it was a continuation of the topic at the travel bureau and was devoted to speaking practice with students performing conversation in dyads. This time each pair of learners was supplied with prompts in the form of role cards written in Polish. In addition, the learners were requested to swap roles and form new dyads once the conversations were finished. It should be noted that as the learner–learner conversation was in progress the teacher walked around the classroom, listened to the students and corrected the mistakes they made.

After the experiment, all the students were asked to fill out the evaluation sheet and some experimental subjects (chosen randomly) were also requested to take part in the individual interview. In addition, the interviewees were informed that the interview concerned the speaking lessons and permission to be recorded was obtained from the subjects.

Results

Oral test

As mentioned above, the analysis of the data gathered from the oral test was subjected to quantitative analysis which involved computing the

mean score, the percentages of the mean score for the whole experimental and control groups and the standard deviation. Furthermore, the
statistical significance of the differences in the means of the experimental
group and the control group on the consecutive tests was evaluated by
means of paired-sample *t* tests and independent-sample *t* tests. Accordingly, paired-sample *t* tests were used when the changes in the
performance of one group on the tests were assessed whereas independent-sample *t* tests were employed whenever the experimental and
control groups were compared. It should be noted that the analysis was
performed by means of the *Statistical Package for the Social Sciences (SPSS
version 17 for Windows)*.

As shown in Figure 17.1, the control students scored slightly higher on
the pre-test than did the experimental learners, with the difference in the
mean score being at 0.17 points (1.88%) and failing to reach statistical
significance ($t = 0.33$, $p = 0.74$). However, the results of the immediate
post-test revealed that this time the subjects in the experimental group
outperformed their control counterparts by 1.76 points or 19.55%, a
difference that was highly statistically significant ($t = 2.96$, $p = 0.005$).
Moreover, the gap between the groups remained wide over time, with
the mean score on the delayed post-test in the experimental group (5.56)
being 1.67 or 18.55% higher than the mean score in the control group
(3.89). In addition, the difference reached the significance value ($t = 2.80$,
$p = 0.008$).

When comparing the mean scores on the successive tests in the
experimental group, which are shown in Figure 17.1 and listed in the

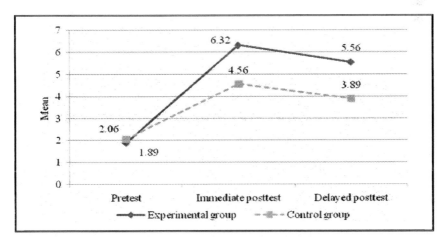

Figure 17.1 The mean scores for the experimental and control groups on the
oral test

Table 17.1 The number of students, mean scores, standard deviations and levels of statistical significance on the oral test for the experimental and control groups

	Number of students	Mean	Percentage	SD	Significance (two-tailed-paired t test)
Experimental group					
Pre-test	27	1.89	21	1.73	
Immediate post-test	25	6.32	70.22	1.86	PreT → IPostT: $t = 11.76$, $p < 0.001$
Delayed post-test	27	5.56	61.77	2.02	IPostT → DPostT: $t = 1.74$, $p = 0.09$ PreT → DPostT: $t = 10.83$, $p < 0.001$
Control group					
Pre-test	18	2.06	22.88	1.51	
Immediate post-test	18	4.56	50.66	2.00	PreT → IPostT: $t = 4.12$, $p < 0.001$
Delayed post-test	18	3.89	43.22	1.84	IPostT → DPostT: $t = 1.61$, $p = 0.12$ PreT → DPostT: $t = 2.89$, $p < 0.01$

first section of Table 17.1, it turns out that the learners improved on the immediate post-test by 4.43 points or 49.22%, although the gain failed to be maintained in the long run and dropped by 0.76 points or 8.44% on the delayed post-test. As for the difference in the mean score from the pre-test to the delayed post-test, it amounted to 3.67 (40.77%). It should also be noted that the pre-test–immediate post-test and the pre-test–delayed post-test differences reached significance values ($t = 11.76$, $p < 0.001$ and $t = 10.83$, $p < 0.001$, respectively). As regards the students in the control group, the pre-test–immediate post-test difference in the mean score amounted to 2.5 points (27.77%), although it dropped on the delayed post-test and equaled 0.67 (7.44%). Moreover, the pre-test–delayed post-test difference in the mean score was 1.83 or 20.33%. Similar to the results in the experimental group, the pre-test–immediate post-test and the pre-test–delayed post-test differences were large enough to reach statistical significance ($t = 4.12$, $p < 0.001$ and $t = 2.89$, $p < 0.01$, respectively).

Results of the learners' logs, the observation, the internet English forum, the individual interviews and the evaluation sheet

The data which emerged from the learners' logs, the observation, the individual interviews and the internet forum were subjected to qualitative analyses which were executed by means of the data analytical software *NVivo version 8*. The analysis of the data revealed that the students in the experimental group enjoyed the lessons and did not consider them to be very difficult. It has to be noted that in the case of problems the students used, for example, online dictionaries or simply asked their classmates. Moreover, the experimental students regarded the speaking activities as useful not only for classroom studies but also in real life. In addition, the students in the experimental group were able to reflect on their own language learning and determine the areas which needed improvement. Thus, for example, the students realized that in order to speak effectively they had to know more vocabulary and remember appropriate expressions, ask more questions and provide full answers as well as ask and answer questions more fluently. Moreover, the learners pointed to the importance of concentration while solving language tasks, self-reliance, spelling and being better prepared for English lessons. It is interesting to note that several students also realized that a successfully conducted conversation depended on the person they were talking to as well as that person's involvement in it and language skills.

The analysis of the data that originated from the learners' logs also revealed that the learners were able to perform self-evaluation of their own learning, although a lot of entries were short and superficial, and in many cases such self-assessment was simply expressed in numbers, that is grades. It should be noted, however, that there were a number of instances in which the students were able to be more specific in the way they assessed their language development. Thus, the subjects considered the number of activities they managed to do, the number of mistakes they made and the amount of time they devoted to studying a particular issue. It could be argued that such self-evaluation and reflection affected the type of homework assignment the subjects were supposed to set for themselves after each lesson since, as the analysis of the data demonstrated, it was usually limited to the revision of the activities performed in the classroom.

Another important finding was related to the way the students performed during the speaking activities. The analysis of the data showed that during online conversations the learners read out loud or quietly the sentences they wrote or even they 'talked to themselves in their thoughts'. Thus, it could be argued that such verbalization of thoughts might, to some extent, resemble a real conversation. It should also be noted that in the first place, the subjects tried to convey the required information in order to be understood, although several students went through great pain to form their sentences correctly and use the right words and expressions.

Since the results of the study presented in this text are part of a larger research project, the findings of the evaluation sheet are limited to those connected with the topic of the chapter. Thus, we will focus here only on the answers to the open-ended question related to the lessons which the participants of the research project liked the most and the Likert-scale question regarding the subjects' assessment of the activities and language materials utilized during the classes, as they provided the relevant data. The analysis of the students' responses to the first question demonstrated that the learners in both groups frequently pointed to the lessons dedicated to the development of speaking skills. It should also be pointed out that all the subjects mentioned various benefits of the speaking activities such as usefulness or practicality. As regards the other question, the mean was higher in the control group than in the experimental group and amounted to 3.50 and 3.42, respectively. It should be noted, however, that the experimental students' responses to that question might be related to some technical problems, that is slow internet connection, which the students did not like and mentioned frequently in their logs or interviews.

Conclusions

The results of the study demonstrate that the use of internet resources together with instant messengers might contribute to the development of speaking skills during English lessons in the Polish educational context. This is especially evident in the results of the mean scores of the immediate post-test and the delayed post-test in the experimental group in comparison with the results of the control group. It should also be kept in mind that the experimental subjects worked on their own without the teacher and, at the same time, were encouraged, for example, to reflect on their learning or self-evaluate their language progress. On the other hand, the control students learned English with their teacher and, for example, had to adhere to his assessment of their performance during the lessons. It could be argued that such a state of affairs might have resulted in better language learning in the experimental group, although the extent to which it contributed to the development of learner autonomy is beyond the scope of this chapter.

Another important contribution to the development of speaking skills might be related to the fact that the experimental students were presented with the opportunity to practice speaking English in the virtual world, which, for young people in particular, seems to be even more attractive than the real one. As a result, this virtual reality might have been a decisive factor in motivating the students to try to use the target language. This was also emphasized by the learners themselves and noted during the analysis of the data. It should be pointed out, however, that in order to make the learning process more efficient, instruction should implement tools which students are accustomed to and know how to use. This very important issue was repeatedly emphasized by some of the experimental subjects.

Despite the fact that the findings discussed in this chapter are positive and seem to augur well for the use of internet resources and instant messengers in the development of speaking skills, there are also such which ought to make us circumspect about taking its benefits for granted. First, the results of the study cannot be generalized because of a small sample size. Second, there were only two lessons dedicated to practice speaking skills, although it has to be remembered that the results presented in this chapter are part of a larger research project devoted to the development of learner autonomy through internet resources and its impact on language attainment.

References

Beatty, K. (2003) *Teaching and Researching Computer-Assisted Language Learning*. London: Longman.

Davis, B. and Brewer, J. (1997) *Electronic Discourse: Linguistic Individuals in Virtual Space*. Albany: State University of New York Press.

Erben, T., Ban, R. and Castañeda, M. (2009) *Teaching English Language Learners through Technology*. New York: Routledge.

Górska, A. (2007) An ICQ message board session as discourse: A case study. *Lodz Papers in Pragmatics* 3, 179–193.

Krajka, J. (2007) *English Language Teaching in the Internet-assisted Environment*. Lublin: Maria Curie-Skłodowska University Press.

Lamy, M. and Hampel, R. (2007) *Online Communication in Language Learning and Teaching*. Palgrave: Macmillan.

MacDonald, P. and Perry, D. (2007) How language learners can develop communication skills in English: An analysis of the structural and interactional aspects of teleconferences in the IDEELS Telematics Simulation Project. *International Conference on Engineering Education (ICEE-2007), Coimbra, Portugal*.

Mullen, T., Appel, C. and Shanklin, T. (2009) Skype-based tandem language learning and Web 2.0. In M. Thomas (ed.) *Handbook of Research on Web 2.0 and Second Language Learning* (pp. 101–118). Hershey, NY: Information Science Reference.

Payne, J.S. and Whitney, P.J. (2002) Developing L2 oral proficiency through synchronous CMC: Output, working memory, and interlanguage development. *CALICO Journal* 20, 7–23.

Teeler, D. and Gray, P. (2000) *How to Use the Internet in ELT*. Harlow: Pearson Education.

Warschauer, M. and Healey, D. (1998) Computers and language learning: An overview. *Language Teaching* 31, 57–71.

Windeatt, S., Hardisty, D. and Eastment, D. (2000) *The Internet*. Oxford: Oxford University Press.

Chapter 18
Investigating the Perception of Speaking Skills with Metaphor-Based Methods

DOROTA WERBIŃSKA

Introduction

Although learners' beliefs have been the object of educational research since the 1980s, the interest in beliefs (personal theories, constructs, subjective philosophies, etc.) referring to important ideas on the language learning and teaching process has been seen only recently. It is believed that the views of individuals can translate into practice and simulta-neously influence the quality of processes and results of learning and teaching foreign languages. Fascinated by subjective theories concerning some language teaching notions (Werbińska, 2004), encouraged by Block (1999: 142) to replicate research in other contexts[1] and inspired by Kramsch's (2006) study, I decided to explore students' beliefs regarding speaking skills in the foreign languages they were learning. As respondents' replies in questionnaires can hardly be considered 'a direct representation of the truth' (Kramsch, 2006: 110) and because of their idiosyncrasy they are difficult to measure (Lundeberg & Levin, 2003: 39), I reached out for the metaphor, an accepted tool in educational and linguistic research (Ellis, 2001: 67). Since the seminal work by Lakoff and Johnson (1980), metaphor has ceased to be regarded solely as a linguistic ornament associated with poetry and is now looked at as an instrument for helping reduce the data through generalising (Katz, 1996: 61), contributing to reflection on action (Ellis, 2001: 67), helping articulate emergent understandings (Mann, 2008) and accessing areas of thinking which other instruments cannot (Thornbury, 1998: 37). Metaphorical exploration could be particularly revealing of beliefs and on this account useful for teacher educators. Therefore, the aim of this chapter is to document students' beliefs in regard to speaking in a foreign language obtained by two methods: (1) the analysis of metaphors given by the respondents and (2) the analysis of their narratives describing their experience connected with the process of learning English and the acquisition of speaking skills in particular.

Theoretical Background

Research studies devoted to creating, understanding and using metaphors refer to different theories of metaphor, among which we can mention those from cognitive psychology (i.e. theory of domains and interaction, theory of conceptual metaphor) and those beyond psychology (i.e. theory of speech acts, theory of semantic field, theory of relevance). As it is easy to become confused while researching metaphors, Gibbs (1999: 30) distinguishes six guidelines, among which he names *processing metaphor* and *metaphoric processing*. The former refers to the conscious elicitation of metaphors and investigation of how learners can construct their different experiences metaphorically. The latter, however, can become a purposefully selected strategy of reading, metaphoric processing of discourse by the reader, although, interestingly, metaphoric material may not appear in the text itself. Such metaphoric processing of a text is a way of reading which calls for cognitive models of reality or mental spaces (see Kramsch, 2006: 112) underlying what the text really says. These two notions will serve as core reference points for us in two research studies discussed below.

Processing Metaphor – Research Study 1

Methods

I asked 184 extramural[2] learners studying at a private higher school of management in Poland to take part in the study and express their opinions on the language they were learning (75 students studying English, 64 students studying German and 45 students studying Russian). In terms of sex, there was a preponderance of female over male respondents (women accounted for 76% of the subjects), and as to the age factor, the average was 29 years old.

Undoubtedly, students' views depend on the teaching context, which is briefly described now. The English course is considered demanding, which is somehow dictated by the school policy viewing communicative competence in English as an important aim to strive for. The German course is conducted by two teachers who also work in secondary schools of technical education, and on this account it can be assumed that their teaching styles resemble the techniques used in their school pro-grammes. The Russian course is delivered by a professor – a researcher specialising in Russian literature. The English groups use books aimed at teaching 'business English' and the German groups learn from course books developing a general knowledge of German, whereas the Russian course is based on a grammar book with an occasional use of video or CDs with Russian music. All the groups have obligatory language lessons for five semesters, with 24 classes in each. The classes are held once every two or three weeks on average and last for three or four 45-minute periods.

All the respondents were asked to complete the following sentence: 'Speaking in English (German, Russian) is like ...'. Just as in Kramsch's (2006: 114) work, the overriding principle of the study was not learning what the subjects thought about speaking skills in general but rather how they constructed their experience, what semantic resources they used and how they expressed their views on speaking skills in the context of the language they were learning. In addition, I assumed that differences in views might emerge with regard to speaking each of the three languages investigated.

The basic step of a metaphor investigator is establishing whether or not the data can be considered metaphorical. Cameron (1999: 13) claims that a metaphorical expression must contain a comparison, in which there is a kind of anomaly between the topic and the vehicle, adding that there exist more verb metaphors than noun metaphors. I based processing metaphors on the following activities, as suggested by Ellis (2001: 70):

- accumulating examples of metaphors and listing them;
- dividing the research data into three groups, according to the languages spoken by the respondents (English, German, Russian);
- categorising the metaphors into three semantically similar groups (looking for key words) representing 'main' metaphors in the research data;
- considering possible implications (*entailments*) of main metaphors and examining to what extent they are expressed in the research data.

Results and discussion

From the study, which was anonymous, I obtained 184 examples of metaphors presenting the understanding of the speaking skill in a foreign language (75 presenting the understanding of speaking in English, 64 in German and 45 in Russian). I divided the metaphors into several groups as defined by subsequent letters of the alphabet in each group and then provided new metaphors to them (called categories), formulated by me on the basis of semantic contents of the students' metaphors, as well as their explanations and similarities to other metaphors. I consulted with two other academics, both of them philologists, regarding the choice of the categories for my metaphors. The divisions of the metaphors into categories in the three languages taught in the researched group of the respondents are presented in Tables 18.1–18.3 of the Appendix.

Generally speaking, the metaphors in the corpora are underexploited because they usually contain only one implication. For example 'writing poems' was considered a difficult task, failing to acknowledge the fact that it can be a pleasure, whereas 'a mountain spring' or 'flying a jet', apart from an aesthetic pleasure of watching or experiencing flying, can mean a risk or even a danger. As in Kramsch's (2006) report, let us discuss them in terms of concept, grammar and discourse.

Conceptually, the investigated subjects tend to associate speaking in English with a difficult challenge, confirmed by the choice of metaphors, such as 'a difficult matter', 'walking along a bumpy road', 'balancing on the line', 'working in the mine', 'torture', 'walking in the swamps', 'interrogation' or 'talking to an Eskimo'. As mentioned before, the English teachers are considered very demanding, and this may be the reason why 'challenge' has become the most ubiquitous concept here. The second popular entailment in the respondents' opinions is 'pleasure', which is indicated by such metaphors as 'pleasant melody', 'a singing bird', 'music, swimming and rippling', 'buying sweets – pleasant and bringing joy' or 'eating chocolate ice cream'. It means that they like this skill, and practising it gives them aesthetic pleasure ('harmony', 'playing the guitar'). For some students speaking in English can be like learning from the beginning because in the examples provided they refer to 'learning how to speak from the beginning', 'the first steps of the child' or 'learning how to walk again'. Several respondents are concerned with the sound of English speech, comparing it with 'speaking with chewing gum' or 'speaking with a mouth full of dumplings'; a few of them perceive speaking English as a natural thing – 'natural conversation in Polish' or 'speaking in Polish', whereas some of them claim that speaking in English touches the issue of identity change – 'being part of England', 'becoming a native English person' or 'trying to be somebody different', and only in the opinion of one person the acquisition of the speaking skill is a step ahead – 'walking one step further in the contemporary world'.

Students learning German also talk about the difficulty they encounter when acquiring speaking skills in German. The metaphors they adhere to seem to be even more picturesque than those used by the students learning English: 'breaking the language', 'crossing the desert', 'calling for help', 'writing in Chinese', 'hard work in the field', 'making sushi for a Japanese', 'reading a boring book' and so on. Speaking as 'a difficult challenge' is followed by, in a sense, two opposing ideas: a shrill sound (suggesting dynamism) and slowness. The association of speaking in German with a shrill sound is expressed by such metaphors as 'a hailstorm', 'a barking dog', 'noise in the city', 'expressing emotions with the help of your jaws' and 'heavy metal songs', whereas association with slowness finds its expression in the choice of the following metaphors: 'moving like a snail on the road', 'Michnik's speech',[3] 'thinking about an answer' to name but a few. Undoubtedly, the idea of a 'shrill sound' refers to the people using German in speech fluently, whereas 'slowness' to the state of a student for whom the achievement of the dynamics of 'a shrill sound' is at the present moment too remote to achieve. Other associations of speaking in German concern systematicity in the process of learning: 'running – the more training, the fewer problems' and 'constant learning of new words', although for a few of the respondents speaking German evokes 'reciting poems' – that is, learning phrases by heart. Then, there are associations related to pleasure, that is 'breaking a tongue, but pleasant', 'talking to your best friend' or something incomprehensible, that is 'baby's babbling', 'muttering something under your breath', 'the sound of conversation of people under the influence of alcohol' or 'gibberish'. Several respondents also notice the pace of the words uttered – 'sport for the tongue when you pronounce very complicated words' or 'making poems at a very fast pace', and the cultural aspect has figured prominently only in the metaphors of two learners – 'changing into another person (from another country)' and 'getting to know a different culture'.

Among the metaphors given by the students of Russian, there are definitely more positive associations than in the other accounts. For the vast majority, the speaking skill in Russian means listening to a nice sound – 'poetry', 'singing', 'a nice melody', 'listening to your favourite music'; experiencing pleasure – 'good fun', 'a walk', 'drifting on the calm sea', 'savouring a delicious dish', 'careless playing with a dog'; or learning something easy – 'bread and butter' or 'talking in your native language', 'speaking "almost" in Polish'. The subjects also provide a communicative aspect linking speaking with communicating – 'approaching other people than Poles', 'a need to communicate' – and the retrospective element – 'returning to the times of primary and secondary school', 'meeting after many years' or 'bringing back the memories of your youth'. Only for three respondents does speaking in Russian turn out to be difficult– 'difficulty', 'breaking the tongue' or 'playing dominoes', although in the case of the last metaphor one more dimension can be seen– logicality and enjoyment. Provided at the conceptual level the metaphors associated with speaking in Russian cast new light on the perception of Russian in Poland (see Johnson, 2008: 195). No longer is it considered an imposed language, but rather a nice sound and a pleasant experience. Considered easy by the respondents, the Russian language seems to recall the arguments of contrastive linguists concerning the significance of similarities/differences between a native and a target language, whereas the nostalgic aspect certainly increases its attractiveness among the oldest students in the study.

To sum up the metaphors defining the speaking skill as a conceptual construct, it can be concluded that, apart from common associations with a foreign language or the speaking skill discussed here (the categories of communicating, getting to know culture, being somebody else), the same speaking skill is perceived in the categories of paradox: easy for some, difficult for others; pleasant for many; incomprehensible for a few; associated with a nice, melodious sound (especially the Russian language) or a rough unpleasant noise (particularly speaking in German). Sometimes, within the same metaphor at the conceptual level, there appear paradoxes, as in the following metaphors: 'breaking your tongue, but pleasant', 'bread and lard – not everybody likes it but sometimes you've got to eat it', 'drinking a bottle of vodka and reciting a poem'. They point out the fact that the perception of speaking in a foreign language can be an ambivalent experience: being in a situation which is hard to manage ('speaking Chinese', 'breaking your tongue', 'making poems at a very fast pace'), ascribing deficiencies to oneself ('an oral exam where an examinee stutters or has another speech defect', 'difficulty because of poor vocabulary', 'agony – I don't know what to say even in Polish'), unpredictability ('interrogation where each utterance is judged and we are waiting for the verdict') or the promise of a reward ('running – the more training, the fewer problems', 'trying to break an ostrich's egg, but not impossible').

Attempting to examine the metaphors as a grammatical construct, I can only agree with Kramsch (2006) that the gerund form *speaking*, given in the instructions, is bound to generate other gerund forms. Analysing the corpora it can be seen that this is often the case, although noun metaphors associated with speaking in a foreign language appear with equal frequency. Despite the fact that the appearance of more verb metaphors was confirmed in my study, there were not so many verb metaphors as to indicate a significant difference. The verbs were mainly used in the active form (*speaking, reading, expressing*), and after some of them, while indicating grammatical complements, the difficulty was suggested ('with a mouth full of dumplings', 'with the help of jaws').

Across the discoursive level, the manifestations of metaphors in most cases convey pragmatic functions. They refer to concrete objects and daily life situations, often eating and drinking ('savouring a delicious dish', 'speaking with a mouth full of dumplings', 'buying sweets', 'eating chocolate ice cream', 'drinking a bottle of vodka', 'bread and butter', 'bread with lard'), working ('working in the mine', 'physical work', 'hard work in the fields') or doing everyday activities ('irritating getting up in the morning', 'driving a car', 'meeting with friends', 'listening to your favourite music'). They sometimes make the impression of narration as in the metaphor 'learning how to speak from the beginning – first I wonder how to build a sentence and then look for proper words for it', refer to famous people ('Michnik's speech') or recall cultural references ('speaking with a mouth full of dumplings – like in the film *Miś*[4]). Some of them are selected in such a way that after producing quiet overtones they change suddenly into a shocking effect ('hacking meat – stretching, catching one's breath at the moment of deliberating where to strike').

Referring to the analysed metaphors, it can be said that all of them express views or expectations of students on their experiences with speaking skills in a new language. There are a few key findings that merit our emphasis. First of all, numerically, most speaking metaphors are used by learners to articulate their difficulties, internal conflicts or tensions. Second, there is some evidence that the languages under discussion are differently received by the learners. In addition, a large number of these metaphors are concerned with expressing other associations of speaking than popular ones, that is communicating or getting to know other cultures.

Taken together as one group, metaphors articulating learners' difficulties offer evidence that students of foreign languages tend to convey their general feelings about speaking, rather than referring to a particular classroom activity. However, the data suggest that they are pulled in different directions, face multiple demands and pressures, and sometimes find it difficult to come to terms with learning speaking. These metaphors provide examples of the existence of tensions between:

- willingness to speak a new language and problems with one's articulation;
- willingness to speak a new language and problems with one's memory;
- being an adult and accepting one's helplessness or awkwardness;
- dislike of complication, uncertainty, one's ignorance and voluntary agreeing to it.

This study also offers evidence that there are considerable differences as to the perception of the language learnt. Of particular interest are so many positive comments directed at Russian. The subjects underscored its pleasant, canorous sound and similarity to Polish, which makes it supreme over the remaining languages in the researched group of students. In contrast to the other languages, the subjects pointed out its relative simplicity, simultaneously contrasted with the difficulty of English or German. These metaphors give a little evidence that the position of Russian in Polish schools seems to be rising in comparison with its status only over a decade ago.

As regards the metaphors on speaking in German, there are fewer positive ones than in the other two languages. Stressing its particularly 'shrill sound' or typical of German consonant clusters, the German language seems to produce more 'rumbling' connotations, which makes it less pleasant in reception than listening to Russian or English. It is worth emphasising that speaking in German was still considered prestigious in mid-1990s in Poland. Social viewpoints and attitudes of the community at large were very positive about German whose position at that time was almost equal to the status of English. Metaphors with negative tinges offered in this study may recognise its decline in status among Polish students.

It is noticeable that very few metaphors are about primary functions of speaking skills, that is communicating with other people. In their metaphors, the subjects prefer pointing to the difficulty of learning a foreign language rather than enriching their personalities through communicating with others, conveying messages in a foreign language or experiencing another culture. Part of the responsibility can be held by the process of teaching in which making use of the students' fledgling communicative competence is not sufficient. Perhaps, the students treat the language learning course just like any other course to be passed, and that is why their metaphors are mostly not about communication.

This metaphor use shows that metaphors may be convenient vehicles to explore learners' tensions, likes and dislikes, perception and reception of speaking in a foreign language. The examples presented here offer but a small window into the worlds of language learners and much more research needs to be conducted to provide any valid conclusions. Yet, just as in giving responses to questionnaires, completing sentences at a given moment, often under the pressure of time, is not enough to learn the learners' true convictions. Sometimes they are difficult to articulate and can be inserted between and beyond the lines. There is also a risk that some metaphors could be given for show and perhaps forced in a way. This is why I also used another instrument – a student-constructed text enabling the reader, as Gibbs (1999: 40–41) says, metaphoric processing of linguistic material.

Metaphoric Processing – Research Study 2

Methods

The essays of 40 extramural students learning English were used as research material in the study based on metaphoric processing. The subjects were asked to describe their experiences connected with learning a foreign language taught during the course of their management studies and share their reflections about other factors influencing, in their opinions, success or failure in the process of language learning. The exact title was: *Describe your story of learning a foreign language as a branched tree. What were the main branches?* No word limit was given and, on average, the students produced one-and-a-half-page essays.

The underlying research aim was to find confirmation for the views on speaking skills from the previous metaphors (Research Study 1) given by the same students indirectly in another research study. Moreover, I believed that metaphoric processing would help me better understand their perception and convictions about learning a foreign language. Since the study was not obligatory, I was able to obtain the research material from only half of the students learning English (40 essays)[5] and failed to collect any work from those learning German or Russian. The average age of the respondents was 35 years. Because of the lack of data from the students of other languages, I will confine the discussion of the results of the second study to the selected fragments of essays written by extramural students learning English.

Results and discussion

Metaphorical reading of students' autobiographic compositions helps reveal the views on what it means to be a mature student subjected to compulsory foreign-language tuition. Below are some fragments of their autobiographies, selected by me at random.[6]

> The ability to use English nowadays is almost a necessity. When I started my studies I didn't hesitate which language to choose. I simply knew that it would be English. Some time ago I used to go to Germany to work, and the lack of language got me back down to the earth, made me realise that in spite of our belonging to EU, we won't be Europeans for a long time until we learn how to communicate. Now, when in almost every Polish town there are buildings of Western companies, when we are surrounded by globalisation from every place, when frontiers are being erased, the knowledge of English has become almost a necessity. I'm a sailor, I go to sea, and entering any harbour outside of Polish borders means the necessity of English. English has become a noose which is tightening more and more around us. Such presence of English has made us know single words, but talking to somebody is a problem and a barrier hard to overcome. ... To speak English I must first get rid of the barriers and fears, but once I've done it (being in Dublin I was able to say what I wanted and do shopping) words come to me, and it's easier. ... The activities that we were assigned to do at home, questioning during the classes, made me feel afraid so as not to be worse than others, but I learnt. English was the subject to which I devoted probably most of my time. ... I'm sure that what I've learnt will be useful at sea; when I'm steering my boat to Bornholm or to another port, when I'm outside of Poland, I'll be using it on a daily basis.
>
> (Marian, 45, sailor)

> My meeting with English – sometimes it's easy, sometimes it's difficult. The greatest problem for me is the difference between spelling and pronunciation. I have problems with understanding 'spoken' English. My 'ears' often don't catch the difference between

the words spoken. I don't have contact with 'living' English. Maybe, if I had, it would be easier for me to overcome this invisible language barrier. I tried to learn words in a variety of ways; I worked with a CD – I tried to work on my pronunciation. Am I learning conscientiously and systematically? I'm trying, but it's not everything. Am I afraid to attend English classes? Yes, I often feel fearful, and after the classes a sense of relief. What does the fright result from? From my being aware that I know what I know or that I don't know, that some things are not to be learnt, and others are. But the fear of being asked in English during the class comes from itself.

(Anna, 37, bank accountant)

My adventure with English has already lasted for over two years. My head is overcome with fear, and there is a strong conviction that I learnt systematically, fear of being ridiculed, and at the same time a feeling of doing my duty well. ... When I don't have to speak, everything in my head is in order and I can say quite a lot in my mind. At the moment of confrontation a barrier is on. I'm afraid if I'll build the sentences correctly, if my vocabulary is rich, and the accent. Won't my pronunciation prevent other students from understanding me? These are the barriers difficult to overcome.

(Katarzyna, 35, unemployed)

When I started my studies and faced the difficult decision of choosing a language, I chose English. I don't regret. Learning this language has turned out easier than I thought. Maybe I don't speak English well, and I've got to think what to say for a long time. But I can see that it's only a matter of time.

(Marzena, 29, shop assistant)

Another stage is the present time; this is my adventure with learning English for the first time. I think that learning here for almost three years has made me feel more secure in lots of situations abroad (communicating on the car park with German attendants, at the airport, on the plane). I don't feel good enough to have a chat with somebody who speaks English fluently, but when I was abroad I didn't feel like a second-class European.

(Tomasz, 31, driver)

Since there are no corpora from the students of German or English in the second study, it is impossible to make sound comparisons between the results coming from both research projects. Yet, from the fragments quoted above it transpires that the metaphor of 'difficult challenge' present in the first study finds its expression in the students' narratives.

There appear phrases such as 'getting rid of fears and fright', 'relief after the classes', 'my head is full of fear' and 'barriers difficult to overcome', most probably associated with students with the speaking skills. Still, in contrast to the first study, there is also some evidence of acknowledging the communicative function of language learning. The same learners simultaneously see the positive consequences of using a foreign language, especially its usefulness in real-life situations ('I am sure that what I've learnt will be useful at sea', speaking is only 'a matter of time', 'when I was abroad I didn't feel like a second-class European'), which was marginally treated in the metaphors intentionally elicited from the students. Also, they give evidence to their awareness of the importance of metacognitive aspects in the process of learning ('I tried to learn words in a variety of ways; I worked with a CD – I tried to work on my pronunciation' and 'I must first get rid of the barriers and fears, but once I've done it ... words come to me, and it's easier'). Such word use means that the students' descriptions are not only registers of their memories about learning a foreign language but their personal reflection about the process of learning. In addition, a small but recurrent note of optimism can be traced in the accounts. No longer are all students overwhelmed by the difficulty of the task, but they start perceiving the benefits of learning speaking and even analysing their own approaches towards it. This may even indicate that the original challenge of the language learning experience starts giving in to finding balance, however slightly. On the other hand, considering the status of English as international *Lingua Franca*, the communicative advantages of learning a language might only appear in the case of students of English. Lack of data from learners studying German or Russian requires the acceptance of this argument with extreme caution.

Lastly, it can be seen that metaphorical reading of narratives reveals that students' beliefs are not stable, that there are multiple themes, even within one text often paradoxical ('after the classes a sense of relief' and 'I can see that [speaking] is only a matter of time'), and that 'mental spaces' which they build in their biographies are not easy to grasp without the knowledge of context and their 'classroom culture' (see Holliday, 1997). A general point can be made about metaphoric processing of the texts. Thanks to learners' implications, digressions and regularly made choices about lexis, grammar and discourse, the reader is offered a deeper understanding of the way extramural students – mature individuals, in most cases already professionals – construct the reality around themselves.

Concluding Remarks

The aim of this chapter was to present extramural students' beliefs concerning their speaking skills on the basis of metaphor theory, as inspired by Kramsch's research. The first study made use of traditional methodology and consisted in completing a sentence provided by the researcher. Although this approach helped to obtain an interesting selection of metaphors about three languages, such methodology is only successful in gathering learners' beliefs that they hold at a particular moment, and not necessarily in learning how they construct the surrounding reality. The second study, relying on metaphorical reading of students' narratives, helped better objectify their beliefs because they were accessed indirectly. Through lack of arbitrariness in belief ascription (Kramsch, 2006: 126), it also made the results more accurate, although because of the context of the setting, perhaps less generalisable. In either study, metaphors proved to be convenient ways of making sense. But using the two research methods to investigate learners' beliefs seems to be the most useful way of obtaining research data because it allows for better exploration of static beliefs of the respondents on a topic interesting for the researcher as well as for deeper interpretation of the dynamic constructions of their worlds.

Notes
1. Block (1999: 142) thinks that replicating research is necessary because it confirms or questions the existing knowledge and, besides, is a useful way to obtain more accurate and reliable results in language acquisition studies.
2. Extramural students are adult learners who have decided to upgrade their qualifications and finish BA studies.
3. Adam Michnik is a famous Polish journalist and a political activist known for his involvement against the communist system. He speaks slowly due to his stuttering problem.
4. *Miś* [*The Teddy Bear*], directed in 1981 by Stanisław Bareja, is a popular Polish comedy which ridicules the communist times.
5. I was one of their English teachers, and this is why some students agreed to write the essays when I asked them.
6. The narratives have been translated into English, but originally they were written in the subjects' native language – Polish.

Appendix

Table 18.1 Speaking in English is like...

Categories	Students' examples of metaphors
Difficult challenge	Bleeding nose (you must think hard before you start responding correctly) Talking about something difficult A difficult matter (you speak in one way, you translate in another and it sounds still different) Walking along a bumpy road – difficult A complicated puzzle that needs time Hopeless film, because nothing comes of this Conversation with an Eskimo Speaking Chinese Torture Ordeal Torment – interrogation where each utterance is judged and we are waiting for the verdict Balancing on the line Agony – I don't know what to say even in Polish Doing something hard Difficult because of poor vocabulary Irritating getting up in the morning Working in the mine Physical work Walking in the swamps Breaking your tongue Drinking a bottle of vodka and reciting a poem Bread and lard – not everybody likes it but sometimes you've got to eat it
Pleasure	Singing (2×) pleasant tune (especially if somebody else is speaking) Palatalising words Bird singing Playing the guitar Music, swimming and rippling Buying sweets – pleasant and bringing happiness Eating chocolate ice cream Riding a bike Flying a jet Harmony Poetry A mountain stream

Table 18.1 (*Continued*)

Categories	Students' examples of metaphors
Learning from the beginning	Learning speaking from the beginning Learning how to speak from the beginning – first I wonder how to build a sentence and then look for proper words for it Learning speaking for the baby Perceiving the world in a new way because the things and words which were pronounced naturally suddenly changed their sounds The first steps of the child Learning how to walk again Teaching three languages to a child at once Putting the familiar words into one correct whole Talking to the baby (2×)
A natural thing	A normal conversation in Polish Speaking Polish Bread and butter Describing and talking about very individual problems A sincere conversation with your mum Meeting with friends
A specific way of expressing yourself	Speaking with chewing gum in the mouth Trying to speak with a full mouth (2×) A conversation with a full mouth (too many words + accent – I don't understand anything Speaking with a mouth full of dumplings! (like in the film *Miś*) Careful pronunciation
Being somebody else	Becoming somebody else, just like a light in the tunnel Being part of England Becoming a native English person Being somebody else, trying out
Risk	A rapid river Flying a jet
A step ahead	One step ahead in the contemporary world

Table 18.2 Speaking German is like ...

Categories	Examples of metaphors
A difficult challenge	Breaking your tongue (2×) Crossing the desert Jumping over an obstacle with a poor effect Writing poems Swotting up on a poem by heart Reading an uninteresting book An ordeal Calling for help Writing in Chinese Watching a bad movie Driving a car for the first time A young child's speech, very hard and unclear Hard work in the fields Climbing the top of the mountain (not always easy) A hard day Making sushi for a Japanese Something that brings trouble A difficulty, better to write than to speak
A shrill sound	A hailstorm A barking dog Expressing your feelings with the help of your jaws A city noise A heavy metal band's songs Hacking meat – stretching, catching one's breath at the moment of deliberating where to strike Chopping down wood – the smaller the bough, the easier it is; bigger it is, the more difficult it gets The rustle of leaves Listening to an echo
Slowness	Moving like a snail on the road Diction Michnik's speech Climbing the top of a mountain Fishing Reading an obligatory and boring set book An oral exam where an examinee stutters or has another speech defect Thinking about an answer Constant checking if we really understand each other Child's speech Talking to a baby who knows what he wants but doesn't know how to express it

Table 18.2 (*Continued*)

Categories	Examples of metaphors
	A little child's unclear speech Tautology
Systematicity	Running – the more training, the fewer problems Difficult to overcome, but you can manage Trying to break an ostrich's hard egg, but not impossible Constant learning of new phrases and expressions
Pleasure	Breaking your tongue, but pleasant The wind's breeze Speaking in my second language Talking to my best friend
Something incomprehensible	Baby's babbling Gibberish (3×) The sound of conversation of people under the influence of alcohol Muttering something under your breath
Pace	Making poems at a very fast pace A fast train Sport for the tongue when you pronounce very complicated words
Getting to know about culture	Getting to know a different culture Changing into another person (from another country)
Learning by heart	Reciting your favourite poem Reciting a poem at a jubilee celebration

Table 18.3 Speaking Russian is like ...

Categories	*Examples of metaphors*
Listening to a nice sound	Poetry (melodiousness, softness, pleasure in reception) Poetry (3×) Singing (3×) Poetics Melody (4×) Singing and poetry A nice melody Listening to your favourite music
Experiencing pleasure	Good fun (2×) A fairy story Pleasure (4×) Magic Pleasure with usefulness, learning and having fun A walk Drifting on the calm sea Savouring a delicious dish Careless playing with a dog
Learning something easy	Bread and butter (2×) implicity and pliability aking in your native language Speaking 'almost' in Polish (2×) Something easy
Communication	Willingness to communicate Approaching other people than Poles A need to communicate – my family comes from Grodno
Learning something difficult	Breaking the tongue Difficulty Playing dominoes
Reminding about the past	Returning to the times of primary and secondary school Meeting after many years Bringing back the memories of your youth

References

Block, D. (1999) Who framed SLA research? Problem framing and metaphoric accounts of the SLA research process. In L. Cameron and G. Low (eds) *Researching and Applying Metaphor* (pp. 135–148). Cambridge: Cambridge University Press.

Cameron, L. (1999) Operationalising 'metaphor' for applied linguistic research. In L. Cameron and G. Low (eds) *Researching and Applying Metaphor* (pp. 3–28). Cambridge: Cambridge University Press.

Ellis, R. (2001) The metaphorical constructions of second language learners. In M.P. Breen (ed.) *Learner Contributions to Language Learning* (pp. 65–85). Harlow: Pearson Education.

Gibbs, R.W. (1999) Researching metaphor. In L. Cameron and G. Low (eds) *Researching and Applying Metaphor* (pp. 29–47). Cambridge: Cambridge University Press.

Holliday, A. (1997) *Appropriate Methodology and the Social Context*. Cambridge: Cambridge University Press.

Johnson, K. (2008) *An Introduction to Foreign Language Learning and Teaching*. Harlow: Longman.

Katz, A. (1996) Teaching style: A way to understand instruction in language classroom. In K. Bailey and D. Nunan (eds) *Voices from the Language Classroom* (pp. 57–86). Cambridge: Cambridge University Press.

Kramsch, C. (2006) Metaphor and the subjective construction of beliefs. In P. Kalaja and A. M. Barcelos (eds) *Beliefs about SLA: New Research Approaches* (pp. 109–127). New York: Springer.

Lakoff, G. and Johnson, M. (1980) *Metaphors We Live By*. Chicago: University of Chicago Press.

Lundeberg, M.A. and Levin, B.B. (2003) Prompting the development of preservice teachers' beliefs through cases, action research, problem-based learning, and technology. In J. Raths and A.C. McAninch (eds) *Teacher Beliefs and Classroom Performance: The Impact of Teacher Education* (pp. 23–42). Greenwich: Information Age Publishing.

Mann, S. (2008) Teachers' use of metaphor in making sense of the first year of teaching. In T. Farrell (ed.) *Novice Language Teachers* (pp. 11–28). London: Equinox.

Thornbury, S. (1998) Images of teaching. *English Teaching Professional* 8, 36–37.

Werbińska, D. (2004) *Skuteczny nauczyciel języka obcego* [The Effective Teacher of a Foreign Language]. Warsaw: Wydawnictwo Fraszka Edukacyjna.

Chapter 19
Phonetically Difficult Words in Intermediate Learners' English

JOLANTA SZPYRA-KOZŁOWSKA

Introduction

Foreign-accented English abounds in numerous phonetically incorrect words, known as local errors, which are stored in learners' memory with phonologically deviant representations, for example *Disney* often pronounced in Polish English as [d'isnej] and *foreign* as [fo'rejn]. In a recent experimental study (Szpyra-Kozłowska, in press), I have demonstrated that such mispronounced items, generally disregarded in pronunciation teaching materials and intelligibility research, are highly detrimental to successful communication in that they significantly decrease the speaker's comprehensibility and intelligibility, create the impression of a heavy foreign accent and are irritating for the listeners. In fact, English native speakers' error gravity judgements show that phonetically seriously deformed words are evaluated as more problematic in all four respects than segmental and prosodic inaccuracies, that is global errors, typical of learners' interlanguage. Consequently, such items deserve to be thoroughly investigated and pedagogically prioritized.[1]

The chapter examines the subjective evaluation of phonetically difficult words by Polish intermediate learners of English, in whose speech they are particularly numerous. It attempts to analyse the major sources of word pronunciation errors and identify several others which have so far escaped notice of pronunciation specialists. This is done on the basis of an experiment carried out by the author in which 100 secondary school pupils, all intermediate learners of English, were asked to list those words whose pronunciation they found particularly difficult as well as to provide comments on the problematic aspects of these items. The obtained data are presented, classified and examined. The analysis hopes to provide some new insights into the interplay between vocabulary and phonetics in the Polish English interlanguage of intermediate learners and carry useful classroom implications.

Pronunciation Errors

One of the striking features of learners' English is a high number of word mispronunciations of different types. A useful distinction between

Table 19.1 Characterizing global and local errors

Global errors	Local errors
Recurring mispronunciations of foreign sounds and prosodies which create a foreign accent and result mainly from L1 phonological and phonetic transfer, for example E *jazz* > PE [džes] E *foreign* > PE [for'in]	Idiosyncratic mispronunciations of individual words in which, apart from global errors, there are other phonological and phonetic deviations from the original because of various interference factors. They are stored in the learner's phonetic memory with the incorrect segmental and/or prosodic structure, for example E *foreign* > PE [fo'rejn] E *Disney* > PE [d'isnej]

global and *local errors* (Sobkowiak, 1996) can be made. Their properties are summarized in Table 19.1, taken from Szpyra-Kozłowska (in press). Global errors typically involve the replacement of foreign sounds with what is felt by the learners to be their closest equivalents, for example the palatoalveolar affricate in *jazz* with the Polish alveolar affricate or the vowel ash in the same word with the Polish mid-open [e]. In addition, such items are subject to phonological processes operating in the learners' mother tongue. Thus, the final fricative in *jazz* is commonly completely devoiced in Polish English and the rhotic in *foreign* is palatalized by the following high front vowel. Local errors, on the other hand, are less predictable and more idiosyncratic in character. They result from a variety of well-known interference factors,[2] of which the high irregularity of English spelling-to-sound rules plays a major role. Because of this, the digraphs < ei > in *foreign* and < ey > in *Disney* are often interpreted in Polish English as [ej] (as in *reign* and *grey*), with stress placed incorrectly on this sequence in the former item.[3]

Words phonetically difficult for foreign learners are those which are error-prone, in terms of both global and local errors but primarily in terms of the latter. As argued by Szpyra-Kozłowska (in press) and Szpyra-Kozlowska and Stasiak (2010), the focus on local errors is justified because of serious consequences they have on linguistic communication mentioned earlier as well as because of a greater ease of reducing their number in learners' speech than of global errors. The proper under-standing of the mechanisms that lie behind such serious errors which contribute to the phonetic difficulty of words is therefore crucial for effective pronunciation training of foreign learners. In spite of this, as argued by Szpyra-Kozłowska (in press), the issue of phonetically difficult words is generally ignored in phonetic manuals and pronunciation practice materials, probably because the majority of them, issued by big publishing houses, are addressed to international users and are not concerned with errors which are L1-specific.[4]

In view of a general disregard of the issue under discussion, Sobkowiak's (1999) work on the Phonetic Difficulty Index (PDI) should be pointed out as a valuable attempt to deal systematically with phonetically difficult words in Polish English. PDI 'is a global numerical measure of the phonetic difficulty of the given English lexical item for Polish learners' (p. 214), meant to be included in machine-readable English as a Foreign Language dictionaries and thus having mainly lexicographic applications. It contains phonetic difficulty ratings of English words carried out by the author on the basis of his observations of Polish learners' pronunciation problems and thus represents a teacher's (or an observer's) perspective. Our study, which deals with the learners' perception of phonetic difficulty, can be seen as both complementing and verifying Sobkowiak's approach.[5]

Experimental Design

In November 2009 about 100 teenagers, aged between 14 and 18 years, of both sex, representing an intermediate level of proficiency[6] and attending a private secondary (junior and senior) school in Lublin, were asked by their English teacher,[7] during regular language lessons, to note down anonymously several English words whose correct pronunciation they found particularly difficult to remember and which they tended to mispronounce in spite of teacher's corrections. They were also requested to point to the problematic aspects of these items, whenever possible. It should be added that the school in which the study took place attaches much importance to teaching foreign languages, including their pro-nunciation. The pupils have six English lessons a week in groups of 10–15. The applied procedure yielded about 400 different words. In order to ensure that a given item was problematic not only to individual learners, it was further analysed when it was found in several pupils' responses. Over 250 such cases are discussed in this chapter.[8]

The participants adopted different strategies when dealing with the second task, that is commenting on the pronunciation difficulties posed by the provided items. In the majority of cases they did not write anything or made a comment such as '*I don't know why I mispronounce this word, I just do*' or '*somehow my tongue refuses to pronounce these letters*', which was to be expected as judgements of this sort require skills of a linguistic analysis, largely unavailable to teenage learners. Thus, the more common method consisted in underlining the problematic parts of words, which the subjects were encouraged to do. In several cases, however, some specific comments on the encountered phonetic difficulty were offered and they are presented in what follows.

A comment on the choice of intermediate learners for this study is in order. While, in terms of pronunciation, for beginners almost everything is difficult (L1 dominates) and for advanced/proficient students there is relatively little that remains problematic (L2 dominates), those who have achieved an intermediate level of proficiency seem to be the most interesting group to study not only because they are probably more numerous than other learners but also because they are at an interesting stage in their linguistic development at which there is a strong tug of war between L1 and L2 influences. In other words, at this stage the learners' interlanguage is bound to display some interesting phonetic and phonological properties.

Results and Discussion

In this section we present and discuss the obtained data, as well as group the collected items into some categories starting with the most numerous and proceeding to the less common types.

Spelling-based forms

The major culprit responsible for learners' phonetic difficulties is English spelling or, to be more exact, irregularities found among spelling-to-pronunciation rules as well as differences between spelling and sounds correspondences in Polish and English. As interference of English orthography is a well-known issue (see Sobkowiak, 1996), in what follows I focus only on those cases which were particularly frequent in the participants' responses. Interestingly, most of them did not concern vowels, notorious for being spelt in a variety of ways, but consonants. Silent letters were only rarely mentioned, probably because of sufficient practice the pupils received in this respect.

The following difficult words were provided by the participants, all of which share multiple phonetic realizations of a given consonant letter or a sequence of letters. The subjects' typical comment was as follows: 'I never know whether to pronounce [s] or [z] in this word'.

(5) $<s>$

   (a) *base, basic, basis, isolate, isolation, crisis, fantasy, ecstasy, bison, philosophy*
   (b) *comparison, curiosity, generosity, consist, insist, increasing, releasing, greasy, inclusive, exclusive, decisive*
   (c) *close* (verb)/*close* (adj.), *loose/lose, use* (verb)/*use* (noun)

What the items in (a) and (b) have in common is that here the letter $<s>$ tends to be pronounced by learners as a voiced fricative, though for different reasons: in (a) because of the presence of [z] in similar Polish words (e.g. *ba[z]a, i[z]olować, kry[z]ys, fanta[z]ja*) and in (b) because of some kind of s-voicing rule (operating mostly intervocalically and next to sonorants) that learners tend to develop.[9] Interestingly, this is not a case of interference from Polish, which allows for both [s] and [z] in the two contexts (e.g. *o[s]a* 'wasp', *kon[s]ekwencja* 'consequence').[10] The items in (c) represent a different problem; here pairs of English words differ in the voicing of the final fricative depending on their grammatical category, which is bound to lead to learning difficulties. It should be added that in such instances in Polish English, a general tendency is to use the voiceless fricative due to word final devoicing operating in Polish.[11]

<g>

The following items containing the letter <g> were claimed by the subjects to be difficult because of confusion whether it should be pronounced as the voiced velar plosive or the palatoalveolar affricate:

(6) *stingy, urgent, gorgeous, gigantic*

This group is not very numerous but is included here since *gigantic* appeared in several papers as particularly difficult due to the different pronunciation of the two <g> letters.

<c> and <cc>

The pronunciation of the letter <c> or a sequence of two such letters was problematic for the learners in the following words:

(7) <c> *civil, scene, cement, cycling*
     <cc> *success, accent, accelerate, accident*

The source of difficulty lies here in the presence of the voiceless dental affricate [ts] in the corresponding Polish words in the first set, for example *[ts]ywil, s[ts]ena, [ts]ement*, and the cluster [kts] in the second set, for example *su[kts]es, a[kts]ent, a[kts]elerator*, and this type of pronunciation is carried over to the English words under discussion.

<ch>

This digraph was often underlined by the subjects as difficult to pronounce in the following words:

(8) *technique, technology, techno (music), chaos, choir, orchid*

in which cases it tends to be pronounced as the voiceless velar fricative spelt in this fashion in Polish.

<ous>, <able>, <ate>, <ace>, <ough>, <augh>

Some suffixes and sequences of letters are known to cause pronunciation difficulties. The pupils who took part in our study underlined these formatives in the words listed below.

(9) < ous > *dangerous, famous, jealous, nervous, marvellous, continuous*

This suffix is frequently rendered as [ows] or [us] in Polish English. A common problem concerns the pronunciation of < a > in < able >, < ate > and < ace >, often interpreted as [ej].

(10) < able > *capable, available, valuable, comfortable, vegetable*

In these instances, there is an additional side effect of the incorrect stress placement on this suffix.

(11) < ate > *delicate, certificate, ultimate, separate* (adj.)

The diphthongal pronunciation of this suffix in verbs often leads to its overgeneralization to all the items with *–ate*, that is nouns and adjectives, such as those provided by the pupils. < ace > in the forms in (12) is also mispronounced as [ejs] (as in *face* or *lace*)

(12) < ace > *surface, preface, necklace, palace*

Two more sequences of letters were mentioned as problematic by the pupils, undoubtedly due to the lack of their uniform pronunciation:

(13) < ough > *tough, enough, brought, fought, thought, although, through, cough*
     < augh > *taught, caught, laugh, draught*

Phonetic 'false friends'

The second largest group of problematic words contains those lexical items which appear in both languages in an identical or very similar orthographic form. While the majority of them are cognates, this is not always the case as in many instances such items are completely unrelated, as shown in the translations of the Polish forms, for example

(1) E *ten* – P *ten* 'this, masc.'   E *pan* – P *pan* 'mister'
     E *brat* – P *brat* 'brother'   E *gnat* – P *gnat* 'bone, augmentative'

Nevertheless, cognates prevail in this group and lead to a strong tendency to be pronounced by learners in the Polish way. The following items in the collected data have been found to belong to this category:

(2) *taxi, karate, alibi, album, chaos, panel, atom, tandem, safari, mania, horror, agent, boa, baobab, jaguar, contact, robot, echo, stereo, video*

Some of the participants commented on such cases in the following way: *'They look like Polish words so when I see them, I pronounce them in the Polish way though I know it's wrong'.*

A large subgroup of such items comprises proper nouns of various types. They include people's names, for example

(3) *Daniel, Audrey, Sara, Naomi, Adrian, Howard, Penelope, Murphy, Turner, Ryan, Britney Spears, Rourke, Einstein, Graham, Spielberg, Shakespeare*

as well as geographical terms, for example

(4) *Nepal, Edinburgh, Geneva, Sydney, Melbourne, Yale, Haiti, Arkansas, Nebraska, Idaho, Illinois*

Word stress

As is well-known, English word stress belongs to the most difficult areas of English phonetics for Poles (e.g. Sobkowiak, 1996; Waniek-Klimczak, 2002), who, with their fixed-stress mother tongue, find the intricacies and irregularities of the former very hard to master. Since this issue is discussed in more detail in other studies, here I will confine myself to listing the items which subjects provided with comments such as *'I keep forgetting how to stress this word correctly'*.[12]

The following bisyllabic items appear in the collected data:

(14) (a) *'guitar,'hotel,'event,'technique,'alarm,'success,'Japan,'exam, 'support,'suspense*
       (b) *e'ffort, fe'male, fo'reign, da'maged, ca'pable* (when pronounced as [e'fo:rt], [fo'rejn], [de'mejčt], [ke'pejbl])

The examples in (a), with ultimate stress, tend to receive penultimate stress in Polish English, partly because of the stress pattern in corresponding Polish words (when they exist) and partly because of the transfer of Polish penultimate stress. The forms in (b) are particularly interesting since here an opposite tendency can be observed, that is stressing the ultimate syllable. It might be the case that learners develop some sensitivity to syllable weight and stress the final syllable as they regard it, correctly or incorrectly, as heavy and therefore stress-attracting.

Problematic stress placement in longer words noted by the participants includes the following cases:

(15) (a) *in'dustry, o'rigin, a'lgebra, valu'able, avai'lable, Janu'ary, Febru'ary, e'nergy, edu'cated, orga'nizer, inte'resting, fasci'nating*
       (b) *unfor'tunately,'successful,'September,'October,'November,'interpret, e'conomic, 'detergent, ar'tificial,'variety* (pronounced as ['verjety])
       (c) *'computer,'museum,'professor*

In the items in (a), with initial stress in English, learners frequently shift stress onto the penultimate syllable, in accordance with the Polish rule. The examples in (b) and (c) depart from this pattern in a curious way; here the antepenultimate syllable tends to be stressed in Polish English, which is particularly surprising in the case of the words in (c) with cognates in Polish stressed on the penultimate syllable like in English, that is *kom'puter, mu'zeum, pro'fesor*. This phenomenon is often viewed as a tendency to avoid too Polish-sounding pronunciation by learners since words with the Polish stress pattern are approached with some suspicion. It seems to me, however, that cases such as those in (b) and (c) contradict this assumption and an alternative explanation can be offered. It might be assumed that in these instances, just like in (14b), learners adopt an English antepenultimate stress rule which operates in numerous items, such as *A'merica, uni'versity,'marvelous*, and employ it to the examples in (15b) and (15c).

To sum up, it appears that a tug of war takes place between Polish and English stress rules in the interlanguage under discussion, with winners on both sides.

Difficult consonant clusters

Polish learners, with their mother tongue abounding in a rich variety of consonant sequences, generally have no major problems with the pronunciation of English clusters, with some exceptions, however. Many participants of our study regard as phonetically difficult those words which contain an interdental fricative in combination with another consonant.

(14) (a) < th + C > *three, throw, threw, through, throat, thriller, threaten, birthday, mathematics, maths, rhythm, truthful, faithful, athletic*

  (b) <C + th > *sixth, seventh, eighth, ninth, tenth, hundredth, thousandth length, strength, month, healthy, wealthy, depth, width, warmth, although, enthusiasm, if they, if the*[13]

Thus, the interdental fricatives, difficult for Poles to learn in any context,[14] are particularly troublesome when they appear next to another consonant. As shown in (16), the order of consonants is irrelevant since in (a) the spirant appears as a first segment while in (b) as the second one. The quality of the other consonant does not seem relevant either; the examples in (16) comprise combinations of 'th' with rhotics, nasals, plosives, laterals and fricatives. It should be pointed out, however, that in my data the most frequently repeated examples involve 'th' followed by $/r/$.[15]

The issues discussed so far, that is the occurrence of cognates, interference from English spelling, word stress and consonant clusters which make English words difficult to learn, belong to well-recognized problems not only for Poles but for learners of other L1 backgrounds as well. In what follows, we focus on lesser known sources of phonetic errors uncovered by our study.

Longer words

The pronunciation of longer words fails to be addressed by the majority of phonetic manuals, which, in fact, do not recognize it as a phonetic issue as such.[16] Yet, such a category has been isolated by several participants of my study, as shown by their comments like *'this word is difficult because it's long'*. Apparently, longer items are problematic for intermediate learners because of a variety of factors they have to control: spelling-to-pronunciation rules, the placement of stress and the articulation of many different new sounds and complex sound sequences.

A question that arises concerns the length of words regarded as difficult. Let us consider the data in (17).

(17) (a) trisyllables: *excitement, adventure, Australia, picturesque, quotation, jewellery, weightlessness*
　　 (b) quadrisyllables: *relaxation, astonishing, surprisingly, competition, desperately*
　　 (c) quintisyllables: *encyclopaedia, occasionally, exaggeration, association opportunity, simultaneously, Mediterranean*

The provided items contain three, four and five syllables. Evidently, for intermediate learners even words which are three-syllable long may be difficult, which does not mean, of course, that every word of this length will be regarded as such. It is not obvious, however, which particular phonetic aspects of the forms listed in (17) makes them troublesome for learners, as this requires a detailed examination of their learners' versions.

Liquids

One of the most surprising results of this study is the discovery that the presence of several liquids, that is both rhotics and laterals, in one word contributes to its considerable difficulty for intermediate learners.

One source of such problems is the failure to master the restrictions on the occurrence of /r/ in RP and a frequent case of articulating it word-finally and preconsonantally. Such realizations of /r/ result in the presence of several rhotics in one item and learners' complaints that it is difficult since *'there are too many r's in this word'*. The following examples have been supplied by the subjects:

(18) *murderers, portray, cartridge, appropriate, library*

Nevertheless, these were forms which contain both laterals and rhotics (found in pronunciation and/or in spelling) that were frequently provided with angry comments such as *'język mi się plącze jak to próbuję wymówić'* (I can't get my tongue around it) or *'od tego robią mi się kluchy w gębie'* (I get my tongue in a twist when I say it).

(19) *regularly, particularly, rarely, barely, burglary, world, girlfriend, rural, elderly, rollercoaster, literally, cellular*[17]

In such cases learners frequently attempt to pronounce all r's present in spelling, which is particularly difficult if this creates two- and three-consonant clusters. The problem with liquids is expressed clearly by one pupil: *'red lorry, yellow lorry – this is a true tongue twister'*.

It should be pointed out that sequences of liquids are problematic for Poles even when they occur in Polish. For example the adjective *kolorowy* 'colourful' belongs to the most frequently mispronounced words in children's speech, where the two liquids get metathesized. The same item appears in the popular tongue-twister: *Król Karol kupił królowej Karolinie korale koloru koralowego* 'king Charles bought queen Caroline colourful coral beads', whose difficulty stems from an accumulation of 14 laterals and trills in a single sentence.

High front vowels

For intermediate Polish learners, difficult English words are also those which contain two different high front vowels, that is [i:] and [ɪ] as in (20)[18]:

(20) *reading, sleeping, feeling, dreaming, cheating, ceiling, greeting, easy, speedy, greedy, sleepy, greasy*

In such instances they tend to employ two [i:] vowels (or rather its shorter and less tense Polish counterpart [i]). Interestingly, when these vowels appear in the reverse order, the pronunciation difficulty of such a sequence is diminished, for example

(21) *believe, receive, deceive, precede, repeat, release*

However, when the progressive –ing suffix is attached to the verbs in (21), a very difficult sequence of [ɪ] – [i:] – [ɪ] is created, as in (22).

(22) *believing, receiving, deceiving, preceding, repeating, releasing*

Here the vowels in the final two syllables are usually pronounced as [i:], as was the case with the examples in (20).

Yet another problem with [ɪ] is created by the following words:

(23) *innocent, image, impression, important, industry*

In these items the initial vowel was indicated by some participants as difficult to pronounce as they usually employ Polish [i] in such instances. Apart from the powerful influence of English spelling, another active factor seems to be the phonotactic constraint of Polish which bans in the word initial position the occurrence of the Polish front centralized vowel [y] - a far more phonetically justified substitute of the English sound in question.

Alternating forms

The collected data contain words regarded as difficult by the respondents because some morphemes they contain are subject to morphological alternations. Since in English such morphophonological changes are often highly irregular and idiosyncratic in character, this fact contributes to the perceived difficulty of items within which they take place. Some examples are given below.

(24) (a) *society* (so*ci*al), *nor*t*hern* (nor*th*), *sou*t*hern* (sou*th*), *longitude, longevity* (lon*g*er), *anxiety* (an*x*ious)

    (b) *can't* (can), *variety* (var*i*ous), *breathe* (br*ea*th), *numerous* (num*b*er), *width* (w*i*de), *depth* (d*ee*p), *southern* (s*ou*th), *sincerity* (sinc*e*re), *bathe* (bathe), *natural* (n*a*ture)

(24a) contains some cases which involve consonant alternations while those in (24b) vowel alternations. It is likely that pupils learn first more frequent words[19] provided in parentheses and when faced with less common related items, transfer the pronunciation of the underlined segments from the former to the latter. The degree of difficulty increases because in the above forms the alternating sounds are spelt in the same way.[20]

Conclusion

Over 250 lexical items presented and analysed in this chapter provide a rich and valuable source of information on the issue of phonetically difficult words for Polish intermediate learners of English. It should be stressed that since we have dealt here with the pupils' subjective judgements, the emerging picture is far from complete and needs to be supplemented by a direct observation of their performance.

According to the participants of this study, what makes English words difficult to pronounce is the presence of phonetic 'false friends' in both languages, the frequently non-phonemic English spelling, lack of fixed word stress, consonant clusters which include interdentals, length of words (three syllables and more), the occurrence of several liquids, a sequence of high front vowels and irregular morphological alternations they are involved in. It should be added that apart from the first three factors which are well-known and discussed in the pronunciation literature, the remaining ones have been uncovered by this study.

It is also interesting which lexical items were most frequently listed by the participants as troublesome. In (25), 15 such words are provided.

(25) *through, valuable, particularly, regularly, certainly, sixth, foreign, gigantic, encyclopaedia, rarely, unfortunately, Australia, early, can't, vague*

These examples involve the majority of problems discussed in this chapter. Thus, three of them are 'false friends' (*encyclopaedia, Australia, gigantic*), three are difficult because of stress (*valuable, foreign, unfortunately*), three are longer words (more than four syllables; *particularly, encyclopaedia, unfortunately*), two contain clusters of interdentals and other consonants (*through, sixth*), three comprise some liquids (*particularly, regularly, rarely*), one involves an irregular morphological alternation (*can't*) and the majority are problematic because of spelling-to-sound correspondences. It should be added that in many cases several factors contribute to the perceived phonetic difficulty of one item. For example *through* contains not only a cluster of an interdental fricative and the rhotic, but also a complex letter combination, that is < ough >. *Valuable* is problematic because of the presence of the suffix < able >, whose mispronunciation results in the incorrect stress placement, as well as the occurrence of two laterals.

There are several important pedagogical implications that stem from this study. First of all, it fully supports claims made by Szpyra-Kozłowska (2010) and Szpyra-Kozłowska and Stasiak (2010) concerning the need to prioritize word pronunciation in phonetic instruction. As evidenced here, there are hundreds of English words perceived as phonetically difficult by learners and many more of which they are not aware. No training which focuses on sounds, usually practised in simple monosyllabic items or minimal pairs, can eliminate error-prone lexemes. Phonetically difficult words deserve to be given a prominent position in language instruction. Secondly, phonetic difficulty is closely connected with learners' language proficiency and should be studied and put into practice in this particular context. This means that we agree with Nation (1990) that the order in which learners are taught vocabulary should take into account the level of phonetic difficulty of English words to reduce part of the learning burden and enhance the effectiveness of this process. In order to implement these ideas, however, more insight is needed into the nature of phonetic difficulty involved in various English words for learners of a different L2 proficiency. This study is meant to be a step in this direction.

Notes

1. Pedagogical implications of local errors are discussed by Szpyra-Kozłowska and Stasiak (in press), where various suggestions are made how to effectively reduce the number of such incorrect form from learners' English.
2. For a more detailed discussion, see Szpyra-Kozłowska (in press).
3. It should be added that the distinction between global and local errors is not always sharp. For instance it is not clear how to classify spelling-related errors which concern many items, for example a common type of overgeneralization that the word final < ey > (*Disney, Audrey, Huxley*) is pronounced as [ej].

4. Some of these books, for example those by Kenworthy (1987) and Hewings (2004), include sections devoted to pronunciation difficulties of specific L1 learners. They deal, however, with selected global errors only.

5. There are other differences between Sobkowiak's ideas and those developed in this chapter. First of all, while Sobkowiak's PDI does not specify the connection between various types of errors and the learners' level of language proficiency, we deal with problems of intermediate learners. Secondly, his PDI excludes 'false friends', borrowings and words with uncommon stress patterns, which, as we shall argue, belong to the most serious sources of phonetic difficulty. Thirdly, while PDI focuses on quantifying the phonetic difficulty of words and adopts a lexicographic perspective, we are concerned mainly with identifying sources of errors and pedagogical implications of this investigation.

6. The participants' level of general English proficiency ranged from pre-intermediate through intermediate to upper intermediate. Each year they are assigned to language classes on the basis of an achievement test which measures their level of proficiency.

7. I would like to express my gratitude to Anna Gryń-Telichowska for her help in carrying out this study.

8. Not all collected words are analysed here since many items appeared in single papers only and could not be regarded as commonly found difficulties. As the experiment had a written form, in some cases it was not clear what type of pronunciation difficulty some of the provided items represented.

9. According to Chomsky and Halle (1968), English has an s-voicing rule which operates on intervocalic stem initial fricatives in *resume* and *resort*, as well as after tense vowels in *music* or *horizon*. Since it has many exceptions, later accounts of English phonology generally do not regard s-voicing as a productive process.

10. This kind of voicing can also be observed in the case of the fricatives in the prefixes *mis-*, *dis-* and *trans-*, which are often pronounced as voiced in Polish English in, for example, *misunderstand, misuse, disappoint, disagree, translate*.

11. While the majority of examples presented here concern the incorrect use of the voiced fricative in English words by Polish learners, in some instances an opposite tendency can be observed, for example in *Oslo, Islam, Missouri*, as in the Polish versions these items are pronounced with the voiceless fricative.

12. The participants did not indicate how they actually stress the provided items. Our discussion is based on observations how such words are mispronounced.

13. The last two examples are not single words but phrases. They are presented here since they appeared in the pupils' papers and since they demonstrate clearly that the source of difficulty is the presence of another consonant – here a fricative – next to the interdental.

14. It should be added that some subjects regarded as difficult words with final 'th', for example *north, south, both, earth, youth, mouth*. No examples with the problematic spirant in word initial or intervocalic position were provided.

15. According to Sobkowiak's (1999) PDI, difficult clusters comprising inter-dentals are those in which these consonants are followed by alveolar fricatives. Our data show that combinations of any consonants with the interdentals are problematic for intermediate learners.

16. The category of long words sometimes appears, however, in the discussion of English word stress (e.g. Sobkowiak, 1996). Sobkowiak (1999) includes words which comprise five or more syllables into his PDI.
17. In the adverbs *regularly* and *particularly*, there is a tendency to drop the lateral in the suffix and retain the preceding rhotic, that is to pronounce them as *regulary* and *particulary*. In *rarely* and *barely* all the letters are pronounced according to the Polish spelling-to-sound rules, which means that the Polish English versions consist of three syllables. Some pupils also listed *early* and *fairly* as '*difficult because of the rl cluster*'. The difficulty of this cluster can also be seen in the pronunciation of borrowings such as *Marlboro* usually simplified by Poles to [malboro].
18. The problems discussed in this section concern those learners who make a distinction between two vowels under consideration. It should be added that many Poles tend to replace most occurrences of English [ɪ] with Polish [i].
19. We mean here word frequency in learners' English which is not the same as word frequency in English.
20. It may be argued that the cases discussed in this section should be subsumed under the heading of spelling-related difficulties, that is various phonetic realizations of the same letter or sequences of letters. It should be observed, however, that no particular problems have been noted in the case of words in which more regular alternations take place, for example *act – action, sex – sexual*, even when the same letters represent the alternating segments.

References

Chomsky, N. and Halle, M. (1968) *The Sound Pattern of English*. New York: Harper and Row.

Hewings, M. (2004) *Pronunciation Practice Activities*. Cambridge: Cambridge University Press.

Kenworthy, J. (1987) *Teaching English Pronunciation*. Harlow: Longman.

Nation, P. (1990) *Teaching and Learning Vocabulary*. New York: Newbury House.

Sobkowiak, W. (1996) *English Phonetics for Poles*. Poznań: Bene Nati.

Sobkowiak, W. (1999) *Pronunciation in EFL Machine-Readable Dictionaries*. Poznań: Motivex.

Szpyra-Kozłowska, J. (in press) On the irrelevance of sounds and prosody in foreign-accented English. In Waniek-Klimczak (ed.) *Issues in Accents of English 3*. Newcastle upon Tyne, UK: Cambridge Scholars Publishing.

Szpyra-Kozłowska, J. and Stasiak, S. (2010) From focus on sounds to focus on words in English pronunciation instruction. *Research in Language* 8, 163–174.

Waniek-Klimczak, E. (2002) Akcent wyrazowy w nauczaniu języka angielskiego. In W. Sobkowiak and E. Waniek-Klimczak (eds) *Dydaktyka fonetyki języka obcego. Zeszyty Naukowe PWSZ w Płocku*, t. III. (pp. 101–114). Płock: Wydawnictwo Naukowe PWSZ w Płocku.

Chapter 20

Transcultural Interference, Communities of Practice and Collaborative Assessment of Oral Performance

PRZEMYSŁAW KRAKOWIAN

Introduction

A community of practice (CoP) is often defined as a network or a forum, both informal and with varying degrees of formal structuring and internal organisation, through which ideas are exchanged and solutions generated (Wenger, 1998). It constitutes a very attractive arrangement for many undertakings as nothing binds people together faster than common interest and pursuit of solutions to common problems. The present chapter reports on one such scheme in which a CoP used a web-based environment collaboratively to evaluate spoken performance as part of the WebCEF project (see http://webcef.eu). It looks, in particular, at the issue of inter-rater reliability in assessing oral production and investigates some possible sources of variability in the ratings, amongst which transcultural interference resulting from the composition of the project's CoP seems to be a major contributing factor.

Background

The WebCEF project was carried out with the support of the Education, Audiovisual and Culture Executive Agency and the European Commission, Directorate-General for Education and Culture under the Socrates Minerva programme. Partner institutions included (alphabetically) the Catholic University of Leuven (Katholieke Universiteit Leuven), Euneos Corporation, Fontys University of Applied Science (Fontys Hogescholen), the Open University in the United Kingdom, the Technical University of Dresden (Technische Universität Dresden), the University of Helsinki – Department of Applied Sciences of Education, the University of Lodz (Uniwersytet Łódzki) and the University of Savoy – Languages Research Group (Université de Savoie). At the last stage of the project, significant contributions were made by the University of Bologna – CILTA (Centre of Theoretical and Applied Linguistics), which became a non-contractual partner in the project.

The project, lasting three years (2006–2009) in its contractual aims and near original wording, constituted an attempt to bring teaching staff across Europe together, provide them with a community where their assessments could be validated by their colleagues and allow them and their pupils and students access to tools to supply and share annotated video and audio materials on the internet. WebCEF additionally focused on the development of a didactic model for web-based collaborative assessment of oral proficiency in accordance with the *Common European Framework of Reference for Languages* (CEFR; Council of Europe, 2001) as well as focused on the collection and joint analysis of oral proficiency samples supported by new and easily accessible technologies and the creation and maintenance of a European CoP of teaching staff and pupils. With the completion of the project, the teachers and learners were to have at their disposal the didactic model for teaching and evaluating oral skills and an operations manual integrated in an *Electronic Performance Support System* (EPSS), as well as an oral proficiency-specific database of validated and annotated video and audio samples (the *Showcase*) together with a proactive CoP geared towards European language teachers, teacher educators and teacher trainees, and a pedagogically justified rationale for future foreign language education assessment.

Overview of Sample Collection

The sample collection started with coordinated efforts to establish parameters for samples for the Showcase in English. Linguistic partners (Belgian, Dutch, Finnish, French, German, Polish) first pooled available audio and video samples – recorded both prior to the project and in its early stages – in an attempt to moderate length, content (exposition, lecture, summary), type of interaction (monologue, dialogue) as well as domain (private, official, educational, leisure, work). Altogether the video and audio recordings, comprising high fidelity/high resolution as well as low bandwidth flash media, spanned several DVD disks, of which several samples were selected as a starting point for discussion and which were included in the annotation tool prior to the Chambéry partner meeting in November 2007. It was assumed that whatever the decisions were to be made concerning the Showcase in English, those would be replicated in the respective partner languages of the Showcase to guarantee comparability across languages – one of the aims of the project as well as an objective related to the didactic model.

During the Chambéry meeting, the Belgian and the Dutch partners expressed dissatisfaction with the CEFR scales and their ease of use in evaluating some more diverse samples from different educational backgrounds, voicing concerns that factors not explicitly present in the

CEFR descriptors may influence the perception of some samples, thus producing undesired effects where satisfactory convergence cannot be reached (compare section on 'Convergence issues'). The two partners additionally suggested assuming an alternative set of scales to include the missing descriptors of performance and allowing one to account for the phenomenon of nativelike performance. While this discussion continued as a peripheral exchange of ideas throughout the project, the majority of the linguistic partners believed that despite the short-comings of the CEFR, the project deliverables demanded that the Showcase needed to illustrate the CEFR scales as they were the centrepiece of the project, and whatever other outcomes of the process of sample collection, evaluation and annotation may be in terms of comparative research, the Showcase would primarily be concerned with explicating and illustrating the CERF scales through a selection of comparable, analogous and, if possible, equivalent samples.

As a result, the major scales for the showcase were those of CEFR for monologue samples, all based on a selection of video clips with minimum language content and explicit situational content, and a short reading task for a dialogue/interaction. The scales for monologue and dialogue/interaction were rendered in the annotation tool first in English and when work was undertaken on Transfer to other Languages (Project Work Package 6) also in respective partner languages (see Figure 20.1). The Dutch and Belgian partners, apart from contributing to the main-stream work on scales, continued their work on alternatives to CEFR, producing what in the annotation tool is now implemented as an assessment wizard, a customisable system for attaching weights to different aspects of oral performance, some of which are verbatim CEFR scales and some of which are categories not present in the CEFR descriptors, such as intelligibility, fluency, which is understood as a mere speed of talking as measured by words per minute, as well as pronunciation and intonation.

The Convergence Issues

The discussion on convergence and discrepancies in evaluating samples was initiated relatively late in the project. While work proceeded on parallel national versions of the Showcase, it became apparent that for the English Showcase the partners could not agree on the choice of suitable samples for the upper bands of the CEFR scales, and addition-ally it could be felt that while an inordinate number of samples was processed, only very few met all of the criteria such as quality of recording, both video and audio, including intelligibility of the speaker or speakers, sufficient length and amount of discourse, but most of all sufficiently convergent assessment from all of the partners participating

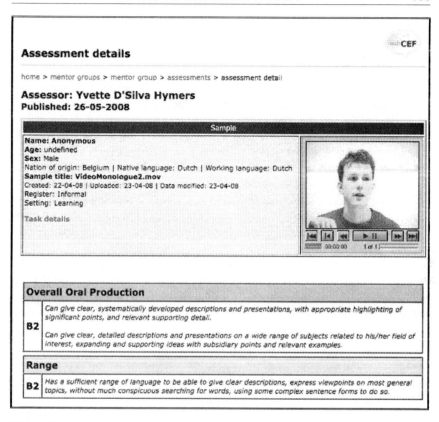

Figure 20.1 Annotation tool showing a fragment of a screen with assessment details

in sample evaluation. All of those issues were discussed at length in a videoconference, which took place only in March 2009. For parties interested in reviewing the discussion, a live link to the recording http://fm.ea-tel.eu/fm/a76037-16318 is maintained by the Open University in the United Kingdom. The topics that were discussed in the partner meeting in relation to the issue of convergence or lack thereof included (1) possible sources of discrepancies in marking by different assessors; (2) cultural differences in the perception of non-native speech related to phonetic accuracy, speed of talking and the ensuing perceived fluency, range and accuracy of student versus native speaker performance; (3) inter- and intra-rater variability affected by external factors as well as by the above.

Inter-rater variability is something that may be partly attributed to fatigue and boredom related to the tediousness of the task, but it also relates to the learning curve and the perception of the rating scales overtime, as it can be concluded that with greater understanding of the mechanics of scoring, the accuracy and reliability of the scorer increases until it reaches a plateau, and the variability there is beyond individual's control and impervious to training effects.

Intra-rater variability may be attributed to a number of factors, the most prominent of which lies in the fact that generally the more complicated the rating scale, the larger the opportunity to make errors of judgment. In relation to the CEFR scales in the project, the inescapable conclusions seem to be that (1) the overall scales for either of the tasks in the Showcase are complicated; (2) they are supplemented by additional scales pertaining to different aspects or facets of performance; (3) the additional scales are complicated. This is perhaps a relative phenomenon and it may be concluded that it is less so in the case of national languages and partner Showcases, but definitely more in the case of the English Showcase, which was constructed on the basis of efforts of individuals of different cultures and backgrounds and with different educational and evaluation histories, where the effects of the intercultural communication and intercultural communication interference were sometimes making the partners read in different ideas into the descriptors as it is succinctly outlined below:

> Intercultural communication is a symbolic, interpretative, transactional, contextual process in which the degree of difference between people is large and important enough to create dissimilar interpretations and expectations about what are regarded as competent behaviours that should be used to create shared meanings. (Lustig & Koester, 1993: 51)

Sources of misunderstandings are numerous and have been pointed out by at least two separate theories. The psychological anthropology theory of intercultural interference (Barna, 1994; Scollon & Scollon, 1995) claims that interference emerges when (1) discourse participants, in our case evaluators who interact with the sample, assume that all humans are essentially similar and therefore behave and interpret behaviour in a similar way; (2) discourse participants incorrectly interpret non-verbal clues and non-verbal communication; (3) discourse participants read into their interpretation of discourse their preconceptions, stereotypes and superstitions; (4) discourse participants assume a stance in which they judge and evaluate elements of the discourse according to their set of values and culture related norms of behaviour; (5) additionally, there is an element which is inherently connected with the language component, namely with the differences between any two or more languages; and (6) ensuing tension, anxiety and other affective factors that appear when a language other than a native one is used by a speaker, a phenomenon also known as culture shock.

Hymes, on the other hand, when outlining his model of communication and the concept of communicative competence (1962, 1974), used the acronym SPEAKING, where the individual letters stand, respectively, for scene, participants, ends, act sequence, key, instrumentalities, norms and finally genres, by which he understood where and how the act of communication is performed, what is the purpose and aim of it, how conventionally the communication unfolds, what is the degree of correctness/ceremoniality/detachment versus casuality/familiarity/intimacy, how the communication is conveyed and what are the overall culturally sanctioned norms of communicating and interacting within the discourse and how they are to be interpreted, and finally what are the characteristics of different types of texts we produce and how they are constructed. The claim here is that the violation or misinterpretation of even one of the above will lead to intercultural interference.

Some additional factors have been identified and postulated as the underlying causes for divergence (O'Sullivan, 2008):

- gender in the perception of speech: effeminate male language tends to be decidedly underscored by male raters and slightly, but statistically significantly overscored by female raters, but only of some nationalities; at the time of the March discussion, in search of a similar trend, a manual search of the samples was performed, which at the time pointed at least to the first of the findings; this was later repeated on a larger number of samples (compare later in the text) with the use of a functionality that was later added to the annotation tool and which allowed all of the sample metadata to be exported in a comma delimited format to be later searched for trends, thus at least partly automating the task;
- gender of the examiner and the alleged claim that female raters rate more leniently: that is overscore the subjects in general and those whom they are familiar with in particular (compare the next section);
- the familiarity with the subjects/examinees under evaluation: a tentative tendency to evaluate more favourably those who are known to us as opposed to those we are not familiar with; some examining bodies (e.g. English for Speakers of Other Languages formerly University of Cambridge Local Examinations Syndicate) require that their oral examiners familiarise themselves with the names of the examinees before the exam and identify those whom they have taught in the past several years;
- the difficulty of the task and the resource intensity of the task: the effect the task has on the complexity of the discourse and range of linguistic resources that have been implemented in an effective and efficient achievement of the task; a task which is not demanding

enough may leave the evaluator with the impression that the performance was of a lesser value and that the level of competence is lower when actually the examinee had no opportunity to show his full potential;

- the effect of the examinee pairing, obviously only in situations involving collaborative tasks, where male versus male and female versus female pairing received more favourable ratings than a setting involving female versus male arrangement, where an additional claim was made that female speakers producing a comparable amount of discourse would tend to be perceived as overbearing and dominating the interaction; unfortunately, such claims remain largely unsubstantiated, as the number of samples with female versus male pairing and the available metadata on the assessors participating in the evaluations is fragmentary and insufficient for performing the type of analysis outlined in the following sections;

- the effect of the native background culture of the assessor that might prove important when evaluating students from other countries and cultures in the sense as it is understood by Hall (1959, 1966) and Hall and Hall (1990) as high and low context culture interference. Some of the characteristics of the high context cultures mean that a culture in which the individual has inter-nalised meaning and information, little is explicitly stated in written or spoken messages. In conversation, the listener knows what is meant; because the speaker and the listener share the same knowledge and assumptions, the listener can piece together the speaker's intentions. In a high context culture, the individual must know what is meant at the covert or unexpressed level and is supposed to know how to react appropriately. Discourse partici-pants are expected to understand without explanation or specific details to the point that explanations may be considered insulting, as if the speaker regarded the listener as not informed or suave enough to understand. High context cultures, therefore, rely on indirect communication and use fewer words, tend to read between the lines and are highly tolerant of silences (Nakane, 2007). A low context culture, on the other hand, is one in which information and meanings are overtly stated and where the individuals expect explanations when statements or situations are ambiguous. Information, context and meanings are not inter-nalised by the individual but instead derived from the actual discourse. Hall (1959, 1966) and Hall and Hall (1990) claim in their work that most of the information missing in the internal and external contexts must be included in the transmitted message or communication breakdown will ensue.

Metadata Analysis

From the onset of the project, all of the partners believed that because the original project's CoP constituted a body comprising individuals from different educational and assessment backgrounds coming from seven different European countries, one of the strengths of the project would be providing a diverse picture of language performance, with speech samples for each of the partner languages coming from a variety of educational and cultural backgrounds being assessed by an equally diverse body of evaluators. It was, therefore, perceived that some form of information capturing such diversity should be recorded alongside with the speech samples. Since the Minerva programme is reluctant to explicitly finance research projects, the original intention was not for such a mode of investigation, but merely to provide any party interested in the samples with a wide, diverse and exhaustive picture of the educational, cultural and social setting of the assessment encompassing the details of both the examinee and the examiners.

To many of the partners, however, it was evident from the start that despite lack of an explicit research deliverable in the project, the data provided immensely attractive research opportunities for a number of reasons. Firstly, large collections of speech samples readily available for any inspection without research effort in the form of collection, processing and storing for later retrieval are rare and exploration opportunities are even rarer because of copyright and privacy issues. If available, however, collections of this sort are usually one-dimensional and capture learner speech characteristics of a particular educational setting of a particular country. The WebCEF database is largely different, being composed not only of samples of learners speaking respective partner languages but also within each of those languages comprising samples from people of different native languages coming from a variety of cultures and a diversity of educational backgrounds. The WebCEF database is also unique because the same can be said about the evaluators, where at the completion of the project the original project's CoP was extended to include several national CoPs working with samples for particular languages and often coordinated by international groups of interest for any given language.

All of the above, despite no original intention of this sort in the project, provide robust research opportunities, and the work on the database was geared towards capturing at least the essentials of the contextual background information. This was done in a number of ways: (1) each person registering for a user account in the annotation tool (EPSS), apart from providing identification and affiliation data was asked to provide metadata on native and working languages, nation of origin and the educational context. In an attempt to make the annotation tool and the registration procedure more user-friendly and more encouraging to lay users, however, the decision to include most of the metadata was left at the discretion of the user; (2) each sample uploaded to the annotation tool, before any instance of assessment could take place, required metadata pertaining to the educational setting, assessment situation, the level of formality and familiarity with the situation as well as relation of the speaking task to the curriculum. Despite similar pressure to simplify the sample logging procedure, providing relatively exhaustive sample metadata is compulsory and additionally the database fields are not filled by a default value, which requires users to enter what is hopefully genuine data; (3) metadata is also collected for each of the tasks, where apart from the task details, support material and the rubric, information is gathered regarding the educational level, domain, type of speech event and the complexity of the task. Owing to similar pressure as above, not all of the metadata is obligatorily required from the user.

The obvious advantage of this arrangement is that any assessment traffic in the annotation tool automatically generates relevant metadata, with the disadvantage that the metadata may be fragmentary, depending on the user involvement in volunteering contextual information. Once, however, present in the system, the metadata is trackable through a combination of manual and semi-automatic procedures such as the metadata export facility added towards the end of the project.

The statistical procedure used to investigate certain rater performance on selected sample sets involved a goodness-of-fit test, with the chi-square test as a statistic of choice as being relatively straightforward to perform and applicable to small datasets. Two separate comparisons of the rater performance were undertaken: one where the model of rater performance consisted of all of the instances of assessment, including the ones selected for goodness-of-fit test (here sig.1); the second where the model consisted of the assessments remaining after the goodness-of-fit group was identified (sig.2). When both calculations yielded results that were at least moderately statistically significant ($p < 0.1$), the rater behaviour was identified as potentially contributing to variability and ensuing lack of convergence. Obviously, the assessor performance was deemed substantially contributing to variability when at least one of the calculations was decidedly statistically significant ($p < 0.05$) (see Figure 20.2).

Results

The following results pertain to the portion of samples accumulated in the annotation tool database relevant to the English-speaking tasks. Similar material, albeit in smaller number, exists for other partner languages, but is not the subject of investigation in the present study.

```
Cmd> chi_sq(M2,RG7).
Using custom macro.
Chi-square      df        p-value    sig..
1.113           10        0.97603    0.02397
```

Figure 20.2 Chi-square goodness-of-fit test for Rater Group 7 and Model 2 (sig.2)

(1) The first of the observations concerns the procedure performed prior to this analysis and relating to the alleged trend identified at the onset of discussion on convergence. The original claim that *effeminate male language tends to be decidedly underscored by male raters* was confirmed on a population of 11 samples involving the assessments of 13 raters, 7 of whom were male raters (RG7, M2, sig.1 = 0.90023, sig.2 = 0.02397).

(2) The second of the postulated trends of the early study, namely that *effeminate male language tends to be statistically significantly overscored by female raters, but only of some nationalities,* was only partly identified for 3 female raters whose native language was English (RG6, M2, sig.1 = 0.89031, sig.2 = 0.75512).

(3) The claim that female raters *rate more leniently* was confirmed at the statistically significant level for 19 female raters of different native languages (RG5, M4, sig.1 = 0.49047, sig.2 = 0.03267).

(4) The tendency to *evaluate more favourably those whom the raters are familiar with* was confirmed at the statistically significant level for 45 raters of all partner native languages (RG11, M7, sig.1 = 0.34021, sig.2 = 0.04175). The familiarity with the subjects was determined on the premise of the authorship of the speech sample if such information was present in the metadata and the sample was not submitted anonymously.

(5) The *effect of the examinee pairing* could not be investigated because of insufficient metadata and a relatively smaller number of samples for interactive tasks compared with the total number of samples.

(6) The *effect of the native background culture of the assessor understood as high and low context culture interference* was investigated in relation to the Finnish project partner (RG8 comprising 3 female raters forming RG9 and 4 male raters belonging to RG10), a decidedly high context culture notorious for exceptional tolerance for silence and ambiguity (Nakane, 2007). RG8 consistently and statistically significantly overrated samples of considerably smaller discourse

size, shorter and/or containing more pauses and hesitations (RG8, M1, sig.1 = 0.40231, sig.2 = 0.08725) and did that irrespective of gender (RG9, M1, sig.1 = 0.44321, sig.2 = 0.08515; RG10, M1, sig.1 = 0.41845, sig.2 = 0.08817).

(7) Finally, a Polish twist in the data, which seems to be pointing in the direction of the 11 Polish raters (RG12) *scoring samples with greater perceived phonetic accuracy more favourably* than the rest of the raters (RG12, M1, sig.1 = 0.83954, sig.2 = 0.04235).

Conclusions

The database behind the annotation tool of the WebCEF project is potentially a very robust source of information on a number of different phenomena related to the mechanics of evaluating oral performance. Based on the available metadata, the notion of assessment convergence and selected issues of inter-rater reliability in assessing oral production and possible sources of variability in the ratings were investigated and seem to be pointing towards transcultural interference resulting from the composition of the project's CoPs. The notions isolated in the database include the perception of effeminate language, the influence of familiarity with the examinees, the effects of gender on adherence to scales and finally interference resulting from national and transcultural features of communication. The WebCEF project data potentially offer opportunities for further research including empirical measures connected with oral performance, especially valuable as they relate to culturally and educationally diverse contexts.

References

Barna, M.L. (1994) Stumbling blocks in intercultural communication. In L.A. Samovar and R.E. Porter (eds) *Intercultural Communication* (pp. 337–346). Belmond, CA: Wadsworth.

Council of Europe (2001) *Common European Framework of Reference for Languages: Learning, Teaching, Assessment*. Cambridge: Cambridge University Press.

Hall, E. (1959) *The Silent Language*. New York: Doubleday.

Hall, E. (1966) *The Hidden Dimension*. New York: Doubleday.

Hall, E. and Hall, M. (1990) *Understanding Cultural Differences: Germans, French and Americans*. Yarmouth, ME: Intercultural Press.

Hymes, D. (1962) The ethnography of speaking. In T. Gladwin and W.C. Sturtevant (eds) *Anthropology and Human Behavior* (pp. 13–53). Washington, DC: The Anthropology Society of Washington.

Hymes, D. (1974) *Foundations in Sociolinguistics: An Ethnographic Approach*. Philadelphia: University of Pennsylvania Press.

Lustig, M.W. and Koester, J. (1993) *Intercultural Competence: Interpersonal Communication across Cultures*. New York: Harper Collins College Publishers.

Nakane, I. (2007) *Silence in Intercultural Communication: Perceptions and Performance*. Amsterdam: Benjamins.

O'Sullivan, B. (2008) *Modelling Performance in Tests of Spoken Language.* Frankfurt: Peter Lang.

Scollon, R. and Scollon, S.W. (1995) *Intercultural Communication.* London: Blackwell.

Wenger, E. (1998) *Communities of Practice: Learning, Meaning, and Identity.* Cambridge: Cambridge University Press.